GUINNESS

The Wine Lists

edited by

Robert Joseph

Glenfiddich Wine Writer of the Year

Assistant editor
Louise Abbott

GUINNESS BOOKS

The Wine Lists

© Robert Joseph and Guinness Superlatives Ltd 1985

Published in Great Britain
by Guinness Superlatives Ltd
33 London Road, Enfield, Middlesex EN2 6DJ

Typesetting by Tradeset Ltd, Wembley Park, London
Printed and bound by R.J. Acford Ltd, Chichester, Sussex

'Guinness' is a registered trademark of
Guinness Superlatives Ltd

Joseph, Robert
  The wine lists.
  1. Wine and wine making—Dictionaries
  I. Title
  641.2'2'0321   TP546

ISBN 0-85112-452-6 Pbk

CONTENTS

Illustrations by
Amanda Ward
pages 5, 8, 13, 14, 16, 35, 36, 62, 99, 102, 104, 116, 119, 123, 125, 126, 139, 143, 161, 168, 170, 171;

Barry Jackson
pages 12, 15, 18, 22, 25, 40, 42, 47, 51, 69, 72, 77, 79, 81, 89, 92, 100, 108, 111, 114, 130, 135, 141, 165, 166.

Maps by
Robert Chapman

THIS IS A VERY DIFFERENT KIND OF WINE BOOK. It is almost certainly the first to list and describe all of the wine producing countries in the world – from Albania to Zimbabwe, describing in detail well over a thousand wines and their producers; it is also the only wine book to include information on both Queen Victoria's favourite aphrodisiac and the world's first nude wine tasting.

Whilst this is essentially a serious reference book, it was produced for readers who do not treat wine with unquestioning reverence. In the course of covering as many aspects of the subject as possible, combining factual information and amusing anecdote, we have also made forthright comments on some of the world's better known but more disappointing wines.

All of the subjects in the book are listed alphabetically, so 'Belgium' will come between 'Barrels' and 'Bolivia'. The entry for each country follows a similar format, detailing the most important regions, the grape varieties grown, local words used on labels and so on. In almost every case a list of producers is also included with an indication of the ones most worth looking out for. Important wine growing regions within a major country are listed alphabetically within that country's section. The opinions expressed in the introductions to these sections and the particular wines and producers recommended are my own responsibility and are bound, on occasion, to arouse differences of opinion. Which is just as it should be: if we all agreed absolutely about every wine, life would be very boring indeed.

A very large number of people helped in its production of this book – far too many for all to be listed individually. I should however like to thank my colleagues on What Wine? for their forebearance and all of the members of the advisory panel for their specific contributions. In particular I must mention Charles Metcalfe for his contributions on Germany and Austria, Margaret Rand for Spain, Chris Milner for Australia, New Zealand and Switzerland and John Livingstone Learmonth for the Loire and Rhône. Oz Clarke provided invaluable advice on Bordeaux; Anthony Hanson MW and Rebecca Wasserman did likewise on Burgundy whilst Don Hewitson spent a transatlantic flight poring over the section on the Antipodes. Jill Goolden was the source of much background information on sparkling wines and Champagne and Martin Symington, Nancy Thomson and Maureen Ashley MW all contributed their specific expertise. Joanna Simon not only proof-read the entire book, but also made a great many suggestions which enabled me hopefully to steer clear of a number of pitfalls.

Four other people deserve special mention for the simple reason that, but for them, this book would never have appeared at all: Louise Abbott, my assistant editor, for uncovering a million facts and figures, researching a large proportion of the book, and achieving the impossible by keeping track of a precarious mountain of manuscript; Michael Stephenson, my editor at Guinness Superlatives for gentle bullying and painless cutting; Roger Pring, the designer, for devising a way to turn 125,000 words into a good-looking book; and Christina Ker Gibson, simply for her patient encouragement during the months it took to write and compile.

All of these people should share any credit for this book; any blame should fall on my shoulders alone.

Robert Joseph

AIRLINE WINES

In 1985 *Business Traveller* magazine organized a blind tasting of wines served to business-class travellers on 21 of the world's best-known airlines. The following are the preferred airlines for both red and white wines, and the best and least liked wines.

Preferred wine air lines

1   Air New Zealand
2   Qantas
3   MAS
4   Austrian Airlines
5   Lufthansa
6   British Caledonian
7   Swissair
8   Singapore Airlines
9   Iberia
10 Finnair
11 Japan Airlines
12 Air Canada
13 Alitalia
14 TWA
15 South African Airways
16 British Airways
17 KLM
18 SAS
19 El Al
20 TAP
21 Olympic Airways

Best whites

1 **Air New Zealand** Chardonnay Montana 1983
2 **Lufthansa** Mosel Wiltiner Schwarzberg Riesling Kabinett 1983
3 **Austrian Airlines** Pinot Blanc
4 **Singapore Airlines** Pouilly Vinzelles 1983
5 **Qantas** Tolleys Riesling

Best reds

1 **Iberia** Rioja Prado Enea Muga 1976
2 **Air New Zealand** Cabernet Sauvignon Montana 1976
3 **Finnair** Château Smith Haut Lafite 1979, Graves
4 **Qantas** Orlando Shiraz Cabernet

5 **British Caledonian** Chablis 1983
6 **MAS** Chablis Premier Cru 1983

Worst whites

1 **El Al** Carmel Sauvignon Blanc
2 **Alitalia** Galestro Frescobaldi
3 **KLM** Chapelle des Mers
4 **British Airways** Bordeaux Cordier White
5 **TAP** Vinho Verde

Worst reds

1 **KLM** Moncadour Bordeaux
2 **SAA** Cabernet Sauvignon 1979 Fleur du Cap
3 **El Al** Carmel Cabernet Sauvignon
4 **SAS** Château Haut-Fourat 1981
5 **Olympia** Montenegro

ALBANIA

FOR several years, before World War II, an Englishman is said to have lived in Albania 'doing research for a book on Albanian wine'. Some people believe him to have been a spy; his book has never appeared. The white and rosé wines produced have been described as 'Yugoslavian' in type, and the Kadarka, one of Eastern Europe's most important grapes, takes its name from the town of Skadarka in Albania.

In Alexis Lichine's *Encyclopaedia of Wines and Spirits,* (1970), Albania was the 20th most prolific wine exporter of the world, sending almost as much wine from its frontiers as the USA and Australia put together. Exactly how a small country which is elsewhere reckoned to produce only 360,000 bottles came to export over 2,500,000 gallons is not entirely clear . . .

ALCOHOLIC STRENGTH OF WINE

	% alcohol by volume
Liebfraumilch	9.0
Vinho Verde	9.0
German Kabinett wines	9.0
French Vin de Table	10.5
German Auslese	10.5
Alsace Riesling	10.5–11.5
Beaujolais	11.0
Valpolicella	11.5
Muscadet*	12.0
Australian Chardonnay	12.0
Bordeaux Cru Classé	12.0
Chablis Premier Cru	12.5
Rioja	12.5
Meursault	12.5
Chianti	12.5
Sancerre	12.5
Californian Chardonnay	13.0
Californian Cabernet	13.0
Châteauneuf-du-Pape	13.0
Barolo	13.0
German Berrenauslese	13.0
Sauternes	13.0
Clos Vougeot	13.0
Zinfandel	13.5

*Muscadet is the only French AOC wine to have a *maximum* alcohol level – 12% – the others all tend to have minimum levels.

ALGERIA

ALGERIA'S wine-producing started in the 1860s and 1870s, when French winegrowers arrived in flight from the Prussian army and the Phylloxera beetle. During the 1880s there was a great deal of plantation, taking the area under vine from 4,600 *ha* (1860) to 22,720 *ha* (1880). Algerian wine was further boosted by the realisation that it was the perfect stuff with which to bolster Burgundy.

Since the closure of the Coteaux de Mascara-Côte de Beaune pipeline – which followed the departure of the French colonists, great efforts have been made to improve the general level of the wines in a variety of ways: by uprooting the poor quality but high yielding grape varieties introduced by the French, and by trying to introduce modern styles of vinification.

From being the fourth largest wine producer in the world in 1962, Algeria has now reduced its dependence on wine considerably.

Production has fallen from 15,000,000 *hl* to 5,000,000 in 20 years, though the area under vine has reduced to a smaller extent – from 360,000 *ha* to 230,000 *ha*.

The government-run Office Nationale de Produits Viticoles recognises seven regions, which are situated in three areas:

Oran (70% of Algeria's wine production; nine of the 12 VDQS's)
Alger (25% of Algeria's wine production; three of the 12 VDQS's)
Constantine (5% of Algeria's wine production)

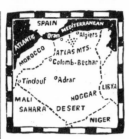

The Grape List

Alicante-Bouschet
Aramon (now being replaced by other varieties)
Cabernet-Sauvignon
Carignan
Cinsault
Clairette
Faramon
Farhana
Gamay
Grenache
Grilla
Hasseroum
Macabeo
Merseguera
Morastel
Mourvèdre
Pinot Noir
Syrah
Ugni Blanc

The Wine Regions

Coteaux de Tlemcen (western border) reds, whites and rosés. Improving methods of cold fermentation to produce longer-living whites and rosés.
Monts du Tessalah (Oran) reds, whites and rosés. Best reds from Sidi bel Abbes.
Dahra (Oran) reds and cherry-flavoured like rosés. Contains former VDQSs of Robert, Rabelais and Renault, now known as Taughrite, Aïn Merane, and Mazouna respectively.
Coteaux du Zaccar (Alger) reds, whites and richly scented rosés.
Coteaux de Mascara (Oran) whites and good wood-aged reds (which used to be sold as Burgundy).

Médéa (south-west of Algiers) Perhaps the best area; has a cooler climate and in certain regions soil similar to Burgundy, e.g. Miliana. Reds from classic French varieties; Cabernet, Pinot Noir, some finesse.
Aïn Bessem Bouir (east of Algiers) light reds and the best rosés.

Old (Pre-Independence) VDQS Zones

Coteaux de Mascara
Mascara
Haut Dahra
Monts du Tesselah
Coteaux de Tlemcen
Mostaganem
Mostaganem-Kenenda
Aïn-el-Hadjar
Oued Imbert
Médéa
Côtes du Zaccar
Aïn-Bessem-Bouira

Old (Pre-Independence) VDQS Wines

Rabelais
Robert
Renault
Château Romain
Domaine de Trappe-Staoueli
Clos de l'Emir
Lismara
Mansourah
The following pre-independence VDQS wines have been renamed:
Robert *has become* Taughrite
Rabelais *has become* Aïn Merane
Renault *has become* Mazouna

Alternative Wine List

The following is a list of alternatives to many of the world's best-known wines. The wines on the right are not, it should be emphasized, substitutes, nor are they necessarily less expensive, or better than the ones on the left. They are selected as being of interest, and with styles or flavours that have some relationship to each other.

Aloxe-Corton	*Ladoix*
Amontillado	*Palo Cortado*
Anjou Rosé	*Carbernet d'Anjou*
Asti Spumante	*Clairette de Die Tradition*
	Moscato
Barbera d'alba	*Bricco Manzoni*
Bardolino	*Chiaretto de Bardolino*
Barolo	*Brunello di Montalcino*
	Montepulciano d'Abruzzi
	Nebbiolo d'Alba
Beaujolais	*Gamay de Touraine*
	Côtes de Forez
Beaujolais Nouveau	*Côtes du Rhône Primeur*
	Vinot (Gaja)
Beaune	*Chorey-les-Beaune*
Bordeaux Blanc (dry)	*Bergerac Blanc*
	Entre-deux-Mers
Bordeaux Rouge	*Bergerac Rouge*
	Coteaux d'Aix en Provence
	Cousino Macul Chilean Cabernet
	Sassicaia
	Australian Cabernert Shiraz
	Californian Cabernet Sauvignon
	Raimat
	Venegazzu
	Bulgarian Cabernet Sauvignon
Bourgogne Blanc	*Marqués de Murrieta Rioja (Blanco)*
	New Zealand Chardonnay
	Aligoté
Bourgogne Rouge	*Pinot Noir (Oregon)*
	Bourgogne Hautes Côtes de Nuits
	Bourgogne Passetoutgrains
	Sancerre Rouge
Champagne	*Blanquette de Limoux*
	Saumur Mousseux
	Crémant d'Alsace
	Crémant de Bourgogne
	Schramsberg (California)
	Domaine Chandon (California)
Châteauneuf-du-Pape	*Australian Cabernet Shiraz*
Cheap Mosel	*Vinho Verde (sweetish)*
Chianti	*Grave de Friuli*
	Carmigniano
Côtes-du-Rhône	*Coteaux de Tricastin*
Crozes-Hermitage	*St-Joseph*
Cru Bourgeois Bordeaux	*Château Vignelaure*
Daõ	*Bairrada*
Dry Sherry	*Vin Jaune*
	Vernaccia di Oristano (Sardinia)
EEC Tafelwein	*Lemonade, water or anything*

Fino Sherry	Old Dry Oloroso
	Manzanilla
Frascati	Marino
	Pino Grigio (Grave del Friuli)
German Auslese	Late Harvest Riesling (New York State)
German Beerenauslese	Austrian Trockenbeerenauslese
Gevrey-Chambertin	Fixin (mature)
Gewürztraminer (Alsace)	Gewurztraminer (New Zealand)
Gigondas	Vacqueryras
Hermitage	Château Musar (Lebanon)
	Cornas
	Shiraz (Australian)
Late Bottled Vintage Port	'Single Quinta' Vintage Port
Liebfraumilch	EEC Tafelwein (qv)
Meursault	St-Aubin
	Australian Chardonnay (especially Rosemount)
Most commercial Lambrusco	Coca Cola with a touch of rum
Moulin-à-Vent	Chénas
Muscadet	Vin de Pays du Jardin de la France
Muscat de Beaumes de Venise	Frontignan
	Moscato di Siracusa
	Moscatel de Setúbal
Pomerol	Lalande de Pomerol
	Californian Merlot (especially Firestone)
Pommard	Auxey-Duresses
	Mercurey Rouge
Port	Bailey's Liqueur Muscat
	Zinfandel 'port' (late picked)
Pouilly-Fuissé	St-Véran
Pouilly Blanc Fumé	Californian Fumé Blanc (especially Mondavi)
Rioja	Raimat
Rosé (still)	Champagne Rosé
Ruby Port	Tawny Port
Sancerre	Sauvignon de Haut Poitou
	Sauvignon de St-Bris
	Quincy
	Sauvignon (Colli Orientali del Friuli)
Sauternes	Monbazillac
	Ste-Croix-du-Mont
	Muscat de Beaumes de Venise
Sweet Sherry (for cooking)	Sweet Montilla
Sweet Vermouth	Pineau de Charentes
Tavel Rose	Listel Gris de Gris
	Rioja Rosé (e.g. Lan, Cáceres)
Tawny Port	Malaga (especially Scholtz Hermanos)
Tokay d'Alsace	Tocai Friuliano
Valpolicella	Recioto de Valpolicella
Vinho Verde	Frizzante
Volnay	Rully
Vouvray	South African Chenin Blanc

ARGENTINA

ANOTHER OF THOSE COUNTRIES which ought to be up there with Bulgaria and Australia as one of the up-and-coming 'New World' wine producers. But politics have played their inevitable part in making Argentinian wine acceptable to a relatively small number of people outside South America. The dispute with Britain over the Falklands removed the British Isles from the list of countries which did import Argentinian wine – only days after a large consignment was delivered to a UK client. If says a great deal for the quality of the wine in question that its fans continued to buy it even whilst most British retailers had removed anything labelled 'Made in Argentina' from their shelves.

In May 1985, a bottle of 1975 Cabernet Sauvignon from Andean Vineyards – part of that last consignment to be allowed into Britain – was placed amongst a range of Australian and Chilean wines judged to be particularly good value for money by What Wine? magazine after a blind tasting. Argentina boasts the most modern winemaking industry in South America; it has enormous potential and only politics and an awesome rate of inflation will hold it back.

The Grape List

26% table grapes
31% white grapes
25% 'pink' grapes
18% red grapes

Red (Malbec)
Sangiavette
Listrac
Cabernet Sauvignon
Barbera
Criolla Chica
Pinot Noir
Lambrusco
Nebbiolo
Bonarda
Tempranillo
Merlot
Syrah

Pink (Criolla/Mission)
Cereza
Ferral
Garnacha

White (Moscatel)
Chenin Blanc
Pedro Ximénez
Sémillon
Malvasia
Sylvaner
Ugni Blanc
Gewürztraminer
Palomino
Chardonnay
Sauvignon Blanc
Torrontes

The Wine Regions

MENDOZA

With 32,000 vineyards (250,000

ha), the region of Mendoza produces over 70 per cent of Argentina's wine. The Malbec reds and Moscatel rosés are some of Argentina's best wines.

Grape varieties

Reds (Malbec)
Cabernet Sauvignon
Lambrusco
Tempranillo
Pinot Noir
Syrah

Pink (Criolla)
Cereza

White (Pedro Ximénez)
Chenin Blanc
Sémillon
Palomino
Moscatel
Chardonnay
Sylvaner

The major areas:
Mendoza (houses 1,300 bodegas)
Maipu
Luyan de Cuy
San Rafael
Lavalle
San Martin

SAN JUAN

Dominant grapes:
Criolla
Cereza
Pedro Ximénez
Moscatel

Black grapes account for only 10 per cent of the total. The hot climate produces heavier wines than elsewhere, sometimes in a sherry style, accounting for 20 per cent of Argentina's production. Grape concentrate, for export to Venezuela, USA and Japan, is produced in large quantities here.

RIO NEGRO AND NEUQU'EN

Grape varieties

Red (Malbec)
Barbera
Syrah
Pinot Noir
Merlot
Cabernet Sauvignon

White (Torrontes)
Pedro Ximénez
Sémillon
Chenin Blanc
Pinot Blanc
Malvasia

The influence of Italian immigrants in the area can often be detected in the styles of wines, which the southerly, cooler climate renders lighter and more acidic, and often more pleasing to the European palate. Five per cent of total production comes from the 3,700 vineyards, with 'Champaña', very popular sparkling wines.

LA RIOJA

Grape varieties

Torrontes
Moscatel
Ferral
Criolla
Cereza

only a small proportion of black grapes.

One of Argentina's oldest wine regions, but the high alcohol, low acidity wines are usually oxidized and flabby.

SALTA, JUJUY AND CATAMARCA

Wines from the Torrontes grape from the Calchaqui Valley, Salta are locally popular, but in the main wine from the 5,500 *ha* of vines is for distillation.

The List of Producers

ARIZU
'Valroy' wines and sparkling wine

BIANCHI
Red and white wines, 'Particular' Cabernet 'Dom Valentin' 'Bianchi Borgogna' (Barbera/Malbec), Argentina's top-selling red

CRILLON
'Crillon' sparkling 'Monitor' 'Embajador'

ESMERALDA
'St Félicien' Cabernet Reds from Malbec, whites from Sauvignon, Sylvaner

FLITCHMAN
Reds from Merlot and Syrah grapes. 'Caballero de la Cepa' white wine, and sparkling wines

FURLOTTI

GARGANTIA
'Emenencia' red.

GIOL (MENDOZA COOP)
'Canciller' branded wines.

GOYASECHEA
'Aberdeen Angus' 'Marques del Nevado'

GRECO

LOPEZ S.A.C.I.
Red and white wines, reds from Cabernet Sauvignon, Malbec, Merlot. Their 'Château Montchenot' is exported as 'Don Federico', and 'Vieux Château' Cabernet as 'Casona Lopez'.

BODEGAS NORTON
Originally English-owned. Cabernet, Sylvaner and Chardonnay red and white wines. 'Pedriel' Cabernet red 'Consechea Especial' 'Norton' sparkling wine.

JOSE ORFILA
'Cautivo' Cabernet

'Extra Dry' Pinot Blanc.

PENAFLOR
A major producer with four bodegas, making good wines from Cabernet Sauvignon and Chenin Blanc, the 'Fond de Cave' Chardonnay, a range of 'Andean' branded wines for export, and a sherry, 'Tio Quina'.

PROVIAR
A Moët & Chandon subsidiary; their 'Baron B' méthode champenoise wine is very popular. 'Castell Chandon' is a blend of Sauvignon, Sémillon and Ugni Blanc, 'Valmont' of Malbec and Cabernet Sauvignon, and 'Valtour' is a Pinot Noir red.

LA RURAL
Wood-aged reds, white wines from Sylvaner and Gewürztraminer.

SANTA ANA
Amongst their grapes are

Barbera, Bonarda and Syrah; 'Val Semina' is made from the latter.

SAN TELMO
'Californian' style wines from Cabernet, Malbec, Chardonnay and Chenin Blanc.

SUTER (SEAGRAMS)
'Etiquetta Blanca' is a brand leader; 'Etiquetta Marron' is the red.

MICHEL TORINO
Cabernet reds, and a Torrontes white, 'Don David'.

PASCUAL TOSO
Their Cabernet Sauvignon has been highly praised; they also make a Sylvaner white and sparkling wines.

WEINERT
Producers of a notable Chardonnay.

GONZALO VIDELA
'Tromel' and 'Panqueha' branded wines.

WINE AUCTION LIST

The largest wine auction was conducted by Christie's of London in Quaglino's Ballroom in 1974. There were 2,325 lots, comprising 432,000 bottles in all, and the sale realised £962,190.

★ ★ ★ ★ ★

In May 1980 Michael Broadbent of Christie's conducted an aution for Heublein's, in San Francisco, where John Grisanti bought a bottle of 1822 Château Lafite for $31,000 (then £13,140).

★ ★ ★ ★ ★

In June 1981 Opus One, the 1979 'Napamedoc' (made by Robert Mondavi and Philippe de Rothschild) was sold at the Robert Mondavi Winery for $24,000 (then £12,000) a case; i.e. £1,000 a bottle. The more patient could buy the same wine in 1984 for a tenth of that sum.

★ ★ ★ ★ ★

On 6 December 1979 at a Christie's auction a bottle of 1748 Rudesheimer Rosewein fetched £260.

★ ★ ★ ★ ★

16 July 1984: a jeroboam of 1870 Mouton Rothschild was bought for resale from Whitwham Wines, Altrincham, England by Bill Burford of Dallas, Texas for £26,500.

★ ★ ★ ★ ★

A bottle of 1806 Château Lafite, only one of two such bottles known, was sold at Heublein's 11th National Auction of Rare Wines in May 1979 in Atlanta, Georgia, for £28,000.

★ ★ ★ ★ ★

A half bottle of 1811 Tokay Essence fetched £220 at a Christie's auction.

★ ★ ★ ★ ★

In 1983, 21 bottles of Biondi-Santi Brunello di Montalcino went on sale at the vineyard for 6m lire (£2,700) each.

★ ★ ★ ★ ★

On 26 September 1983 an imperial of Château Mouton Rothschild 1924 was sold at Sotheby's for £8,500, approximately £40 per mouthful. Possibly the only surviving example of only three such bottles produced, it attracted particular interest as being Baronne Philippe de Rothschild's first successful vintage, and the first for which he commissioned an artist (in this case Jean Carlu) to design the label (see p.126 for the list of de Rothschild's commissioned wine labels).

★ ★ ★ ★ ★

Cheapest wine ever? In 1983 surplus wine from the EEC wine lake was sold to the USSR at less than 7p a litre. The Russians have recently bought 25 million gallons of Argentinian wine at 1 US cent per litre, for sale in the USSR.

★ ★ ★ ★ ★

The 1982 Napa Valley Wine Auction, which was conducted by Michael Broadbent of Christie's, attracted a record attendance and realised over $250,000:
A nebuchadnezzar of Beringer Cabernet Sauvignon 1978 fetched $1,450
A salamanazer of Domaine Chandon Napa Valley Brut fetched $1,100
A jeroboam of Robert Mondavi Cabernet Sauvignon fetched $2,600
A jeroboam of Buehler Cabernet Sauvignon 1978 fetched $3,000
A jeroboam of Chappelet Cabernet Sauvignon 1970 fetched $3,300
A case of Diamond Creek Lake Cabernet Sauvignon 1978 fetched $5,400

★ ★ ★ ★ ★

AUSTRALIA

AUSTRALIA is, without question, the most exciting new wine-producing country in the world. Hyperbole? Not a bit of it. No other country has as much potential, and as few handicaps:
The list of Australian assets:

1. Inexpensive land – and plenty of it.
2. Reliable climate, varying from baking heat in some regions to relatively cool temperatures in others.
3. Up-to-date technology.
4. Open minds, enthusiasm and an antipathy to pretension in any form.

Whilst not a few Californians have been busy convincing themselves and each other that they have already achieved so much that they can ask more for their wine than is charged for the finest bottles from the old vineyards of Europe, the Australians have been following a more humble track. Almost all will admit that they still have a great deal to learn; but there is one essential difference between the attitude of the Australian and that of the Californian – the Australian is not looking over his shoulder at Europe. It is no accident that whilst California's great vinous successes have almost all been with Cabernet Sauvignons and Chardonnays which mimicked the wines of Bordeaux and Burgundy, the Aussies have been breaking new ground with the Shiraz and Sémillon, using these grapes in ways the Europeans never imagined. Of course the Europeans have to be given some credit for today's Australian wines. Even now there are winemaking regions where the local dialect is a form of 'Australianized' German, but the Fatherland is a long way away, and the settlers arrived rather a long time ago. Until recently,

few wine lovers in the rest of the world could take the idea of Antipodean beer-swilling wine producers seriously, so there was every reason to get on with the job of proving those foreigners wrong. For many years, the heritage of heavy 'Port' style wines did slow progress, but this has now been relegated to the past.

Another feature of interest in Australia is the fact that no single region has yet been allowed to hog the limelight. There is no 'Australian Napa Valley'; there are five regions, each subdivided into smaller areas, each busily working to establish its own identity. One way in which the local winemakers are achieving this is by holding literally scores of local tasting competitions. We did contemplate listing these and their winners – but doing so would not have left us much space for any of this book's other contents.

The Grape List

RED WINES

Cabernet Sauvignon	4,151ha: major premium quality grape
Carignan	182ha: not a true Carignan – poor quality
Cinsault	152ha: used for table wines and port-style wines
Frontignan	417ha: produces the best of the Muscat dessert wines
Grenache	6,301ha: average quality table and port-style wines
Malbec	467ha: rare – average quality – mostly in irrigation areas
Mataro	1,924ha: similar to Mourvèdre grape – average quality
Pinot Noir	120ha: mainly in the Hunter Valley in small quantities
Shiraz	10,387ha: the Syrah – good quality wines often blended

WHITE WINES

Chardonnay	176ha: being increasingly planted for quality wines
Chasselas	74ha: rare – often used for sparkling wine
Chenin Blanc	259ha: becoming increasingly planted for dry white table wine
Clairette	46ha: mainly found in NSW – blended medium quality
Crouchen	1,111ha: French origin – Clare Riesling – used for dry table wine
Doradillo	2,230ha: mostly used as a base wine for fortified and distilled wines
Irvine's White	177ha: mainly for sparkling wine production in Victoria
Marsanne	44ha: rare – used for white table wines mainly in north Victoria
Muscadelle	466ha: principally in South Australia – fortified sweet dessert wines
Muscat Gordo Blanco	4,000ha: used for dry table wines or sweet fortified wines
Palomino	1,187ha: very popular for dry fortified wines
Pedro Ximénez	1,574ha: also used for dry fortified wines
Rhine Riesling	2,937ha: quality variety – best in South Australia – also in the Hunter Valley
Sauvignon Blanc	122ha: mostly in South Australia – used for dry white table wines

Sémillon	2,554 *ha*: at its best in the Hunter valley – often blended
Sercial	60 *ha*: same as Irvine's White, used for blends and fortified
Sultana	19,690 *ha*: for distillation and cheap table and fortified wines
Traminer	214 *ha*: mainly in NSW – good quality table wines
Trebbiano	1,496 *ha*: used as blending wine or for distillation
Verdelho	88 *ha*: used in 'white Burgundy' style blends
White Grenache	44 *ha*: all in South Australia – blending wine

The List of Australian Wineries

NEW SOUTH WALES

The Hunter Valley

The fame of the Hunter rests on its dry red and white table wines, chiefly made from the Shiraz and Sémillon grapes. The older and more well-known vineyards are situated in the parishes of Pokolbin and Rothbury, whereas the more recent expansion has been in the Upper Hunter area, west of Muswellbrook. The soils are very varied with outcrops of volcanic among alluvial and sandstone with occasional patches of limestone. The climate is moderate, with the heaviest rainfall occurring during the summer.

Major growers:

Arrowfield With over 500 *ha* of vines, this estate is not only one of the largest in Australia but is also relatively new, the first vintage having been harvested in 1975, and it is best known for its Sémillon and Rhine Riesling.

Brokenwood A small boutique winery near Pokolbin planted in 1971, with a reputation for producing excellent blended red wines.

Château Douglas Owned by 300 shareholders, the estate started planting in 1970 with a preponderance of Shiraz and Sémillon, together with Cabernet and a number of other smaller plantings.

Château François Another very small vineyard, situated close to Tyrrell's. Beside a number of varietals, it also produces a port-style wine from the Cabernet.

W. Drayton & Sons Pty Ltd The Drayton family has been at Bellevue since 1850, situated in the foothills of the Mt View range, and has been producing

wine since the 1870s. The family now concentrates on Shiraz and Sémillon, with the recent addition of Cabernet Sauvignon and Rhine Riesling.

Elliott's Wines Pty Ltd Another old-established Hunter Valley family, the Elliotts first arrived in 1893 and bought the Oakvale property. Owning a number of vineyards in the area, the family sells all its wines bottled at source and has a particular reputation for wines made from the Shiraz and Sémillon.

Hermitage Estate Although a vineyard for over 70 years, the estate has only recently been developed, and now has more than 325 *ha* under vine, including some Chardonnay. It also owns the Elliotts' Oakvale vineyards.

Hollydene A 200 *ha* property first planted in 1969 by Henry Tulloch, one of Australia's leading viticulturalists. It is famous for its circular winery and the quality of its Sémillons and Shiraz Cabernet blend.

Hungerford Hill Vineyards This company owns one of the largest vineyard areas in the Hunter Valley, as well as an estate in Coonawarra in South Australia. First vintaging in 1970, the estate is a proponent of the modern methods of vinification with cold fermented whites and reds aged for a year in Limousin oak.

Lake's Folly One of the most well-known vineyards in the Valley, it was first planted by Dr Max Lake in 1963, one of the first people to concentrate on Cabernet Sauvignon, matured in new oak. He also produces an excellent Chardonnay.

Lindemans Wines Pty Ltd at Ben Ean. The Lindeman family first started planting vines in the Hunter Valley in 1843, and have since grown to become of national importance – one of the 'big four'. The Ben Ean estate is particularly well-known for its dry white wines, owned by Lindemans.

McWilliams Wines Pty Ltd at Mt Pleasant. Many of McWilliams top quality wines, mainly Sémillon and Shiraz, are sold under this name, where they have had an interest since 1932.

Murray Robson's Squire Vineyard A nine-hectare property near Mt View, well

known for the quality of its wines and the number of more unusual varieties planted in the vineyards.

Oakdale Vineyards Pty Ltd This historic Pokolbin vineyard has recently been expanded after remaining for over 100 years in the same family. While still supplying grapes to other companies, the present owners have started bottling and selling wines under their own label.

Penfolds Wines Pty Ltd at the Dalwood Estate. Though they have been associated with the Valley since 1904, the Dalwood Estate was only planted in the 1960s, when they developed more than 500 hectares near Muswellbrook, where a wide variety of vines are grown.

Pokolbin Estate Vineyard A quality vineyard situated in the heart of the traditional Pokolbin area, mainly planted with Shiraz, Cabernet Sauvignon and Sémillon.

Roberts Rothbury Pty Ltd at Belbourie. First started in the 1960s, this property aims soon to have 80 hectares under vine, with many varieties being included. The wine is sold directly to the public and is noted for its unusual labels and Aboriginal names.

Saxonvale Pokolbin One of the vineyards originally owned

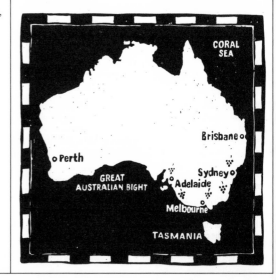

by a member of the Drayton family, it now belongs to Saxonvale, though is still marketed under its own label.

Saxonvale Wines With three vineyards in the Hunter Valley, this company now has close to 300 hectares of vines, planted with a variety of the classic grape types.

Seppelts Hunter 40 hectares are situated just outside Cessnock, is planted entirely with Shiraz, which came into full production in 1978.

Sobels Queldinburg Wines A winery without vineyards, this operation is situated near Muswellbrook and vinifies grapes from the upper Hunter area, which are marketed under their own label, mostly as straight varietals.

J.Y. Tulloch & Sons Pty Ltd at Glen Elgin. The Tulloch family was one of the four in the Valley who managed to survive the Depression. Now part of Gilbeys Australia, it is particularly known for its Sémillon wines, though it makes some excellent Cabernet as well.

The Rothbury Estate With its associated vineyards, the estate now controls more than 300 hectares of vines. It is owned by a syndicate that was formed in 1968. Sold under a distinctive label, the wines undergo a vigorous selection by, among others, Len Evans and Murray Tyrrell, and are sold mainly through their Wine Club.

Tamburlaine Wines Started as a hobby in 1967, this vineyard near Pokolbin is a family venture which vinifies and bottles its own wines, and has been particularly successful with Cabernet and Cabernet/Shiraz blends.

Tyrrell's Vineyards Pty Ltd at Ashmans. The Tyrrell family first came to the Valley in 1858, when they bought the land on which the vineyards now stand. The present owner, Murray Tyrrell, has established the vineyard as one of the best-known in Australia.

Wollundry Wines Begun in 1971, this estate now covers 23 hectares. Growing both red and white varieties, the owner, Ron Hansen, has established a particular reputation for his old style Sémillon wines.

Wyndham Estate Wines from this estate were among the first Australian wines to be shown at European competitions during the second half of the 18th century. After a period under Penfold ownership, it has now returned to its original title and has been replanted and extended to become one of the larger producers in the area.

The Murrumbidgee Irrigation Area. Situated around the towns of Griffith, Leeton and Yenda in the south-west of New South Wales, this area accounts for about a sixth of the total Australian wine production. Traditionally associated with sweet dessert and port-style wines, the region is now concentrating on making light table wines (sold either in bulk or wine casks) using the most modern techniques available and is having a considerable success.

Major companies:

McWilliam Wines Pty Ltd. at Hanwood. The McWilliams family was one of the first in the area to plant vines once the main irrigation channels were built. Still a family business, it now processes more than 16 million litres a year.

Penfolds, Griffith. Another of the original families to arrive in the area after the introduction of irrigation, the company first started processing grapes in 1921. They now have facilities to handle over 250 tonnes a day.

Seppelts, Griffith. Seppelts own a winery near Bilbul where they ferment wines prior to sending them to Rutherglen for blending and maturation.

Wynn Winegrowers Ltd. at Yenda. Wynn's is unusual among the large companies in the region in that they own a number of vineyards. The family first decided to start operating in the area in the early 1960s, and are now producing a whole range of wines and styles.

Calamia Wines, Griffith. Specialises in the production of dry reds.

Calabria Wines, Griffith. A family affair, this business produces a range of wines of different styles from grapes bought from the surrounding farmers, as well as some good quality wines from their own estates.

De Bortoli, Griffith. An Italian company producing more than 50 styles of wine.

Fairefield Winery. Belongs to a cooperative of winegrowers.

McManus Wines. A small estate which only produces wine from its own grapes, and has started winning a good reputation for the quality of its wines.

Rossetto's Wines. Owned by an Italian immigrant who makes a range of wines and liqueurs.

San Bernadino Wines. A small company producing a full range of wines including sparkling, this business is working hard to improve the quality image of the area.

Sergi's Wines. Another relatively new arrival that produces a full range of wines.

Toorak Wines. A small company that has acquired a considerable reputation for its wines made from the Cabernet Sauvignon.

Rooty Hill

Penfolds Wine Pty Ltd. Situated at Minchinbury just 30 miles from Sydney, this estate has now been reduced by urban development to about 14 hectares. Producing grapes for use in sparkling wine for which the name 'Minchinbury' is a brand name, the estate also grows some Traminer.

Other areas

Corowa. Being on the border with Victoria, this area is more closely associated with Rutherglen in Victoria. It is famous for the production of sweet dessert and port-style wines, mainly coming from the house of Lindemans.

Mudgee. This area lying over 140 miles to the west of the Hunter Valley on the other side of the Continental Divide has a similar climate though rather cooler as a result of the higher altitude. After a period of stagnation following the Depression, the region is experiencing a revival and is rapidly gaining a reputation for producing excellent quality wines: Botolbar. At over 600 metres, this is the highest vineyard in the area, founded in 1970 and making a range of varietal wines.

Craigmoor. A property with a growing success in shows, this is one of the only estates in that area to survive the Depression.

Miramar Vineyards.

Huntingdon Estate Wines, Montrose Wines, Mudgee Wines Pty Ltd, Young, Barwang Pastoral Co. An estate lying half-way between Sydney and Griffith, and though small has been winning a lot of medals, especially for its Cabernet Sauvignon.

Cobbitty. Cobbitty Wines

Cowra. Cowra Vineyards.

Namoi Valley. Cubbaroo Vineyards.

Buronga, Hungerford Hill Pty Ltd. An offshoot of the Hunter Valley winery.

Denman. A town situated in the upper Hunter Valley: Denman Estate Wines. Started in 1969, this property now has over 200 hectares of vines. Rosemount Estates. Originally purchased as grazing land, this company first began to plant vines in 1970 and now has over 60 hectares as well as other vineyards purchased in the surrounding areas. The enterprise is rapidly gaining an excellent reputation for its varietal wines.

Barooga. Close to Rutherglen in Victoria, this area has been used by Seppelt to produce port-style wines as well as some white table wines.

Forbes. The Sand Hills Vineyard.

VICTORIA

Rutherglen and the North-East

Centred on Rutherglen which lies on the Murray river, the area has made its reputation with excellent dessert and port-style wines as well as full-bodied reds. The climate is continental in character with hot, dry summers and cold, frosty winters when most of the precipitation occurs. The vineyards are to be found around the valleys of the Murray, King and Ovens rivers where the soil is a well-drained sandy loam.

Baileys' Bundarra Vineyards. For over 100 years, the vineyards remained in the hands of the Bailey family until they were purchased in 1972. The estate is particularly famous for its big gutsy red wines and its Muscats and port-style wines; it is now owned by Davis Gelatine.

Booth Brothers, Taminick Vineyards. This family-run business has mainly made wines to sell in bulk, but they have recently started to market their own hefty reds.

Brown Bros Milawa Vineyard Pty Ltd. This family business now has the fourth generation working on the premises. Owning a number of estates around Milawa and vinifying and marketing the produce from a number of others, the family concentrates on selling a range of varietal wines of high reputation with the most modern viticultural and wine-making techniques.

R.L. Buller & Son Pty Ltd, Calliope Vineyards. The Buller family has about 38 hectares under vine near Rutherglen and has been in the area since 1921. Their most famous wines are vintage and ruby port-style wines (including a straight Cabernet port-style) and a fine Muscat.

A.D. Campbell, Bobbie Burns Winery. The Campbell family has owned vines near Rutherglen since the 1880s and now has 44 hectares planted with a number of different varieties.

W.H. Chambers & Sons, Rosewood. Another small family-owned winery, it is situated close to. Rutherglen and produces a wide range of wines including a straight Cabernet Sauvignon.

R.N. & K.B. Gayfer, Chitern Winery. This winery grew out of the demise of the goldmining industry, using the old engine-houses as cellars. Now owning nearly 30 hectares of vines, they are well-known for their full reds and fortified wines.

G.T. Gehrig, Barnawartha Vineyards. Another old-established family business now working 20 hectares of vines near Rutherglen, growing a range of different grape varieties.

L. Jones, Rutherglen. A property just outside Rutherglen, notorious for the first discovery of phylloxera in 1897.

Markwood Estate. One of the newer properties in the area situated near Milawa, which is owned and run by a member of the Rutherglen family, mentioned above.

Morris Wines Pty Ltd. This family has been making wine in the area since the middle of the 19th century, and is especially famous for the quality of its Liqueur Muscats. The business is now owned by Reckitt & Colman.

B. Seppelt & Sons Ltd. Seppelts are the only large national company to be found at Rutherglen, where they own 200 hectares. They specialise in the production of fortified wines including a full range of sherry-style wines.

G.S. Smith & Sons, All Saints. This property, which contains over 100 hectares of vines, was bought by the Smith family in the 1860s, and has remained in their hands ever since. Originally having a reputation for making very masculine wines, they were one of the first wine-makers to start leading the way to a lighter, fresher style.

Stanton and Killeen, Gracerray Vineyards. Another family business with origins in the middle of the 19th century, it owns a small vineyard just outside Rutherglen. A good reputation has been built for traditional styled wines including some excellent fortifieds.

Goulburn Valley. This area is situated around the town of Seymour about 80 miles north of Melbourne. The climate is extreme with very hot summers and the danger of frosts in the winter. The soil is a mixture of sandy loams and alluvial.

Château Tahbilk. By far the most famous property in the area, it was begun in 1860 with the clearance of 60 hectares of scrub. There are now over 70 hectares of vines, and only table wines are produced which have traditionally been sold under their varietal names. The wines are individual in style and excellent in quality.

Other Wineries. With the exception of the Darveniza Brothers' Excelsior Vineyard, most of the properties in the Goulburn Valley are of fairly recent origin, and include the following:

Cottage Vineyard
Gravina Bros
Mitchelton Vintners (Aust) Pty Ltd
Osicka's Vineyard
Rosebercon Vineyard
Virgin Hills
C. Conte, Ardmona
V. Curcio, Ardmona
Goulburn Valley Winery, Shepparton
G. & V. Scrimizzi, Ardmona

Great Western and Environs

This small region situated about 140 miles west of Melbourne lies between 280 and 360 metres, and is reckoned to have the climate most similar in Australia to that of the best European sites. The soils are among the poorest in Australia being mainly volcanic, broken down into loams or sand. The area is best-known for the quality of its sparkling wines, the still wines being more

normally used for blending with other areas.

Seppelts. The vineyards situated just south of the small township of Great Western had already built a considerable reputation for sparkling wines when they were taken over by Seppelt in 1918. There are now almost 300 hectares under vines and about four miles of tunnels for the maturation of the wines. Some still varietal wines are also now being produced. Seppelts' Great Western sparkling wine is the best known in Australia.

Best's Wines Pty Ltd, Concongella. This property has a history as old as that of Seppelt and is now known for its light table wines.

Balgownie Vineyard at Bendigo. A vineyard that was first started in 1969, it has achieved an excellent reputation for the quality of its 100 per cent varietal wines produced on the estate.

Nathan and Wyeth at Avoca. This recent and large estate uses at least half its production to make an excellent sparkling wine using traditional French methods only, which is marketed under the 'Quelltaler' label.

Redbank at Avoca. A new development specialising in producing varietal wines from its own and neighbouring vineyards.

Seppelts at Drumborg. Finding their property near Great Western too small to meet their requirements, Seppelts have recently begun planting an area of 190 hectares near Drumborg. The climate and soil is very similar to that found at Great Western though it tends to be somewhat cooler. The grapes grown are all vinified at Great Western.

The North-West
This region of Victoria lying around the town of Mildura which is on the banks of the Murray river is undulating, with red sandy soils and a hot continental climate. Most of the wines produced rely on irrigation and have been of medium to lower quality or used for distillation, but with recent research into hot climate vinification, there has been a great deal of improvement.

Lindemans at Karadoc. Lindemans bought a large property in this area in 1973 and started to plant vines as well as to construct one of the largest wineries in Australia.

Mildara Wines Ltd. This company has its roots in a business which started in 1891, just after the town of Mildura was founded. It makes some outstanding wines and is particularly famous for its brandies and sherry-style wines.

McWilliams at Robinvale. McWilliams moved into the area in 1961, and have since begun the production of a variety of table wines and brandies.

Other Areas:
Swan Hill – Bullers

Lake Boga – Best Wines Pty Ltd.
Anakie – near Geelong
Mooorabool, near Geelong –
Idyll Vineyard
Wantirna Estate – close to Melbourne
Yarck Vineyards Estate
Yarra Yering Vineyard – near Melbourne.

SOUTH AUSTRALIA

The vineyards of Adelaide are almost as old as the city itself, the first vines being planted just one year after the colony was founded in 1836. Many of the vineyards have since disappeared under the advancing suburbs, but many of the famous names who originally started in the area are still there. The climate is mild with a great deal of sunshine and rain, and the soil fertile.

Angle Vale Vineyards Pty Ltd. This 280 hectare estate was started in 1969 and fully planted by 1975. The mix is 70/30 red/white and the company has already built a reputation for good Cabernet and Shiraz as well as a vintage port style.

Angoves Pty Ltd at Tea Tree Gully. Founded during the second half of the 19th century, this vineyard has been reduced to a few hectares only by urban development, and the main centre has moved to Renmark.

Hamilton's Ewell Vineyards Pty Ltd at Glenelg. Claimed to be the first winemaker in South Australia, Richard Hamilton started making wine in 1839. Though only seven hectares have survived the onslaught of buildings, the company is still controlled by the same family, with estates in Springton and Eden Valley in the Barossa,

Nyah near Swan Hill and at Nildottie on the Murray river.

H.M. Martin and Son Pty Ltd at Stonyfell. This estate is now owned by Dalgety Australia Pty Ltd, having previously been in the Martin family since the beginning of the century.

Norman's Wines. This family business has been in existence since 1853, and has built a reputation for making consistently good wines.

Penfold's Wines Pty Ltd at Magill. The Penfold family first settled in the Grange at Magill in 1844. The company headquarters are still there and 'Grange Hermitage' has become one of the most prized wines in Australia.

Auldana. An old estate which was purchased by Penfolds in 1944, it is now the centre of

production of the famed St Henri wines.

Seaview Champagne Cellars at Romalo, Magill. Belonging to the Wynns since 1929, this winery is famous mainly for its excellent sparkling wine production, much of which is sold under the Seaview label and made by the Champagne method.

D.A. Tolley Pty Ltd at Tea Tree Gully. Since 1892 the

The Southern Vales
Lying to the south of Adelaide, this area is a mixture of rolling hills and rich plains. The soils are varied to match and the climate is temperate with cool autumns, warm summers and infrequent frosts.

Alcheringa Winery. A new development, this vineyard specialises in a variety of fortified wines.

Genders McLaren Park. Until 1968 the Gender family used to sell their grapes to the local wineries, but now they are making their own wines in small quantities but of good quality and including both table and fortified styles.

Thomas Hardy and Sons Ltd at Tintara. The Tintara vineyard was purchased by the Hardy family in 1876 and has since acted as a base for their expansion into being a major force in the Australian wine trade. Their fame rests mainly with their blended wines.

Richard Hamilton's Willunga Vineyards. A new vineyard, it is owned and run by a member of the Hamilton family that first started wine making near Adelaide in 1839. It is very small and one of the few in the area that specializes in white wines.

A.C. Johnston Ltd at Pirramimma. This family concern has about 90 hectares

Tolley family has been involved in growing vines in the Hope Valley. They also own estates now in Modbury and the Murray Valley and have started to market their own wines under the Pedare label.

Woodley Wines Pty Ltd at Glen Osmond. Though no vines remain, the cellars are still in existence having taken over the tunnels left by a worked-out silver-lead mine.

under vine, with a preponderance of Shiraz. They produce both table and fortified wines.

Kay Brothers Pty Ltd at Amery. Another family business which has had in the past considerable exports to the UK, this vineyard was established in 1890 and has concentrated mainly on red wine production.

Marienberg Winery. A small winery begun in 1966 by the husband and wife team, Ursula and Geoffrey Pridham, who have rapidly built up a reputation for the excellence of their wines and especially their handling of oak-cask maturation.

F.E. Osborn & Sons Pty Ltd at d'Arenberg. Dating to 1912 the estate is well-known for its range of full-bodied red wines as well as some port-style wines.

Walter Reynelly & Sons Wines Ltd at Reynella. The family first settled in the area in 1840, when they planted with vines brought from South Africa. Reynella remained in the family until 1976, and is best known for its reds though it does produce a full range of wines.

Roxton Estate. First planted by the Hull-based wine-merchants, B.B. Mason, in the 1930s, to supply port-style wines for the British market, the estate has gone through many vicissitudes and is now owned by Dalgety and produces 75 per cent reds.

Ryecroft Holdings Pty Ltd. Best-known as the property from which Jim Ingoldby spread the fame of the McLaren Vale wines

13

during the 1960s and especially the quality of its reds; previously it had been a major area for the supply of sweet wines to the export market.

Seaview Winery Pty Ltd. The vineyards at Seaview cover more than 240 hectares, of which the majority is Cabernet Sauvignon and Shiraz. Unusually for Australia, there are some plantings of Sauvignon Blanc.

Southern Vales Co-operative Winery Ltd. Formed during the period of grape surplus in the 1960s by almost 200 growers, this cellar now produces a full range of wine styles.

Other properties in the Southern Vales

G. & G. Berenyi at McLaren Flat
Chalk Hill Wines
Coriole Vineyard
Dridan Skottowe Estate
Egerton Dennis
Light Wines, Coolawin
Merrivale Wines
Palladio Wines Pty Ltd
G. Patritti & Co
Santa Rosa Wines
The Settlement Wine Co
Torresan's Happy Valley Vineyards
Trennert Wines
Woodstock Wine Cellar

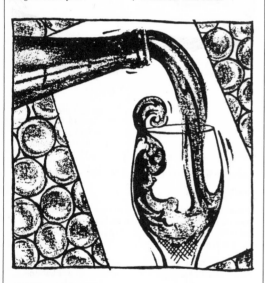

The Barossa Valley
The Barossa lies about 30 miles north-east of Adelaide and has long been synonymous with the production of wine in Australia. First settled by German immigrants in the middle of the last century, it has become famous for the range of fortified wines, though increasingly the production of table wines is taking over, especially in the hills. The climate is hotter and drier than most European wine-growing areas, though it varies a great deal throughout the valley, as does the soil which varies from light sand to heavy loam.

Barossa Co-operative Winery Ltd at Kaiser Stuhl. The sole co-operative in the valley, it was founded in 1931 and now has 520 members. Besides producing a full range of wine styles, it also sells a number of wines under their individual vineyard names.

Wolf Blass Wines of Bilyara. Though only formed in the

1960s, this company has become well-known for the quality of its wines, especially its reds, and the strong personality of its owner.

Leo Buring Pty Ltd at Château Leonay. This property remains a monument to one of the pioneers of the 20th century Australian wine trade. It is now owned by Lindemans and is chiefly known

for its excellent white wines.

Château Yaldara Pty Ltd. Founded by Hermann Thumm, a German who had been interned in Australia during the last war, this estate has acquired a reputation particularly for its sparkling wines and for the beauty of the property.

G. Gramp & Sons Pty Ltd at Orlando. The involvement of the Gramp family in the area began in 1847 when Johann Gramp moved to Jacob's Creek. This century they were among the first to introduce cold fermentation for white wines. The company is now owned by Reckitt & Colman.

Hamilton's Ewell Vineyards Ltd. Hamiltons own two wineries in the area, one at Springton and the other at Eden Valley.

Thomas Hardy and Sons Pty Ltd at Siegersdorf. Siegersdorf has been in the hands of the company since just after the First World War, and though originally producing fortified wines, it now makes almost exclusively white table wines.

C.A. Henschke and Co at Keyneton. This property is situated in an area which has a much cooler climate than the valley in general. It is well-known for the quality of its red and white table wines, produced from over 100 hectares of vines.

Hoffman's North Para Wines Pty Ltd. This small estate is now being run by the sixth generation of the Hoffman family, and makes mainly fortified and red table wines.

Penfolds Wines Pty Ltd. Penfolds own estates at Nuriootpa and Kalimna where they make a great deal of their brandy and fortified wines. Kalimna vineyard, which covers nearly 300 hectares, is one of the sources for the Cabernet used in the famous St Henri wines.

W. Salter and Son Pty Ltd at Saltram. Part of the Dalgety empire, this property has over 100 hectares under vine which constitutes only about 10 per cent of their total output.

B. Seppelt and Sons Ltd. Seppelts have their head-quarters at Seppeltsfield where they also produce vast quantities of fortified wines. Their other property in the valley is Château Tanunda where they concentrate on table wines.

S. Smith & Son Pty Ltd at Yalumba. The Smiths first settled in the Valley in 1847, and the fifth generation of the family now owns over 160 hectares in the Valley as well as further parcels in the Murray Valley and at Pewsey Vale high up in the Barossa hills. They are best-known for their oak matured reds and fresh, crisp Rhine Rieslings.

Tolley, Scott and Tolley Ltd. Until the 1960s, this company was known mainly for its brandies but now, after extensive investment, they also have large table-wine production, with nearly 600 hectares of newly planted vines; their wines are marketed under the Tollana brand name.

Wynn's High Eden Estate. This property has been developed to replace their Modbury Estate which was lost to Adelaide's suburbs in 1975. The vineyards are high in the Barossa hills and have been planted with Pinot Noir, Chardonnay, Cabernet Sauvignon and Rhine Riesling.

Other Estates

O. Basedow Wines Ltd
Bernkastel Wines Pty Ltd
Château Rosevale Winery
Chattertons Wine Cellars
Karslburg Wines
Karrawirra
B. Liebich & Sons, Rovalley Wines
St Hallett's Wines Pty Ltd
Veritas Winery
Wilsford Wines

Clare, Watervale

The towns of Clare and Watervale are situated in a small area of wooded hills, lying about 90 miles north of Adelaide and very close to sea level. The climate is hot with restricted rainfall and a variation of soils similar to those found in the Barossa.

A.P. Birks, Wendouree Cellars. This small estate had been in the same family since it was first planted in 1892, until 1974. It makes big, old-fashioned styled wines.

Château Clare Estate. Although only planted in 1969, this vineyard under the direction of the Taylor family has already achieved notable distinction for the quality of its oak matured Cabernet Sauvignon and Shiraz.

Manresa Society Inc. Sevenhill Cellars. Begun in 1845 by two Jesuit brothers, it now produces most of the altar wine used in the Pacific and SE Asia. The excess production has been sold commercially since 1954.

Quelltaler Wines Ltd. This vineyard has a history stretching back to 1865, and with about 240 hectares of vines, it is best-known for the quality of its white wines.

Stanley Wine Co Pty Ltd. The vineyards were purchased by H.J. Heinz in 1971, and have since concentrated increasingly on marketing their own wines, including the premium range of Leasingham Estate wines.

Other Estates

Clarevale Co-operative Winery
St Clare Cellars

Coonawarra

This region is the most southerly of Australian wine-making areas with a climate that is cooler than the majority of European centres, with the attendant problems of frosts, late harvesting and variable vintage characteristics. Lying 260 miles SE of Adelaide, the region has rapidly acquired a reputation for the production of quality wines, thanks to its moderate climate and to the famous red soil, a lime-rich loam, which lies in an island nine miles long and one mile wide in the centre of the area. This red island is completely covered with vines, which also spread out to the surrounding areas of related black soil, that are more clay-like in formation but still with the same calcareous subsoil and unusually high water table. With an area of over 1,300 hectares under vines, Coonawarra is most famous for the quality of its Cabernet Sauvignons and Rhine Rieslings.

Eric Brand. Having for many years been selling his grapes to Rouge Homme, Eric Brand decided in 1965 to start marketing his own wines. He makes a range of red wines both blended and straight which are sold under the Laira label.

Hungerford Hill Ltd. This Hunter Valley based company purchased over 160 hectares in the valley in the early 1970s, which have been planted with Cabernet Sauvignon, Shiraz and Rhine Riesling.

Lindemans Wines. Lindemans own almost 200 hectares in the area. It is the centre of their famous Rouge Homme brand as well as a range of individual vineyard wines.

Mildara Wines Ltd. Mildara owns over 300 hectares of vines situated in the prime red soil, planted with a variety of red and white grapes. The knowledge-able note a difference between the fuller style of their reds and the lighter more elegant style of the Wynn's or Redman wines.

O.D. & E.M. Redman. At the time of the Second World War, Redman's was virtually the only winery in the area, though they did not start to market their own wines until 1954. Sold under the Rouge Homme label, the wines quickly spread word of the region's potential, and by 1965 the Redmans had sold out to Lindemans. The family is still making wine, though on a much smaller scale.

Wynn's Coonawarra Estate. Wynn's took over where Redmans left off in increasing the reputation of the area's wines. Samuel Wynn bought vineyards in 1951 that were destined to become grazing land, and from which he now makes some of Australia's finest wines from the Shiraz and Cabernet Sauvignon (both straight and blended) Chardonnay and Rhine Riesling.

Keppoch, Padthaway

One of the newest vineyard areas in Australia, the region was not planted until the late 1960s. Lying just 40 miles north of Coonawarra, it is a dry area with sparse vegetation and a soil that is rather heavier than the red soil of Coonawarra. The following four big companies have been building up large estates in the area:

Lindemans Wines Pty Ltd, Thomas Hardy, Wynn's, Seppelts

Langhorne Creek

25 miles west of Adelaide on the Bremer river can be found the region known as Langhorne Creek, where wines have been made since the mid 1860s. The soil is a rich alluvial loam and the climate warm with low rainfall requires irrigation.

Bleasdale Vineyards Pty Ltd
The Potts family has owned vineyards in the Creek since the earlier 1860s, which are now under the control of the fourth generation.

Metala. A small vineyard planted solely with Cabernet Sauvignon and Shiraz, Metala has become well-known as a blended wine sold in numbered bottles.

The Murray Valley – Renmark, Berri, Loxton, Waikerie

The conditions for growing grapes in the Southern Australian sector of the Murray Valley are very similar to those found in Victoria and New South Wales, with alluvial soils and dry, hot weather necessitating irrigation. Traditionally a region for producing grapes for drying or distilling, the introduction of new technology has resulted in some very acceptable table wines now being made along with a wide range of sweet and fortified wines.

The major companies:

Angoves Pty Ltd, Renmark
Renmano Wines Co-operative Ltd
Barossa–Waikerie Co-operative Winery Ltd
Berri Co-operative Winery & Distillery Ltd
County Hamley
Thomas Hardy & Sons Pty Ltd., Waikerie
Loxton Co-operative Winery and Distillery Ltd

Lubiana Winery
B. Seppelt and Sons Pty Ltd, Qualco
S. Smith & Son Ltd, Yalumba River Estates
Tarawein Ltd
Tolley Scott and Tolley
Vindana
Gramps
Douglas A. Tolley
Greenways
Hamiltons

WESTERN AUSTRALIA

Swan Valley

Lying north-east of Perth and close to the city, the Swan Valley has long been planted with vines. The climate is hot, with rain only falling during the winter, and the soil is a deep alluvial sandy loam, resulting in wines that are full and high in alcohol but low in acid.

Houghton Wines. Houghton is another property dating back to the origins of viticulture in Western Australia and now belongs to Thomas Hardy & Sons of South Australia, together with another W.A. company, Valencia Vineyards at Caversham. Together their properties total about 300 hectares, from which are produced a full range of fortified and table wines including Houghton's famous 'White Burgundy'.

Sandalford Vineyards Pty Ltd. Western Australia's oldest vineyards with a history stretching back to 1840, they now cover more than 40 hectares and have one of the best reputations in the state. They have become well-known for the quality of their table wines which are mainly sold as varietals.

Other Growers

Evans and Tate Pty Ltd
Waldeck Wines
Swanville Wines

Other Areas

Since the 1960s various other regions have been opened up for viticulture, lying in the south-west corners of Western Australia, where the climate is cooler than the Swan Valley. The main plantings are in the Margaret and Frankland River Valleys.

The main holdings:
Cape Mentelle Vineyards, Margaret River
Cullen's Willyabrup Wines, Margaret River
Leeuwin Vineyards, Margaret River
Pannell W.D., Moss Wood, Margaret River
Redbrook, Margaret River

Vasse Felix, Margaret River
Château Barker, Frankland River
Forest Hill Vineyard, Frankland River
Plantagenet Wines, Frankland River
Sheldon Park, Frankland River
Alkommi Wines, Frankland River
Frankland River Grazing Co, Frankland River

QUEENSLAND

Though the climate being hot and dry is not very suitable for the production of good quality wines, one or two wineries have been set up near the border with New South Wales. They include:

Elsnore Wines
Romavilla Vineyards Pty Ltd, Roma

TASMANIA

In the past, winemaking never established itself commercially on the island, but with modern techniques and the modern demand for cool-fermented wines some people are now making the attempt with some very positive results which are being watched closely by the larger companies. They include:

Heemskerk Vineyards
John F. Miguet, La Provence
Claude Alcorso, Moorilla Estate

Pipers Brook Vineyards
Windemere Vineyards
Château Legana

The Major Australian Wine Companies

Hamilton's	Craigmoor
★ ★ ★ ★ ★	★ ★ ★ ★ ★
Lindemans	The Rothbury Estate
★ ★ ★ ★ ★	★ ★ ★ ★ ★
McWilliams	Rosemount
★ ★ ★ ★ ★	★ ★ ★ ★ ★
Mildara Wines Ltd	**VICTORIA**
★ ★ ★ ★ ★	Baileys
Penfolds	★ ★ ★ ★ ★
★ ★ ★ ★ ★	Château Tahbilk
Seppelts	★ ★ ★ ★ ★
★ ★ ★ ★ ★	Brown Bros.
Thomas Hardy & Sons	★ ★ ★ ★ ★
★ ★ ★ ★ ★	Balgownie
Tolley, Scott and Tolley Ltd	★ ★ ★ ★ ★
★ ★ ★ ★ ★	Buller
WINES TO WATCH OUT FOR	★ ★ ★ ★ ★
NEW SOUTH WALES	**SOUTH AUSTRALIA**
Arrowfield	Penfolds Grange Hermitage
★ ★ ★ ★ ★	★ ★ ★ ★ ★
Tyrrell's	Lindemans Rouge Homme
★ ★ ★ ★ ★	★ ★ ★ ★ ★
Lakes Folly	Wynn's Coonawarra
★ ★ ★ ★ ★	★ ★ ★ ★ ★

AUSTRIA

AUSTRIA is one of those white wine producing countries everyone has heard of but whose wines are rarely drunk. How many restaurants offer a half bottle of Austrian Beerenauslese at the end of a meal? It would be a far more affordable treat than its German or French counterpart . . . For basic whites, Austria has a number of cheap wines which could readily compete with Liebfraumilch. Austria's handicap has always been its grapes. That Beerenauslese could be made from one of a number of varieties, but it probably won't be a Riesling. Even so, the Austrians mostly do care about the quality of their wines and are making every effort to move them out of the 'inexpensive alternative' class and into one of their own. Only the activities of the minority who have been illegally adding glycol to sweeten up their wine, and the thirst of the Germans who mix Austrian wine into their own Beerenausleses will slow the progress of these wines.

THE WINE REGIONS AND PRINCIPAL VILLAGES

NIEDER-ÖSTERREICH

THE most diverse of Austria's four wine-growing regions, Nieder-Österreich (Lower Austria) is, confusingly, the most northerly of all. The climate, types of soil, and vineyard sites vary enormously, and, in consequence, so do the wines. Nieder-Österreich is the most productive region in Austria, supplying almost two-thirds of the country's wine, from the steely, acidic wines of the Wachau to the full, alcoholic wines of Gumpoldskirchen.

Wachau. The character of the wines of the Wachau is dictated by the steeply sloping sides of the valley in which they are grown. The toughest sites often make the finest wines, and the precipitously terraced vineyards of the Wachau can produce some of the most stylish dry Rieslings in all Europe. Grüner Veltliner, Müller-Thurgau, Sylvaner and Neuburger are also grown.

Principal villages	Joching
Spitz	Weissenkirchen
St Michael	Dürnstein
Wösendorf	Loiben

Krems. The town of Krems gives its name to the surrounding district, and is the location of Austria's largest annual wine fair, the Österreichische Weinkost. Production in the district is dominated by the Krems cooperative, but there are fine sites near the Danube, and the region is the home of two of the most respected names in Austrian winemaking, Lenz Moser at Rohrendorf and the Salomon estate at Undhof. Half the wines made in the region are from Grüner Veltliner; other grapes grown are Müller-Thurgau and Riesling.

Principal villages	Kamp
Krems	Rohrendorf
Imbach	Gedersdorf
Rehberg	Sittendorf
Senftenberg	Nussdorf
Stratzdorf	Hollenburg
Haitzendorf	

Langenlois. Similar wines to those of Krems are made here, and there has always been friendly competition between the two communities. Good Grüner Veltliners are produced in pockets of loess soil, and the rocky sites of Heiligenstein can make Rieslings which rival the best from the Wachau.

Principal villages	Schönberg
Langenlois	Mollands
Heiligenstein	Gobelsburg
Strass	Hadersdorf

Klosterneuburg. A district split in two by Austria's capital, Vienna (Wien), a wine-growing region in its own right. To the west of Vienna is Klosterneuburg itself, famous for its Abbey and its Viticultural School, where much of the country's most important research into new grape varieties and crossings has been carried out. The district's vineyards stretch westwards to Krems on both sides of the Danube, producing mainly Grüner Veltliner wine. To the south-east of Vienna, in the other half, formerly named Carnuntum, many of Austria's red wines are made, from the Blauburgunder, Blau Portugieser and Blaufränkischer varieties.

Principal villages	Gross-Weikersdorf
Klosterneuburg	Königsbrunn
Feuersbrunn	Traismauer
Gösing	Nussdorf an der Traisen
Kirchberg	Hainburg
Gross-Riedenthal	Bruck an der Leitha
Ottenthal	

Retz. Despite its northerly position, the region enjoys a very mild climate, with a surprisingly high incidence of sunshine. Retz itself is noted for its red wine, but the production of the region as a whole is of white wines, particularly Grüner Veltliner of a fairly high acidity, much of which is used in Austria's growing sparkling wine industry.

Principal villages	Haugsdorf
Retz	Hadres
Retzbach	Mailberg
Röschitz	Hollabrunn
Hohenwarth	Windpassing

Falkenstein. The largest of the wine districts in Nieder-Österreich, and the source of much of the anonymous wine drunk in taverns, guest houses and private homes throughout eastern Austria. The white Grüner Veltliner and Welschriesling predominate, but good red wines are made from the Blaufränkisch grape around Matzen.

Principal villages	Höbersbrunn
Falkenstein	Wolkersdorf
Poysdorf	Bockfliess
Herrnbaumgarten	Zistersdorf
Mistelbach	Gaiselberg
Ebenthal	Matzen
Hörersdorf	

Gumpoldskirchen. Within easy driving distance south of Vienna, the picturesque village of Gumpoldskirchen has recently given its name to the whole of the surrounding area. As Gumpoldskirchen is one of the best known wine names in all Austria, this makes good commercial sense. Not long ago, in fact, the producers of Gumpoldskirchen wines banded together to impose strict bottling and labelling controls in order to ensure that the contents of a bottle labelled Gumpoldskirchener really *did* come from the village, so much had the name been abused. The best Gumpoldskirchen wines are full and alcoholic, benefitting from a wonderfully sunny climate, and made from two local grapes, the Zierfandler and Rotgipfler.

Principal villages	
Gumpoldskirchen	Mödling
Baden	Pfaffstätten
Perchtoldsdorf	Guntramsdorf
	Sooss

Vöslau. Mainly known for its red wines, although some white wine is made for the sparkling wine industry. The main grape variety is the Blau Portugieser, although one enterprising company, Schlumberger, has plantings of Cabernet and Merlot which produce small quantities of firm, long-lived wine.

Principal villages	
Bad Vöslau	Schönau
Wiener Neustadt	Eggendorf
Leobersdorf	Kottingbrunn

WIEN (VIENNA)

One of the pleasures that any Viennese enjoys is a trip out on Sunday to one of the many taverns selling 'heurige', young wine from the previous harvest. Everyone has his favourite, and wine-loving visitors to Vienna soon catch on. Many capitals have good taverns, or bars, or pubs, but Vienna is unusual in having the vineyards to produce the wines as well. The suburbs to the north-west of the city are wine villages, thronged with taverns, each of which advertises its wares by hanging a branch of fir above the entrance.

Vienna's wines are not great, but they are seldom given the chance to improve with age! Most are made from the Grüner Veltliner, some from the Riesling and Müller-Thurgau, and they are light, supremely unserious wines, intended to be drunk while sitting under a canopy of vines listening to a schmaltzy Viennese waltz.

Principal villages	
Grinzing	Cobenzl
Heiligenstadt	Kahlenberger Dorf
Sievering	Nussdorf

BURGENLAND

From Burgenland come the wines which many consider Austria's finest, sweet botrytised wines from around the Neusiedler See. The factors influencing their production are principally climatic: the summers are long and hot, and the vast inland lake, the Neusiedler See, stores up the heat from the blazing summer days, releasing it very gradually throughout the autumn. Evaporation from the lake creates ideal conditions for the formation of botrytis, noble rot, which concentrates the already ripe grape juice to a point where the manufacture of wines of Beerenauslese quality is commonplace.

The grapes from which these wines are made have to reach higher degrees of potential alcohol than in neighbouring Germany, and much of the production is exported there, where the chance to buy dessert wines of this quality at relatively low prices is welcomed. When compared to the great sweet wines of Germany and France, however, the Burgenland wines are usually rated less highly, as only rarely do they contain sufficient acidity to mature for decades into complexity and subtlety like the great wines of Sauternes and the Rheingau.

Rust-Neusiedler See. The more important of the two districts of Burgenland, in which all the great sweet wines are made. Indeed, such is the quality of the wines from two of the towns, Rust and Eisenstadt, that they have both been granted the status of 'free' towns, independent of the surrounding political areas. The principal grape planted in the region is the Welschriesling, successful because of its relatively high acidity. The Grüner Veltliner and Müller-Thurgau varieties follow hard on its heels, but some of the very best wines are made from the Weissburgunder (the Pinot Blanc of Alsace).

The district lies on both the east and west banks of the Neusiedler See, although most of the well-known wine villages are on the west. Bordering Hungary (and prior to the First World War Burgenland was Hungarian) east of the lake is the Seewinkel (lake corner). Apetlon is the best wine producing town here, and Podersdorf, with the only sandy beach on the whole lake, a popular resort. To the south-west of Eisenstadt is a district specialising in *red* wine. Pöttelsdorf and Mattersburg, and, further south still, the Oberpullendorf district, are the most reliable villages.

Principal villages	
Rust	Illmitz
Eisenstadt	Apetlon
Donnerskirchen	Pöttelsdorf
Purbach	Mattersburg
Mörbisch	Horitschon
Podersdorf	Deutschkreuz

Eisenberg Although a separate wine district, Eisenberg is of less importance than the northern half of Burgenland, both in volume and quality of the wines. Both white and red wines are made, from the Müller-Thurgau, Welschriesling and Grüner Veltliner for whites, and Blaufränkisch for reds.

Principal villages
Eisenberg
Rechnitz

STYRIA

Styria (Steiermark) is a province of forests and hills. Conditions for vine cultivation are far from ideal, and only a relatively small acreage has been replanted since oïdium and phylloxera ravaged vineyards in the second half of the last century. Despite a high average rainfall, vineyard sites, most of which are on hills to escape frosts, suffer from a shortage of water, which washes down to lower ground, often taking precious soil with it. Protection against hail, deer from the forests and birds adds to the costs, and it can be seen why the Austrian government has to subsidise wine making in Styria.

Klöch-Oststeiermark. Unusually in Austria, it is the Traminer grape which produces the best wines in this district, from the town of Klöch. Rounder and fuller than most other Styrian wines, they exhibit all the spiciness of this variety.

Principal villages	
Klöch	Tieschen
Feldbach	St Anna

Südsteiermark. The wine road in the district of South Styria would make an excellent basis for a touring holiday. Running very near the border with Yugoslavia, it meanders through little wine villages whose wines are amongst the best in the province. Riesling is the most important variety, although the Welschriesling, Weissburgunder and Müller-Thurgau are also grown.

Principal villages	
Ehrenhausen	Silberberg
Berghausen	Gamlitz
Pössnitzberg	Leibnitz
	Leutschach

Weststeiermark. West Styria is Schilcher country. This is a light, acid rosé wine, made from the Blau Wildbacher grape. Not much is exported, and it is a wine to drink where it is made. It varies in colour from the palest of onion-skin pinks to quite a deep fuschia. White wines are also made, principally from the Welschriesling and Müller-Thurgau.

Principal villages	
Stainz	Deutschlandsberg
St Stefan	Sulz-Laufenegg

1983 Good year, with a harvest above average in quantity. Ripe grapes perhaps a little lacking in acidity. Lack of humidity (a dry autumn) in Burgenland meant that less top-quality sweeties were made.

1982 The biggest yield ever. Like so many other European winemaking countries, the wines are light and should be drunk early.

1981 Good year. Higher acidity

levels made for longer-lived wines. Keep quality Prädikat wines until 1987.

1979 Average sized, good quality harvest. Most wines should already have been drunk, but some higher quality Wachau and Krems wines are still delicious after six years..

1976 A great vintage. Opulent in both quality and quantity, this year will be talked about for a long time to come. Burgenland top-quality Prädikat wines are splendidly mature, but have lots of life in them yet.

Anton, Weingut Ernst	Oggau, Burg
Bründlmayer, Weingut	Langenlois, N-Öst
Carli, Dieter	Klöch, St
Elfenhof, Weingut	Rust, Burg
Esterhazy'sche Schlosskellerei	Eisenstadt, Burg
Feiler, Weingut	Rust, Burg
Geymüller, Schlossweingut Freiherr von	Krems, N-Öst
Graber-Schierer, Weingut	Gumpoldskirchen, N-Öst
Haimer, Weingut Gunter	Poysdorf, N-Öst
Halbturn, Schlosskellerei	Halbturn, Burg
Heidebodenhof, Weingut	Pamhagen, Burg
Heiss, Franz & Maria	Illmitz, Burg

Hirtzberger, Weingut Franz	Spitz, N-Öst
Hofbauer, Weingut	Retzbach, N-Öst
Hofer, Weingut Rudolf	Gumpoldskirchen, N-Öst
Holler, Weingut Johannes	Rust, Burg
Gumpoldskirchen, Winzergenossenschaft	Gumpoldskirchen, N-Öst
Jamek, Weingut Josef	Joching, N-Öst
Kattus, Johann	Vienna
Klosterneuburg, Kelleramt Chorherrenstift	Klosterneuburg, K1
Liechtenstein'sches Weingut, Prinz	Gross St Florian, St
Loiben, Winzergenossenschaft	Unter Loiben, N-Öst
Lust, Weingut Josef	Haugsdorf, N-Öst
Mad, Weingut Franz	Oggau, Burg
Mantlerhof, Weingut	Gedersdorf, N-Öst
Marienhof, Weingut	Rust, Burg
Mayer, Weingut Franz	Vienna
Metternich'sche Weingüter	Krems, N-Öst
Moser, Lenz	Rohrendorf, N-Öst
Nikolaihof, Weingut	Mautern, N-Öst
Paul, Winzerhof	Klosterneuburg, K1
Prager, Weingut Franz	Weissenkirchen, N-Öst
Raubal, Weingut Fritz	Gumpoldskirchen, N-Öst
Roiss, Weingut Josef	Podersdorf, Burg
Sandhofer, Michael	Purbach, Burg
Sattlerhof, Weingut	Samlitz, St
Schlumberger, Weingut Robert	Bad Vöslau, N-Öst
Schröck, Weingut Wilhelm	Rust, Burg
Schwamberg, Weingut	Gumpoldskirchen, N-Öst
Siegendorf, Klosterkeller	Siegendorf, Burg
St Martinus, Winzergenossenschaft	Donnerskirchen, Burg
Stürgk'sches Weingut, Gräflich	Klöch, St
Thallern, Freigut	Gumpoldskirchen, N-Öst
Thiel, Weingut Othmar	Gumpoldskirchen, N-Öst
Torok, Ladislas	Rust, Burg
Traismauer, Hauerinnung	Traismauer, N-Öst
Tscheppe, Weingut Eduard	Leutschach, St
Uhleim, Schlosskellerei	Ilz, St
Undhof, Weingut Salomon	Stein, N-Öst
Wachau, Winzergenossenschaft	Dürnstein, N-Öst
Wimmer, Weingut Eugen	Oggau, Burg
Zens, Josef	Mailberg, N-Öst
Zimmerman, Weingut R.	Vienna

Amtliche geprüfter Qualitätswein Superier quality wine selected through official tasting and chemical tests. Corresponds to German QbA wine.

Ausbruch Quality level between Beerenauslese and Trockenbeerenauslese with no German equivalent. Wine must be made from grapes affected by botrytis and then partially dried, and the must weight has to reach 27°K M W.

Auslese As in Germany, the third grade up the Prädikat scale. Wine made from selected late-harvested grapes, which have to reach a must weight of 21°K M W.

Beerenauslese Wine made from even riper, late-harvested grapes, usually affected by botrytis. Minimum must weight 25°K M W.

Buschenschank Wine tavern outside Vienna attached to a winemaker's house, where his own wine is on sale.

Heuriger Either wine from the most recent harvest or, the wine tavern where such wine is sold, particularly in the Viennese suburbs.

Kabinett Lowest on the Prädikat scale. Superior quality wine with a minimum must weight of 17°K M W.

Klapotetz Wooden, wind-powered bird scarer common in Styria.

Klosterneuburger Mostwaage Usually written as degrees (°) K M W. The Austrian measurement scale for specific gravity, and hence sugar content, of grape must. Similar to the Oechsle scale in Germany. To convert degrees Oechsle into degrees K M W, the rough method is to divide by 5 (i.e. 85° Oechsle equals 17°K M W).

Prädikatswein Superior categories of wine (Kabinett, Spätlese, Auslese, Beerenauslese, Ausbruch and Trockenbeerenauslese) made from grapes ripe enough to need no enrichment. Strictly supervised by the Austrian Ministry of Agriculture and Forestry.

Spätlese Wine made from late-harvested grapes, with a minimum must weight of 19°K M W.

Spitzenwein Top-quality wine.

Sturm New wine that has not finished its fermentation.

Tafelwein Ordinary wine, suitable for everyday drinking.

Trockenbeerenauslese (often abbreviated to TBA): The highest quality of Prädikat wine. Made from super-ripe grapes which have been concentrated in flavour and sugar content by botrytis. Minimum must weight 30° K M W.

Weingütesiegel Seal awarded to wines of superior quality officially selected through tasting tests and chemical analysis. Corresponds to German QbA.

Weinwirtschaftsfond The Austrian wine industry's promotional body.

The Grape List

Blauer Burgunder

Blaufränkischer Imported into Austria by Charlemagne's Franks in the Middle Ages, this is Burgenland's most popular red variety.

Blauer Portugieser A grape of no great distinction but Austria's most widely grown red variety. It makes light wines to be drunk young.

Blauer Wildbacher The Schilcher grape of Western Styria. The Blauer Wildbacher has a high acidity and, depending on the length of the skin contact with the fermenting must, can yield rosés of varying colours.

Grüner Veltliner Austria's most characterful grape produces white wines with good acidity and a spicy, peppery fragrance. Particularly in Nieder-Österreich, the Grüner Veltliner makes an ideal carafe wine, served in heurigen and buschenschenken throughout Austria.

Müller-Thurgau

Muskat-Ottonel Perfumed, muscatty variety peculiar to Austria, and found above all in Burgenland. Said to take its name from a corruption of the Irish name O'Connell. Why, no-one seems to know.

Neuburger First planted in the 1860s, this variety has been through a number of name changes (Neue Rebe von der Burg, Neue Rebe vom Burgberg, Burgler and Burglerrebe) before settling down to Neuburger. Flourishes on chalky soil.

Riesling Usually referred to as Rheinriesling in Austria.

Rotgipfler Speciality variety (together with the Zierfandler) of the Gumpoldskirchen region, where the two are blended to give full-flavoured, alcoholic wines.

St Laurent A variety of Pinot Noir and nothing to do with the St Laurent of Bordeaux. Named after St Lorenz, on whose saint's day the grapes usually start to ripen. Grown in Nieder-Österreich and Burgenland.

Traminer   Weissburgunder   Welschriesling

Zierfandler (or **Spätrot**): *see* Rotgipfler.

BARREL SIZES

		Metric capacity in litres	British Imp. gallons
FRANCE			
Alsace	Foudre	varies	varies
	Aume	108	25.1
Beaujolais	Pièce	216	47.5
	Feuillette	108	23.7
	Quartaut	54	11.9
Bordeaux	Barrique (hogshead)	225	49.5
	Tonneau (a measure [4 barriques] rather than a barrel) Prices are quoted in *tonneaux*)	900	197.9
	Demi-barrique (feuillette)	112	24.6
	Quartaut	56	12.3
Burgundy	Pièce	228	50.1
	Queue	456	100.3
	Feuillette	114	25.1
	Quartaut	57	12.6
Chablis	Feuillette	132	29
Champagne	Feuillette (or pièce)	205	45.1
Loire	Pièce	varies	varies
Maconnais	Pièce	215	47.3
Midi	Demi-Muid	6-700	145 (approx)
Rhône	Pièce	225	49.5
GERMANY Rhine and Mosel			
	Ohm	150	33
	Doppelohm	300	66
	Fuder (Mosel)	1000	219.9
	Stück (Rhine)	1300	264.0
	Doppelstück	2400	527.8
	Halbstück	600	132
	Viertelstück	300	66
AUSTRALIA & S. AFRICA	Hogshead	295.3	64.9
SPAIN AND PORTUGAL			
Lisbon	Pipe	531.4	117
Madeira	Pipe	418	92
	Hogshead	209	46
Marsala	Pipe	422.6	93
	Hogshead	209	46
Port	Pipe	522.5	115
	Hogshead	259	57
	Quarter Cask	127.7	28
Sherry	Butt	490.7	108
	Hogshead	245.4	54
	Quarter Cask	122.7	27
	Octave	61.4	13.5

In the 1930s, Limousin, Memel, Lübeck, Danzig and Bosnia were the chief suppliers of oak for barrels. Nowadays, Californian winemakers still mortgage their souls to afford Limousin oak casks. The largest wooden wine cask in the world is the Heidelberg Tun, completed in 1751, in the Friedrichsbahn cellars in Heidelberg, W. Germany. It has a capacity of 1855 hl. (40,790 gallons).

BELGIUM

THE Belgians are the world champion claret drinkers. Belgium is, in terms of value rather than volume, traditionally the Number One importer of red Bordeaux, only recently overtaken by the USA. Even so, this small country still consumes – per capita – far more good quality claret – per capita – than anywhere else.

The existence of a vineyard here has long been rumoured in France, but since, to the French, Belgian jokes are not unlike Polish jokes to the Americans, and Irish jokes to the English, we have decided not to take this too seriously.

Countries exporting to Belgium:

France
Germany
Greece
Italy
Portugal
Spain
Tunisia

BOLIVIA

WITH inflation currently running at 200 per cent, no wonder the Bolivians need a drink. Suitably high-alcohol wines are produced here, along with sherry-type wines, mainly from the La Paz area, from grape varieties originally brought from the Canary Islands – 5,000 acres are planted, with an average annual production of around 10,000 hl.

The Bottle List

The impressive Biblical names used to describe the larger Champagne bottles are perhaps the most widely known – a 'jeroboam' is mentioned in the Scriptures as 'A large drinking cup', but the origins of the other names are obscure. Winston Churchill found a 'pint' (half-bottle) of Pol Roger, his favourite brand, ideal for solitary consumption. However, many other wines have their own individual names for the bottle sizes in which they are available.

CHAMPAGNE

Split	¼ bottle
Pint	½ bottle
Quart	bottle
Magnum	2 bottles
Jeroboam	4 bottles
Rehoboam	6 bottles
Methuselah	8 bottles
Salamanazar	12 bottles
Balthazar	16 bottles
Nebuchadnezzar	20 bottles

BEAUJOLAIS

Pot	⅔ bottle

BORDEAUX

Fillette	½ bottle
Magnum	2 bottles
Marie-Jeanne	3 bottles
Double Magnum	4 bottles
Jeroboam	5 litres
Imperial	8 bottles

PORT

Quart	bottle
Magnum	2 bottles
Tappit hen	3 bottles
Jeroboam	4 bottles

SHERRY

Pint	½ bottle
Quart	bottle

U.S. SIZES

Tenth*	½ bottle
Fifth*	bottle
Magnum	2 bottles

*These more particularly for spirits.

countries. In 1981 the average was 8.6 litres per head which is less than a tenth of the average consumption in France and little more than a third of the amount drunk in Germany which, in turn, drinks less than Spain, Italy and Portugal among others. Consumption in most of these countries, notably in France and Italy, has fallen away in recent years.

Wine consumption in Europe by country (litres per capita)

	1978	1979	1980	1981	1982	1982 (Bottles per week)
European Average	50	49	50	51	45	
France	96	93	95	90	89	2.3
Portugal	95	86	91	85	88	2.25
Italy	98	90	93	74	80	2.05
Spain	71	70	65	60	62	1.60
Switzerland	45	45	47	48	48	1.20
Greece	41	41	45	46	48	1.20
Australia	35	36	35	35	35	0.9
Germany	26	25	26	25	25	0.6
Belgium	17	19	20	20	20	0.5
Denmark	12	14	14	16	18	0.5
Netherlands	12	12	13	13	13	0.3
Sweden	9	9	9	10	10	0.25
UK	8	8	8	9	9	0.25
Finland	5	5	5	7	8	0.2
Ireland	3	4	4	4	4	0.1
Norway	3	4	5	4	3	0.08

BRAZIL

ONE of the very few countries in the world where Dallas flopped; the Brazilians, apparently, preferred their own home-grown brands of soap operas – a taste the outside eye might find baffling. So it is with their wine – a substantial quantity is produced, and though the small number of vinifera varietals have a certain following in the USA and Germany, the labrusca-based bulk of it has little appeal to the foreign palate. But the Brazilians like it. And such major concerns as Heublein, Martini and Rossi, Cinzano and Moët and Chandon have had enough faith in the country's vinous potential to establish wineries there; with Heublein in particular beating a path towards a wider market with new, distinctly 'European' styles that are showing great promise.

The Grape List

Labrusca hybrids make up 80 per cent of Brazil's grapes, with 50 per cent of all vines planted being the Isabella. Other grapes are:

Red

Cabernet Franc
Merlot
Barbera
Niagara
Folhe de Figos
Black July
Sangiovese
Bonarda
Syrah
Concorde
Delaware
Jacques Gaillard
Gothe
Bordo

The Brahms Liszt

Despite the growth in wine drinking in the UK, far less wine than beer is consumed and only a fraction of the amount drunk in other

White

Moscatel
Malvasia
Riesling
Trebbiano
Povarel
Tercy
Herbemont
Duchesse
Bertille-Seyve
Cintiana

The Wine Regions

Rio Grande do Sul

Garibaldi, Benito Gonzales, Caxidis

San Roque

São Paolo State

Santa Caterina (the influence of German settlers here is still detectable in the wine)

The Wine Producers

Sociedade Viticola Rio Grandense Ltda

The main Brazilian producer, with the red and white 'Grandja União' brand.

Carlos Dreher Neto
Owned by the US company Heublein, this firm produces varietal wines, including good Cabernet and Barbera, a red 'Marjollet' blend, and a notable, almost 'European' style blended white.

Luiz Antunes & Cia
Luiz Michielon S.A.
Sociedade Vinho Unic. Ltda
E. Mosele S.A.
Sociedade Brasileira de Vinhos Ltda
Almaden Vineyards
Coop. Aurora
Coop. Garibaldi
Companhia Monaco
Vinhos Finos de Santa Rosa Profivin

BULGARIA

THIS is one of the world's most exciting wine producing nations. Interestingly unworrying to those whose political sensibilities bar them from drinking wines from undemocratic right-wing nations, Bulgaria's reds and whites now represent some really remarkable value. The story goes that one of the giant American Cola concerns, having been granted the licence to sell their pop in Bulgaria then discovered themselves in the classic situation of being offered payment in tractors, soft East European currency, or wine . . . The liquid in question was, at that time, mostly made of the local Mavrud grape which, though quite characterful, seemed less than ideally suited to the palates of downtown Los Angeles. The answer to everyone's problem lay in the smaller areas of vines planted in Cabernet Sauvignon, a grape which the folks back home not only knew all about, but were often ready to spend a lot of money on.

A few visits by experts from the University of California's renowned Davis school of viticulture and winemaking, and the redesign of a few cooperative wineries were all that it took to give the Bulgarians the means to produce a world-beating, inexpensive clarety wine. Bulgarian winemakers will now grinningly inform you that there are four times as many Cabernet Sauvignon vines planted in their country as in California – and that their wines have done remarkably well in a number of blind tastings throughout the world.

Another feature of being relatively new to the game is that Bulgaria is in the rare position of making almost equal quantities of red and white wine. Amongst the other particularly successful varieties have been

the Merlot, Chardonnay and Sauvignon.

As you might expect in Eastern Europe, all the wine is produced in cooperatives, and marketed by the state, but the variations of climate and style from winery to winery can be quite notable – a fact which people who are attracted by the generic 'Bulgarian Cabernet Sauvignon' (or whatever) label would be wise to bear in mind. Whichever winery the wine does come from however, the chances are that it will be well-made – those Californians have seen to that.

The Grape List

Red
Mavrud*
Cabernet Sauvignon* (55% of black grapes planted)
Merlot* (20% of back grapes planted)
Pamid (or Plovdina)* (11% of black grapes planted)
Cabernet Franc*
Kadarka*, also known as Gamza*
Pinot Noir
Gamay (very little)

White
Rcatsiteli* (50% of all whites grown. Also cultivated in the USA)
Red (sic) Misket* (14% of all whites grown)
Dimiat* (14% of all whites grown)
Muscat Ottonel (11% of all whites grown)
Chardonnay*
Riesling
Aligoté
Ugni Blanc
Tamianka*
Gewürztraminer
Sauvignon*
Perla (Sparkling)*
Sylvaner*
Furmint*
Welschriesling*
Feteasca*
Iskra (Sparkling)
*grapes used for varietals

The Wine Regions

North
The following towns are known for the wines which bear their names:
Sukhindol (Cabernet Sauvignon, Kadarka)
Pleven (Cabernet Sauvignon, Kadarka)
Turnover (red wines)
Lyas Kovets (red wines)
Pavlikeni (Cabernet Sauvignon, Kadarka)

Kramolin (Kadarka)
Upper Maritsa Valley
Asenovgrad (Mavrud)
Plovdiv (rosé made from Pamid)

South West

Melnik (red wines)
Stara Zagora
Slavyantsi (some reds, mostly whites)

Amongst the white are:

Karlovo (The Valley of the Roses)
Hemus Misket
Rosenthaler Riesling
Chardonnay
Gewürztraminer
Sauvignon
Tamianka dessert wine

East

Shumen, or Choumen (known for Chardonnay)
Sungurlare (where Sonnenkuste Muscat is made. Also Riesling and Klosterkeller, made from Dimiat).
Varna (Dimiat)
Preslav (Dimiat)
Pomorie (Dimiat)

Branded wines

Much of Bulgaria's wine is sold to East Germany, hence a large variety of Germanic branded wine names. Best known amongst these are:

Donau Perle ('Pearl of the Danube', a sparkling wine made from the Fetieska)
Sonnenkuste (made from Dimiat and Rcatsiteli)
Rostenthale Riesling (made from Welschriesling and Riesling)
Klosterkeller (made from Sylvaner or Dimiat)
Euxinograd

Other wines

Balgarske Slanske ('Bulgarian Sun', made from Furmint)
Slantchev Birag ('Sunshine Coast', made from Rcatsiteli)
Kramolinska (made from Gamza)

Slavianka (made from Muscat)
Sakar Mountain (Cabernet
Sauvignon)

THE GREAT CABERNET SAUVIGNONS

Everyone wants to make claret,
wherever their vineyard. The
Cabernet Sauvignon is *the* claret
grape, so everyone plants it.
These producers are amongst
the most successful outside
France.

Andean Vineyards
Argentina

★ ★ ★ ★

Antinori-Tignanello
Italy

★ ★ ★ ★

Babich Wines
New Zealand

★ ★ ★ ★

The Bergkelder
South Africa

★ ★ ★ ★

Beringer
California

★ ★ ★ ★

Bowen Estate
South Australia

★ ★ ★ ★

Brand's Laira
South Australia

★ ★ ★ ★

Brown Brothers Milawa
Australia

★ ★ ★ ★

Buena Vista
California

★ ★ ★ ★

Byrd
Maryland, USA

★ ★ ★ ★

Château Musar
Lebanon

★ ★ ★ ★

Château Reynella
Australia

★ ★ ★ ★

Clos du Bois
California

★ ★ ★ ★

Bruno Colacicchi-Torre Ercolano
Italy

★ ★ ★ ★

Columbia
Washington, USA

★ ★ ★ ★

Conte Loredan-Gasparini 'Venegazzu'
Italy

★ ★ ★ ★

Cooks
New Zealand

★ ★ ★ ★

Cousinho Macul
Chile

★ ★ ★ ★

Durney
California

★ ★ ★ ★

Estrella River
California

★ ★ ★ ★

Flora Springs
California

★ ★ ★ ★

Franciscan
California

★ ★ ★ ★

Freemark Abbey
California

★ ★ ★ ★

Gallo 'Limited Release'
California

★ ★ ★ ★

Groot Constantia
South Africa

★ ★ ★ ★

Hargreave
Long Island, New York, USA

★ ★ ★ ★

Haywood
California

★ ★ ★ ★

Hungerford Hill – Coonawarra
New South Wales, Australia

★ ★ ★ ★

Inglenook
California

★ ★ ★ ★

Kenwood
California

★ ★ ★ ★

Heitz
California

★ ★ ★ ★

Lake's Folly
New South Wales, Australia

★ ★ ★ ★

Jean Leon
Spain

★ ★ ★ ★

Lohr
California

★ ★ ★ ★

Marchese Incisa della Rocchetta – Sassicaia
Italy

★ ★ ★ ★

Marietta
California

★ ★ ★ ★

M. Marion
California

★ ★ ★ ★

Meerlust
South Africa

★ ★ ★ ★

Michtom
California

★ ★ ★ ★

Mildara
Victoria, Australia

★ ★ ★ ★

Mondavi
California

★ ★ ★ ★

Mount Mary
Victoria, Australia

★ ★ ★ ★

Moss Wood
Western Australia

★ ★ ★ ★

Newton
California

★ ★ ★ ★

Opus One
California

★ ★ ★ ★

Orlando-Coonawarra
New South Wales, Australia

★ ★ ★ ★

Pine Ridge
California

★ ★ ★ ★

Preston
California

★ ★ ★ ★

Quinta da Bacalhão
Portugal

★ ★ ★ ★

Raimat 'Clos Abadia'
Spain

★ ★ ★ ★

Redman
South Australia

★ ★ ★ ★

Renmano 'Chairman's Selection'
South Australia

★ ★ ★ ★

Ridge
California

★ ★ ★ ★

Rosemount Show Reserve
Australia

★ ★ ★ ★

Round Hill
California

★ ★ ★ ★

Rutherford Hill
California

★ ★ ★ ★

St Hubert's
Victoria, Australia

★ ★ ★ ★

Saltram
South Australia

★ ★ ★ ★

Sebastiani
California

★ ★ ★ ★

Seppelt Reserve Bin
Australia

★ ★ ★ ★

Sequoia Grove
California

★ ★ ★ ★

Smith's Yalumba *South Australia*	Tisdall-Mount Helen *Victoria, Australia*
★ ★ ★ ★	★ ★ ★ ★ ★
Stag's Leap *California*	Torres 'Gran Coronas' *Spain*
★ ★ ★ ★	★ ★ ★ ★ ★
Robert Stemmler *California*	Torres 'Santa Digna' *Chile*
★ ★ ★ ★	★ ★ ★ ★ ★
Stony Ridge *California*	Vasse Felix *Western Australia*
★ ★ ★ ★	★ ★ ★ ★ ★
Taltarni *Victoria, Australia*	Wantirna Estate *Victoria, Australia*
★ ★ ★ ★ ★	★ ★ ★ ★ ★
Te Mata *New Zealand*	Whitehall Lane *California*
★ ★ ★ ★ ★	★ ★ ★ ★ ★
Tenuta di Capezzana- Carmignano *Italy*	Wynn's *Victoria, Australia*
★ ★ ★ ★ ★	★ ★ ★ ★ ★

CANADA

ONE factor which seems to be inhibiting Canada's progress towards the production of wines of quality is the ever-widening gap between the larger companies and smaller producers. The former are quite content to plough their considerable resources back into the frightful menagerie of infant animals, after which they name their wines, whilst the latter group which *is* beginning to master the problems of vinification cannot afford the bottle ageing which would improve it. Until the bigger firms see the sense in giving a hand to the more imaginative, smaller winemaker, it is difficult to see how the industry as a whole can develop.

Wine legislation could also do with an overhaul – at the moment it is both clumsy and seems to miss the whole point of what wine is all about. Marketing is an important concept to the Canadians, keen to enlarge the home market for their wines, yet although wine may be advertised on television, no-one may be seen drinking, let alone *enjoying* drinking wine. As one Canadian wine-writer put it, a passing visitor from Mars, glimpsing a commercial for a  Canadian wine, might well come away with the impression that it was a proprietary agent for washing glasses.

Canada could also do with some serious standards for grapes and appellations, rather than a system which tells you how much water you may legally add to your wine 'product'. Luckily, the more scrupulous firms make their wines as though such rules already exist. Another good idea would be to drop a rather deferential attitude to all things European, as visible in the endless 'Italian', 'Spanish', 'German' sounding names, and to improve their label designs, which range from the boringly informative – with about as much aesthetic appeal as a parking ticket – to the dog's dinner variety – Watteau reproductions and unreadably contorted Gothic script.

The Wine Regions

ONTARIO

Ontario's wine history stems in part from the prohibition era, when it used to take grapes off the hands of the Californian vine-growers. Since then, the grape growers have been moving steadily from growing American labrusca strains to more familiar European hybrids, but Californian grapes and juices are still used to stretch the native crop. In the case of the low-alcohol wines such as 'Baby Duck', water is one of the chief ingredients – permitted by Ontario's wine legislation, which allows a yield of 258 litres of product per ton of grapes; bizarrely high by European standards. The 'product' (a recurring word in Canadian winespeak) must now, however, contain at least 70 per cent native grapes – a step in the right direction towards encouraging the efforts of those grape-growers, and winemakers who are trying to produce authentically 'Ontarian' wines, some of which are now achieving a recognizable degree of quality.

BRITISH COLUMBIA

Wine-making in British Columbia is relatively recent, dating from the 1930s. Stealing a march on already-established areas, it was able to start with vinifera strains and move quickly on to the second generation of European hybrids, and so has progressed rapidly to the forefront of developments. Okanagan Valley is on the same latitude as Champagne and the Rheingau, though with greater extremes of climate, and the white wines made there tend more towards the style of the Rhine than of California. The BC crop represents 65 per cent of the total grapes used for wine, though technically each blend must contain at least 80 per cent BC grapes.

The British Columbians drink more wine than other Canadians – 13.5 litres per head as opposed to a national average of 9.5, and prefer the home-grown product, with two glasses of domestic wine being drunk for every glass of imported wine.

QUEBEC

One striking anomaly springs to the forefront when considering Quebec as a wine region – no grapes are grown there. This has not deterred the sturdy Québécois, who travel the world in search of spare grapes to freeze, flash-freeze and pulp, and then bear them home by the container-load to vinify.

The 'product' here must be 70 per cent fermented in the province, with a permitted addition of 20 per cent 'finished' wine from Europe, or 30 per cent from California.

The Grape List

Agawam	Maréchal Foch
Aligoté	Niagara
Auxerrois	Okanagan Riesling
Baco	Perle de Csaba
Catawba	Pinot Noir
Chancellor	Ravat
Chardonnay	Riesling
Chelois	Seibel
Concord	Seyve-Villard
De Chaunac	Ventura
Delaware	Vidal
Dutchess	Villard Noir
Elvira	
Gamay Beaujolais	
Gewürztraminer	
Isabella	
Landot	

> The French and Italian wine industry lose more wine by evaporation than is produced by all Canada's wineries.

The List of Producers

ONTARIO

Andres. Mostly hybrid grapes plus some Rhine Riesling, from which a varietal wine is made. Famous for their 'Baby Duck', an enormously successful pink sparkling wine made from labrusca grapes, and described as 'fowl' by an English taster.

Barnes. Again, hybrids and a Rhine Riesling, also some Californian Petite Sirah. Make a 'Still Cold Duck' and a 'Crackling Wild Duck'.

Brights. Hybrids, including the Baco Noir. Rhine Riesling and Gewürztraminer varietal wines, plus a Chardonnay 'Champagne'.

Charal. Hybrids plus Rhine Riesling, and a still Chardonnay (which was a gold medal winner in the USA).

Château Des Charmes. Classic European varieties, including varietal Cabernet Franc, Pinot Noir, Aligoté, and Chardonnay vintage wines.

Château Gai. Hybrid blended wines plus a Merlot and a Gamay rosé. Also something called 'Canadian Sauternes' in a screw-top bottle.

Colio. Hybrid wines with Italianate names, and a varietal Rhine Riesling.

Hillebrand Estates. Hybrid blends with vintage Rhine Riesling and Gewürztraminers.

Inniskillen. Hybrid varietal wines, and vintage Riesling, Gewürztraminer, Chardonnay, Merlot, Gamay Noir and an unusual Gamay Blanc from European varieties. Exports to Germany, Switzerland, UK, USA and Japan.

Jordan. Hybrid blends, Rhine Riesling and a Chardonnay blend. Sparkling wines include Cold Duck, Luv-a-Duck, Cold Turkey, Baby Deer, Baby Bear, Spumante Bambino and Lonesome Charlie.

London. Brand-name hybrid blends – Dinner Red, Dinner White, Buffet Sauternes, a Chablis made from Chenin Blanc plus hybrids.

Podamer (Montravin Cellars). Best known for quality method champenoise wines, including a 100% Chardonnay Brut Blanc de Blanc.

BRITISH COLUMBIA

Andres. Good vintage wines from classic varieties – Cabernet Sauvignon, Riesling, Gewürztraminer, Auxerrois – and a prize-winning 'sherry'.

Brights. 'Ordinaire' hybrid reds, and blended Chenin Blanc whites.

Calona Wines. Large selection of hybrid blends plus some interesting 1981 50th anniversary bottlings of European varietal wines brought from Washington State.

Casabello. Medal-winning Canadian 'Burgundy', varietal Riesling, Gewürztraminer, Pinot Noir. Suspicious 'Burgonay' – "in the French Burgundy tradition" – made entirely from American hybrid grapes.

Claremont. Hybrids, vintage Pinot Blanc, 'limited edition' Gewürztraminer and Blanc Fumé (Sauvignon).

Gray Monk. Varietal whites from European varieties including a Pinot Gris and a medal-winning Gewürz-traminer.

Jordan & Ste Michelle. Hybrid varietals and blends, a 'Spätlese'-style Riesling, and 'Slingers White'.

Mission Hill. Several different cellar names, with brand names from the corresponding European countries hinted at e.g. 'Réserve Speciale Blanc' from Caves Chauvignon, 'Schloss Weinberg' from Klosterberg Cellars.

Sumac Ridge. Red and rosé hybrid blends and European varietal whites.

Uniacke Estate Wines. Good European varietals (Merlot, Chasselas, etc.) and one medal-winning hybrid Riesling.

QUEBEC

Les Entreprises Verdi. Reds from a number of mooted Californian grapes, and a range of Kosher whites.

Julac Inc. One Italian-style white wine, not unattractive.

Lubec Inc. Wines made from imported concentrates from Rioja, Argentina, Greece and California, plus a number of aperitifs.

La Maison Secrestat Ltee. Inoffensive (except for the rosé) table wines from blended concentrates.

Les Vignobles Chantecler. More blended concentrates, some using Italian Merlot and packaged in fiascos.

Les Vignobles de Quebec. Grocery chain brand wines made from fresh and sulphited Californian grape juice.

Vin Geloso Inc. Proprietor Vincent Geloso holds Permit 001, the first wine-making licence issued by the Quebec Government. He makes frequent trips to his native Italy to select the grape juices he uses in his blends.

Les Vins Andrés du Quebec Ltee. Blended wines, often for the restaurant trade, made from refrigerated grapes and juice shipped in from Ontario and California, some for a local version of Baby Duck.

Les Vins Bright/Les Vins Lasalle. Highly commercial concentrate blends, uninspiring.

Les Vins Corelli. Pleasant wines made entirely from grapes and juices imported from Italy.

ALBERTA

Andres, Château Gai and Jordan all have processing plants here for producing their national blends.

Andrew Wolf Wine Cellars. Varietal wines from classic Californian varieties 'flash-frozen' in the fields. Andrew Wolf claims the dubious distinction of having 'invented' Baby Duck for Andres.

NOVA SCOTIA

Grand Pré Wines. Tiny winery with its own vineyard, growing exotic varieties – two Russian grapes provide the basis for Grand Pré's most successful wines.

Andres Wines (Atlantic). Accounts for huge proportion of NS sales mainly from sparkling wines and Californian blends.

CELLAR LIST

THERE are several ways to start a cellar. If you have several thousand crisp new banknotes to spare, you can wave your hand around at every available auction and buy yourself a sufficiency of ready-to-drink fine wine. Of course that won't help you a great deal with your future drinking (some of those 1959s may be looking a little tired in the year 2000), so perhaps it's worth including a few wines which aren't ready yet, but which will improve with keeping.

And then there's the question of your day-to-day drinking. Do you really want to drink your 1982 Lafite and 1961 Latour while watching Dallas and gobbling a hamburger? Well maybe, but for those with less expensive taste, or less expansive wallets, there will have to be at least a few more humble bottles.

Inexpensive Wine List

Château l'Etoile Graves
Bulgarian Cabernet Sauvignon
Côtes du Rhône
French white Vin de Pays
Vina Faustino

Touraine Sauvignon
French red Vin de Pays
White Rioja (Marques de
  Caceres)
Pinot Grigio
Wente Bros Chardonnay
Burgundy Passetoutgrain
  (Leroy)
New Zealand Müller-Thurgau
  (Cooks)
Saumur Mousseux
Chinon (O. Raffault)
Dry sherry
Single Quinta Port
German Kabinett
Ste Croix du Mont
Muscat de Beaumes de Venise
Raimant Abadia

Medium Price Wine List

Chardonnay Vino da Tavola
  (Tiefenbrunner)
Louis Roederer champagne
Beaune Les Vignes Franches
  (Germain)
Bourgogne Hautes Côtes de
  Nuits (Moillard)
St Joseph (La Grande Pompée)
Clairette de Die
Blanc Fumé (Mondavi)
Carmignano (Bonacossi)
Château Doisy-Védrines
Château Chasse-Spleen
Lancorta Reserva Rioja
Morgon (Janodet)
Pernand Vergelesses (Thiely)
Torres Gran Coronas
Cousinho Maćul Chilean
  Cabernet
St Véran (Duboeuf)

Fleurie La Madonne (Duboeuf)
Meursault (Jadot)
Pouilly Fuissé (Ferret)
Palo Cortado Sherry (Lustau)

Luxury Wine List

Château Léoville-Barton
Château Pichon-Longueville-
  Lalande
Pouilly Blanc Fumé (Châtelain)
Sauternes (Château d'Yquem)
Hargrave New York State
  Chardonnay
Krug Grande Cuvée
Pommerer Sonnenuhr Riesling
  Kabinett
Gewürztraminer (Cuvée
  Christine Schlumberger)
Châteauneuf-du-Pape Domaine
  du Vieux Télégraphe
Hermitage La Chapelle
Chablis ler Cru Chapelot
  (Raveneau)
Gran Reserva Rioja
Bailey's Australian Liqueur
  Muscat
Niedermenninger Herrenberg
  Riesling Auslese
Bienvenue Bâtard Montrachet
  (Leflaive)
Romanée Conti
Château Petrus
Volnay Clos de la Bousse d'Or
  (Potel)
Bairrada (Cantanhede)
Tignanello (Antinori)
White Rioja (Marques de
  Murrieta)
Opus One
Cabernet Sauvignon (Taltarni)

7th. **Australia,** William Jacob
8th. **S. Africa,** KWV Chenin Blanc 1983
9th. **Germany,** Blue Nun 1982
10th. **England,** Bruisyard St Peter Müller-Thurgau 1982
USA, Paul Masson California Carafe
12th. **England,** Astley Kerner 1983
13th. **Switzerland,** Fendant de St Leonard Provins Valais 1981
England, Staple St James Huxelrebe 1982
Germany, Wehlener Sonnenuhr Kabinett (Z. Prum) 1983
New Zealand, Cook's Müller-Thurgau 1981
Germany, Deinhard Green Label Berncastel 1982
18th. **China,** Dynasty
19th. **Italy,** Soave Campagnola 1983
Zimbabwe, Vat 10 Colombard
Bulgaria, Chardonnay
22nd. **France,** Chablis ler Cru Fourchaume. Ch de Maligny. (Durup)
23rd. **France,** Muscadet de Sèvre et Maine Cuvée du Cardinal
  (Sauvion) 1983
24th. **Portugal,** Vinho verde Gazela
France, Piat d'Or
26th. **Austria,** Schluck
27th. **Germany,** Schloss Vollrads Halbtrocken Kabinett 1982
28th. **Canada,** Inniskillin Chardonnay 1982
29th. **Chile,** Concha y Toro Sauvignon/Sémillon
30th. **Argentina,** Franchette
31st. **Greece,** Côtes de Meliton, Cava Carras
Luxembourg, Clos des Rochers, Auxerrois 1981
33rd. **Spain,** Olarra Bianco Seco 1980
34th. **Romania,** Murfatlar Riesling 1982
35th. **France,** Châteaux Loudenne 1982
36th. **Yugoslavia,** Lutomer Riesling
37th. **Hungary,** Olasz Riesling
38th. **Israel,** Carmel Negev Sauvignon

CHEESES AND ACCOMPANYING WINES

Brie
English Müller-Thurgaus, Beaune (Burgundy) and Graves (Bordeaux)

★ ★ ★ ★ ★

Camembert
English white wines, light Burgundies, Valpolicella, Barolo,
Zinfandel, Gigondas, Châteauneuf-du-Pape, Tawny Port

★ ★ ★ ★ ★

Chaumes
Müller-Thurgaus, Gewürztraminer, Californian Chardonnay, Chianti

★ ★ ★ ★ ★

Cheddar
German Mosels, Rioja, Zinfandel, Madeira

★ ★ ★ ★ ★

Cottage
English and Austrian white wines, Beaune

★ ★ ★ ★ ★

Emmenthal
Mosel, Gewürztraminer, Californian Chardonnay, Bordeaux (Listrac),
Beaune, Sauternes, Madeira

★ ★ ★ ★ ★

Explorateur
English Müller-Thurgau, Beaune, Rioja, Châteauneuf-du-Pape,
Madeira, Port

★ ★ ★ ★ ★

THE 'WHAT WINE?' INTERNATIONAL CHALLENGE

In July 1984, *What Wine?* magazine's first International
Challenge set eight English Wines against a field drawn from
around the rest of the world, with an international panel of
tasters which included three Masters of Wine. All the wines in
the blind tasting were white, and as similar as possible to the
'English' style. France and Spain were represented by four
wines each; other countries included ranged from Argentina to
Zimbabwe, and the wines from commercial brands such as Blue
Nun to a Premier Cru Chablis. The English wines swept the
board, taking first, second, fourth and fifth places – and one of
the most remarkable results was the sixth place, awarded to a
Welsh wine, produced from the first vintage of a tiny
one acre vineyard.

Results
1st. **England,** Magdelen Pulham St Mary Rivaner 1982
2nd. **England,** Lamberhurst Schönburger 1982
3rd. **Italy,** Goldmuskateller (Tiefenbrunner) 1983
4th. **England,** Three Choirs Huxelrebe 1983
5th. **England,** Wootton Schönburger 1982
6th. **Wales,** Monnow Valley 1983

Goat Cheese
Gewürztraminer, Barolo, Beaune, Châteauneuf-du-Pape, Sancerre, Jura vins jaunes

★ ★ ★ ★ ★

Leiden
Californian Chardonnay, Madeira, Rioja

★ ★ ★ ★ ★

Roquefort
Oloroso sherry, Mosel, Sancerre, Gewürztraminer, Californian Chardonnay, Sauternes, Monbazillac, Tokay

★ ★ ★ ★ ★

Smoked Cheeses
Austrian and Luxembourg white wines, Montilla, Sauternes

★ ★ ★ ★ ★

Stilton
Beaune, Chianti, Bulgarian Cabernet Sauvignon, Tokay, Port

★ ★ ★ ★ ★

Münster
Gewürztraminer, Beaune

★ ★ ★ ★ ★

Reblochon
English white wines, Chianti, Valpolicella, Graves

★ ★ ★ ★ ★

Red Cheshire
Beaune, Rioja, Sauternes

CHILE

CHILE produces the finest red wines in South America, rich, almost Bordeaux-style Cabernets and even the occasionally creditable Pinot Noir. It is however also one of those countries where even the most apolitical of wine lovers may find themselves pausing to consider how great a part low wages have played in the low price they are paying for their bottle of excellent wine. Those of liberal attitudes and with appreciative palates can only hope that the growing success of these wines will eventually help their peasant producers' incomes in the way in which the popularity of Spain's wines has transformed the lives of the winegrowers in that country.

There is one very important link between winemaking in Spain and Chile, in the form of Miguel Torres. The son of the Penedès' most famous and successful wine producer, Miguel has invested heavily in the Central Valley, concentrating on a number of ambitious varietals, including several dry whites, for which he is already winning international acclaim. But Torres has only been in Chile since the late 1970s.

The modern wine industry dates from 1851, when Silvestre Ochagavia, 'the father of Chilean wine', brought experts and cuttings from France. The vineyards he helped to establish were to be the source of the industry's moment of glory – having escaped oïdium and phylloxera, they were able to send millions of healthy vines back to

France to restock the ravaged vineyards. Chile's vinestocks are still ungrafted, and stringent border restrictions now exist to keep phylloxera at bay.

White wines are harder to produce successfully for the climate induces a natural lack of acidity and 'flabbiness', though progress is being made. But Chile has long had a reputation for 'quality' red wines (Chilean 'claret' could often be found in England around the time of the Second World War) and the wine-makers have always had an eye for the export market, which is considerable. Owing to the cheapness of the wine, the domestic market is also vast. In an effort to combat alcoholism, the Chilean government now restricts consumption to 60 litres per head per year, which still represents a bottle and a half for every man, woman and child in the country.

The Grape List

The 'pink' Pais (alias the Mission/Criolla) is by far the dominant grape. Others are:	Moscato
	Sauvignon
	Riesling
Red	Chardonnay
Cabernet Sauvignon	Gewürztraminer
Cabernet Franc	Pinot Gris
Malbec	
Merlot	
Pinot Noir	
Petit Verdot	
Torrontes	
White	
Sémillon	

Chilean classification

Vinas Courant	–1 year old
Special	–2 years old
Reserve	–4 years old
Reservado	–6 years old

The Wine Regions

'Central Valley' (provinces of Aconcagua, Santiago, O'Higgins, Valparaiso, Curico, Talca, Colchaqua)

Grape varieties

Cabernet Sauvignon	Sauvignon Blanc
Cabernet Franc	Sémillon
Malbec	Chardonnay
Merlot	Riesling

Virtually all Chile's good wine comes from the irrigated vineyards of the Central Valley. The province of Aconcagua is noted for producing Chile's finest wine, particularly from the Cabernet Sauvignon grape. The towns of Pirque, Linderos and Santa Aña have a deserved reputation for 'quality' wines.

Coastal region
Considerable acreage, but producing inferior wine. The Pais and the Torrontes grapes predominate.

Linares valley
Extremes of temperature make wine-making problematical. Much wine is produced from the Pais grape, but of a very poor standard. In irrigated areas a little good white wine is made from the Sauvignon Blanc and Sémillon.

Atacamba and Coquimbo
Despite semi-desert conditions the Pais and the Moscatel are grown, producing high alcohol, low-acidity wines which are usually fortified.

Maule, Concepcion, Nubile, Bio Bio, Malleca, Cautin
Pais and Moscatel predominate, producing cheap, low-alcohol wine for blending and distillation. Low yields, and the rock-bottom prices paid for their grapes make vine-growing a miserable business for the thousands of smallholders.

Recommended producers

Concha Y Toro S.A.
With 4,000 acres under vine, and an average production of a million cases, Chile's biggest producer. Employ a German oenologist. Their best known wines are the Castillero del diablo and Marques de Casa Concha brands, a 'St-Emiliana' Cabernet, and Sauvignon and Riesling whites.

Vina Santa Helena/Vina San Pedro
A major exporter, owned by the Wagnerstein group.

'Santa Helena' Semillon	'Santa Helena' Merlot/Malbec
'Santa Helena' Riesling	'San Pedro' Cabernet Sauvignon
'San Pedro' blended white	'Llave de Oro'
'Gato Blanco' Sauv/Semillon	'Las Encinas'
'Gato Negro' Cab/Malbec	
'Santa Helena' Cabernet Franc	

Vina Underraga S.A.
An old family firm, the first to export to the USA. Red wines from Cabernet and Pinot Noir, whites from Sauvignon, Semillon and Riesling. Sparkling wines.

Vina Cousino Macul
Have a reputation for fine wines, made 'in the French tradition'. Have stocked their vineyards with cuttings from Pauillac and Martillac.

'Dona Isadora' Riesling Chardonnay	'Antiguas Reserva' Cabernet Sauvignon
'Don Luis' Cabernet Sauvignon	'Palacio Cousina' blended white
'Don Matias' Cabernet Sauvignon	

José Canepa y Cia
'Gran Brindis' Semillon
'Pommard'
Moscatel/Semillon blends

Viña Linderos
'Para Guarda' Cabernet
'Subterraneo XII' red, white and rosé

Viña Manquehue
Use the Cabernet and Semillon grapes, amongst others:

Wines: all sold under the 'Jose Rabat' name

Premium
Alcalde Jufre
Reservado Rabat

Santa Carolina
Wines from the Cabernet, Merlot, Malbec, Sauvignon, Semillon, Chardonnay grapes

Santa Rita
'120'
'CasaReal'
'Real Audiencia'
'Gran Libertador'

Miguel Torres
A new venture; 'Santa Digna' Cabernet Sauvignon won first prize at the 1985 International Food & Wine Exhibition in London. Torres' Cabernet Rosé did equally well, coming first in its class.

CHINA

AS the bamboo curtain finally lifts, there are clear signs that China is preparing to compete on very level terms with what its leaders might once have called the 'decadent west'. Despite a long history of wine production—Vitis Chunganensis is one of the world's oldest recorded wine-making vines – China had, until very recently, grown its 30,000 ha of grapes for eating and for medicinal purposes. This last use for wine has its own well-established tradition which has been traced back to 2140 BC.

Today however, just as China's first vinifera vines are supposed to have been imported to Sinkiang from Persia in the second and first centuries BC, modern expertise and grape varieties are being brought in from France. Experiments are being carried out on crosses between vinifera, labrusca and chunganensis varieties at the Peking and Nanking research stations, as well as at individual wineries, and the French Cognac company, Rémy Martin, has helped to create a potentially 'international' wine called Dynasty.

The Wine Regions

Sinkiang (north-west)	**Hebei** (north-east of Peking)
Kiangsu (north of Shanghai)	**Liaoning** (in Manchuria, near
Shensi (near Sian, on the	the Great Wall)
Yellow River)	**Shantung Peninsula** (possibly
Shansi (also near Sian, on the	the best-known region)
Yellow River)	

The Chinese Wine List

P'u T'ao Chiu: The generic term for wine made from grapes (Chaosing and Pai Chiu respectively refer to wines made from rice and grain).

Chefoo and Tsing Tao
Both on the Shantung Peninsula, and produce high alcohol wines: port-like reds, and sherry-like whites.

Hebei
'Dynasty'. A modern, almost 'European-type' wine, produced with assistance from Rémy Martin, and successful in two western wine competitions: Highly Commended in the 1984 *What Wine?* International Challenge (London) and Silver Medal winner in the 1984 International Wine & Spirit Competition.

Meikuishanputaochu
Sweet Muscat-like wine made from a local hybrid grape.

Great Wall
The first Chinese wines to be imported into the UK, in 1980.

CLASSIFICATIONS AND RE-CLASSIFICATIONS

*'Most of the experts consulted were of the opinion that, in assessing the position of the vineyards, price would still be (as it was in 1855) the most reliable indicator; and it was on this basis that (my) classification was prepared',
Alexis Lichine, speaking of his reclassification of the Médoc.

★★★★★

*'The wines of the world characterised and classed',
Henry Vizetelly, 1875.

★★★★★

*'Topographie de tous les vignobles connus',
A. Jullien, 1848.

★★★★★

*Wilhelm Franck's guide to the wines of Bordeaux in 1824

*'The Wine Aristocracy',
T.E. Carling, 1957

★ ★ ★ ★ ★

*'Variétiés Bordelaises',
Abbé Barein, 1786.

★ ★ ★ ★ ★

*M. B. Reis, the Portuguese Consul in Newcastle in the early 20th century, made an elaborate classification of all the world's wines, no trace of which seems now to exist.

57 Wine Cocktails

There is a surprising number of cocktails which include wine of some kind (after all Vermouth *is* wine). The following is a list of 57 varieties we found of interest.

1
Americana

1 part Bourbon
½ teaspoon sugar
1 dash Angostura Bitters
Champagne

2
Aquilas

1 part Spanish brandy
1 part Grand Marnier
1 part Orange Curaçao
1 part Maraschino
Cava (Spanish sparkling wine)

3
Badminton Cup

½ Cucumber, peeled and sliced
strips of cucumber peel
5 oz. sugar
1 bottle claret
Pinch nutmeg
Soda water

4
Balaklava Nectar

Juice of 1 lemon
grated lemon peel
2 tablespoons castor sugar
1½ measures Maraschino
½ cucumber, thinly sliced
2 bottles Bulgarian Cabernet-
Sauvignon (or similar)
1 bottle Champagne
Assorted fresh fruit.

5
Bellini

3 parts peach juice or nectar
Champagne

6
Beretta

2 parts Dry Martini
1 part gin
1 part Orange Curaçao
6 parts medium-dry white wine
2 dashes Angostura bitters

7
Black Lace

Dry Sparkling Wine
1 dash Murelle

8
Black Velvet

Guinness
Champagne

9
Blenheim (10 glasses)

½ bottle scotch whisky
½ bottle tawny port
1 glass fresh orange juice
1 glass Malvern water
3 cloves
2 oranges
Simmer for 10 minutes. Pour on
a dash of soda before serving.

10
Buck's Fizz

Orange Juice
Champagne

11
California Dreaming

3 parts pineapple juice
1 dash lemon juice

2 dashes Kirsch
Champagne

12
Camp Champ

2 parts Campari
1 part orange juice
Champagne

13
Chablis Cup

1 part Cognac
1¼ parts Curaçao
1¼ parts raspberry syrup
1 bottle Chablis (Californian)
Fruit in season
Cucumber peel
Sprig of mint

14
Champagne Normande

1 teaspoon Calvados
1 dash Angostura bitters
½ teaspoon sugar
Champagne

15
Champoo

1 part Amaretto
1 part Orange Curaçao
1 dash lemon juice
Champagne

16
Classic Champagne Cocktail

1 part Cognac
1 lump white sugar
2 dashes Angostura bitters
Champagne

17
Cool Cucumber

2 parts Benedictine
1 part lemon juice
Cucumber
Champagne

18
Coronation

1 part dry sherry
1 part dry vermouth
1 dash Maraschino
2 dashes Angostura bitters
3 parts Mosel
Soda

19
Damn the Weather

2 parts ruby port
1 part pineapple juice
1 part orange juice
1 dash lemon
Soda

20
Dolores

2 parts dark rum
1 part Dubonnet
1 part dry sherry

21
East & West

1 part port
1 part Cognac
1 part Orange Curaçao
1 dash lemon juice

22
The General (36 glasses)

1 bottle claret
1 bottle Champagne
½ bottle brandy
½ bottle Orange Curaçao
2 glasses soda

23
Ginger Punch (18 glasses)

1 bottle dry white wine
4 glasses ginger beer
2 glasses orange juice
1 glass pineapple juice
3 dashes Angostura bitters

24
Gordon

5 parts gin
1 part dry sherry

25
Haiti Punch (12 glasses)

2 parts de Kuyper
Nassau Orange
2 parts Cognac
1 bottle dry white wine
2 glasses soda

26
Happy Youth

2 parts cherry brandy
6 parts orange juice
1 part Cognac
Champagne

27 Honeydew

¼ cup diced honeydew melon
2 parts gin
1 dash Pernod
1 part lemon juice
Champagne

28 Iced Bishop

2 glasses lime-blossom tea
1 sliced orange
½ sliced lemon
Gomme Syrup
Champagne

29 Iced Punch

1 bottle Sauternes
¼ lb sugar
lemon rind
1 clove
4 tablespoons tea.
Heat: then add
1 thinly sliced orange
1 thinly sliced lemon
1 glass dark rum
Ignite, then chill

30 Inigo Jones

1 part Marsala
1 part Cognac
1 part rosé
1 dash lemon juice
1 dash orange juice

31 Invigorator (hangover cure)

1 egg
½ cup strong black coffee
1 part Cognac
1 part ruby port
sugar

32 Jerez

1 part Amontillado sherry
1 part peach brandy
1 part dry white wine
1 dash Prunelle
1 dash Orange Bitters

33 Jubilee

1 part Sloe Gin
1 dash Triple Sec

---

1 dash lemon juice
1 dash orange bitters
Champagne

34 Kir

Dry white wine (Aligoté)
½ measure Cassis

35 Kir Royale

Crémant de Bourgogne
½ measure Cassis

36 Lovett

1 part redcurrant juice
1 part apple juice
Champagne

37 Madeira Cocktail

1½ measures Malmsey
2 dashes Gomme syrup
2 dashes Orange Curaçao
2 dashes orange bitters

38 Mantegazza (12 glasses)

½ bottle cherry brandy
¼ Orange Curaçao
1 bottle Lambrusco
2 lb black cherries
2 finely diced lemons
Heat before serving

39 Maxim's à Londres

4 parts Cognac
1 part Cointreau
1 part orange juice
Champagne
(Add a dash of Framboise for a
Maxim's de Paris)

40 Memphis Belle

1 apricot
1 part Southern Comfort
2 parts Port, sherry or Marsala

41 Mimosa

Blood orange juice
Champagne

---

42 Mitre

2 parts full-bodied red wine
1 part orange juice
1 dash lemon juice
1 dash Gomme syrup
Ginger ale

43 Never on Sunday

2 parts Greek brandy
1 part Ouzo
1 dash Angostura bitters
1 dash lemon juice
Ginger beer
Champagne

44 Ojos Verdes

2 parts Midori
1 part Spanish brandy
1 dash orange bitters
Cava (Spanish sparkling wine)

45 Operator

5 parts dry white wine
1 dash lime juice
Ginger ale

46 Pennsylvania (12 glasses)

1 part peach brandy
1 part bourbon
1 part brandy
1 part Southern Comfort
1 bottle Californian red wine
4 glasses ginger ale
2 chopped apricots
2 chopped peaches

47 Pineapple Cooler

2 oz Pineapple juice
½ cup diced pineapple
1 dash lemon juice
1 glass dry white wine
Soda

48 Pink Chevrolet

½ cup fresh strawberries
1 part Fraise
1 dash lemon juice
Champagne

---

49 Port in a Storm

3 parts ruby port
1 part brandy
4 parts claret

50 Quarter Deck

2 parts dark rum
1 part dry sherry
1 dash lime juice

51 Reid's Flip

2 parts Malmsey
1 egg
1 part double cream
1 dash Angostura bitters
Blend and add cinnamon

52 Restoration

4 parts red wine
1 part Cognac
1 part Framboise
1 dash lemon juice
Soda

53 Saint Charles (12 glasses)

2 parts Cognac
2 parts Orange Curaçao
1 part ruby port
1 part lemon juice
1 dash Gomme syrup
1 bottle dry white wine

54 Sherry Cobbler

3 parts Orange Curaçao
2 teaspoonful castor sugar
Dry sherry
Crushed ice

55 Strawberry Fields (18 glasses)

1 bottle dry white wine
1 bottle Anjou rosé
½ bottle Cognac
2 parts Fraise
1 lb strawberries
1 dash lemon juice
2 oz castor sugar

56
Twister

2 parts dry sherry
2 parts orange juice
1 part scots whisky
1 dash Triple-Sec
Dry white wine

57
Wine Cobbler

16 parts dry white wine
4 parts Orange Curaçao
1 part lemon juice
1 part orange juice
Soda

COLUMBIA

COLOMBIA's torrid climate produces an interesting phenomenon; the grapes mature several times a year. Even so, the Colombians only manage to produce an annual 2,000 gallons, reportedly of 'sherry' and 'port' styles, and some hideously sweet dessert wines – in which case it may well be a mercy that they lack the resources to exploit this viticultural vicissitude.

CYPRUS

SUPPLIER of sherry-style wine to the British Empire for a century or more, Cyprus has fought to hold its position in the expanding export markets of the world. At the moment, it's a losing battle. Most of the wines which escape from Cyprus's shores are made in an old-fashioned style which the wine drinkers of today recognize for what it is: technologically out-of-date. There are hopeful signs, however. Many drinkers insist on a freshness and fruitiness hitherto undreamt of in Cyprus, and the industry is trying to adapt itself to the changes.

'Commandaria' is a reliable name, though, with its concentrated, raisiny fruit, and some of the sweeter 'sherries' share this quality, if to a lesser degree. But there is a long way to go before the overall quality of Cyprus table wines improves enough to compete in an ever more sophisticated world market.

List of Wineries

There are four large winemaking companies in Cyprus, and between them they produce all the Cyprus wine commercially available.

Keo. Not the biggest, but the most technically innovative, and thus the company to watch most closely. Not only has Keo already done research into a low-alcohol, ultra cool-fermented white wine made from Cyprus's indigenous white grape, the Xynisteri, but it has also started to apply this method to some high-quality reds. It will be some time before the world sees these, but it must be a step in the right direction.

Etko. Ranking third in size, and producer of some respectable if unexciting wines. Their 'Graves' is not dissimilar to the old-fashioned Sémillon-based white Bordeaux from which it takes its name, and their off-dry 'Fair Lady' is much enlivened by a dash of local Muscat.

Sodap. Run entirely as a cooperative, and the largest producer on the island, Sodap has a lot of modernisation to do before its wines have any real attractions for the modern wine lover.

Loel. Smallest of the four companies, Loel has taken some steps towards updating its operation, as their low-alcohol, Muscat-scented, slightly fizzy wine recently launched proves. They also have plans for

a small winery up in the mountains (Keo already has two of these), near prime grape-growing areas, instead of having to transport the harvested grapes miles to their winery in Limassol.

The Grape List

Black Muscat
Cabernet Franc
Cabernet Sauvignon
Carignan
Chardonnay
Grenache
Malvasia Grossa

Maratheftikon
Local black variety that could turn out to be a star. Carefully vinified, can make red wine with real fruit, acid and tannin. It's hard to harvest, though, as it grows in among the Mavro vines, and growers are unwilling to pick it separately.

Mataro

Mavro
The local black variety, mainstay of most red wines produced on the island, although some producers are making single variety wines from imported foreign grapes. Mavro rarely seems to make anything but over-alcoholic, coarse wines, at best with a raisiny fruit, but modern fermentation techniques and more careful control of the harvest might yield better results.

Palomino
Plant X
Riesling
Riesling Italico
Sémillon

Sultana
Mainly grown as an eating grape, but sometimes used to make rather neutral flavoured white wine.

Ugni Blanc

Xynisteri
The local white variety. Carefully picked and vinified, this can make aromatic, fresh white wines, as Keo are beginning to show. Too often, though, Cypriot white wines are made from grapes that should have been harvested months earlier, and hot fermentations lose any aroma the wine might have had.

CZECHOSLOVAKIA

THE one wine which visitors to Czechoslovakia remember is 'Champagne' of which copious quantities seem to be drunk at every opportunity. The quantity would seem to be a good idea, in view of the tiny resemblance which the Czechoslovakian version bears to the real thing. Elsewhere, the style of the wines depends partly on the region in which they are made; partly on the grape variety/ies used. The style of most is as reminiscent of Austria as it is of Hungary, Czechoslovakia's other vinous neighbour. Despite the modernity of the cooperative wineries, wines are often let down by the quality

and size of the corks used when they are bottled. Little effort has been made to export any of these wines westwards, so your only chance of tasting most of them is by visiting the country yourself.

The Wine Regions

SLOVAKIA
70 per cent of total production. Major areas are Bratislava, Modra, Pezinok. Others are Nove Zamky, Hurbanova, Skalica, and Hlohovec-Trnava.
This is a small enclave in the South-East bordering on

Hungary's Hegyalia region and which makes a quasi-Tokay, using virtually identical grapes. Mala Trna is the best known name in this area.

Grape varieties
Müller-Thurgau
Grüner Veltliner
Italian Riesling
Neuberger

Sylvaner
Muscat Ottonel

MORAVIA
Bordering on the Austrian Weinviertel, this region produces very similar styles of wine, light acidic whites and light acidic roses.

Grape varieties
Grüner Veltliner
Rhine Riesling
Italian Riesling
Traminer
Weiss Burgunder
Ruländer
Neuberger
Frankovka

BOHEMIA
Some of the best wines come from this area – reds and whites, the latter being very much in the German style. Quality zones include:
Litomerice
Roudnice
Melnik
Brezanky
Velke Zemoseky

The Grape List

Three quarters of the grapes planted are white, and divided into two categories:

First Class A
Gewürztraminer
Muscat Ottonel
Pinot Blanc
Rhine Riesling
Sauvignon

First Class B
Grüner Veltliner
Müller Thurgau
Welsch Riesling

> The original 'Good' King Wenceslaus was in fact a notorious alcoholic who once had his cook spitted and roasted for spoiling his wine.

> After France, Czechoslovakia is the second largest producer of Gewürztraminer wines in the world, with 1,520 ha (France 2,010 ha) planted. Switzerland, by way of contrast, has only 7 ha planted with the grape.

DENMARK

UNLIKE some of their Scandinavian neighbours, the Danes are really very keen indeed on wine, boasting the fifth highest consumption in Europe: 20 litres per head each year.

Countries exporting to Denmark
Algeria
Bulgaria
France
Germany
Hungary
Italy
Spain
UK
USA

EGYPT

THE renaissance of Egyptian wine in the twentieth century owes its origins to one man: Nestor Gianaclis. After careful study of ancient texts, Gianaclis decided that it was possible to plant vines and make wine of the quality described by Virgil and Horace. Tests were carried out with nearly 75 different grape varieties, whilst soil analyses were effected in various parts of the Nile Delta. These proved that one site, beneath its superficial covering of sand, had almost exactly the same chalky soil as Champagne. This was at Marisyut, close to Alexandria, and to the west of the Nile Delta. If some historians are to be believed, this was also the source of the *vinum mereoticum* which Julius Caesar enjoyed with Cleopatra. Over the first three decades of this century, vines were planted here, and elsewhere, so successfully that in the early thirties, wines from the Mariout vineyard were compared with Montrachet, Meursault and Rhine when they were tasted by Parisian gourmets.

More recent reports of these wines describe them as heavy and sweet, and rarely of any great interest. The one exception is supposed to be Omar Khyam, a Muscaty success.

There are approximately 20,000 *ha* of vines producing around 65,000 *hl*, much of which is exported to the USSR.

The Grape List

Chasselas
Pinot Blanc
Pinot Noir
Chardonnay
Gamay
Muscat Hamburg
Fayumi
Guizazi
Rumi

Egyptian Wine List (est. 1935)
Arsinoe (q.v. Greece)
Mendes
Mareotis
Delta Sebenytus

Reds
Gianaclis Abyad
Gianaclis Ahmar
Omar Khayyám

Whites
Reine Cléopâtre
Cru des Ptolomées
Clos Mariout

Grape varieties
Rhine Riesling
Traminer
Sylvaner
Müller-Thurgau
Chardonnay
Blauer Burgunder (Pinot Noir)
Blau Portugieser
St Laurent

SHERLOCK HOLMES STORIES IN WHICH WINE FEATURES

The Sign of Four
(Chaps 1, 4, 9, 10)

★ ★ ★ ★ ★

The Hound of the Baskervilles
(Chap. 2)

★ ★ ★ ★ ★

The Valley Of Fear
(Pt. 2, Chap. 2)

★ ★ ★ ★ ★

The Adventures of Sherlock Holmes
('A Case of Identity', 'The Noble Bachelor')

★ ★ ★ ★ ★

The Casebook of Sherlock Holmes
('Shoscombe Old Place,' 'The Creeping Man', 'The Veiled Lodger')

His Last Bow
('The Cardboard Box', 'The Dying Detective', 'His Last Bow')

★ ★ ★ ★ ★

The Return of Sherlock Holmes
('Abbey Grange')

★ ★ ★ ★ ★

Wines mentioned:
Beaune
Chianti
Port
Imperial Tokay (from Franz Josef's 'special cellar')
Champagne
Claret
Montrachet

We are indebted to Mr Stanley Mackenzie of The Sherlock Holmes Reference Collection, London, for this information.

ENGLAND

THEY MUST BE CRAZY. Otherwise, why should anyone even dream of making wine in England's uncertain and often unfriendly climate, and in the face of a rigorously unsympathetic government. English (and Welsh) vinegrowers and winemakers have been faced with a lack of official support matched only in the USA. Socialist politicians see no reason to help what they see as a rich man's hobby; Conservatives believe that – unlike other forms of coddled agriculture – winemaking has to stand on its own barely formed feet. And it is a *new* form of agriculture in England, despite the stories of huge amounts of wine being made before the arrival of the Romans: the stuff being made then would bear little comparison with the wine we enjoy today.

In the more recent early days of English winemaking – the beginning of the 1970's – the socialists were not entirely wrong: many of the people who were planting vines did do so as a hobby, just as they might have decided to grow roses in the back garden. Far too often, the wrong grape varieties were planted in the wrong places by people who knew less about wine than about fox-hunting and bee-keeping. Matters have changed radically since then however. The hobbyists have become bored (or gone broke) and a serious industry has been created. There is a considerable level of expertise now both in which kinds of vines should be grown where, the ways to blend different varieties and the method to make wine of the highest quality.

There is still a long way to go. The British themselves are hardly helping – they still prefer to continue drinking commercial German and East European wine rather than even to try a bottle of the home-grown product. If only 10% of British wine drinkers bought just one bottle of English wine each year, the wineries would be far less reliant on tourism (still an essential source of income) and could build the base for a healthy industry.

THE Vintners Company, formed in the 14th century, when Edward III granted letters patent to the 'Misterie of Vintners', had their own wharf, 'Three Cranes Vault', and City Ward 'The Vintry'. Both William of Malmesbury and Geoffrey Holinshed, the renowned 12th and 16th century historians, make note of English wines, the latter comparing them favourably with 'the best German sweet wines'.

When David Carr-Taylor put his English wines on show in Paris for the first time, their very existence was a continual source of amazement to the French wine trade throughout the Exhibition. Indeed, the phenomenon of an English wine was considered sufficiently startling to warrant *four minutes* of peak airtime on France's national television news.

The Grape List

White
Müller-Thurgau
Reichensteiner
Seyval Blanc
Kerner
Madeleine Angevine
Sylvaner
Sieggerebe
Huxelrebe
Chardonnay
Gewürztraminer
Seibel
Chambourcin
Ortega
Scheurebe
Optima
Ortega
Perle
Findling
Albalonga
Auxerrois
Pinot Blanc
Würzer
Seyvé Villard
Ehrenfelser
Pinot Gris

Pinot Meunière
Gütenborner
Gutedel
Faber
Chasselas
Bacchus
Schönburger
Triomphe d'Alsace
Pinot Chardonnay
Septima
Riesling
Sauvignon Blanc
Morio Muscat

Red
Zeiggeltrebe
Pinot Noir
Gamay de Beaujolais
Wrotham Pinot
Blau Portugieser
Gamay
Gagarin Bleu

Gamay Hatif
Blauberger
Leon Millot

Key to Grape Varieties

GWT.	– Gewürztraminer
Hux.	– Huxelrebe
MA	– Madeleine Angevine
MS –	Madeleine Sylvaner
MT	– Müller-Thurgau
PB	– Pinot Blanc
PN	– Pinot Noir
SB	– Seyval Blanc
Scheur.	– Scheurebe
Schön.	– Schönburger
Sieg.	– Sieggerebe
WP	– Wrotham Pinot
Zweig.	– Zweiggeltrebe

The List of English Vineyards

ADGESTONE
Sandown, Isle of Wight.
25¼ acres
Wines first sold 1970
65,000 bottles
MT 40%, Reich. 25%, Seyval Blanc 25%, Kerner 10%
Vinified on premises.
MT/Reich/SB 1982 won Gore-Browne trophy. 1976, 1978 and 1980 won silver medal in English Vineyard Association (EVA) championships

ALDERMOOR
Ringwood, Hants.
6 acres
Wines first sold 1979
10,000 bottles
mainly MT, and Reich.
Vinified Lamberhurst
Recent varietal Aldermoor MT

ASCOT FARM
Ascot, Berks.
2.5 acres
Wines first sold 1980
5,000 bottles
MT 50%, Reich. 35%, and MA, MS, PN, Sieg. and Zweig.
Vinified Westbury
Red, white, rosé

ASTLEY
Stourport, Worcs
4 acres
25% each MT, MA, Hux., Kerner

BARNSGATE MANOR
Uckfield, E. Sussex
20 acres
Wines first sold 1980
50,000 bottles
MT, PN, Chard., SB, Reich., Kerner
Vinified on premises
Exports to Channel Islands, Germany
Barnsgate Manor White, Kerner 1983

BARTON MANOR
Cowes, Isle of Wight
6 acres
Wines first sold
15–20,000 bottles
MT, SB, Reich, Zweig., Hux. and trials with GWT
Vinified on premises.
2 whites and a rosé
1983 still and sparkling rosés won gold medals and dry white won Gore-Browne trophy

BEAULIEU
Beaulieu, Hants
5.5 acres
First sold 1975
3,600 bottles
MT 55%, Hux. 15%, Reich. 15%, and Chambourcin, Seibel
Vinified Biddenden

BERWICK GLEBE
Polegate, E Sussex
2 acres
75% MT, Reich. 25%
5,000 bottles
Vinified Biddenden

BIDDENDEN
Ashford, Kent
18 acres
First vintage 1972
60–85,000 bottles
Mainly MT and Ortega and Reich., Hux., Scheur., Zweig.
Vinified on premises
Biddenden 1983 MT, Biddenden 1983 Hux. – won bronze medal EVA

BOSMERE
Chippenham, Wilts
2 acres
MA 25%, PN 25%, and MT, SB, Gamay de Beaujolais, Hux., Ortega and others
Vinified Lamberhurst

THE BOTHY
Abingdon, Oxon.
3.25 acres
600 bottles

Optima, Ortega, Perle, Findling, Hux., Albalonga
Not sold commercially
Vinified on premises

BOYTON
Halstead, Essex
4.5 acres
First sold 1979
8,000 bottles
MT 80%, Hux. 20%
Vinified Pulham Market or Bruisyard
Boyton MT dry and Boyton Hux. dry

BRANDESTON PRIORY
Woodbridge, Suffolk
7 acres
1,200 bottles
MT 90% and Schön., Auxerrois, PB
Vinified on premises

BREAKY BOTTOM
Lewes, Sussex
4 acres
First sold 1977
5,000 bottles
SB, MT, PN, Würzer, Schön. and trials with Loire varieties
Vinified on premises
SB. 1979, 1983, MT 1979, 1983, Reich. 1983, Würzer 1983

BROADFIELD
Bodenham, Herefordshire
10 acres
First sold 1977
2,500 bottles
mainly Reich. and Hux., MT, Seyve Villard
Vinified Pilton Manor

BROADWATER
Framlingham, Suffolk
Not presently in production but hoping to vinify 1985
9 acres
First sold 1981
2–3,000 bottles
Seyval Blanc
Broadwater SB 1981 and 1982

BRUISYARD
Saxmundham, Suffolk
19 acres
First sold 1977
8,000 bottles
MT
Vinified on premises
Bruisyard St Peter 1980, 1981, 1982, 1983

BRYMPTON D'EVERCY
Yeovil, Somerset
1 acre
First sold 1977
2,000 bottles
MT, Reich.
Vinified Pilton Manor
Brympton D'Evercy blended white

CARR TAYLOR
Westfield, Hastings, E. Sussex
21 acres
108,000 bottles
Wines first sold 1977
Schon, Gutenborner, Hux, MT, Kerner, Reich, Mullerebe. And Spatburgunder (2 acres)
Varietals and blends are vinified on the premises, as are wines for other vineyards.

CASTLE CARY
Castle Cary, Somerset
2.5 acres
First sold 1982
4,000 bottles
MT, SB, MA, Hux., Ehrenfelser
1982 and 1983 white table wine
SB/MT, MA medium
Vinified on premises

CAVENDISH MANOR
Sunbury, Suffolk
10 acres
First sold 1975
8,000 bottles
MT
Vinified Chilford Hundred
Cavendish Manor 1982, 1983

CHALK HILL
Salisbury, Wilts
6.5 acres
1984
3,000 bottles
MT, Bacchus, Kerner
Vinified on premises
3 varietal wines

CHICKERING
Hoxne, Suffolk
6–7,000 bottles
2.5 acres
Wine first sold 1980
MT – all vinified on premises.

CHILFORD HUNDRED
Linton, Cambs.
29 acres

First sold 1974
15,000 bottles
Mainly MT and Sieg., Ortega, Hux. Schon., and trials
Vinified on premises
All grapes organically grown
Chilford Hundred MT/Hux. dry 1982
Chilford Hundred MT/Schön. dry 1981

CHILSDOWN
Chichester, Sussex
10.5 acres
First vintage 1974
Production varies – max. 56,000 bottles
Mainly MT and SB, Reich.
Vinified on premises
Chilsdown dry white 1978, 1983, 1984
2nd wine – Chalklands white – made with bought in grapes

CONGHURST
Hawkhurst, Kent
½ acre
First sold 1982
1,490 bottles
Chasselas, Regner, SB
Vinified Lamberhurst
Conghurst Chasselas 1982, 1983

COSTYN
Pembroke Dock, Dyfed
1 acre
MT, SB, MS, MA, Reich., Wrotham Pinot, Morio Muscat
Vinified on premises

COURT LANE
Ropley, Hants
2 acres
First sold 1983 unbottled
MT, MA, Reich, Hux.
Vinified Lamberhurst
2 wines: MT/Reich. Hux. Reich.

CRANMORE
Yarmouth, Isle of Wight
6 acres
First sold 1971
MT 85% and PB, Gutenborner, Würzer
Vinified on premises
Cranmore MT 1982 and 1983

CROFFTA
Pontyclun, Glamorgan
3 acres
First sold 1982
7,000 bottles
MT, MA, Seyve Villard

Vinified Pilton Manor
Blended white 1983

CUCKMERE
Alfriston, Sussex.
4.5 acres (+some experimental)
Wines first made 1975
8,000–9,000 bottles
MT (medium dry)
Wines are vinified at Biddenden by Christopher Lindler

CUFIC VINES
Cheddar, Somerset
0.5 acre
First sold 1977
300 bottles
Mainly MT and SB, GWT, MA, Hux., Reich.
Vinified Wootton
MT white

DEVILS CAULDRON
High Haden, Kent
3.5 acres
3,000 bottles
Gutedel
vinified Lamberhurst
Gutedel dry 1983

DITCHLING
Hassocks, Suffolk
5 acres
First sold 1982
11,000 bottles
MT, Reich., Ortega
Vinified Biddenden
MT/Ortega, MT 1982, Reich. 1982

DOWNERS
Henfield, Sussex
6 acres
Wines first sold 1980
4,000 bottles
Müller-Thurgau
Vinified at Biddenden
Downers 1982 and 1983

EGLANTINE
Loughborough, Leics.
3.4 acres
First sold 1984
Mainly MA, with MT, MS, SB and some N. American hybrids
Vinified on premises

ELHAM VALLEY
Canterbury, Kent
1.6 acres
Wine first sold 1984
Mainly MT, with SB, Kerner, MA, Chasselas
Vinified Lamberhurst
MT 1983, and Pendant – a blended white

ELMHAM PARK
Dereham, Norfolk
7 acres
Mainly MT, and MA, Scheur.,
Reich., Kerner
4,000 bottles
Vinified on premises
Elmham Park dry and medium
dry 1983

ELMS CROSS
Bradford-on Avon, Wilts
3 acres
Wine first sold '82
10,000 bottles
100% MT, – 0.25 acre red
planted though not producing
yet.
Vinified on premises
MT Dry and medium dry 1983
and 1984

FELSTAR
Felsted, Essex
10.5 acres
Wines first sold 1969
8,000 bottles
MT, SB, Chardonnay, Pinot
Noir, MA, Wrotham Pinot,
Reich., Scheur., MS
Vinified on premises
SB/Chard. 1982, MA/SB 1983,
MT 1983, MT/Sieger 1983,
Chard./SB 1983, MS 1983,
Wrotham Pinot 1983, WP/PN
1983

FRITHSDEN
Hemel Hempstead, Herts
2.5 acres
Wine first sold 1974
1,500 bottles
80% MT, 10% MA and Reich.,
Kerner, Faber, PN, Siegger
Vinified on premises
MT white, Sieg./Reich white and
a rose

GAMLINGAY
Sandy, Beds
8 acres

First sold 1973
7,000 bottles
MT, Reich., Scheur.
Vinified on premises
Rosé, Reich. white, Scheur. dry
white

GREENS VINEYARD
Moreton, Essex
3 acres
First sold 1983
1,200 litres
Mainly Schön. and MT with
Würzer, Scheur., Kerner, Hux.
Vinified Chilford Hundred
Greens Vineyard 1983.

HAMBLEDON
Portsmouth, Hants.
7 acres
First sold 1958
15,000 bottles
SB, PM, Auxerrois,
Chardonnay, PN
Vinified on premises
Hambledon 1982, 1983
Exported to Dallas

HARBOURNE
Ashford, Kent
3 acres
1,000 bottles
MT, MA, SB, Blau Portugieser
and other reds

HELIONS
Haverhill, Suffolk
1 acre
Wine first sold 1983
2,500 bottles
Mainly MT and Reich., plus
Zweigel.
Vinified Biddenden
Dry white and a rosé to come

HENDRED
Wantage, Oxon.
3.5 acres
Wine first sold 1977
500 bottles
Reich.
Vinified on premises

HIGHWAYMANS
Bury St Edmunds, Suffolk
24 acres
wines first sold 1980
80,000 bottles
MT, PN, Hux. MA, PG, Bacchus,
Perle, Optima
Vinified on premises
Abbey Knight MT and Hux.
whites, and a PN rosé

HILLFOOT
Reading, Berks
8 acres
Wine first sold 1982
12,000 bottles
MT, SB, PN
Vinified on premises
MT 1981, 1983, MT/SB 1983,
1982

THE HOLT
Newbury, Berks
1 acre
First vintage 1980
Mainly MA, with MT, Sieg.
Vinified on premises
Woodhay 1981, 1982, 1983

HOOKSWAY
N. Marden, E. Sussex
3.5 acres
Wines first sold and 1982
10,000 bottles
MT, MA
Vinified on premises
Varietals from both grapes

HORAM MANOR
Heathfield, E. Sussex
4.5 acres
Wine first sold 1969
1,400 bottles
95% MT, 5% Hux.
Vinified on premises
Horam Manor 1980 and 1981

IGHTHAM
Sevenoaks, Kent
3 acres
Wine first sold 1977
6,000 bottles
MT, Hux., Reich., Schön., SB
Vinified Lamberhurst
Ightham 1982, 1983

ISLE OF ELY
Ely, Cambs
2.5 acres
Wine first sold 1975
2,000 bottles
MT, MA, Chard. WP
MT and Chard. varietals

JESSES
Salisbury, Wilts
1 acre

MA, MT, Triomphe d'Alsace
Jesses red chosen by Jordan
Govt. for visit of Queen

JOYOUS GARDE
Wargrave, Herts
2.5 acres
Wine first sold 1982
6,000 bottles
50% Bacchus, 49% MT, 1% Hux.
Vinified Wootton

KENTISH SOVEREIGN
Maidstone, Kent
2.5 acres
Wine first sold 1969
4,500 bottles
MT, Seyve Villard, Seibel
Vinified Lamberhurst
Kentish Sovereign red, white,
rosé. Jubilee 1976 sweet white

KINGS GREEN
Gillingham, Dorset
4 acres
First sold 1985
3,000 bottles
Mainly Zweig. and MT, Gamay,
Pinot Chardonnay, PN, GWT

KINVER VINEYARD
Kinver, Worcs
2 acres
2,000 bottles
MT, MA, PN, Bacchus,
Auxerrois, Findling,
Chambourcin, Gagarin Bleu
Vinified on premises
Dry white and rosé

KNOWLE HILL
Ulcombe, Kent
2 acres
Wine first sold 1974
600 bottles
MT, PN
Vinified Lamberhurst

LAMBERHURST
Tunbridge Wells, Kent
35 acres
Wine first sold 1975
150,000 bottles
45% MT, 20% SB and Reich.,
Schön, Riesling, Chasselas
Vinified on premises
MT, Reich., SB and Schön.
varietals and a blended white

LA MARE
St Mary, Jersey
6 acres
Wines first sold 1976
10,000 bottles
SB, Hux., Reich., Schön.,
'Clos de Seyval' white, Clos de la
Mare Hux/Reich.

LANGHAM
Colchester, Essex

4 acres
Wine first sold 1975
2,600 bottles
MT
Vinified Bruisyard
Langham MT 1979, 1980, 1981

LYMINGTON,
Lymington, Hants
6 acres
Wine first sold 1982
MT, Hux., Schön., Gut.
Vinified on premises

MAGDALEN
Diss, Norfolk
6 acres
Wine first sold 1977
10,000 bottles
Mainly MT and Auxerrois,
Bacchus, Optima
Magdalen Rivaner 1980, and
winner of the 1984 International
Challenge Auxerrois and
Bacchus varietals

NASH
Stoywing, Sussex
1.5 acres
500 bottles
50% MT, and Seyve Villard, MA,
Hux., Ortega
Vinified Biddenden

NEVARDS
Colchester, Essex
1 acre
Wine first sold 1980
700 bottles
Reich., Hux.
Blended white

NEWHALL
Chelmsford, Essex
24 acres
36,000 bottles
Mainly Hux.; and MT, with PN,
PG, Zweig., Bacchus, Reich.
Vinified on premises
MT and Hux. varietals, and
Pinot Selection and PN/Zeig.

PENSHURST
Penshurst, Kent
12 acres
Wine first sold 1976
20,000 bottles
MT, SB, Ehrenfelser, Reich.,
Scheur.
Vinified on premises
MT dry and medium dry, Reich.
and Scheur. whites

PILTON MANOR
Shepton Mallet, Somerset
6.5 acres
Wine first sold 1967
20,000 bottles
MT, MA, SB, Hux.

Vinified on premises
Pilton Manor MT, SB, Hux.
varietals

PINE RIDGE
Robertsbridge, E. Sussex
1.5 acres
Wine first sold 1982
50% MT, 20% Gut., and Kerner,
MS, MT, Scheur., Hux.
Vinified on premises
Organic methods
Reich. dry and medium dry, Gut.

POLMASSICK
St. Austell, Cornwall
1.5 acres
1,500 bottles
Vinified on premises
MT, Seyve Villard

PULHAM
Diss, Norfolk
6 acres
Wine first sold 1977
15,000 bottled
mainly MT, and Auxerrois,
Optima, Bacchus
Vinified on premises
Rivaner 1981, 1982, 1983,
Auxerrois 1980, 1982, Bacchus
1980
Twice winner of Gore-Browne
trophy

RENISHAW
Sheffield, Yorks
2 acres
Wine first sold 1979
200 bottles
SB, PM, PN, Hux., Reich.,
Schön.
Renishaw white 1979, PN red

ROCK LODGE
Scaynes Hill, Sussex
3.5 acres
Wine first sold 1970
17,000 bottles
MT, PN, Reich., Zweig.
Vinified on premises
Reich. and MT varietals

ROPELEY
Ropeley, Hants
2 acres
First sold 1982
35% MT, 40% Reich., 20% Hux.,
5% MA
Vinified Lamberhurst

ROWNEY
Sawbridgeworth, Herts
2 acres
4,000 bottles
MT, MA, SB, Zweig.
Vinified on premises

ST ANNES
Newent, Glos.

2 acres
Wine first sold 1984
50% MA, 20% MT, 30%
Triomphe d'Alsace and other
varieties for research
Vinified on premises

**ST GEORGES (WALDRON
VINEYARDS)**
Heathfield, E. Sussex
5.5 acres
Wine first sold 1982
MT, SB, Kerner, Reich., Ortega,
Schön., GWT and Kanzler.
30,000 bottles
Vinified on premises
MT 1983, Reich. 1983 and
blends

ST NICHOLAS
Canterbury, Kent
2.5 acres
Wine first sold 1982
8,000 bottles
MT, Schön.
Vinified on premises
Blended white. MT varietals
rating medium

SANDPITTS
Gastard, Wilts
0.5 acre
Wine not yet sold
Chambourcin, Leon Millot,
Zweig.

SHARPHAM
Totnes, Devon
2 acres
MA, PN, Hux., Reich.

SHERSTON EARL
Malmesbury, Wilts
3.5 acres
Wines first sold 1984

5–7,000 bottles
MT, ST, Bacchus, Ortega,
Würzer
Vinified on premises
Sherston Earl blended dry white

SNIPE
Woodbridge, Suffolk
1.5 acres
Wine first sold 1980
2,500 bottles
MT
Vinified Bruisyard
Silver Snipe MT

SOUTHCOTT
Pewsey, Wilts
1 acre
400 bottles
80% MT, 20% Septima, Ortega

SPRING FARM
Bridgewater, Somerset
12 acres
SB, MT, MA, Schön.
Medium dry and dry white

STAPLE
Canterbury, Kent
7 acres
Wine first sold 1978
Mainly MT, and Hux., Reich
Vinified Biddenden
Staple St James varietal whites

STAPLEGROVE
Taunton, Somerset
4 acres
Wine not yet sold 1985
7,000 bottles
MA, Hux., Reich., Sieg., Kerner,
Ehrenfelser
Vinified on premises
'Staplecombe' MA/Reich.
varietal and Hux. varietal

STERT
Devizes, Wilts
1 acre
Wine first sold 1980
1,500 bottles
MT, WP
Vinified Wootton
MT dry, WP rosé

STITCHCOMBE
Marlborough, Wilts
5.5 acres
Wines first sold 1982
8–10,000 bottles
MT, Reich., Sieg.
Vinified on premises
Blended dry white

STOCKS
Suckley, Worcs
11 acres
Wine first sold 1975
MT
Vinified Pilton Manor

SYNDALE VALLEY
Faversham, Kent
5 acres
12,000 bottles
MT, SB, Reich., Wurzer, Zweig.,
Weissburgunder
Vinified Lamberhurst
MT white

TAPESTRY WINES
Apperley, Glos.
5 acres, between 2 vineyards
Wine first sold 1984
8,000 bottles
MT, MA, SB, Reich.
Vinified on premises
Corinium blend MT, SB, Reich.,
MA/Reich. varietal

TENTERDEN
Tenterden, Kent
10 acres
Wine first sold 1980
25,000 bottles
30% MT and SB, and Gut.,
Reich., Schön. and 0.5 acre red
grapes
Vinified on premises
7 varietal Spots Farm wines,
and Tenterden rosé
Winners of Gore-Browne trophy,
1980 1st, 2nd, 3rd best dry white
1982
Gut, gold medal winner

THORNBURY CASTLE
Thornbury, Avon
1 acre
Wine first sold 1975
1,000 bottles
MT
Vinified on premises

THREE CHOIRS
Newent, Glos.
17.5 acres
Mainly, MT, with Hux., Schön.,
Reich., SB, Ortega, Riesling
Vinified on premises
Medium dry and Hux. white
Three Choirs 1979 bronze medal
at Vinexpo 1981. 1983 Hux.
Silver medal EVA

THREE CORNERS
Woodnesborough, Kent
1 acre
Wine first sold 1984
100 bottles
Mainly Sieg. and Reich., with
MA
Vinified Biddenden
Tricorne English white

WENDEN
Saffron Walden, Essex
2.5 acres
Wines first sold 1980
9,000 bottles
MT
Vinified Chilford Hundred
Dry and medium 'spritzig' MT
whites

WESTBURY
Reading, Berks.
16 acres
First harvest 1975, first sold
1976
100,000 bottles
MT, SB, MA, PN, PM, Seibel,
Sieg., Reich.
Vinified on premises
Varietal and blends from all
grapes, Seibel rosé, red blend
MT/SB 1982, gold and bronze
medal winner MT/SB 1983, best
in English Wine Race

WHATLEY
Frome, Somerset
1 acre
Wine first sold 1984
5,500 bottles
SB, MA, Hux., Reich.
Vinified Pilton Manor
Whatley St George white blend

WHITSTONE VINEYARDS
Bovey Tracey, Devon
1.5 acres
Wine first sold 1980
3,000 bottles
75% MT, 25% MA
Vinified Wootton
2 varietal whites

WICKENDEN
Taplow, Bucks
2¼ acres
Wine first sold 1981

49% MT, 39% Reich., 11% Sauv.,
1% Sieg.
Vinified on premises
Blended whites matured in oak

WOOTTON
Shepton Mallet, Somerset
6 acres
Wine first sold 1974
26,000 bottles
Mainly MT and Schön. and SB,
Auxerrois
Vinified on premises
Varietal whites from all 4
grapes

WRAXALL
Shepton Mallet, Somerset
6 acres
Wine first sold 1976
20,000 bottles
33% each MT, SB, MA
Vinified on premises
Blended dry white.

YEARLSTONE
Tiverton, Devon
2 acres
Wine first sold 1981
5–6,000 bottles
50% MA, 25% Sieg., 25% black
PN grapes and Chard., Riesling
Vinified on premises
Varietal whites and blended red
MA, Sieg. and Chard.

ETHIOPIA

THERE are many references
to 'Ethiopian Soave' in wine
books written earlier this
century. This may refer to the
influence of Mussolini's
occupying troops during their
sojourn in the region. Ethiopian
'chiante' also earned a reputation for itself. There were
recently reported to be some 500
ha of vineyards, whose produce,
plus concentrates, yielded an
annual production of around
50,000 *hl*. Famine and drought
have sadly made these figures of
academic interest. Still, they
show Ethiopia's potential for the
future.

List of Wine Regions

The principal regions are:
Abadir
Dukem
Eritrea
Guder

The Grape List

Black Muscat
Sultana
Cabernet (very little)

Principal wineries

Alexandris
Altavilla
Elaberet Estate
Makanissa

Food with Wine List

Starters/Snacks

Black Pudding	Castilian Red
Boston Baked Beans	White Zinfandel
Boudin Blanc	Champagne, Vouvray
Charcuterie	Corbières, Rosé d'Anjou
Cheese Omelette	Sancerre, Californian Cabernet Sauvignon
Cheese Soufflé	Chinon, Red Sancerre
Chitterlings	Pouilly Fuissé, Beaujolais
Escargots	Meursault, Aligoté
Frankfurters	Mosel Halbtrocken
Fresh Pasta	Pinot Grigio, Pinot Bianco
Frogs' Legs	White Graves, White Burgundy
Hors d'Oeuvres	Fino or Amontillado Sherry
Moussaka	Retsina, Sancerre
Paella	White Rioja, Penedès
Pâté de Foie Gras	Sauternes, Gewürztraminer
Pizza	Valpolicella, Chianti

Quiche Lorraine	Riesling (Alsace)
Salade Niçoise	Corbières
Salami	Chianti
Scrambled Eggs	Buck's Fizz (Champagne and Orange Juice)
Stuffed Peppers	Barolo, Gigondas
Terrine de Foie Gras	Gewürztraminer, Tokay (Alsace)
Tripe	Mâcon Rouge, Hock
Welsh Rarebit	English Müller-Thurgau

Soups

Bouillabaise	Provençal Red
Clam Chowder	Pinot Gris, White Graves
Consommé	Dry Sherry
Garlic Soup	Mâcon Blanc, Australian Chardonnay
Gazpacho	Vinho Verde, Manzanilla
Lobster Soup	Dry Oloroso Sherry
Oxtail Soup	Medium Sherry
Turtle Soup	Verdeilho (Madeira)

Shellfish

Clams	Riesling, Californian Chardonnay
Crab Salad	Riesling (Alsace, Moselle)
Curried Oysters	Pinot Blanc, White Rioja
Moules Marinières	Saumur, Muscadet
Mussels à la Bordelaise	White Graves, Montilla
Octopus in Ink	Ribeiro
Oysters	Chablis, Sancerre
Squid	Tavel Rosé, Rosé de Provence

Fish

Beluga Caviar	Dry Champagne
Freshwater Fish	White Graves, Australian Sémillon
Grilled Sardines	Dry Sherry, White Rioja
Rollmop Herrings	Soave, White Graves, Dão
Salmon	White Graves
Salmon Trout	Moselle, Meursault
Salt Cod	Vinho Verde, White Dão
Smoked Mackerel or Trout	Dry Sherry, Sancerre
Smoked Salmon	Dry, Medium Sherry, Hock, White Graves
Sole Meunière	Sancerre, Chablis
Swordfish	White Dão
Trout with Almonds	Californian Chardonnay

White Meat

Cold Roast Chicken	Hock, Mâcon Blanc
Coq au Vin	Bourgogne Rouge, Beaujolais, New Zealand Pinot Noir
Escalope of Veal	Hock, Gewürztraminer
Roast Pork	Mosel, Grüner Veltliner (Austria)
Roast Turkey	Claret, Chinon

Spare Ribs	Zinfandel, Gewürztraminer
Sweet and Sour Pork	Rosé de Provence, Asti Spumante

Red Meat

Boeuf Bourguignonne	Bourgogne Rouge, New Zealand Pinot Noir, Passetoutgrain
Beef Stroganoff	Pinotage (S. Africa, New Zealand)
Beef Wellington	Claret, Californian Cabernet Sauvignon
Hamburger	Zinfandel, Chianti
Meat-loaf	Californian Cabernet Sauvignon, Zinfandel
Osso Bucco	Montepulciano, Barolo
Pot au Feu	Beaujolais, Côtes du Rhône
Roast Lamb	Claret, Bourgogne Rouge
Steak and Kidney Pie	Australian Cabernet/Shiraz

Game

Goose	Châteauneuf-du-Pape
Grouse	Hermitage, Shiraz (Australia)
Hare	Côte Rôtie, Shiraz (Australia)
Hung Game	Zinfandel, Pinotage, Claret
Partridge	Claret, Gigondas, Gevrey-Chambertin
Pheasant	Châteauneuf-du-Pape, Californian Cabernet
Pigeon Stew	Bourgogne Passetoutgrain
Rabbit	Chinon, Italian Cabernet Sauvignon, Rioja
Venison	Blanc de Noirs Champagne, Palatinate
Wild Boar	Nuits-St-Georges, Châteauneuf-du-Pape

Vegetables/Vegetarian Dishes

Asparagus	Californian Chardonnay, Rosé Rioja
Guacamole	Zinfandel, White Rioja
Ratatouille	White Graves, Minervois

Desserts

Apple Crumble	Riesling, Muscat de Beaumes de Venise
Baked Alaska	Asti Spumante
Christmas Pudding	Muscat de Beaumes de Venise
Gâteaux	Sauternes, Spätlese Hock
Pecan Pie	Late-picked Gewürztraminer
Strawberries and Cream	Sauternes, Late-picked Cabernet, Vouvray
Treacle Tart	Verdeilho Madeira, Champagne

FRANCE

SAY wine and most people's Pavlovian response is to think French. And then there are all those grape varieties. Spaniards and Italians have had to make do with grape varieties which no one else really wants (how many vineyards full of Tempranillo and Nebbiolo do you see planted in the Napa Valley) whilst the French have generations of experience with almost all the world's greats: Cabernet

Sauvignon, Sauvignon, Pinot Noir, Chardonnay, Muscat, Gewürztraminer, Syrah, Merlot . . .

There is the climate: you want it cool – in Alsace, Champagne, the Loire and even Burgundy, you've got cool. You want hot – take your pick between the southern Rhône, Provence and the south-west. The would-be wine grower in France is quite literally spoiled for choice.

Despite a few (self-inflicted) bruises (Burgundy, though no longer tainted by North African wine, is still far from beyond reproach; Muscadet can be disappointing too) France can still see off the rest of the world when it comes to variety and value for money. Bordeaux, after its cathartic scandals is more vibrant than it has ever been; the Rhône is almost a byword for reliable reds; Alsace is as quality-conscious about its basic whites as the German vineyards across the river ought to be. VDQS's and Vins de Tables are producing an ever-growing number of individual wines. Previously unheard-of regions are suddenly coming up with estates and cooperatives and exciting new wines. The quality of France's most basic wines has never been higher.

The picture is not universally rosy – how could it be in a country with so many different wines? – but France is certainly a fighter ready and able to defend its corner.

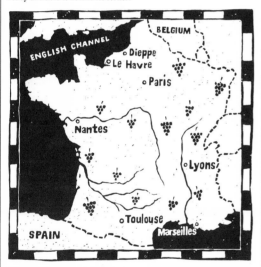

ALSACE

INTRODUCING ANYONE who doesn't already know them to the wines of Alsace is always a nerve-wracking process, rather like taking a prospective spouse to meet your parents for the first time. It's very easy to see why some people will never like these wines: their fans like them *because* of their odd, quirky, character which the uninitiated often find an unacquirable taste. And Alsace doesn't taste the way many people expect it to: in their tall green bottles, why aren't they undemandingly sweet like their cousins from the Mosel. On the other hand, if they are going to be dry, why can't they be bone dry like Chablis or Sancerre? There are all sort of words to describe these wines ('overt', 'mouthfilling', 'nutty', 'steely' and so on) but none can truly convey the spicy richness of a good Alsace, from whichever grape variety it is made. To say that these wines are only really appreciable with the highly flavoured foods which the Alsatians so relish is little help – few of these kinds of charcuterie are easily found outside the region itself.

The wine trade throughout the world, who often seem to be Alsace's only loyal supporters, continue to drink the wine copiously

themselves whilst trying to persuade their reluctant customers to try just a bottle or two. Still, Alsace's day may soon dawn: a growing number of wine bars in Britain and elsewhere are beginning to offer Pinot Blanc as an inexpensive white for customers who feel themselves just a little too sophisticated for Piesporter Michelsberg. And if a taste for fine sweet wine were ever to return, the best of the Vendanges Tardives will stand up as being good value for money against their Bordeaux and German counterparts. There are dull bottles of Alsace to be found, but very rarely a really poor one.

The Grape List

Chasselas
More often found in Switzerland these days, but once one of the staple varieties of Alsace, it is used in Edelzwicker and other blends, and, as a single variety, by Keintzler at Ribeauville.

Edelzwicker
Often thought to be a grape in its own right, but in fact a blend of Alsatian grapes. Once it was known as 'le Gentil' and placed only below Tokay in the Alsace hierarchy, Edelzwicker is now often simply the producer's standard blend. Equally often the name Edelzwicker does not appear on the label (e.g. Hugel describes its version as 'Sporen'.) Most cooperatives produce good Edelzwickers.

Gewürztraminer
Perhaps the most 'Alsatian' of Alsace wines, its name describes its taste: 'spicy' *(gewürz)* Traminer. The Traminer and Gewürztraminer were once made separately in Alsace, but nowadays only the latter variety is used. It is at once perfumed, oily and spicy; it clings to the surface of the mouth and lingers. Too much and what you have is a really blowsy glass of Parma Violets; get the balance right though, and the result is one of the richest, most *interesting* wines in the world – dry and yet so rich that it almost tastes sweet. Gewürztraminer is also very successful in its late-harvest version.

Recommended Gewürztraminer villages	Kientzheim
Ammerschwihr	Mittelwihr
Barr	Orschwihr
Beblenheim	Rorschwihr
Bergheim	Sigolsheim
Eguisheim	Turckheim
Kayserberg	Westhalten
Ingersheim	Wintzenheim

Recommended Gewürztraminer producers	Exceptionelle')
Lucien Albrecht ('Cuvée Martine')	Heim ('Zinnkoepfle')
	Hugel ('Réserve Personelle')
Ph. & M. Becker	Jos. Meyer ('Hengst')
Leon and Marc Beyer (Cuvée des Comtes d'Eguisheim)	Joseph Freudenreich
	Gaschy ('Réserve Exceptionelle Comtes des Martinsbourg)
Blanck ('Furstentum')	Louis Gisselbrecht
Bott-Geyl	Willy Gisselbrecht
Marcel Deiss ('Altenberg')	Hauller ('Cuvée Saint-Sebastian Vendange Tardive')
Dopff au Moulin ('Eichberg')	
Dopff & Irion ('Les Sorcières')	Ingersheim Cooperative
Cave Vinicole Eguisheim ('Cuvée St Leon')	Kayserberg Cooperative ('Kaefferkopf')
Henri Erhardt ('Kaefferkopf')	Klipfel ('Freiberg', 'Clos Zisser')
Joseph Freudenreich ('Cuvée	Kuehn ('Cuvée St Hubert)

Kuentz-Bas
Gustave Lorentz
Jérôme Lorentz
Mosbach
Marcel Mullenbach
Mure
Preiss-Henny
Preiss-Zimmer ('Réserve Comte Jean de Beaumont')
Paul Reinhart
Rolly-Gassmann
Charles Schleret
Sick-Dreyer ('Kaefferkopf')
Schlumberger ('Cuvée Christine Schlumberger')

René Schneider ('Kaefferkopf')
Jean Sipp ('Cuvée Particulière')
Louis Siffert
Sigolsheim Cooperative ('Mambourg')
Pierre Sparr ('Mambourg')
Trimbach ('Cuvée des Seigneurs de Ribeaupierre')
Charles Wantz ('Réserve')
Domaine Weinbach
Westhalten Cooperative
Willm ('Clos Gaensbroennel')
Wunsch & Mann ('Cuvée Steingrubler')
Zind-Humbrecht ('Hengst')

Klevener de Heigenstein
The forbear of the Gewürztraminer, rarely found in Alsace nowadays, but grown by Charles Wantz and sold by A. Willm.

Knipperle
Used in blends only.

Muscat
In a style now being earnestly copied by winemakers in countries as diverse as Portugal and Australia, in Alsace this makes one of the grapiest *dry* wines in the world. However, there is more than one kind of Muscat: Muscat d'Alsace (also known as the Muscat à Petits Grains) which is traditional to the region, and the Muscat Ottonel, a finer variety which has, in recent years been taking its place. Both have their good and bad points. The Muscat d'Alsace makes full-flavoured wine and is less vulnerable to bad weather. The answer seems to be a blend of two thirds Ottonel, one third Muscat d'Alsace.

Recommended Muscat villages
Gueberschwihr
Mittelwihr

Voegtlinshoffen
Wettolsheim

Recommended Muscat producers
Bott Frères ('Cuvée Exceptionelle')
Théo Cattin ('Cuvée de l'Ours Noir')
Dopff au Moulin
Dopff & Irion ('Les Amandiers')
Jean-Paul Eckle
Cave Vinicole Eguisheim (Cuvée de la Comtesse)
Heim ('Cuvée Speciale')
Kuentz-Bas ('Cuvée Reservée')
Marcel Mullenbach

Mure
Victor Peluzzi ('Steingrubler')
Preiss-Henny
A. Seltz ('Réserve Particulière')
Schaller
Charles Schleret
Sigolsheim Cooperative
Jean Sipp
Antoine Stoffel
Westhalten Cooperative ('Cuvée Reservée')
Zind-Humbrecht

Pinot Auxerrois
Usually sold as Pinot Blanc (see below) but a different, north Burgundian variety.

Recommended producers of Pinot Auxerrois
Cleebourg Cooperative ('Pinot d'Alsace')

Louis Hauller
Jos. Meyer ('Les Lutins')
Sick-Dreyer

Pinot Blanc
Also known as the Clevner or Klevner.
Once widely grown in Burgundy, this grape is rapidly finding a new home in Alsace (as it is in Italy) where it is used for méthode Champenoise sparklers as well as for attractive, light, single-grape varietals.

Recommended Pinot Blanc producers
Blanck ('Klevner Réserve')

Cave Cooperative de Beblenheim
Marcel Deiss

Heim ('Strangenberg')
Hugel ('Réserve Personelle')
Louis Gisselbrecht
Louis Hauller
Kayserberg Cooperative
Kuehn
Kuentz-Bas
Preiss-Henny
Xavier Rentz

A. Seltz
Charles Schleret
Schlumberger
Traenheim Cooperative
Trimbach
Domaine Weinbach
Westhalten Cooperative ('Strangenberg')

Pinot Gris
See Tokay d'Alsace.

Pinot Noir
The Alsace climate is far too tough to permit this grape to produce anything even approximating to the great red Burgundies for which it is best known. In Alsace it is used to make prettily fruity rosé which is usually sold as red. Special heated fermentation vats are used in the attempt to maximize colour.

Recommended Pinot Noir producers
Bott Frères ('Réserve')
Cleebourg Cooperative
Hunawihr Cooperative
Kuentz-Bas ('Réserve Personelle')
Laugel ('Rosé de Marlenheim')
Mosbach ('Vorlauf')
Mure
Paul Reinhart
Xavier Rentz (White 'Pinot Réserve Particulière')
Ribeauville Cooperative

Rolly-Gassmann
GAEC Saint-Fulrade
Charles Schleret
Louis Siffert
Antoine Stoffel
Traenheim Cooperative
Turckheim Cooperative ('Cuvée Réservée')
Charles Wantz ('Rouge d'Ottrott')
Westhalten Cooperative ('Cuvée Réservée')
Wunsch & Mann
Zind-Humbrecht

Riesling
Like the Muscat, this is a grape most familiar in its sweet form, here made into a dry wine. It has no real counterpart across the Rhine or elsewhere and makes an exciting comparison with Rieslings from other parts of the world. At its best it is big, deep and full of fruit, flower and spice. The Alsatians have a saying: 'He who knows Riesling, knows Alsace; he who loves Alsace, loves the Riesling'.

Recommended Riesling villages
Ammerschwihr
Dambach-la-Ville
Hunawihr
Husseren-les-Châteaux

Kayserberg
Orschwihr
Ribeauvillé
Thann
Wolxheim

Recommended Riesling producers
Lucien Albrecht ('Clos Himmelreich')

Leon and Marc Beyer ('Cuvée Particulière', 'Cuvée des Ecaillers')
Blanck ('Furstentum')

Boeckel ('Brandluft', 'Wibelsberg', 'Réserve')
Bott Frères ('Réserve Personelle')
Albert Boxler
Alfred Burghoffer ('Mandelberger')
Marcel Deiss ('Altenberg')
Dopff au Moulin ('Schoenberg')
Dopff & Iron ('Les Murailles', 'Vendange Tardive')
Robert Faller ('Geisberg')
Heim ('Les Eglantiers')
Louis Hauller ('Réserve')
Hugel ('Cuvée Tradition', 'Réserve Personelle')
Hunawihr ('Clos St Hune')
Jos. Meyer ('Hengst')
Gaschy ('Steingruber')
Louis Gisselbrecht
Willy Gisselbrecht
Francois Kientzler ('Geisberg')
Kuehn ('Kaefferhopf')
Kuentz-Bas ('Cuvée Reservée', 'Réserve Personelle')

Preiss-Henny ('Mandelberg')
Preiss-Zimmer ('Cuvée Particulière')
Paul Reinhart ('Bollenberg')
Joseph Riefle
Louis Siffert
Jean Sipp ('Kirchberg')
Louis Sipp ('Kirchberg')
Schaller
Schlumberger ('Kitterle')
René Schmidt ('Schoenberg', 'Cuvée Exceptionelle')
Stempfel
Sigolsheim Cooperative
Pierre Sparr ('Altenbourg')
Antoine Stoffel
Trimbach ('Cuvée Frédéric Emile')
Turckheim Cooperative
Domaine Weinbach ('Cuvée Théo')
Willm ('Kirchberg')
Zind-Humbrecht ('Clos St Urbain')

Francois Kientzler ('Clos du Zahnacker')
Klipfel ('Freiberg',)
Kuentz-Bas ('Réserve Personelle')
Mittnacht Frères ('Réserve Particulière')
Mosbach
Preiss-Henny ('Mandelberg')
Rolly-Gassmann

Schlumberger
Sigolsheim Cooperative
Pierre Sparr ('Altenbourg')
Antoine Stoffel
Trimbach ('Cuvée des Seigneurs de Ribeaupierre')
Turckheim Cooperative
Domaine Weinbach
Wunsch & Mann ('Cuvée de la Reine Clothilde')

Traminer
See Gewürztraminer

Sylvaner
Imported from Germany, or more romantically perhaps, Transylvania, this is Alsace's workaday variety. Its wines are never really great, but they are reliable and a good introduction to Alsace in general.

Recommended Sylvaner villages
Barr
Dambach-la-Ville
Epfig
Mittelbergheim

Recommend Sylvaner producers
Beblenheim Cooperative
Jean Beyer
Jean Hauller ('Réserve')
Louis Gisselbrecht
Willy Gisselbrecht
Hunawihr Cooperative
Ingersheim Cooperative
Kayserberg Cooperative
Kuehn
Preiss-Henny
A Seltz ('Zotzenberg')
Traenheim Cooperative
Charles Wantz ('Zotzenberg')
Westhalten Cooperative
Willm ('Cordon d'Alsace')

Tokay d'Alsace (or Pinot Gris)
Often confused with Hungarian Tokay of which it is no relation, the origins of the variety are unclear. An Alsatian soldier, Lazare de Schwendi, certainly stormed and took the fortress of Tokaj in Hungary in 1565. And he certainly took 4,000 vats of Hungarian Tokay home with him. Some say he brought back some vines too. If he did, they were not Hungarian Tokay vines, because they would have been the Furmint from which that country's Tokay is made, not the Pinot Gris which is used in Alsace. The wine itself is the heaviest of Alsaces and the one which, in a good year, needs most time to develop. At best, it is at once smoky and nutty.

Recommended Tokay villages
Cleebourg
Beblenheim
Kientzheim
Obernai
Millelwihr

Recommended Tokay producers
Léon and Marc Beyer ('Réserve')
Blanck ('Réserve Speciale')
Cave Cooperative de Cleebourg
Cave Vinicole Eguisheim ('Cuvée du Schlossherr')
Heim ('Réserve')
Hugel ('Réserve Personelle')

28 recommended growers, merchants and cooperatives of Alsace

Andlau-Barr (Barr)
197-member cooperative. Specialities: 'Zotzenberg' Sylvaner, Klevner de Heiligenstein.

Les Caves Adam (Ammerschwihr)
Grower/merchant with 12 *ha*, selling 150,000 cases. Specialities: Gewürz 'Kaefferkopf'; Riesling 'Kaefferkopf'.

Caves Becker (Zellenberg)
Grower/merchants with 10 *ha* selling 40,000 cases per year and using the brand name Gaston Beck. Specialities: 'Zellenberg' Muscat, Gewürz.

Léon Beyer (Eguisheim)
Family firm of grower/merchants with 30 *ha*, selling around 800,000 bottles per year, supplying some of France's finest restaurants. Specialities: Tokay, Tokay 'Réserve', 'Vendange Tardive'; Riesling 'Cuvée des Ecaillers', 'Cuvée Particulière'; Gewürztraminer 'Cuvée des Comtes'.

Bennwihr
250-member cooperative, one of the biggest in Alsace, selling around 350,000 cases per year. Labels include:
Poème d'Alsace
Victor Preiss
Réal
Rêve d'Alsace
Specialities: Riesling 'Rebgarten'; Gewürztraminer 'Réserve', 'Côtes de Bennwihr'.

E. Boeckel (Mittelbergheim)
Grower/merchant with 20 *ha* selling 55,000 cases per year. Specialities: Sylvaner 'Zotzenberg'; Gewürz 'Zotzenberg', Château d'Isembourg'; Riesling 'Zotzenberg', 'Brandluft', 'Wibelsberg'.

Bott Frères
Grower/shipper with 12 *ha*, selling 25,000 cases per year. Specialities: Riesling 'Cuvée Exceptionelle', 'Réserve Personelle'.

Dambach-la-Ville
163-member cooperative. Specialities: Pinot Blanc, Sylvaner, Riesling.

Dopff & Irion (Riquewihr)
Grower/merchants with 125 *ha* selling 350,000 cases per year, including around 18,000 cases of Riesling from their own vineyard. The company also uses the names:
Charles Jux
Kugler
Ernest Preiss
and sells wines from its own estate under the name Domaines du Château de Riquewihr.
Specialities: Riesling 'Les Murailles', 'Vendange Tardive'; Gewürztraminer 'Les Sorcières' Vendange Tardive; Muscat 'Les

Amandiers'; Pinot Gris 'Les Maquisards'.

Eguisheim
470-member cooperative, selling 450,000 cases. Also uses the names:
Pierre Meierheim
Pierre Rotgold
Wolfberger
Specialities: Riesling 'Cuvée des Seigneurs'; Gewürz 'Cuvée St-Léon
IX; Pinot Noir 'Prince Hugo'; Tokay 'Cuvée du Schlossherr'; Muscat
'Cuvée de la Comtesse'; Crémant.

Dopff au Moulin (Riquewihr)
Established in the 17th century, this firm, with 75 *ha*, now sells
200,000 cases per year. Other names used include:
Caves Dolder
P.E. Dopff & Fils
Mergy
Specialities: Riesling 'Schoenberg'; Muscat 'Schoenberg'; Gewürz
'Eichberg', 'Cuvée Exceptionelle'; Crémant.

Theo Faller (Kayserberg)
Theo Faller died some years ago and is now buried amongst his vines.
The 27 *ha* estate is run by his widow and son and produces around
14,000 cases per year. Wines are labelled:
Clos des Capucins
Domaine Weinbach
Specialities: Riesling 'Vendange Tardive', 'Schlossberg Gewürz
'Vendange Tardive'.

Louis Gisselbrecht (Dambach-la-Ville)
Grower/merchant with 6 *ha*, selling 60,000 cases. Speciality:
Sylvaner, Riesling.

Willy Gisselbrecht (Dambach-la-Ville)
Grower/merchant with 15 *ha*, selling 120,000 cases. Speciality: Pinot
Blanc, Gewürztraminer 'Réserve'.

Caves de Hoen (Beblenheim)
220-member cooperative selling 210,000 cases. Labels include:
Baron de Hoen
Cave de Beblenheim
Eugène Deybach

Heim (Westhalten)
Grower/merchant with 5 *ha*, selling 180,000 cases. Labels include:
Ann d'Alsace
Anne Koehler
Meyer
Mittnacht
Specialities: Pinot Blanc 'Clos du Strangenberg'; Riesling 'Les
Eglantiers'; Gewürz 'Zinnkoepfle'; Muscat 'Réserve'; Tokay 'Réserve';
Crémant.

Hugel (Riquewihr)
Grower/merchant with 25 *ha*, selling 120,000 cases. Labels include:
Couronne d'Alsace
Cuvée des Amours
Flambeau d'Alsace
Fleur d'Alsace
Les Vignards
Specialities: Edelzwicker 'Sporen'; 'Tokay'.

Ingersheim et Environs (Colmar)
160-member cooperative, selling 180,000 cases. Other label:
Florimont.
Specialities: Pinot Blanc, Gewürz, Riesling.

Kientzheim-Kayserberg (Kayserberg)
125-member cooperative. Specialities: Gewürz 'Kaefferkopf'; Riesling
'Schlossberg'.

Regulations and characteristics of Alsace Grand Cru

Alsace has recently started its own Grand Cru denomination:
An Alsace grand cru must:
1. Satisfy all the conditions of ordinary AOC Alsace
2. Be made from Riesling, Gewürztraminer, Pinot Gris (Tokay) or
Muscat grapes, 100 per cent single variety
3. Contain (for Pinot Gris and Gewürztraminer) 187 g/1 minimum of
sugar natural, and have a minimum of 11° after fermentation or
(for Riesling and Muscat) contain 170 g/1 natural sugar and 10°
minimum alcohol after fermentation
4. Come from a vineyard producing no more than 70 *hl* per *ha* of
vines in production (though this is the basic yield, and in some years
may be increased by a small percentage, like ordinary AOC Alsace)
5. Come from the same vintage
6. Come from one of the following vineyards:

Lieuxdits (vineyards)	In the commune(s) of
Altenberg de Bergbieten	Bergbieten
Altenberg de Bergheim	Bergheim
Brand	Turckheim
Eichberg	Eguisheim
Geisberg	Ribeauvillé
Gloeckelberg	Rodern et Saint-Hippolyte
Goldert	Gueberschwihr
Hatschbourg	Hattstatt et Voeglinshoffen
Hengst	Wintzenheim
Kanzlerberg	Bergheim
Kastelberg	Andlau
Kessler	Guebwiller
Kirchberg de Barr	Barr
Kirchberg de Ribeauvillé	Ribeauvillé
Kitterlé	Guebwiller
Moenchberg	Andlau (67) et Eichhoffen
Ollwiller	Wuenheim
Rangen	Thann (68) et Vieux-Thann
Rosacker	Hunawihr
Saering	Guebwiller
Schlossberg	Kaysersberg et Kientzheim
Sommerberg	Niedermorschwihr et Katzenthal
Sonnglanz	Beblenheim
Spiegel	Bergholtz et Guebwiller
Wiebelsberg	Andlau

Klipfel (Barr)
Grower/merchant with 30 *ha*, selling 90,000 cases. Domaine wines are sold under the name Louis Klipfel, the rest under that of Eugène Klipfel. Specialities: Louis Klipfel Gewürz 'Clos Zisser', 'Freiberg'; Tokay 'Freiberg'; Riesling 'Kirchberg', 'Kastelberg'.

Kuehn (Ammerschwihr)
Grower/merchant with 8 *ha*. Specialities: Pinot Blanc, Riesling 'Kaefferkopf'; Gewürz 'Cuvée Saint-Hubert'.

Kuentz-Bas (Husseren-les-Châteaux)
Grower/merchant with 12 *ha*. Specialities: Pinot Noir (maceration carbonique); Edelzwicker 'La Mariette'; Riesling 'Cuvée Tradition', 'Cuvée Réservée', 'Cuvée Personelle'.

Michel Laugel (Marlenheim)
Grower/merchant with 5 *ha* of Pinot Noir, selling 350,000 cases. Specialities: Pinot Noir Rosé 'Marlenheim'; Edelzwicker 'Pichet d'Alsace'.

Gustave Lorentz (Bergheim)
Grower/merchant with 20 *ha*, selling 80,000 cases. Under the same ownership, though independent of, Jérôme Lorentz. Specialities: Gustave Lorentz Gewürz 'Altenberg'; Riesling 'Altenberg'; Jérôme Lorentz Gewürz 'Kanzlerberg'.

Mure (Rouffach)
Grower/merchant with 17 *ha* (including 15 *ha* of the Clos Saint-Landelin), selling 40,000 cases. Domaine wines are sold under the Mure label; Mure-Ehrhardt is used for the rest. Specialities: Gewürz 'Clos Saint-Landelin'.

Orschwiller (Selestat)
138-member cooperative, selling 85,000 cases.

Pfaffenheim-Gueberschwihr (Rouffach)
190-member cooperative selling 120,000 cases. Specialities: Gewürz 'Bergweingarten'; Pinot Blanc 'Schneckenberg'.

Preiss-Henny (Mittelwihr)
Grower/merchant with 45 *ha*. Specialities: Pinot Gris 'Réserve'; Riesling 'Cuvée Marcel Preiss'; Gewürztraminer 'Cuvée Camille Preiss'; Muscat.

BORDEAUX

IN THE EARLY 1970's Bordeaux looked a very sick region indeed. Scandal and world financial crisis coincided and conspired to raise doubts in many minds over the authenticity and prices of even the most vaunted wines. In retrospect, that 'mauvais quart d'heure' did Bordeaux an enormous amount of good. It destroyed a complacency bred of centuries, forced owners of neighbouring chateaux to cooperate with each other instead of bickering, obliged the Bordelais themselves to take a fresh look at the quality of their wines. The improvement in the way in which wines are made can be seen across the board, from the humblest Bordeaux Rouge to the once disappointing classed growth.

Of course, outsiders can still criticise this estate or that, and complain of prices demanded on account of the producers' economic need (some call it greed) rather than the quality of the vintage. But, compared with Burgundy and indeed with some of the more insatiable Californians, Bordeaux can still offer excellent value for money.

In white wines the revolution has been both more recent and more dramatic still. A region which, a few decades ago procued 80% sweet wine has been transformed into one which now increasingly specialises in crisply *dry* wines. There is still a great deal of progress to be made – far too much of the region is still planted with the Semillon, ideal for sweet wine, poor for dry – but the introduction of temperature-controlled fermentation vats has done much to do away with the dish-clothy staleness of so many of the white Bordeaux which used to be sold. But the scope is there: as the Sauvignon takes over, the clean, fruity wine made here will leave many a Loire winemaker looking sourly envious.

The sweet whites are still underpriced – when one considers their limited production – but there are signs that the unfashionability of Barsac and Sauternes may be beginning to fade. Pudding wines could make a comeback at any time, and when they do, the better-made Bordeaux ought to make a killing; at least here, unlike Germany, the region's most traditional wines are still made from the region's most traditional grapes.

The Grape List

Cabernet Franc
Cabernet Sauvignon
Malbec (or Pressac)
Merlot
Petit Verdot
Sauvignon
Sémillon
Muscadelle
Ugni Blanc

Bordeaux Words

Assemblage
The blending of different grape varieties to produce claret.

★★★★★

Barrique
Cask holding 225 litres.

★★★★★

Bordeaux
Any wine, red or white, produced within the Appellation Bordeaux area.

★★★★★

Bordeaux Supérieur
As above, but with 1–2% more alcohol.

★★★★★

Chai
Literally the winery storage building, as opposed to a cellar.

★★★★★

Château
Almost all estates in Bordeaux call themselves Château – there does not have to be a building.

★★★★★

Chef de Culture
The man responsible for the vineyard.

★★★★★

Cru Artisan
Defunct designation for sub-Cru Bourgeois estates.

★★★★★

Cru Bourgeois
A class above basic Bordeaux, but still confused in its coverage. Although several hundred Châteaux can use the description, having been permitted it by law, the list on page 46 includes all of the current members of the Syndicat des Crus Bourgeois which operates its own set of quality standards. Crus Bourgeois have to be in the Médoc.

★★★★★

Cru Bourgeois Supérieur
As above, but matured in barrel.

★★★★★

Cru Classé
Indicates a wine which features in one of the several quality classifications created for the separate communes and regions of Bordeaux.

★★★★★

Cru Exceptionnel
Limbo designation for Châteaux which are not quite Classés.

★★★★★

Cru Grand Bourgeois Exceptionnel
A Cru Bourgeois from the same area as the Crus Classés of Médoc, bottled at the estate.

★★★★★

Cru Paysan
Defunct designation for humble estates. See Petits Châteaux.

★★★★★

Domaine
Possibly a blend of wines from more than one château.

★★★★★

Grand Cru
A difficult term. If the word Classé does not also appear (and

it is not mandatory) it is quite
meaningless.

★ ★ ★ ★ ★

Régisseur
*The person responsible for the
running of a Château and the
making of its wine.*

★ ★ ★ ★ ★

Maître de Chai
The cellar-master

★ ★ ★ ★ ★

Petits Châteaux
*Unofficial description to describe
sub-Cru Bourgeois properties.*

★ ★ ★ ★ ★

The Wine Regions

The vineyards of Bordeaux follow the Gironde and is tributaries. The
region is divided between sizeable regions and communes.

Barsac
See Sauternes.

Canon-Fronsac
To the west of St-Emillion, producing good to very good red wine. See
also Fronsac.

Ch. Bodet
Ch. Canon
Ch. Canon de Brem

Ch. Junayme
Ch. Moulin-Pey-Labrie
Ch. Toumalin

Cérons
Not a great deal of Cérons is made, and even less leaves France, but it
is worth watching out for if you want a sweet wine which might once
have done credit to the Graves Supérieur appellation.

Côtes de Blaye
See Premières Côtes de Blaye.

Côtes de Bordeaux Saint-Macaire
Source of sweetish white wine, little seen outside the region.

Côtes de Bourg
Not all Bordeaux is built on Cabernet Sauvignon: Bourg combines
Merlot with Cabernet Franc, producing some very respectable results.

Ch. de Barbe

Côtes de Castillon
A prime contender for the title of 'Affordable Bordeaux', the Côtes de
Castillon lack the St-Emilion tag of their neighbours, Montagne and
Parsac, but arguably offer better wine.

Ch. de Pitray

Coutras
Wine used to be distilled for Cognac.

Ch. de Meaume

Cubzac
Small, rarely seen appellation for flat land with reasonable red and
white wine.

Ch. de Terrefort-Quancard

Entre-Deux-Mers
'Between two seas' – but which? In fact the name should really be
'Entre-Deux-Rivières', because the water which runs along both sides
of these vineyards flows along the rivers Dordogne and Garonne.
Quite recently the appellation was used for sweet white wine of little
distinction; following the international trend, the flavour is now dry
white. And quite good too.

Fronsac
Just beneath the vineyards of Canon-Fronsac, this appellation's wines
are compared with St-Emilion, though with a rather tougher quality.
These can be bargains.

Graves
Cheap and rather nasty white wine. Not all of it – just the stuff for
which Graves became known. There *are* some extremely good
properties producing excellent whites – Carbonnieux is one lesser
known example – but it is the reds which are worth paying particular
attention to. Ready to drink earlier than Médocs they are often of just
as high a class.

Ch. de Fieuzal
Ch. Carbonnieux
Domaine de Chevalier
Ch. Guitres
Ch. Haut-Bailly

Ch. Haut-Benauge
Ch. Haut-Brion
Ch. Malartic-Lagravière
Ch. Pape-Clément
La Tout-Martillac

Haut-Médoc
A large appellation which includes wine of the level of Château La
Lagune as well as quite a few very ordinary properties indeed. Look at
the communes such as Moulis and Listrac which fall within its
boundaries.

Ch. Barreyres
Ch. Cantemerle
Ch. Caronne-Ste-Gemme
Ch. Cissac
Ch. Citran
Ch. Coufran

Ch. La Lagune
Ch. Lanessan
Ch. Liversan
Ch. Malescasse
Ch. La Tour-Carnet
Ch. Victoria

Lalande-de-Pomerol
Not quite comparable with Pomerol across the River Barbanne – the
Malbec sometimes influences the flavour of the wine, much as the
Merlot does in Pomerol itself – these are nonetheless usually wines of
a good standard at a good price.

Ch. Bel-Air

Ch. Tournefeuille

Médoc
The name of a whole chunk of land, and an appellation of pretty basic
aspirations. These wines are often unfairly not reckoned to be up to
the standard of good Haut-Médocs, but they should be reasonably
sound and can offer really attractive claret to drink young. Look for
the Cru Bourgeois.

Ch. Blaignan
Ch. La Clare
Ch. La Tour de By

Ch. La Tour St-Bonnet
Ch. Loudenne
Ch. Potensac

Listrac
Very much in the shadow of the better known, and better classed
communes Listrac, like Moulis its neighbour, deserves closer
attention. It is a place to find Crus Bourgeois.

Ch. Fonréaud
Ch. Fourcas-Dupré

Ch. Fourcas-Hosten
Ch. Lestage

Loupiac
Ste-Croix-du-Mont's lesser brother, largely in the hands of the
cooperative. Still there are some nice, basic sweet Bordeaux to be
found at pretty low prices.

Lussac-St-Emilion
A 'satellite' of St Emilion itself, like Parsac, Puisseguin, Montagne
and St Georges-St-Emilion, this is a place to look for pretty soft,
reasonably undemanding claret which can, in good examples, be
worth keeping for a while.

Ch. de Lussac

Margaux
With a higher number of Crus Classés (over 20) than any other
Bordeaux appellation, and with Château Margaux itself to serve as a
flagship, this could be thought to be the Harrods of the region.
Actually, there are some rather disappointing wines from other

villages which still have the right to call their wine Margaux, but the great wines are just that – great. Delicate and long-lived.

Ch. Brane-Cantenac
Ch. Cantenac-Brown
Ch. d'Angludet
Ch. Giscours
Ch. d'Issan
Ch. d'Issan

Ch. Malescot-St-Exupéry
Ch. Palmer
Ch. Prieuré-Lichine
Ch. Rausan-Ségla (from 1983)
Ch. Siran
Ch. Du Tertre

Montagne-St-Emilion
See Lussac-St-Emilion.

Moulis
A good place to look for the unjustly overlooked. This commune has several properties which, in many experts' view, could leap into any revised classification of Bordeaux.

Ch. Brillette
Ch. Chasse-Spleen
Ch. Grand Poujeaux

Ch. Maucaillou
Ch. Poujeaux

Parsac-St-Emilion
See Lussac-St-Emilion.

Pauillac
The cream of the Bordeaux crop, with Lafite, Latour and Mouton, to name but three. The two words to bear in mind here are *Cassis* and *Cash*. A lot of the latter will buy you a lot of the former – in the shape of deliciously and unashamedly blackcurrant wine.

Ch. Batailley
Ch. Clerc-Milon
Ch. Fonbadet
Ch. Grand-Puy-Lacoste
Ch. Haut-Bages-Monpelou
Ch. Haut-Batailley
Ch. Lafite-Rothschild
Ch. Latour

Ch. Lynch-Bages
Ch. Lynch-Moussas
Ch. Mouton-Baronne-Philippe
Ch. Mouton-Rothschild
Ch. Pichon-Longueville au
   Baron de Pichon-Longueville
Ch. Pichon-Longueville,
   Comtesse de Lalande

Pomerol
Are these the richest Bordeaux? There are two real success stories here: firstly there is the region which came in from the cold of obscurity, and then there's the tiny property (4,000 cases) which, with no classification to bolster its claim, rose to become one of the world's most highly prized, and priced, red wines. If you cannot afford Château Pétrus, try some of its honeyed, plummy neighbours before their prices go through the roof too.

Ch. Certan-de-May
Ch. La Conseillante
Ch. Evangile
Ch. Feytit-Clinet
Ch. Lafleur
Ch. Le Gay

Ch. Lagrange
Ch. La Grave Trigant de Boisset
Ch. l'Eglise-Clinet
Ch. La Fleur-Gazin
Ch. La Fleur-Petrus

St Emilion
St Emilion has always envied the Médoc for its 1855 classification system. It was not until 1954 that any kind of hierarchy was established here, and the list which then appeared – and has since been amended – is generally disdained; how can there be 72 Grands Crus Classes and over 150 Grands Crus? As we go to print the system is being revised once more. Which should help to encourage the makers of what can be deliciously mellow-Merlot-y wines.

Ch. Canon-La-Gaffelière
Ch. Cheval-Blanc
Ch. Dassault

Ch. Figeac
Ch. Fombrauge
Ch. Fonroque

Ch. Pavie
Ch. Magdelaine
Ch. La Tour-Figeac

Ch. La Tour-du-Pin-Figeac
Ch. Larcis-Ducasse
Ch. La Clusière

St-Estèphe
If it tastes a bit tougher when young, a little less ready to show its charms, the chances are it could be a St-Estèphe. But that's not to say that a wine from this appellation has to look up to its 'classier' neighbours – given time, these slightly rustic clarets can easily rival many a well-born contender.

Ch. Andron-Blanquet
Ch. Beau-Site
Ch. Calon-Ségur
Ch. Capbern-Gasqueton
Ch. Cos d'Estournel
Ch. Cos Labory
Ch. Haut-Marbuzet
Ch. Huissant

Ch. Lafon-Rochet
Ch. de Marbuzet
Ch. Meyney
Ch. Montrose
Ch. Les-Ormes-de-Pez
Ch. de Pez
Ch. Phélan-Ségur

Ste-Foy-Bordeaux
Unexciting wine better than most plain Bordeaux, but not much.

St-Georges-St-Emilion
See Lussac-St-Emilion.

St-Julien
If the wines of this appellation are not quite the royalty of Bordeaux, they are right up there amongst the top levels of the aristocracy. Class is the keynote. That, and a depth and richness of fruit which make these wines the epitome of claret: cedar and deep ripe fruit.

Ch. Beychevelle
Ch. Branaire-Ducru
Ch. Ducru-Beaucaillou
Ch. Du Glana
Ch. Gloria
Ch. Gruaud-Larose
Ch. Lagrange

Ch. Langoa-Barton
Ch. Léoville-Barton
Ch. Léoville-Las-Cases
Ch. Le Léoville-Poyferre
Ch. St Pierre-Sevaistre
Ch. Talbot
Ch. Terrey-Gros-Caillou

Sauternes
You can make a few glasses of wine from each vine – only one glass at Yquem. And people still pay less for a fine Sauternes than they would spend on a bottle of California Chardonny, where the yield is at least

ten times greater. Sauternes will have to come back into fashion one day, and when it does, those who have bought a case or two now will smile as they sip. A word of warning though: Sauternes can vary from property to property and from year to year. None of these properties should ever be less than good – and sometimes they will be magic.

Ch. Bastor-Lamontagne	Ch. Liot
Ch. Broustet	Ch. Nairac
Ch. Climens	Ch. Rieussec
Ch. Coutet	Ch. Sigalas-Rabaud
Ch. Doisy-Daëne	Ch. Suau
Ch. Guiraud	Ch. Suduiraut
Ch. La Chartreuse.	Ch. d'Yquem
Ch. Lafaurie-Peyraguey	

The Merchant List

Unlike other areas of France where merchants can, to a great extent, control the wine trade by buying wine in bulk from producers, Bordeaux is now very much in the hands of the estate owners themselves, the *châtelains*, who bottle their own wine and establish their own prices. Most merchants, however, still buy in and bottle 'generic' wines which they sell under their own labels.

Castel Frères
Biggest in Bordeaux.

Cordier
Own Ch. Gruaud-Larose, Lafaurie-Peyraguey, Meyney, Talbot. Ch. Cantemerle, Clos des Jacobins and Ch. Plagnac.

Barton & Guestier
Belong to Seagrams. Own Ch. Langoa-Barton.

La Baronnie
The trading arm of the Baron Philippe de Rothschild.

Borie-Manoux
Owners of Chx Batailley, Beau-Site, Haut-Bages-Monpelou.

C.V.B.G.
Consortium of companies, including Dourthe and Kressman.

Calvet

Ginestet

Lebègue & Cie

S.D.V.F.
Young company selling exclusively châteaux Bordeaux

Yvon Mau
Dynamic company making particular efforts to promote Bergerac.

Cruse & Fils Frères
The company caught up in the 'banana wine' scandals of the early 1970s. Still one of Bordeaux's biggest shippers of fine wine.

Pierre Dulong

Louis Eschenauer
British-owned company with Ch. La Garde, Olivier, Rausan-Ségla, Smith Haut-Lafitte.

Gilbey de Loudenne
Owned by IDV (thus Grand Metropolitan) distribute Chx Branaire, Giscours, Loudenne, de Pez.

Nathaniel Johnston
Sell Haut-Brion's second wine, Ch. Bahans.

Les Fils de Marcel Quancard

Alex Lichine
No longer any connection with the great author and wine-maker – belongs to UK brewers Bass Charrington. Owns Ch. Lascombes Castér.

A. De Luze
Owned by Rémy Martin, with Chx Cantenac-Brown and Paveil-de-Luze. Markets Chx Filhot, Beauséjour.

Mahler-Besse
Part-owns Ch. Palmer.

Mestrezat-Preller
Has shares in Chx Chasse-Spleen, Grand-Puy-Ducasse.

Schröeder & Schyler
Own Ch. Kirwan

Sichel
Peter Sichel owns Ch. d'Angludet. Part-own Ch. Palmer.

List of the Bourgeois Growths of the Médoc

Ch. d'Agassac, *Ludon*	Ch. Colombier Monpelou, *Pauillac*
Ch. Andron Blanquet, *Saint-Estèphe*	Ch. Coufran, *Saint-Seurin*
Ch. Aney, *Cussac*	Ch. Coutelin-Merville, *Saint-Estèphe*
Ch. Anthonic, *Moulis*	Ch. Le Crock, *Saint-Estèphe*
Ch. Balac, *Saint-Laurent*	Ch. Duplessis-Fabre, *Moulis*
Ch. Beaumont, *Cussac*	Ch. Duplessis-Hauchecorne, *Moulis*
Ch. Beausite, *Saint-Estèphe*	Ch. Dutruch-Grand Poujeaux, *Moulis*
Ch. La Bécade, *Listrac*	Ch. l'Estruelle, *Saint-Yzans*
Ch. Bellerive, *Valeyrac*	Ch. La Fleur Milon, *Pauillac*
Ch. Bellerose, *Pauillac*	Ch. Fonréaud, *Listrac*
Ch. Bellevue, *Valeyrac*	Ch. Fontesteau, *Saint-Sauveur*
Ch. Bel Orme, *Saint-Seurin*	Ch. Fort Vauban, *Cussac*
Ch. Les Bertins, *Valeyrac*	Ch. Fourcas-Dupré, *Listrac*
Ch. Bonneau-Livran, *Saint-Seurin*	Ch. Fourcas-Hosten, *Listrac*
Ch. Bonneau, *Avensan*	Ch. La France, *Blaignan*
Ch. Le Boscq, *Saint-Christoly*	Ch. Gallais Bellevue, *Ordonnac*
Ch. Le Bourdieu, *Vertheuil*	Ch. du Glana, *Saint-Julien*
Ch. Bournac, *Civrac*	Ch. Goudy la Cardonne, *Ordonnac*
Ch. du Breuil, *Cissac*	Ch. Grand Moulin, *Saint-Seurin*
Ch. de la Bridane, *Saint-Julien*	Ch. Greyssac, *Bégadan*
Ch. Brillette, *Moulis*	Ch. Grivière, *Blaignan*
Ch. de By, *Bégadan*	Ch. Hanteillan, *Cissac*
Ch. Cailloux de By, *Bégadan*	Ch. Haut Bages Monpelou, *Pauillac*
Ch. Canuet, *Margaux*	Ch. Haut Canteloup, *Couquèques*
Ch. Capbern-Gasquelon, *Saint-Estèphe*	Ch. Hauterive, *Saint-Germain d'Esteuil*
Ch. Cap Léon Veyrin, *Listrac*	Ch. Haut Garin, *Prignac*
Ch. Carcannieux, *Queyrac*	Ch. Haut Logat, *Cissac*
Ch. la Cardonne, *Blaignan*	Ch. Haut Marbuzet, *Saint-Estèphe*
Ch. Caronne-Ste-Gemme, *Saint-Laurent*	Ch. Houbanon, *Prignac*
Ch. Chambert-Marbuzet, *Saint-Estèphe*	Ch. Hourtin Ducasse, *Saint-Sauveur*
Ch. Charmail, *Saint-Seurin*	Ch. de Labat, *Saint-Laurent*
Ch. Chasse-Spleen, *Moulis*	Ch. Lafon, *Listrac*
Ch. Cissac, *Cissac*	
Ch. Citran, *Avensan*	
Ch. La Clare, *Bégadan*	
Ch. Clarke, *Listrac*	
Ch. La Closerie, *Moulis*	

Ch. Lalande, *Listrac*
Château de Lamarque, *Lamarque*
Ch. Lamothe-Cissac, *Cissac*
Ch. Lamothe-de-Bergeron, *Cussac*
Ch. Le Landat, *Cissac*
Ch. Landon, *Bégadan*
Ch. Larose Le Trintaudon, *Saint-Laurent*
Ch. Lartigue de Brochon, *Saint-Seurin*
Cru Lassalle, *Ordonnac*
Ch. Laujac, *Bégadan*
Ch. Lestage, *Listrac*
Ch. Lestage Simon, *Saint-Seurin*
Ch. Liouner, *Listrac*
Ch. Liversan, *Saint-Sauveur*
Ch. Loudenne, *Saint-Yzans*
Ch. MacCarthy, *Saint-Estèphe*
Ch. MacCarthy-Moula, *Saint-Estèphe*
Ch. Magnol Dehez, *Blanquefort*
Ch. Malescasse, *Lamarque*
Ch. de Malleret, *Le Pian*
Ch. Malmaison, *Listrac*
Ch. Marbuzet, *Saint-Estèphe*
Ch. Martinens, *Cantenac*
Ch. Maucaillou, *Moulis*
Ch. Maucamps, *Macau*
Ch. Meyney, *Saint-Estèphe*
Ch. le Meynieu, *Vertheuil*
Ch. Monbrison, *Arsac*
Ch. Du Monthil, *Bégadan*
Ch. Morin, *Saint-Estèphe*
Ch. Moulin à Vent, *Moulis*
Ch. Moulin de la Roque, *Bégadan*
Ch. Moulin Riche, *Saint-Julien*
Ch. du Moulin Rouge, *Cussac*
Ch. Moulis, *Moulis*
Ch. Les Ormes-de-Pez, *Saint-Estèphe*
Ch. Les Ormes-Sorbet, *Couquèques*
Ch. Panigon, *Civrac*
Ch. Patache D'Aux, *Bégadan*
Ch. Paveil de Luze, *Soussans*
Ch. Pey Martin, *Ordonnac*
Ch. Peyrabon, *Saint-Sauveur*
Ch. Peyredon Lagravette, *Médrac-Listrac*
Ch. Phélan Ségur, *Saint-Estèphe*
Ch. Pibran, *Pauillac*
Ch. Plantey de la Croix, *Saint-Seurin*
Ch. Pontet, *Blaignan*
Ch. Pontoise Cabarrus, *Saint-Seurin*
Ch. Potensac, *Ordonnac*
Ch. Poujeaux, *Moulis*
Ch. Puy Castera, *Cissac*
Ch. Ramage la Batisse, *Saint-Sauveur*
Ch. Reysson, *Vertheuil*

Ch. de la Ronceray, *Saint-Estèphe*
Ch. la Roque de By, *Bégadan*
Ch. la Rose Maréchale, *Saint-Seurin*
Ch. Saint-Bonnet, *Saint-Christoly*
Ch. Saint-Paul, *Saint-Seurin*
Ch. Saint-Roch, *Saint-Estèphe*
Ch. Ségur, *Parempuyre*
Ch. Sestignan, *Jau Dignac-Loirac*
Ch. Sigognac, *Saint-Yzans*
Ch. Sociando-Mallet, *Saint-Seurin*
Ch. Soudars, *Saint-Seurin*
Ch. du Taillan, *Le Taillan*
Ch. Tayac, *Soussans*
Ch. Terrey-Gros-Cailloux, *Saint-Julien*
Ch. La Tour Blanche, *Saint-Christoly*
Ch. la Tour de By, *Bégadan*
Ch. Tour du Haut Moulin, *Cussac*
Ch. la Tour du Mirail, *Cissac*
Ch. Tour du Roc, *Arcins*
Ch. La Tour du Haut-Caussan, *Blaignan*
Ch. la Tour Saint-Bonnet, *Saint-Christoly*
Ch. la Tour Saint-Joseph, *Cissac*
Ch. des Tourelles, *Blaignan*
Ch. Tourteran, *Saint-Sauveur*
Ch. Tronquoy Lalande, *Saint-Estèphe*
Ch. la Valiere, *Saint-Christoly*
Ch. Verdignan, *Saint-Seurin*
Ch. Vernoux, *Lesparre*
Ch. Vieux Robin, *Bégadan*

Classification of Sauternes and Barsac

Premier Grand Cru
Ch. d'Yquem   *Sauternes*

Premiers Crus
Ch. la Tour Blanche   *Bommes*
Ch. Peyraguey   *Bommes*
Ch. Vigneau   *Bommes*
Ch. Suduiraut   *Preignac*
Ch. Coutet   *Barsac*
Ch. Climens   *Barsac*
Ch. Bayle   *Sauternes*
Ch. Rieussec   *Fargues*
Ch. Rabaud   *Bommes*

Deuxièmes Crus
Ch. Myrat   *Barsac*
Ch. Doisy   *Barsac*
Ch. Pexoto   *Bommes*
Ch. d'Arche   *Sauternes*
Ch. Filhot   *Sauternes*

Ch. Brouster-Nérac   *Barsac*
Ch. Caillou   *Basac*
Ch. Suau   *Barsac*
Ch. de Malle   *Preignac*
Ch. Romer   *Preignac*
Ch. Lamothe   *Sauternes*
Ch. Dubroca   *Barsac*

1855 Classification of Grands Crus Rouges de Bordeaux

First Growths
Ch. Lafite-Rothschild *Pauillac*
Ch. Margaux *Margaux*
Ch. Latour *Pauillac*
Ch. Haut-Brion *Pessac, Graves*

Second Growths
Ch. Mouton-Rothschild: became a First Growth in 1973 *Pauillac*
Ch. Rausan-Ségla *Margaux*
Ch. Rauzan-Gassies *Margaux*
Ch. Léoville-Las-Cases *St Julien*
Ch. Léoville-Poyferré *St Julien*
Ch. Léoville-Barton *St Julien*
Ch. Durfort-Vivens *Margaux*
Ch. Gruaud-Larose *St Julien*
Ch. Lascombes *Margaux*
Ch. Brane-Cantenac *Cantenac-Margaux*
Ch. Pichon-Longueville-Baron *Pauillac*
Ch. Pichon-Lalande *Pauillac*
Ch. Ducru-Beaucaillou *St Julien*
Ch. Cos d'Estournel *St Estèphe*
Ch. Montrose *St Estèphe*

Third Growths
Ch. Kirwan *Cantenac-Margaux*
Ch. d'Issan *Cantenac-Margaux*
Ch. Lagrange *St Julien*

Ch. Langoa-Barton *St Julien*
Ch. Giscours *Labarde-Margaux*
Ch. Malescot-St-Exupéry *Margaux*
Ch. Boyd-Cantenac *Cantenac-Margaux*
Ch. Cantenac-Brown *Cantenac-Margaux*
Ch. Palmer *Cantenac-Margaux*
Ch. La Lagune *Ludon-Haut-Médoc*
Ch. Desmirail *Margaux*
Ch. Calon-Ségur *St Estèphe*
Ch. Ferrière *Margaux*
Ch. Marquis d'Alesme-Becker *Margaux*

Fourth Growths
Ch. St-Pierre *St Julien*

Fifth Growths
Ch. Pontet-Canet *Pauillac*
Ch. Batailley *Pauillac*
Ch. Grand-Puy-Lacoste *Pauillac*
Ch. Grand-Puy-Ducasse *Pauillac*
Haut-Batailley *Pauillac*
Ch. Lynch-Bages *Pauillac*
Ch. Lynch-Moussas *Pauillac*
Ch. Dauzac *Labarde-Margaux*
Ch. Mouton-Baronne-Philippe: formerly known as Mouton Baron Philippe *Pauillac*
Ch. du Tertre *Arsac-Margaux*
Ch. Haut-Bages-Libéral *Pauillac*
Ch. Pédesclaux *Pauillac*
Ch. Belgrave *St Laurent-Haut-Médoc*
Ch. de Camensac *St Laurent-Haut-Médoc*
Ch. Cos Labory *St Estèphe*
Ch. Clerc-Milon-Rothschild *Pauillac*
Ch. Croizet-Bages *Pauillac*
Ch. Cantemerle *Macau-Haut-Médoc*

Classed Growths of the Médoc: Grapes used

The following list was compiled from various sources. Chateaux can alter the proportions from year to year.

First Growth

Ch. Lafite-Rothschild *70% Cab. Sauv., 13% Cab. Franc, 12% Merlot, 5%; Petit Verdot.*
Ch. Latour *75% Cab. Sauv., 10% Cab. Franc, 10% Merlot, 5% Petit Verdot.*
Ch. Margaux *75% Cab. Sauv, 20% Merlot, 5% Petit Verdot.*
Ch. Mouton Rothschild *85% Cab. Sauv., 10% Cab. Franc, 5% Merlot.*
Ch. Haut Brion *55% Cab. Sauv., 22% Cab. Franc, 23% Merlot.*

Second Growth

Ch. Rausan-Ségla *66% Cab. Sauv., 27% Merlot, 5% Cab. Franc, 2% Petit Verdot.*
Ch. Rauzan-Gassies *36% Merlot, 30% Cab. Sauv., 20% Cab. Franc, 4% Petit Verdot.*
Ch. Léoville Las Cases *65% Cab. Sauv., 18% Merlot, 14% Cab. Franc., 3% Petit Verdot.*
Ch. Léoville Poyferré *66% Cab. Sauv., 34% Merlot.*
Ch. Léoville Barton *70% Cab. Sauv., 15% Merlot and Malbec, 8% Petit Verdot, 7% Cab. Franc.*
Ch. Durfort Vivens *82% Cab. Sauv., 10% Cab. Franc, 8% Merlot.*
Ch. Gruaud Larose *62% Cab. Sauv., 25% Merlot, 9% Cab. Franc, 4% Petit Verdot.*
Ch. Lascombes *46% Cab. Sauv., 32% Merlot, 10% Petit Verdot, 8% Cab. Franc, 4% Malbec.*
Ch. Brane Cantenac *70% Cab. Sauv., 15% Cab. Franc. 13% Merlot, 2% Petit Verdot.*
Ch. Pichon Longueville *60% Cab. Sauv., 30% Merlot, 10% Cab. Franc, Petit Verdot and Malbec.*
Ch. Pichon Lalande *45% Cab. Sauv., 35% Merlot, 12% Cab. Franc, 8% Petit Verdot.*
Ch. Ducru Beaucaillou *65% Cab. Sauv., 25% Merlot, 5% Cab Franc., 5% Petit Verdot.*
Ch. Cos d'Estournel *56% Cab. Sauv., 31% Merlot, 13% Cab. Franc.*
Ch. Montrose *65% Cab. Sauv., 25% Merlot, 10% Cab. Franc.*

Third Growth

Ch. Kirwan *45% Cab. Sauv., 25% Merlot, 20% Cab. Franc, 10% Petit Verdot.*
Ch. d'Issan *75% Cab. Sauv., 23% Merlot, 2% Cab. Franc.*
Ch. Lagrange *65% Cab. Sauv., 35% Merlot.*
Ch. Langoa-Barton *70% Cab. Sauv., 15% Merlot, 8% Petit Verdot, 7% Cab. Franc.*
Ch. Giscours *66% Cab. Sauv., 34% Merlot.*
Ch. Malescots St-Exupéry *50% Cab. Sauv., 35% Merlot, 10% Cab. Franc, 5% Petit Verdot.*
Ch. Cantenac-Brown *70% Cab. Sauv., 30% Merlot.*
Ch. Boyd-Cantenac *70% Cab. Sauv., 20% Merlot, 5% Cab. Franc. 5% Petit Verdot.*
Ch. Palmer *55% Cab. Sauv., 40% Merlot, 3% Cab. Franc, 2% Petit Verdot.*
Ch. la Lagune *50% Cab. Sauv., 25% Cab. Franc, 20% Merlot. 5% Petit Verdot.*
Ch. Desmirail *80% Cab. Sauv., 10% Merlot, 9% Cab. Franc, 1% Petit Verdot.*
Ch. Calon-Ségur *60% Cab. Sauv., 20% Cab. Franc, 20% Merlot.*
Ch. Ferrière *47% Cab. Sauv., 33% Merlot, 8% Cab. Franc 12% Petit Verdot.*
Ch. Marquis d'Alesme Becker *40% Cab. Sauv., 30% Merlot, 20% Cab. Franc, 10% Petit Verdot.*

Fourth Growth

Ch. St Pierre *70% Cab. Sauv., 20% Merlot. 10% Cab. Franc.*
Ch. Talbot *71% Cab. Sauv., 20% Merlot, 5% Cab. Franc, 4% Petit Verdot.*
Ch. Branaire-Ducru *60% Cab. Sauv., 25% Merlot, 10% Cab. Franc, 5% Petit Verdot.*
Ch. Duhart-Milon Rothschild *63% Cab. Sauv., 18% Merlot, 15% Cab. Franc, 4% Petit Verdot.*
Ch. Pouget *66% Cab. Sauv., 30% Merlot, 4% Cab. Franc.*
Ch. La Tour Carnet *53% Cab. Sauv., 33% Merlot, 10% Cab. Franc, 4% Petit Verdot.*
Ch. Lafon-Rochet *70% Cab. Sauv., 20% Merlot, 8% Cab. Franc, 2% Malbec.*
Ch. Beychevelle *58% Cab. Sauv., 28% Merlot, 11% Cab. Franc, 3% Petit Verdot.*
Ch. Prieuré-Lichine *52% Cab. Sauv., 32% Merlot, 3% Cab. Franc, 3% Petit Verdot.*
Ch. Marquis du Terme *45% Cab. Sauv., 35% Merlot, 15% Cab. Franc, 5% Petit Verdot.*

Fifth Growth

Ch. Pontet Canet *70% Cab. Sauv., 20% Merlot 10% Cab. Franc.*
Ch. Batailley *70% Cab Sauv., 22% Merlot, 3% Petit Verdot, 5% Cab. Franc.*
Ch. Haut-Batailley *66% Cab. Sauv., 24% Merlot, 10% Cab. Franc.*
Ch. Grand-Puy-Lacoste *70% Cab. Sauv., 25% Merlot, 5% Cab. Franc.*
Ch. Grand-Puy-Ducasse *70% Cab Sauv., 25% Merlot, 5% Petit Verdot.*
Ch. Lynch-Bages *70% Cab. Sauv., 18% Merlot, 10% Cab., Franc, 2% Petit Verdot.*
Ch. Lynch-Mousses *70% Cab. Sauv., 25% Merlot, 5% Cab. Franc.*
Ch. Dauzac *70% Cab. Sauv., 20% Merlot, 5% Cab. Franc, 5% Petit Verdot.*
Ch. Mouton-Baronne-Philippe *65% Cab. Sauv., 30% Merlot, 5% Cab. Franc.*
Ch. du Tertre *80% Cab. Sauv., 10% Merlot, 10% Cab. Franc.*
Ch. Haut-Bages Libéral *70% Cab. Sauv., 25% Merlot, 5% Petit Verdot.*
Ch. Pédesclaux *70% Cab. Sauv., 20% Merlot, 10% Cab. Franc.*
Ch. Belgrave *50% Cab. Sauv., 30% Merlot, 18% Cab. Franc, 2% Petit Verdot.*
Ch. de Camensac *60% Cab Sauv., 20% Merlot, 20% Cab. Franc.*
Ch. Cos Labory *40% Cab. Sauv., 35% Merlot, 20% Cab. Franc, 5% Petit Verdot.*
Ch. Clerc Milon *78% Cab. Sauv., 20% Merlot, 2% Petit Verdot.*
Ch. Croizet Bages *37% Cab. Sauv., 30% Merlot, 30% Cab. Franc, 3% Petit Verdot.*
Ch. Cantemerle *40% Cab. Sauv., 40% Merlot, 18% Cab., Franc, 2% Petit Verdot.*

Up-and-coming Bordeaux Châteaux

There are innumerable great actors and actresses who, having failed to garner an Oscar, remain largely unknown. Bordeaux is very similar: unless you are amongst the most famous names, to many people you are really little better than an also-ran. The following properties are ones which deserve closer attention.

Ch. Andron-Blanquet *Médoc*
Ch. d'Angludet *Médoc*
Ch. Balestard-La-Tonnelle *St-Emilion*
Ch. Bastor-Lamontagne *Sauternes*
Ch. Beau-Site-Haute-Vignoble *St-Estèphe*
Ch. Berliquet *St-Emilion*
Ch. Cadet-Piola *St-Emilion*
Ch. Chartreuse *Sauternes*
Ch. Chasse-Spleen *Moulis*

Ch. Cissac *Cissac*
Clos du Marquis *St-Julien*
Ch. Clos Fourtet *St-Emilion*
Ch. Colombier-Monpelou *Médoc*
Ch. Couhins *White Graves*
Ch. Doisy-Daëne *Sauternes*
Ch. Doisy-Védrines *Sauternes*
Ch. la Dominique *St-Emilion*
Ch. Feytit-Clinet *Pomerol*
Ch. Fieuzal *Red and white Graves*
Ch. Fonplégade *St-Emilion*
Ch. Guiteronde *Sauternes*
Ch. la Grave Trigant de Boisset *Pomerol*
Ch. Haut-Bages-Averous *Pauillac*
Ch. Haut-Bages-Monpelou *Pauillac*
Ch. Hortevie *Médoc*
Ch. Labégorce-Zédé *Margaux*
Ch. Lamothe *Sauternes*
Ch. Lanessan Haut Médoc
Ch. Liot *Sauternes*
Ch. Malartic-Lagravière *Red and white* Graves
Ch. Malescasse *Haut Médoc*
Ch. Malescot-St-Exupéry *Margaux*
Ch. de Malle *Sauternes*
Ch. Maucamp
Ch. Meyney *St. Estèphe*
Ch. Monbousquet *St-Emilion*
Ch. Nairac *Sauternes*
Ch. Patache d'Aux *Médoc*
Ch. Potensac *Médoc*
Ch. Les Ormes-de-Pez *St-Estèphe*
Ch. Ramage-La-Batisse *Haut Médoc*
Ch. St-Amand *Sauternes*
Ch. St-Georges *St-Emilion*
Ch. la Serre *St-Emilion*
Ch. Siaurac *Lalande de Pomerol*
Ch. Siran *Labarde-Margaux*
Ch. Suau *Sauternes*
Ch. les Templiers *Lalande de Pomerol*
Ch. la Tour à Pomerol *Pomerol*
Ch. la Tour de By *Médoc*
Ch. Tour-Martillac *Red Graves*
Ch. la Tour Pibran *Médoc*
Ch. la Tour St-Joseph *Médoc*
Ch. Villegeorge *Avensan*

The first mention of a Bordeaux vineyard by name in England was Château Margeau (sic.) by Christie's in 1788.

Châteaux to watch

As newly replanted vines mature, a château changes hands, or experts (generally Professor Emile Peynaud, Bordeaux's vinous flying doctor) are called in to sort things out, the quality of a wine can change remarkably quickly. The following list is of châteaux whose stars are in the ascendant.

Ch. Arricaud *Graves*
Ch. Belgrave *Haut-Médoc*
Ch. Bouscaut *Graves*
Ch. Clarke *Listrac*
Ch. la Conseillante *Pomerol*

Ch. Dauzac *Margaux*
Ch. Desmirail *Margaux*
Ch. Duhart-Milon-Rothschild *Pauillac*
Ch. Grand-Puy-Lacoste *Pauillac*
Ch. Lagrange *St-Julien*
Ch. Lynch-Moussas *Pauillac*
Ch. du Tertre *Margaux*

Liste Exceptionelle

One of the first facts any novice wine drinker learns as she or he begins to read about wine is that red Bordeaux is made from the Cabernet Sauvignon grape,

along with the Malbec, Merlot, Petit Verdot and Cabernet Franc. True enough, but not always. There are fine red Bordeaux which because of their soil contain not a single drop of Cabernet Sauvignon.

Ch. Ausone Premier Grand Cru Classé, St-Emilion.
50% Merlot, 50% Cabernet Franc.

Ch. Belair Premier Grand Cru Classé, St-Emilion.
60% Merlot, 40% Cabernet Franc.

Ch. La Cabanne, Pomerol.
60% Merlot, 30% Cabernet Franc, 10% Malbec.

Ch. Certan-de May, Pomerol.
70% Merlot, 30% Cabernet Franc.

Ch. Certain Giraud, Pomerol
70% Merlot, 30% Cabernet Franc.

Ch. Cheval Blanc, Premier Grand Cru Classé, St-Emilion
66% Cabernet Franc, 32% Merlot, 2% Malbec.

Ch. Clos René, Pomerol
60% Merlot, 30% Cabernet Franc, 10% Malbec.

Ch. la Conseillante, Pomerol
45% Merlot, 45% Cabernet Franc, 10% Malbec.

Ch. Curé-Bon-la-Madeleine, Grand Cru Classé, St-Emilion
80% Merlot, 20% Cabernet Franc.

Ch. du Domaine de l'Eglise, Pomerol
65% Merlot, 25% Cabernet Franc.

Ch. l'Eglise-Clinet, Pomerol
60% Merlot, 30% Cabernet Franc, 10% Malbec.

Ch. l'Enclos, Pomerol
80% Merlot, 20% Cabernet Franc.

Ch. l'Evangile, Pomerol
66% Merlot, 34% Cabernet Franc.

Ch. Feytit-Clinet, Pomerol
85% Merlot, 15% Cabernet Franc.

Ch. la Fleur Gazin, Pomerol
80% Merlot, 20% Cabernet Franc.

Ch. la Fleur Pétrus, Pomerol
75% Merlot, 25% Cabernet Franc.

Ch. Franc-Mayne, Grand Cru Classé, St-Emilion
70% Merlot, 30% Cabernet Franc.

Ch. le Gay, Pomerol
50% Merlot, 50% Cabernet Franc.

Ch. Grand-Barrail-Lamarzelle-Figeac, Grand Cru Classé, St-Emilion
90% Merlot, 10% Cabernet Franc.

Ch. la Grave Trigant de Boisset, Pomerol
85% Merlot, 15% Cabernet Franc.

Ch. La Fleur, Pomerol.
50% Merlot, 50% Cabernet Franc.

Ch. Magdelaine, Premier Grand Cru Classé, St-Emilion
80% Merlot, 20% Cabernet Franc.

Ch. Moulinet, Pomerol
70% Merlot, 30% Cabernet Franc.

Ch. Pavillon-Cadet, Grand Cru Classé, St-Emilion
50% Merlot, 50% Cabernet Franc.

Ch. Pétrus, Cru Exceptionnel, Pomerol
95% Merlot, 5% Cabernet Franc.

Ch. La Pointe, Pomerol
55% Merlot, 40% Cabernet Franc, 5% Malbec.

Ch. La Prieuré, Grand Cru Classé, St-Emilion
70% Merlot, 30% Cabernet Franc.

Ch. La Serre, Grand Cru Classé, St-Emilion
80% Merlot, 20% Cabernet Franc.

Ch. Taillefer, Pomerol.
66% Merlot, 34% Cabernet Franc.

Ch. Tertre-Daugay, Grand Cru Classé, St-Emilion
70% Merlot, 30% Cabernet Franc.

Ch. La Tour-du-Pin-Figeac, Grand Cru Classé, St-Emilion.
50% Merlot, 50% Cabernet Franc.

Ch. La Tour-Figeac, Grand Cru Classé, St-Emilion.
60% Merlot, 40% Cabernet Franc.

Ch. Trotanoy, Pomerol
85% Merlot, 15% Cabernet Franc.

98 Second Labels

The expression 'second label' is often used in Bordeaux. It refers to wines produced by many of the major châteaux, which, because of the youth of the vines, or the quality of the wine in a particular vintage, are not considered worthy to bear those châteaux' own labels. The use of second labels dates back to the arrival of phylloxera and the enforced re-plantation of all the great properties. Whilst some of the second labels bear the names of châteaux which once existed in their own right, in all cases these properties have now either ceased to exist or have been assimilated into the principal property. Second labels can be bargains.

Second label	First label
Ch. Artigue-Arnaud	Ch. Grand-Puy-Ducasse, Pauillac
Ch. Bahans-Haut-Brion	Ch. Haut Brion, Graves
Ch. Barthez	Ch. Malleret, Le Pian
Ch. Baudry	Ch. Desmirail, Margaux
Ch. Beau-Mazaret	Ch. Grand-Mayne, St-Emilion
Ch. Bellegarde	Ch. Siran, Labarde
Ch. Bellerose	Ch. Pedesclaux, Pauillac
Ch. Bellevue-Laffont	Ch. Fourcas-Dupré, Listrac
Dom. Boisgrand	Ch. Ségur, Médoc
Bouquet de Monbousquet	Ch. Monbousquet, St-Emilion
Ch. Cantereau	Ch. Rouget, Pomerol
Ch. Cassevert	Ch. Grand-Mayne, St-Emilion
Ch. Chambert-Marbuzet	Ch. Marbuzet, St-Estèphe
Ch. de Clairefont	Ch. Prieuré-Lichine
Ch. du Clos Renon	Ch. Millet, Graves
Connetable-Talbot	Ch. Talbot, St-Julien
Ch. Coquilles	Ch. de France, Graves
La Cour Pavillon	Ch. Loudenne, St-Yzans-de-Médoc
La Croix	Ch. Ducru-Beaucaillou, St-Julien
Dom de Curé-Bourse	Ch. Durfort-Vivens, Margaux
Ch. Demereaulemont	Ch. Montabert, St-Emilion
Enclos de Moncabon	Ch. Croizet-Bages
Dom. de l'Estremade	Ch. Rabaud-Promis
Ch. Fonpetite	Ch. Phélan-Ségur, St-Estèphe
Ch. Fonseche	Ch. Lamothe-Cissac, Cissac
Dom. de Fontarney	Ch. Brane-Cantenac, Cant-Margaux
Les Forts de Latour	Ch. Latour, Pauillac
Ch. Galais-Bellevue	Ch. Potensac, Médoc
Ch. la Gombaude	Ch. Lascombes, Margaux
Ch. Grand-Canyon	Ch. Colombier-Monpelou
Ch. Grand-Duroc-Milon	Ch. Pédesclaux, Pauillac
Ch. du Grangeneuve	Ch. Figeac, St-Emilion
Les Gravilles	Ch. Coufran, Haut-Médoc
Haute-Bages-Averous	Ch. Lynch-Bages, Pauillac
Haut-Prieuré	Ch. Prieuré-Lichine, Margaux
Ch. des Hormes	Ch. Liversan, St-Sauveur
Jean-Blanc	Ch. Sigalas-Rabaud
Ch. Labarde	Ch. Dauzac, Lab-Margaux
Clos Labère	Ch. Rieussec, Bommes
Ch. Labory-de-Tayac	Ch. Tayac, Margaux
Ch. la Labut	Ch. Caronne-Ste-Gemme
Ch. Lamarzelle-Figeac	Ch. Grand-Barrail-Lamarzelle-Figeac, St-Emilion
Ch. Lartigue de Brochon	Ch. Sociando-Mallet, St-Seurin
Ch. Lemoyne-Nexon	Ch. Malleret, Le Pian
Ch. de Lognac	Ch. Ferrande, Graves
Ch. MacCarthy-Moula	Ch. Haut-Marbuzet, St-Estèphe
Ch. Magnan-la-Gaffelière	Clos la Madeleine, St-Emilion
Ch. Malmaison	Ch. Clarke, Listrac
Ch. Marbuzet	Ch. Cos d'Estournel
Clos du Margins	Ch. Léoville-Las-Cases
Dom du Martiny	Ch. Cissac, Cissac
Cotes Mauvezin-Badette	Ch. Haut-Sarpe, St-Emilion
Ch. Mayne d-Artignan	Ch. Cap de Mourlin, St-Emilion

Clos du Monastère	Ch. de Doms, Médoc
Moulin d-Arolgny	Ch. Beaumont, Cussac
Moulin de Calon	Ch. Calon-Ségur, St-Estèphe
Moulin des Carruades	Ch. Lafite-Rothschild, Pauillac
Ch. Moulin de Duhart	Ch. Duhart-Milon-Rothschild, Pauillac
Ch. Moulin-Riche	Ch. Léoville-Poyferré, St-Julien
Ch. Moulin de St-Vincent	Ch. Moulin-à-Vent, Moulis
Ch. des Moulinets	Ch. Ch. Liversan, St-Sauveur
La Parde de Haut Bailly	Ch. Haut-Bailly, Graves
Pavillon Rouge	Ch. Margaux, Margaux
Ch. Perroy	Ch. Sigalas-Rabaud
Ch. Peymartin	Ch. Gloria, St-Julien
Ch. Peyrelebade	Ch. Clarke, Listrac
Ch. Plantey-de-la-Croix	Ch. Verdignan, St-Seurin
Le Prieur de Meyney	Ch. Meyney
Ch. Le Priourat	Ch. La Commanderie
Réserve de la Comtesse	Ch. Pichon-Longueville-Lalande, Pauillac
Ch. Romefort	Ch. La Cardonne, Blaignan
Ch. La Roque	Ch. La Tour de By, Bégadan
Ch. de Roquefort	Ch. La Caffelière, St-Emilion
Ch. La Rose de Faurie	Ch. Cap de Mourlin, St-Emilion
Ch. La Rose Goromey	Ch. Livran, St-Germain
Ch. La Rose Maréchal	Ch. Verdignan, St-Seurin
Cru St. Estèphe-la-Croix	Ch. Le Crock, St-Estèphe
Dom. du St-Gemme	Ch. Lanessan, Cussac
Dom-de-Ste-Hélène	Ch. de Malle, Fargues
Ch. St-Jacques	Ch. Siran, Labarde
Cru St-Marc	Ch. La Tour Blanche, Bommes
Ch. St-Roch	Ch. Andron-Blanquet
La Salle de Pez	Ch. de Pez, St-Estèphe
La Salle de Poujeaux	Ch. Poujeaux, Moulis
Sarget de Gruaud-Larose	Ch. Gruaud-Larose, St-Julien
Ch. de Ségur	Ch. Broustet, Médoc
Ch. des Templiers	Ch. Larmande, St-Emilion
Clos Toulifaut	Ch. Taillefer, Pomerol
Ch. La Tour d'Aspic	Ch. Haut-Batailley, Pauillac
Clos de la Tournelle	Ch. Soutard, St-Emilion

BEAUJOLAIS

BEAUJOLAIS is a very complicated region – like the Côte d'Or to the north. Its wines are made by thousands of growers, many of whom rent their vines in return for the right to vinify half their harvest, thus doubling the potential number of slightly different wines. Most of the wine is still sold by merchants, some of whom now print the name of the original producer on the labels of particular cuvées. The *négociants* of Beaune are notoriously bad at buying good Beaujolais – perhaps they want it to taste like Burgundy, perhaps they hark back to the days of Algerian Beaujolais, or perhaps they just do not care. If you steer clear of Beaujolais from Beaune you will avoid more disappointments than happy surprises. Fortunately, the merchants of the Beaujolais itself are a far better lot; the region's cooperatives are pretty good too.

Vintages

These are of relatively little historic interest, since most Beaujolais should be drunk within a year of the harvest. Even so, it is worth mentioning that the region is very dependent on plentiful sun if it is to avoid having to pour a surfeit of sugar into the vats to raise the alcohol level; and that each year, some villages seem to be affected quite differently to others, depending on their altitude. So beware of thinking a vintage exclusively 'good' or 'bad'.

The merchants

Aujoux	Mommessin
Paul Beaudet	Ph. Moreau
Bouchacourt	Pasquier Desvignes
Caves de Champclos	Pellerin
Chanut	Piat
Chevalier	Mathelin
David & Foillard	Sarrau
Depagneux	Louis Tête
Georges Duboeuf	Thorin (also known as Faye)
Pierre Ferraud	Trenel
Gobet	Valette
Loron	

Beaujolais Nouveau
Technically wine of the most recent harvest, though in practice used to describe Beaujolais Primeur. Nouveau used to leave the region on or after 15 November; the date has now been switched to the third Wednesday in November.

Beaujolais Primeur
New wine, sold before December 15th.

Beaujolais Supérieur
Beaujolais with a little more alcoholic strength.

Beaujolais Villages
Usually more than a cut above plain Beaujolais, this comes from a specified set of villages in the heart of the region. One of these, Regnie-Durette is now trying to become the tenth Beaujolais Cru, alongside Morgon, Fleurie et al. Look out for its name on labels.

Henri Fontaine	Monternot
Etienne Jambon	Dom Gilles Perroud
Dom Joubert	André Vernus
Durieu de Lacarelle	Société Viticole Beaujolaise
René Miolane	Tissier-Depardon

Beaujolais Crus
The name used to describe the nine finest villages in Beaujolais.

Brouilly
Good Brouilly is a great example of pure Gamay. It rarely achieves the height of Fleurie, Morgon and Moulin-à-Vent, but drunk young, it is one of the most refreshingly fruity wines you could ever want to find. By the way, do not go looking for the village of Brouilly – there isn't one; the wine takes its name from a hill.

Ch. de Briante	André Large
Ch. de la Chaize	Ch. de Nervers
Georges Duboeuf	Ch. de Pierreux
('Dom de Combillaty')	André Ronzière
Philippe Dutraive	Jean Ruet
Ch. de Fouilloux	Dom Verger
Claude Geoffray	
Hospices de Beaujeu	
('Cuvée Pissevieille')	

Chénas
The least well-known of the 'Crus', and frequently sold as Bourgogne Rouge. Deserves more attention.

Paul Beaudet	Georges Duboeuf
Bouchacourt	('Dom de la Combe Remont')
Louis Champagnon	Château de Jean Loron
Fernard Charvet	Pierre Perrachon
Ch. de Chénas (cooperative)	Emile Robin

Chiroubles
Certainly the wine closest to the style of Beaujolais Nouveau which the world has grown used to, Chiroubles is the one to drink before those of the other Beaujolais villages.

René Bouillard	Ch. Javernand
Dom Emile Cheysson	Christian Lafay
Chiroubles (cooperative)	Mathelin ('Cuvée Plaforet')
Dessalle ('Les Martins')	Dom du Moulin
Jean-Pierre Desvignes	Georges Passot
Georges Duboeuf	Ch. les Près
Philippe Govet	René Savoye

Côtes de Brouilly
Often confused with Brouilly from which it can easily be differentiated, this can be a particularly attractive mixture of ripe fruit and flowers, standing somewhere between Fleurie and Moulin-à-Vent in style.

Cave Cooperative de Bel-Air	Mathelin
Ch. Delachanal	Dom Sanvers
Georges Duboeuf	Dom du Ch. Thivin
Mme Veuve Joubert	Lucien Verger

Fleurie
To some people, the epitome of what Beaujolais can, and should be. Good Fleurie is as fresh and fragrant as its name would lead you to hope for.

Maurice Bruone	Dom de la Grand Cour
Chauvet Frères	Dom Bernard Paul
Dom Yvonne Couibes	Société Civile du
Georges Duboeuf	Ch. de Poncié
Fleurie (Cooperative)	Dom de la Presle
Caveau de Fleurie	Marcel Rollet
Ch. de Fleurie	

Juliénas
One of the original winegrowing communes of Beaujolais. At its best Juliénas can be perfect Beaujolais, packed with plummy-cherry flavour, enjoyable young but worth keeping for a year or three.

Ernest Aujas	Loron ('Clos des Poulettes')
Ch. des Capitans	André Pelleier
Georges Duboeuf	M. Perrachon
M. Foillard	M. Poulachon
Ch. de Juliénas	Louis Tête
Juliénas cooperative	Dom de la Vieille Eglise
('Ch. du Bois de la Salle')	

Morgon
Is this the only wine to give its name to a verb? 'Morgonner' is the expression for what this commune's does when it matures. It takes on a flavour of dark chocolate and wild cherry, and a character

somewhere between that of the Gamay grown in neighbouring villages and the Pinot Noir grown further north in the Côte d'Or. Sometimes this process takes years. Sometimes it never happens at all. Even so, good Morgon is worth maturing.

Georges Brun	Mathelin
Paul Collonge ('Dom de Ruyère')	Pierre Piron ('Dom de la Chanaise')
Dom Demont	
Louis Desvignes	Pierre Savoye
Jean Descombes	Louis Tête
Georges Duboeuf	Marcel Vincent ('Morgon Charmes')
Louis Genillon	
Jacky Janodet	Gen. Jacques de Zelicourt
Dom Lieven, Ch. de Bellevue	

Moulin-à-Vent
Taking its name from the windmill can still be seen there, this is often thought to be the finest of all Beaujolais. It's certainly – with Morgon – one of the only two which warrant keeping for longer than a few years. Good Moulin-à-Vent is big, rich stuff.

Jean Brugne	Ch. des Jacques
Propriété Bourisset	Propriété Labruyère
Chauvet Frères	Dom Monrozier
Ch. de Chénas	Ch. du Moulin-à-Vent
Raymond Degrange	Hospices de Moulin-à-Vent
Héritiers Devillaine	Alphonse Mortet
Georges Duboeuf	Raymond Siffert
Ch. de Gimarets	

St-Amour
Possibly the prettiest named of all wines (the locals attribute its origins to a Roman soldier who married a girl from the village). The wine tends to be more delicate and light than those of the other villages.

Cave cooperative du Bois de la Salle	Loron ('Dom des Billards')
	Dom Patissier
Maurice Delorme ('Dom du Paradis')	M. Perrichon
	Piat ('Ch. de St-Amour')
Georges Duboeuf	Francis Saillant
Dom Duc	Caveau de St-Amour
Dom Finaz Devillaine	Ch. de St-Amour
Dom Janin	Paul Spay

BURGUNDY

Burgundy is divided between Chablis, an island of vines about 100 miles south of Paris; the Côte d'Or, extending southwards from Dijon to Santenay; the Côte Chalonnaise which runs from Bouzeron, just beyond Santenay down to the Mâconnais and the Beaujolais.

Its wines are produced by literally thousands of individual growers who, increasingly, bottle and sell their own wines as well as selling to merchants – *négociants* – who blend, mature and sell the wine under their own name. As the number of domaine-bottled wines grows, the *négociants* find it more and more difficult to find good wine. Amongst their best, therefore, are wines made from grapes harvested in their own vineyards, over which they have full control. Each grower will tend to produce several different wines, which will often vary in quality. The number of growers and *négociants* who can offer a whole range of really first-class wines every vintage is very small indeed. The list on p. 000 shows the most

important producers for each appellation, and indicates those most worth looking out for.

The Grape List

Pinot Noir
For all fine Burgundy and all Bourgogne Rouge, with a small number of exceptions. See below.

Gamay
The Beaujolais grape, also used with the Pinot Noir to make Passetoutgrains, and by itself in Bourgogne Grand Ordinaire and Mâcon Rouge.

César
Only grown in the Chablis region, and legally used for Bourgogne Rouge there.

Tressot
Only grown in the Chablis region, and legally used for Bourgogne Rouge there.

Chardonnay
The fine white Burgundy grape.

Aligoté
Burgundy's 'supplementary' white grape, used for daily-drinking wines, and as a base for Kir.

Sauvignon
Grown in Chablis to make Sauvignon de St Bris, that region's white VDQS.

Burgundy Words

Bourgogne Grand Ordinaire The most basic of all Burgundy – made from any of the above grapes. Increasingly rare.

Chaptalisation The legal (up to a point – usually surpassed) addition of sugar to fermenting Burgundy to raise its alcohol level.

Côte de Beaune Small appellation covering vineyards in and around Beaune itself, as well as the description for the strip of villages from Santenay to Ladoix. Do not confuse with Côte de Beaune Villages.

Grand Cru The finest vineyards, which are thought so fine that they can displace the village name on the label. So whereas the Premier Cru Perrières vineyard in Meursault appears as Meursault Perrières, the Grand Cru Montrachet vineyard in Chassagne simply, and grandly, features as 'Montrachet'. Incidentally, a Premier Cru made by a good producer in a good vintage can be a far better wine than a Grand Cru made by a poor winemaker in a rainy year. Or even a fine one, come to that.

Hautes Côtes de Beaune (or Nuits) the area of vineyard in the hills above the great vineyards of the Côtes de Beaune and Nuits. Can produce very nice, and (relatively) reasonably priced wine. In ripe vintages.

Hospices as in 'de Beaune' and 'de Nuits'. Two hospitals funded by the sale at auction of wine produced from vineyards donated to them over the centuries. Buyers should pay attention to the name of the merchant who purchased and bottled the wine.

Négociant-Eleveur A merchant who has bought, 'matured' *(élevé)* wine and bottled it.

Passetoutgrains Wine made of two thirds Gamay, one third Pinot Noir.

Premier Cru Wine from vineyards historically deemed of higher quality, and subject to stricter rules of production (lower yield per hectare).

Propriétaire-Récoltant (or Viticulteur) the man who grew the grapes and made the wine. Not a merchant.

Tastevin Refers to the gaudy label adorning wines which have been deemed good examples of their appellation in a blind tasting organised by the Chevaliers de Tastevin.

List of Recommended Négociants

Albert Bichot *(Beaune)*
The man with a thousand names, Bichot specialises in using a multitude of different labels. Wines range from dull to good. Chablis is excellent. Other labels:

Jean Bouchard	Fortier-Picard
Paul Bouchard	Labaume Aîné & Fils
Bouchot-Ludot	Lupe-Cholet (a subsidiary)
Caves Syndical de Bourgogne	Rémy-Gauthier
Maurice Dard	Léon Rigault
Charles Drapier	

Jean-Claude Boisset *(Beaune)*
A young company which has yet to establish a reputation for really high-quality wines. Best wines are from Gevrey-Chambertin, Nuits St Georges and Bourgogne Rouge. Other labels:

Blanchard de Cordambles	Honoré Lavigne
Louis Deschamps	Georges Meurgey

Bouchard Aîné *(Beaune)*
25 *ha* of vines, but few really exciting wines. The Mercurey and Fixin are good though. Other labels:

H. Audiffred

Bouchard Père & Fils *(Beaune)*
Burgundy's largest merchant, with an impressive set of Beaunes, some Montrachet and good Aligoté de Bouzeron.

Pierre Bourrée
Little known, small, Gevrey-based merchant with apparently reliable wines, e.g. Bourgogne Rouge.

Brenot Père & Fils
Santenay-based family firm with delicious Bâtard-Montrachet.

Chandesais
Small firm outside the Côte d'Or, but with some first-class wines, particularly Gevrey-Chambertin.

Champy *(Beaune)*
Good, small, frequently 'Tastevin' merchant.

Chanson *(Beaune)*
Adequate rather than classy, but with some nice Beaunes, Pernand Vergelesses and Chablis.

F. Chauvenet
Best wines possibly at lower price levels. Also some good sparkling wines and Pouilly Fuissé. Labels include:

Marc Chevillot
Louis Max

Raoul Clerget
Good small firm with particularly fine whites, e.g. St Aubin.

Coron
Small company with fine vineyards in Beaune. Other label:

Amsler-Lecouvreur

Doudet-Naudin *(Savigny-les-Beaune)*
'Traditional' Burgundy for those who like thick black wine, the way it used to be made. Other labels:

Albert Brenot
Georges Germain

Joseph Drouhin
Possibly the most reliable of the larger Burgundy houses (Leroy apart), with good wines from throughout the region, and excellent Montrachet.

Geisweiler *(Nuits-St-Georges)*
Never renowned for the quality of its top-of-the-range wines, Geisweiler is now proving a good source of basic Bourgogne Rouge and Blanc. Other labels:

Colcombet Frères	Larbelestier
Duret	A. Roussigneux
J. Goubard	

Jaboulet-Vercherre *(Beaune)*
Big, velvety wines – for those who like them that way. Not for lovers of characterful modern Burgundy.

Louis Jadot *(Beaune)*
One of the better merchants, but still not beyond reproach. Good whites, Beaune and Rully.

Jaffelin *(Beaune)*
Under the same ownership as, but independent from, Joseph Drouhin. Good wines, e.g. Clos de Vougeot.

Raymond Javillier
Meursault based broker/merchant/grower with particularly good white wines.

Labouré-Roi *(Nuits-St-Georges)*
Excellent small merchant, selling wines from the domaines Chantal Lescure, René Manuel and Jean Paul Droin in Chablis. Very good Pommard.

Louis Latour *(Beaune)*
Superlative whites and occasionally disappointingly dull reds. Nonetheless, one of the best.

Leroy
Almost certainly Burgundy's finest sizeable merchant, with stocks of excellent (very pricy) old wines and a range whose quality is sustained from the simple Bourgogne Rouge to Musigny. Mme Bize-Leroy is co-owner of the Dom de la Romanée-Conti.

P. de Marcilly Frères
Owners of several very fine vineyards, and makers of very good basic Bourgogne Rouge and Blanc.

Prosper Maufoux
Based in Santenay, this company does produce excellent wines – and some disappointing ones. Pick and choose. Other label:

Marcel Amance

Moillard
'Burgundy's banker' supplying other merchants with wine. Whites can be fair; reds are frequently dull. Other labels:

Henri de Bahezre	Thomas Frères
Javelier-Laurin	Toursier
Pierre Olivier	

Mommessin
Mâcon-based firm which owns the Clos de Tart Grand Cru vineyard in Morey St Denis. Other label:

J. Curtil

Veuve Henri Moroni
Small company run by Mme Moroni for around 40 years. Good Bâtard-Montrachet.

Patriarche *(Beaune)*
A commercial success, with commercial non-Burgundy table wines. Wines from Patriarche's Château de Meursault estate though can be excellent. Particularly 'Clos du Château'. Other labels:

Noémie Vernaux (a subsidiary)

Pierre Ponelle
Smallish company with nicely situated vineyards, and which used to be a good source for mature Burgundy.

La Reine Pedauque *(Aloxe-Corton)*
Like Patriarche, more commercial than classy. Now moving towards printing growers' names on labels and upgrading the image.

Remoissenet *(Beaune)*
Whites are often particularly good.

Antonin Rodet
Côte Chalonnaise merchant, well liked by French restaurateurs. Good Mercurey. Other labels:

Alain Constant
Pierre Desruelles

Ropiteau Frères
Meursault-based firm, specialising in wines from that village and gradually producing creditable wines from elsewhere in Burgundy.

Trébuchet Chartron
Recently launched merchant with some potential. M. Trébuchet previously ran Jaffelin.

Charles Vienot
Smallish company, based in the Côte de Nuits, but with some vines in Aloxe Corton.

Léon Violland
Small company, little known outside mainland Europe, but with some good Beaune.

Henri de Villamont
Swiss-owned merchant, based in Savigny-les-Beaune. Good wine from that village and the Hautes-Côtes. Labels include:

Barolet	Louis Serrignon
Brocard & Fils	Caves de Valclair
Mesnard	Etienne Vergey
Paul Rolland	

List of Wines and Principal Producers

Aligoté *(See also Bouzeron)*

Aloxe-Corton
Village with the only red Grand Cru – Corton – in the Côte de Beaune, as well as the white Corton Charlemagne. Wines are notoriously slow to show their qualities; nowadays there are those who would say that some of these Grands Crus have too little quality to show.

Pierre André (La Reine Pedauque)
Dom Bonneau de Martray
Bouchard Père & Fils ('Corton Charlemagne')
Domaine Chandon de Briailles ('Corton Blanc'; 'Corton Bressandes')
Louis Chapuis ('Corton Perrières')
Domaine Chevalier
Roger Clerget

Doudet-Naudin
Joseph Drouhin
Pierre Dubreuil-Fontaine (Corton 'Clos du Roi')
Faiveley ('Clos des Cortons Faiveley')
Dom Goud de Beaupuis
Dom Antonin Guyon
Hospices de Beaune ('Corton Charlemagne – Cuvée François de Salins')
Dom Lucien Jacob Leroy
Louis Jadot ('Corton Charlemagne'; 'Corton-Pougets')
Dom de la Juvinière
Louis Latour (Corton 'Clos de la Vigne au Saint'; 'Corton Charlemagne'; 'Château Corton Grancey')
Dom Lequin-Roussot
Dom Machard de Gramont (part now sold as Dom Chantal Lescure)
Moillard ('Corton Clos du Roi')
Pierre Ponnelle
Domaine du Prince Florent de Mérode ('Corton les Maréchaudes'; 'Corton Clos du Roi')
Domaine Quenot Fils & Meuneveaux
Remoissenet (Corton 'Clos du Roi')
Daniel Senard (Corton 'Clos des Meix'; 'Corton Bressandes'; 'Aloxe Corton Blanc')
Domaine du Baron Thénard (Corton 'Clos du Roi')
Tollot-Beaut ('Corton')
Dom Tollot-Voarick
Charles Viénot (Corton)
Michel Voarick ('Corton Renardes'; Corton 'Clos du Roi')

Auxey-Duresses
Often under-rated village in the Côte de Beaune, tucked away beyond Meursault. Reds can be tough when young, but achieve attractive raspberry complexity when mature. White Auxey is often a good alternative to Meursault itself.

Robert Ampeau & Fils
Gérard Creusefond ('Le Val')
Bernard Fèvre
Alain Gras
Hospices de Beaune ('Cuvée Boillot')
Lafouge-Clerc et Fils ('La Chapelle'; 'Les Duresses')
Henri Latour ('La Chapelle'; 'Les Grands Champs')
Leroy
Naudin-Grivelet
Jean Prunier & Fils ('Clos du Val')
Domaine du Duc de Magenta ('Les Bretterins')
Dom Guy Roulot
Dom Reñe Roy ('Les Duresses'; 'Le Val')
Roland Thévenin ('Clos du Moulin aux Moines; 'Les Ecusseaux')

Beaune
Beaune has no Grands Crus 'because they would have had to allocate too many', say some of the town's supporters. Wines are more reliable than from many other communes, ranging from the tough Teurons Premier Cru to the more delicate Vignes Franches and Cent Vignes. The recognizeable mark of good mature Beaune is a smell of fading roses.

Robert Ampeau
Besancenot-Mathoullet
Albert Bichot & Cie
Dom Gaston Boisseaux
Bouchard Aîné & Fils
Bouchard Père & Fils ('Les Grèves Vigne de l'Enfant Jesus', 'Beaune du Château')
Louis Carillon
Champy Père & Fils ('Clos des Mouches'; 'Les Avaux')
Chanson Père & Fils ('Les Fèves')

Coron Père & Fils
Dom Darviot
Doudet-Naudin
Joseph Drouhin
Dom Duchet
Dom Michel Gaunoux
Dom François Germain
Dom Goud de Beaupuis
Hospices de Beaune
Jaboulet-Vercherre
Louis Jadot
Dom Michel Lafarge
Jaffelin
Louis Latour
Lycée Viticole
Dom Machard de Gramont
Maire & Fils
Mallard-Gaullin

P. de Marcilly Frères
Mazilly Père & Fils
Ch de Meursault
Moillard
Jean Monnier & Fils
Dom René Monnier
Ets André Morey
Maison Albert Morot
Dom Mussy
Patriarche
Dom Jacques Prieur
Remoissenet Père & Fils
Dom Daniel Senard
René Thévenin-Monthélie & Fils
Tollot-Beaut
Tollot-Voarick
Leon Violland
Dom Voiret

Blagny (see Meursault)

Bouzeron
Village in the Côte Chalonnaise specialising in Aligoté and uniquely allowed to add its name to that of the grape on the label.

Bouchard Père & Fils
Dom Chanzy
Dom A. & P. de Villaine

Chambolle-Musigny
One of the finest communes in the Côte de Nuits, producing rich, deeply flavoured wines.

Bouchard Père & Fils
Dom Clair Dau
Dom Clerget
Joseph Drouhin
Dom Drouhin-Laroze
Dufouleur
Dom Dujac
Faiveley
Dom Grivelet
Jean Grivot

Dom Antonin Guyon
Paul Hudelot & Fils
Alain Hudelot-Noëllat
Leroy
Dom Machard de Gramont
Pierre Ponnelle
Georges Roumier & Fils
Dom des Varoilles
Henri de Villamont
Dom Comte Georges de Vogüé

Chassagne-Montrachet
One of the two villages which share the honours of the Montrachet Grands Crus between them. White Chassagne can be at once grassily fresh and biscuity-rich; red Chassagne (of which more is made) is also very attractive, with a rich wild raspberry flavour. It is often difficult to sell and so can prove good value.

Dom Amiot Père et Fils
Bachelet-Ramonet Père & Fils
Baudrand & Fils
Soc Louis Carillon Fils
François Colin
Delagrange-Bachelet
Georges Deleger
Joseph Deléger
Jean-Noël Gagnard
Gagnard-Delagrange
Gagnard-Dupont
Dom Lequin-Roussot
Marquis de Laguiche
(See Joseph Drouhin)

Dom du Duc de Magenta
Château de Maltroie
Marcel Moreau & Fils
Albert Morey
Dom Marc Morey & Fils
Michel Niellon
Dom Alphonse Pillot
Paul Pillot
Dom Jacques Prieur
Ramonet-Prudhon
Claude Ramonet
Dom Etienne Sauzet

Chorey-les-Beaune
Once upon a time the wines of this village were sold as Côte de Beaune Villages. Now though, despite its situation in the plain, Chorey is beginning to prove its own worth.

Arnoux Père & Fils
Dubois-Goujon
Dom Gay
Dom Germain
Dom Goud de Beaupuis

Daniel Maillard-Diard
Maldant-Pauvelot & Fils
Dom Maurice Martin
Dom Tollot Beaut
Dom Tollot-Voarick

Côte de Beaune

Côte de Beaune Villages

Côte de Nuits Villages
Philippe Rossignol

Fixin
Generally termed 'uncommercial', the wines of this village of the Côte de Nuits are unpalatably hard and tannic when young. Give them time though, and they have often got more to offer than most 'commercial' Gevrey-Chambertin.

André Bart
Guy Bertheaut
Bouchard Aîné & Fils
Ernest Bourgeot
Louis Brocard
Société Civile du
  Clos Saint-Louis

Clemency Frères
Camille Crusserey
René Defrance
Derey Frères
Dom Pierre Gelin
Dom de la Perrière
Charles Quillardet

Flagey-Echézeaux
Surprisingly sited on the wrong (flat) side of the road, this village is not on the wine-tourist's map. Its red wines are amongst the finest that the Côte de Nuits has to offer.

Coquard-Loison ('Echézeaux'; 'Grands Echézeaux')
Henri Gouroux ('Grands Echézeaux')
Louis Gouroux ('Echézeaux'; 'Grands Echézeaux')

Gevrey-Chambertin
This ought, judging by its renown, to produce some of the best of all Côte de Nuits Burgundies. Unfortunately, widescale plantation of high-yielding young vines in the 1960s and 1970s, coupled with the greed of the growers and the amount of flat land within the appellation, all conspire to make for some very disappointing wine indeed.

Thomas Bassot
Albert Bichot
J.C. Boisset
Bouchard Père & Fils
Pierre Bourrée
Alain Burguet
Camus Père & Fils
Dom Pierre Damoy
Joseph Drouhin
Dom Dujac
Dom Drouhin-Laroze
Duroche
Faiveley
E. Geantet-Pansiot
Dom Pierre Gelin

Geoffroy Père & Fils
Dom Antonin Guyon
Henri Magnien
Moillard
Naigeon-Chauveau
Fernand Pernot
G. Poulleau-Muet
Charles Quillardet
Philippe Rossignol
Dom Joseph Roty
Dom Armand Rousseau
Thomas-Bassot
Dom F. Tortochot
Dom Louis Trapet Père & Fils.
Dom des Varoilles

The Grands Crus of Burgundy

Aloxe Corton *r.* red, *w.* white
Les Chaumes (part) *r*
Le Charlemagne *r&w*
Les Combes (part) *r*

Corton-Charlemagne *r*
Corton Bressandes *r*
Corton Maréchaudes *r*

Corton Perrières r
Corton Renardes r
Corton Clos du Roi r
Les Fiètres (part) r
Le Corton r&w
Les Grèves (part) r
Les Languettes r&w

Les Meix (part) r
Les Meix Lallemand (part) r
Les Paulands (part) r
Les Pougets r&w
Les Renardes r&w
La Vigne au Saint (part) r
Le Village (part) r

Chambolle Musigny
Bonnes Mares r   Musigny r

Chassagne-Montrachet
Bâtard-Montrachet w   Clos de Vougeot r&w
Criots-Bâtard-Montrachet w

Gevrey Chambertin
Chambertin r   Griotte-Chambertin r
Chambertin Clos de Bèze r   Latricières-Chambertin r
Chapelle-Chambertin r   Mazis-Chambertin r
Charmes-Chambertin r   Ruchottes-Chambertin r
Mazoyères-Chambertin r

Puligny-Montrachet
Bâtard-Montrachet w   Chevalier-Montrachet w
Bienvenues-Bâtard-Montrachet w   Montrachet w

Vosne Romanée
Echezeaux r   Romanée-Conti r
Grands Echezeaux r   Romanée-St-Vivant r
Richebourg r   La Tâche r
La Romanée r

Givry
Once one of the best known of all red Burgundies, Givry has, in more recent times, suffered from being situated in the Côte Chalonnaise rather than the Côte d'Or, and is rarely seen. The wine is not the classiest of Burgundy, but it *is* good Pinot Noir.

Société Civile du Dom Thénard   Dom Steinmaier

Ladoix-Serrigny
Another Côte de Beaune village (the closest to the Côte de Nuits) which is little known outside Burgundy. At their best, these wines can easily compete with many a dull Aloxe-Corton.

Bouchard Père & Fils   Michel Mallard
Capitain-Gagnerot   Dom Prince Florent de Mérode
Chevalier-Dubois   André Nudant

Mâcon-Villages
Wine bearing this label, or Mâcon, Lugny, Clesse, Vire and Prisse can be some of the best affordable Chardonnay anyone could ever wish for. Drink it young.

Marsannay-la-Côte
Almost in Dijon, this village was once the heart of the 'Côte Dijonnaise'. Nowadays, it produces Bourgogne rouge and rosé.

Dom Clair-Dau   Dom Huguenot
Jean Fournier   Charles Quillardet

Mercurey
The Côte Chalonnaise's answer to Pommard – with white wine as well. The reds can be tough at first, but they *are* worth waiting for; the whites can be nutty and rich.

Dom Bordeaux-Montrieux   Yves de Launay
Bouchard Aîné   Paul Marceau
Roland Brintet   Jean Maréchale
Faiveley   François Protheau
Michel Juillot   Dom Raquillet

Antonin Rodet   Emile Voarick
Dom Hughes de Suremain

Meursault
With 300 individual growers, each making as many as two or three different Meursaults, there is little reason to expect consistency. The soil plays its true role: Meursault Perrière is hard and unyielding when young, glorious when mature. Meursault Charmes is as attractive as its name, even when freshly fermented in its barrel. This is one village where even vineyards without Premier Cru status are increasingly named on labels. Look out for some of these wines, they can be bargains.

Charles Allexant   Dom Leflaive
Robert Ampeau   Leroy
Dom Marquis d'Angerville   Dom du Duc de Magenta
Ballot-Millot   Dom Pierre-Yves Masson
Dom de Blagny   Dom Joseph Matrot
Bouchard Père & Fils   Mazilly Père & Fils
André Brunet   Château de Meursault
Dom Clerget   Bernard Michelot-Buisson
Dom Coche-Deborde   Jean Monnier & Fils
Dom Coche-Dury   Dom René Monnier
Heritiers Darnat   Berthe Morey
François Gaunoux   Dom Jean Pascal
Henri Germain   Dom Pitoiset-Urena
Sélection Jean Germain   Henri Potinet-Ampeau
Dom Charles Giraud   Dom Jacques Prieur
Dom Albert Grivault   Ropiteau Frères
Dom Antonin Guyon   H. Rougeot
Raymond Javillier   Dom Guy Roulot
Dom Jean Joliot & Fils   Dom Etienne Sauzet
Dom Michel Lafarge   René Thévenin-Monthélie
Dom des Comtes Lafon   Joseph Voillot

Montagny
A tiny commune in the Côte Chalonnaise, put on the map by Louis Latour, the first Beaune merchant to promote its wines. These whites are not great Burgundy, but they are certainly a match for many Pouilly Fuissés.

Caves des Vignerons de Buxy   Bernard Michel
Dom Martial de Laboulaye   Dom Steinmeier
Louis Latour   Jean Vachet

Monthélie
These wines are sometimes described as a little 'rustic' but anyone who has tasted a good example of the Hospices de Beaune Cuvée Lebelin (Mothélie Les Duresses) will have realised that this Côte de Beaune Village can produce reds and whites of some style.
Charles Boussey ('Les Champs Fuilliot')
Dom Monthélie-Douhairet
Henri Potinet-Ampeau
Dom Ropiteau-Mignon
Dom Thévenin-Monthélie & Fils
R. de Suremain ('Château de Monthélie')

Morey St Denis
Sandwiched between Gevrey and Chambolle, Morey sometimes seems a little unsure of itself. At their best, its wines are deeply fruity and richly smooth, even when young. At their least good, Morey's wines can be simply rather dull.

Ets Bertagna   Dom Dujac
Dom Bryczek   Héritiers Cosson
Dom Clair Dau   Dom Dujac

Dom Robert Groiffier
G. Lignier & Fils
Dom Mommessin
Henri Mauffre

Dom Ponsot
Maison Henri Rémy
Dom G. Tortochot

Nuits-St-Georges

To taste 'real' young Nuits-St-Georges is to understand just how great a part additions of Algerian wine played in its commercial success. Good Nuits is glorious stuff, but it is also tough and ungiving when young (hence the addition of Clos d'Algiers). Go for the genuine article and be patient with it.

Maison Jules Belin
Jean-Claude Boisset
L.J. Bruck ('Les St Georges')
F. Chauvenet
J. Chauvenet ('Les Vaucrains')
Maurice & Robert Chevillon ('Les Cailles'; 'Aux Chaignots'; 'Les Pruliers'; 'La Roncière'; 'Les St-Georges')
Auguste Chicotot ('Les Proces'; 'Les Pruliers'; 'Les St-Georges'; 'Les Vaucrains')
Lucien Chicotot ('Les St-Georges'; 'Les Vaucrains')
D. Chopin-Gesseaume ('Les Cailles'; 'Les Chaignots'; 'Les Pruliers')
Jean Confuron & Ses Fils
Robert Dubois & Fils
Gérard Elmerich
J.H. Faiveley ('Clos de la Maréchale'; 'Les Porets'; 'Les St-Georges)
Geisweiler & Fils
Dom Henri Gouges ('Aux Chaignots'; 'Clos des Porets St-Georges'; 'Les St-Georges'; 'La Perrière'; 'Les Pruliers')

Hospices de Nuits St-Georges
      'Cuvée Cabet' (Didiers St-Goerges)
      'Cuvée Jacques Duret' (Didiers St-Georges)
      'Cuvée Fagon' (Didiers Monopole)
      'Cuvée Grangier'
      'Cuvée Guyard de Changey' (Murgers)
      'Cuvée Guillaume Laby'
      'Cuvée Mesny de Boisseaux' (Boudots)
      'Cuvée Antide Midan' (Porets)
      'Cuvée Mignotte'
      'Cuvée Claude Poyen'
      'Cuvée Camille Rodier' (Rues de Chaux)
      'Cuvée Saint-Laurent' (Corvées Paget)
      'Cuvée Soeurs Hospitalières'
      'Cuvée des Sires de Vergy' (Saint Georges)

Dom Georges Jeanniard
Jouan-Marcillet
Laboure-Roi
Liger-Belair
Lupe-Cholet (Bichot)
Dom Machard de Gramont
Dom Tim Marshall
Dom Héritiers Emile Michelot
P. Misserey & Frère

Moillard-Grivot
Morin Père & Fils
Bernard Mugneret-Gouachon
Dom de la Poulette
Henri Remoriquet
Dom Rion
Trapet-Lalle
Charles Vienot

Orches

Burgundy's other rosé village, tucked away atop some very impressive cliffs close to Saint Romain in the Hautes Côtes de Beaune.

Cave Cooperative des Hautes Côtes

Passetoutgrains

Dom Rion

Michel Lafarge

Pernand Vergelesses

Pernand's reds (with the exceptions of those of a few producers) tend to be over-sugared and jammy; far less classy than those of neighbouring Savigny-les-Beaune. The whites however are amongst the best buys

in the Côte d'Or. Some of them would shame the Corton Charlemagnes produced in Aloxe-Corton, Pernand's other illustrious neighbour.

Dom Bonneau de Martray
Chanson Père & Fils
P. Dubreuil-Fontaine Père & Fils
Doudet-Naudin
Dom Germain
Dom Antonin Guyon
Laleure-Piot

Louis Latour
Dom Lucien Jacob Leroy
Rober Rapet & Fils
André Thiely
Tollot-Beaut
Tollot Voarick

Pommard

One local winemaker compared Pommard wines to the village church: solid and rather austerely impressive. There are a great many old vines in Pommard which should make for good wine; unfortunately it also makes for a certain amount of to-ing and fro-ing across the Route Nationale where the flat land is blessed with younger vines. Of course this sometimes means that wine which really ought to be called Bourgogne Rouge suddenly 'becomes' Pommard.

Robert Ampeau & Fils
Dom Marquis d'Angerville
Comte Armand – Dom du
  Clos des Epeneaux
Bidot-Bourgogne
Dom Billard-Gonnet
Bouchard Père & Fils
Bernard Caillet
Félix Clerget
Roger Clerget
Lahaye Père & Fils
Dom de Mme Bernard de Courcel
Dom François Gaunoux
Dom Michel Gaunoux
Dom Goud de Beaupuis
Dom Bernard Glantenay
Dom Jules Guillemard
Dom Lejeune

Héritiers Raoul Leneuf
Dom Lequin-Roussot
Leroy
Dom Machard de Gramont
Mazilly Père & Fils
Château de Meursault
Dom Michelot-Buisson
Dom Michelot
Dom Jean Monnier & Fils
Dom René Monnier
Dom de Montille
Dom Mussy
Dom Parent
Dom Jean Pascal & Fils
Château de Pommard
Dom V. Pothier-Rieusset
Dom de la Pousse d'Or
Dom Ropiteau-Mignon

Pouilly-Fuissé

Very attractive Mâconnais wine. But why did its price have to rise higher than that of Meursault? Because it is a transatlantic success. If you cannot get hold of the very best Pouilly Fuissé, try Pouilly Vinzelles, Pouilly Loché, or Saint Véran instead and save money.

Bouchard Aîné & Fils
Château de Beauregard
Georges Duboeuf
Château Fuissé

Dom Ferret
Maurice Luquet
Gilles Noblet
Louis Latour

Pouilly-Vinzelles

Not really up to the level of good Pouilly Fuissé, but not up to its price level either. Most Pouilly Loché is sold under this name.

Georges Duboeuf
H. Mathias
The local cooperatives

Puligny Montrachet

This is the finest example of the laws of supply and demand: every drop of Puligny is accounted for within weeks of the harvest. Most of it is subsequently drunk far too young; unlike Meursault, Puligny can be grassily steely when young, taking time to really open out into its full richness.

Robert Ampeau & Fils
Bouchard Père & Fils
Dom Carillon
Joseph Drouhin
Dupard Aîné

Dom Guérin
Louis Jadot
Dom Leflaive
Leroy
Lycée Viticole

Dom du Duc de Magenta
Dom Jean Monnier & Fils
Dom René Monnier
Veuve Henri Moroni
Dom Jean Pascal & Fils
Dom Jacques Prieur

Dom de la Romanée-Conti
Ropiteau Frères
Dom St Michel
Dom Etienne Sauzet
Roland Thévenin

Rully

If Mercurey is the Pommard of the Côte Chalonnaise, this is the Volnay. Much white Rully goes to make sparkling Crémant de Bourgogne; the red can be attractively floral – and attractively priced.

Comte J. d'Aviau de Ternay
René Brelière
Emile Chandesais
Dom Chanzy
Les Caves Delorme-Meulien
('Dom de la Renarde')

Dom de la Folie
Henri & Paul Jacqueson
Louis Jadot
René Ninot-Riguad
Armand Monassier

St-Aubin

Yet another of those under-rated villages. The red can be a little disappointing but the white, when well made, is at once flinty and nutty; Meursault's leaner country cousin.

Blondeau-Danne
Raoul Clerget
Jean Lamy & Fils

Roux Père & Fils
Dom Thomas

St-Romain

High up in the hills of the Hautes Côtes, this can be the source of surprisingly fine white wine and some rather rustic red. Some of the reds though can also achieve a certain style. As elsewhere in the Hautes Côtes, the ripeness of the harvest is crucial.

Fernand & Armand Bazenet
Henri Buisson
Bernard Fèvre
Alain Gras

Emile Grivelet
Roland Thévenin
('Clos des Ducs')
Germain Théviot

St-Véran

The rising star of the Mâconnais – thanks to Georges Duboeuf who, almost alone, has championed its cause. Every Pouilly Fuissé drinker should try it. Delicious young, it can even benefit from a year or two in bottle – unlike more humble Mâcon Villages.

Georges Chagny
Dom Corsin
Georges Duboeuf

Dom Duperron
Henry-Lucius Gregoire
Union des Producteurs

Santenay

Almost forgotten, tucked away at the southern end of the Côte d'Or, this is the source of good, if not incredibly stylish, reds, and the occasional pretty white.

André Bart
Dom de l'Abbaye de Santenay
Dom Joseph Belland
Brenot Père & Fils
Paul Chapelle
Philippe Chapelle
Société Civile du
    Château de Santenay
Clair-Cautain
Dom Fleurot-Larose

Jessiaume Père & Fils
Joly Père & Fils
Dom Lequin-Roussot
Prosper Maufoux
Mestre Père & Fils
Dom René Monnier
Jean Moreau
Dom de la Pousse d'Or
G. Prieur
Dom St Michel

Savigny-les-Beaune

Hiding in a valley just behind Beaune, Savigny produces some really delicious plummy red wine which is on a level with Beaune itself. The white can be good too, but is rarely fine.

Pierre André
    (La Reine Pedauque)

P. Bitouzet
GAEC Simon Bize

Dom Bonneau de Martray
Bouchard Père & Fils
Valentin Bouchotte
Dom Capron-Mannieux
Chandon de Briailles
Chanson Père & Fils
Dom Clair-Daü
Doudet-Naudin
Paul Dubreuil-Bize
Dom Dubreuil Fontaine
Louis Ecard-Guyot

Dom Goud de Beaupuis
Dom Antonin Guyon
Dom de la Juvinière
Dom Lucien Jacob Leroy
Dom Machard de Gramont
Château de Meursault
Dom Pavelot Père & Fils
Seguin-Manuel
Tollot-Beaut
Tollot-Voarick
Henri de Villamont

Volnay

One of the really great villages, and one which is blessed with a good number of excellent winemakers. The wines achieve a delicacy and complexity which set them aside from their neighbours. Describing them is not easy, but mention of violets and black cherry is not too fanciful.

Robert Ampeau & Fils
Marquis d'Angerville ('Caillerets'; 'Champans'; 'Clos des Ducs';
    'Fremiet'; 'Taille-Pieds'.
Henri Boillot ('Les Angles'; 'Caillerets'; 'En Chevret')
Bouchard Père & Fils
Mme Buffet ('Champans'; 'Clos du Verseuil'; 'les Santenots')
Bidot-Bourgogne
Dom Clerget
Bernard Delagrange ('Caillerets'; 'Champans')
Joseph Drouhin
Jacques Gagnard-Delagrange
Dom François Gaunoux
Georges Glantenay ('Les Brouillards'; 'Clos des Chênes'; 'Les
    Santenots')
Dom Antonin Guyon
Michel Lafarge ('Clos des Chênes')
Dom Joseph Matrot
Château de Meursault
Dom René Monnier
Henri Monnot ('Caillerets')
Mme François de Montille ('Champans'; 'Les Mitans'; 'Taille-Pieds')
Dom Jean Pascal & Fils
Michel Pont – Château de Savigny/Cellier Volnaysien ('Caillerets';
    'Clos des Chênes')
Henri Potinet-Ampeau
Dom de la Pousse d'Or ('Clos d'Audignac'; 'Bousse d'Or'; 'Cailleret
    Dessous'; 'Cailleret Dessus, Clos des 60 Ouvrées')
Dom Jacques Prieur
Dom Ropiteau Mignon
F. Rossignol-Boillot
R. Rossignol-Changarnier
P. Rossignol-Simon
Joseph Voillot

Vosne-Romanée

Home of the most expensive red in the world – the Romanée-Conti – and some rather more (though not readily) affordable village wines. As elsewhere, there is a tendency towards dullness amongst second-grade producers, so buy carefully.

Albert Bichot
Dom Clair-Daü
Dom G. Clerget
J. Confuron-Jayer ('Les Suchots')
Coquard-Loison
Dom René Engel ('Les Brulées')
Jean Grivot ('Les Beaumonts'; 'Les Suchots')
Dom Gros Frère & Soeur

Jean & François Gros ('Clos des Réas')
Henri Gouroux ('Les Suchots')
Dom Henri Lamarche ('La Grande Rue'; 'Aux Malconsorts'; 'Les Suchots')
Liger-Belair – sold by Bouchard Père & Fils ('La Romanée'; 'Les Reignots')
Dom Machard de Gramont
Jean Méo ('Les Chaumes')
Moillard
Mongeard-Mugneret ('Les Suchots')
René Mugneret ('Les Suchots')
A. Mugneret-Gibourg
Dom Mugneret-Gouachon
Charles Noëllat ('Les Beaumonts'; 'Aux Malconsorts'; 'Les Suchots')
Henri Noëllat ('Les Beaumonts'; 'Les Suchots')
Manière-Noirot ('Les Suchots')
Dom de la Romanée-Conti ('Romanée-Conti'; 'La Tache'; 'Romanée St-Vivant')
Charles Vienot

Vougeot

A truly impressive sight – but not such an impressive site – the Clos de Vougeot made sense when the monks who founded it could combine grapes from the flat bits with grapes from the slopes. Nowadays, though, there are so many individual owners (some with hill, some with plain) that there is no such thing as a single level of quality – even if all the winemakers were equally skilful.

Albert Bichot	L'Héritier Guyot
Pierre André	Jaffelin
(La Reine Pédauque)	Dom Henri Lamarche
Ets Bertagna	Leroy
Champy Père & Fils	Dom Machard de Gramont
Dom Clair-Daü	Mugneret-Gibourg
Dom G. Clerget	Charles Noëllat
Joseph Drouhin	Pierre Ponnelle
Dufouleur Frères	Dom Jacques Prieur
Dom René Engel	Dom G. Roumier
Faiveley	Dom des Varoilles
Jean Grivot	

BURGUNDY SHOPPING LIST

Affordable Red Burgundy

Auxey Duresses (Duc de Magenta or Alain Gras)
Bourgogne Rouge (Louis Jadot or Geisweiler or Leroy)
Chassagne (Albert Morey or Bachelet-Ramonet or Roland Rapet or Dubreuil Fontaine)
Chorey (Tollot-Beaut or Domaine François Germain)
Côte de Beaune (La Grande Châtelaine, Chantal Lescure)
Côtes de Beaune Villages (Albert Morey)
Côtes de Nuits Villages (Philippe Rossignol)
Fixin (Joliet or Bertheaut)
Givry (Steinmaier)
Hautes Côtes de Beaune (Cave des Hautes Côtes or Geisweiler or Dom Cornu or Mazilly)
Hautes Côtes de Nuits (Cave des Hautes Côtes or Geisweiler or Dom Cornu)
Ladoix (Domaine Chevalier)
Mercurey (Bouchard Aîné or de Suremain)
Meursault Rouge (Laboure-Roi)
Montagny (Louis Latour or Cave de Buxy or Michel Vachet)
Monthélie (Denis Boussey or Dom Thévenin-Monthélie)
Passetoutgrains (Leroy)
Pernand-Vergelesses (Chandon de Briailles)
Rully (Louis Jadot or Brelière)

St-Aubin (Thomas Père & Fils or Roux)
St-Romain (Alain Gras)
Savigny Les Beaune (Dom Simon Bize or Pavelot or Tollot Beaut or Henri de Villamont)

Chablis

Anything from La Chablisienne, Louis Michel, Pinson, Fèvre or Droin, Sauvignon de St Bris (Brocard or Albert Pic or Verret)

Mâconnais

St-Véran (Duboeuf or Corsin)
Pouilly Vinzelles
Pouilly Loché

Beaujolais

Georges Duboeuf, Ch. Gaillard, Loron

Beaujolais Villages

Georges Duboeuf, Sarrau, Trenel, Ferraud, Loron, Piat, Pasquier Desvignes

Brouilly

Georges Duboeuf, Ch. de Fouilloux

Chénas

Georges Duboeuf or Trenel or Champagnon, Sélection Eventail, Ch. de Chénas

Chiroubles

Georges Duboeuf, La Maison des Vignerons, Sarrau

Côte de Brouilly

Ch. de Grand Vernay

Names to trust

Dom de la Pousse d'Or	Jayer
Ramonet Prudhon	Ponsot
Etienne Sauzet	François Germain
Dom des Comtes Lafon	Leroy
Laboure Roi	Joseph Drouhin
Duboeuf	Louis Latour
Raveneau	(whites more than reds)
Tollot-Beaut	

Good, less well-known merchants

Chandesais	Jaffelin
Pierre Bourrée	Naigeon Chauveau
Thomas La Chevalière	

CHABLIS

CHABLIS is one of the few really first class winemaking regions in France which still has space in which to grow. Recent laws have permitted the expansion of the appellation to cover land which lacks the 'Kimmeridgian' limestone subsoil which – to many traditionalists – plays an essential role in giving Chablis its recognizeable steely character. But it is perhaps the very absence of that character which has so endeared this wine to an international public in recent years: warm summers have helped to produce a succession of 'soft' vintages. Still, with a name known to wine drinkers around the world, who's to worry. As prices rise to levels far beyond those asked for often unarguably better wines from the great villages of the Côte d'Or, few buyers are deterred. Go for Grand or Premier Cru wines – they're still the best value, and worth paying the extra for.

The Premiers Crus

Beauroy (includes Beauroy and Troesmes)
Côte de Lechet

Fourchaume (includes Côte de Fontenay, Fourchaume, l'Homme Mort, Vaupulent and Vaulorent)
Les Fourneaux (includes Côte

des Prés-Girots, Les Fourneaux and Morein)
Mélinots (includes Les Epinottes, Mélinots and Roncières)
Montée de Tonnerre (includes Chapelot, Montée de Tonnerre and Pied d'Aloup)
Montmains (includes Butteaux, Forêts and Montmains)
Monts de Milieu
Vaillons (includes Beugnons, Châtains, Les Lys, Séché and Vaillons)
Vaucoupin
Vaudevey
Vosgros (includes Vaugiraut and Vosgros)

The Grands Crus

Blanchots	Preuses
Bougros	Valmur
Les Clos	Vaudésir
Grenouilles	

La Moutonne (in both Vaudesir and Preuses)

Recommended growers/merchants

René Dauvissat
Paul Droin
Dom. Duplessis
William Fèvre
Lamblin & Fils
Henri Laroche
Long-Depaquit
Louis Michel
J. Moreau et Fils
Dom. Pinson

Francois Raveneau
A. Regnard & Fils
Dom. Rottiers-Clotilde
Simmonet-Febvre & Fils
Gérard Tremblay
Jacques Tremblay
Robert Vocoret
Cave Coopérative 'La Chablisienne'.

CHAMPAGNE

CHAMPAGNE is a very confusing segment of the wine world. On the one hand, quality is often confused with personal taste and snob-appeal and on the other hand, prices vary enormously, as do styles. None of which is surprising when you consider that there are well over 5,000 individual producers who make their own fizz, a handful of super-dynamic cooperatives and 100 or so shippers who blend and make Champagnes to sell under their own, and frequently their clients' labels. This list includes all the principal Champagne houses.

The Grape List

Champagne is made from three grape varieties. It can be a blend of two or three, or the produce of a single variety.

Pinot Noir the same variety as is grown in Burgundy to produce that region's great red wines, and in Alsace to make rosé, here produces white (Blanc de Noirs) and pink (Rosé) Champagne. Its presence is often recognizable by a (dark) chocolatey flavour.

Pinot Meunier a related variety, little grown elsewhere – though now found producing white wine in England where it is known as the Wrotham Pinot.

Chardonnay the great white Burgundy grape, and the one which, in Champagne, is responsible for all Blancs de Blancs. Its keynote is a buttery, nutty flavour.

Ch – Chardonnay	
f. – Founded	
NM – Négociant-Manipulant	
PM – Pinot Meunier	
PN – Pinot Noir	

Peter Dowdeswell, the English gluttony-record setter, can drink a pint of Champagne upside down in 3.3 seconds.

128 Champagne Producers

Ayala & Co (Ay)
A Grande Marque, f. 1850, owning no land, but making wine from 23 *ha* belonging to Champagne Montebello, whose label it still uses. Produces 900,000 bottles per year
Non-Vintage: PN 50%, Ch 25%, PM 25% (Av. bottle age 2.5 years);
Vintage: PN 75%, Ch 25%
Cuvée de Prestige: Brut Blancs de Blancs Millésime – Ch 100%
Rosé: 'mostly PN-blended'.

Bauget-Jouette (Epernay)

Beaumet-Chaurey (Epernay)
NM, f. 1878, producing 90% from its own 62 *ha*
Non-Vintage: PN 66.6%, Ch 33.3% (Av. bottle age 3 years);
Vintage: PN 66.6%, Ch 33.3%
Cuvée Prestige: Cuvée Malakoff – Ch 100%
Rosé: PN 100% SC.

Paul Berthelot (Dizy)

Besserat de Bellefon (Reims)
NM, f. 1843, belongs to Pernod-Ricard, prod. 2,000,000 bottles, 5% from own vineyards. Famous for Crémants
Non-Vintage: PN 70%, Ch 30% (Av. bottle age 3 years)
Vintage: PN 50%, Ch 50%
Cuvée Prestige: Cuvée Besserat de Bellefon (blend of vintages) – PN 50%, Ch 50%
Rosé PN 40%, Ch 60%

Bichat (Reims)

Billecart-Salmon (Mareuil-sur-Ay)
NM, f. 1818, prod. 450,000 bottles
Non-Vintage: PN 25%, PM 25%, Ch 50% (Av. bottle age 3 years)
Vintage: PN 60%, Ch 40%
Cuvée Prestige: N.F. Billecart Cuvée
Rosé: PN 25%, PM 25%, Ch 50%

Billiard (Epernay)

Boizel (Epernay)
NM, f. 1834, producing 300,000 bottles. Uses the names Louis Krémer and Camuset.
Non-Vintage: PN 55%, PM 15%, Ch 30%, (Av. bottle age 3 years)
Vintage: PN 65%, PM 5%, Ch 30%
Cuvée Prestige: Joyau de France – PN 65%, Ch 35%
Rosé: PN 70%, PM 30%

Bollinger (Ay)
NM, f. 1829, producing 2,000,000 bottles, 70% from own 140 *ha*
Non-Vintage: PN 60%, PM 10%, Ch 30% (Av. bottle age 3 years)
Vintage: PN 70%, Ch 30%
Cuvée Prestige 1: Bollinger R.D. – PN 70%, Ch 30% (has spent at least 7 years on its lees)
Cuvée Prestige 2: Vieilles Vignes – from pre-phylloxera PN vineyard
Rosé: PN 70%, Ch 30%

F. Bonnet et Fils (Oger)
NM, f. 1922 producing 160,000 bottles 2/3 from own 9 *ha*

Non-Vintage: (Av. bottle age 4–5 years)
Vintage: Ch 100%

Bouche Père & Fils (Pierry)

A. Bricout (Avize)

Edouard Brun (Ay)

René Brun (Ay)

Burtin (Epernay)

> **Longest Champagne cork flight (32.23 m. (105ft 9ins) from unheated bottle held 4' above ground level was set by Peter Kirby, at Ildewild Park, Reno, Nevada on 4 July, 1981**

Canard-Duchêne
NM, f. 1868. Has belonged to Veuve Clicquot since 1978, producing 2,500,000 bottles, 4% from own 15 *ha*
Non-Vintage: PN and PM 85%, Ch 15%
Cuvée Prestige: Charles VII – PN 34%, Ch 66%

De Castellane (*Epernay*)
NM, f. 1895, producing, 1,000,000 bottles
Non-Vintage: PN 30%, PM 50, Ch 20% (Av. bottle age 3 years)
Vintage: PN 45%, PM 35%, Ch 15%
Cuvée Prestige: Cuvée Commodore – PN 75%, Ch 25%
Rosé: PN 45%, PM 30%, Ch 25%

De Castelnau (Epernay)

De Cazenove (Avize)

Chanoine Frères (Rilly-la-Montagne)

A. Charbaut et Fils (Epernay)
NM, f. 1948 producing 1,200,000 bottles, 33% from own 56 *ha*

Chauvet (Tours-sur-Marne)
NM, f. 1848, producing 50,000 bottles, 80% from own 10 *ha*
Non-Vintage: PN 66.6%, Ch 33.3% (Av. bottle age 2.5 years)
Vintage: PN 50%, Ch 50%
Rosé: a blend of red and white wine

Emile Clerambault (Neuville-sur-Seine)
Cooperative with members' 115 *ha*, producing 250,000 bottles
Vintage 'Carte d'Or': PN 50%, Ch 50%

Collery (Ay)
NM, f. 1893, producing 150,000 bottles, 50% from own 8 *ha*
Non-Vintage: PN 70%, PM 20%, Ch 10% (av. bottle age 3 years)
Vintage: PN 90%, Ch 10%
Rosé: PN 100%

Compagnie Française des Grand Vins (Reims)

Comptoir Vinicole de Champagne (Reims)

De Courcy (Epernay)

Marcel Defond (Reims)

Delamotte Père & Fils (Avize)

A. Desmoulins (Epernay)
NM, f. 1908 producing 180,000 bottles
Non-Vintage: (Av. bottle age 2.5 years)
Cuvée Prestige: PN 50%, Ch 50%

Deutz & Geldermann (Ay)
NM, f. 1838, producing 800,000 bottles, 40% from own 42 *ha*
Non-Vintage: PN 60%, PM 25%, Ch 15% (Av. bottle age 4 years)
Vintage: PN 60%, PM 25%, Ch 15%
Cuvée Prestige: Cuvée William Deutz – PN 60%, PM 10%, Ch 30%
Rosé: PN 80%, PM 20%

Noël Doré (Rilly-la-Montagne)

André Drappier (Bar-sur-Aube)
NM, f. early 19th century, producing 22,000 bottles, 100% from own 24 *ha*.

Non-Vintage: PN 75%, PM 25%, (Av. bottle age – 2 years)
Vintage: PN 40%, PM 5%, Ch 55%
Cuvée Prestige: Grande Sendrée – PN 40%, PM 5%, Ch 55%
Rosé: PN 100% (skin contact)

Emile Driant (Ay)

Robert Driant (Ay)

Michel Dubois (Epernay)

Dueil (Reims)

Duval Leroy (Vertus)
NM, f. 1859, producing 170,000 bottles, 25% from own 80 *ha*
Non-Vintage: PN 30%, Ch 70% (Av. bottle age 3–4 years)
Vintage: PN 20%, Ch 80%
Cuvée Prestige: Cuvées des Roys – PN 5%, Ch 95%
Rosé: PN 20%, Ch 80%

Roland Fliniaux (Ay)
NM, f. 1938, producing 80,000 bottles from own 4 *ha*
Non-Vintage: PN 80%, Ch 20% (Av. bottle age 3–5 years)
Vintage: PN 100%
Rosé: PN 100% (skin contact)

Fournier and Co (Reims)

France Champagne (Epernay)

Gardet & Co. (Rilly La Montagne)
NM, f. 1895, producing 600,000 bottles
Non-Vintage, PN 70%, Ch 30% (Av. bottle age 3 years)
Vintage: PN 50%, Ch 50%
Cuvée Prestige: Selected Réserve – PN 70%, Ch 30%
Rosé: PN 100% (skin contact)

> **The record for tallest stack of Champagne glasses placed one on top of the other and filled was set by Carl Groves and Peter Sellers on 19 April 1983 on the Australian Channel 9 programme 'The Daryl Somers Show' at 23 glasses.**

Lucien Gentils (Dizy)

René Gentils (Dizy)

H. Germain and Fils (Rilly La Montagne)
NM, f. 1898, producing 280,000 bottles, 25% from own 23 *ha*
Non-Vintage: PN 45%, PM 35%, Ch 20% (Av. bottle age 2 years)
Vintage: PN 55%, Ch 45%
Cuvée Prestige: Grand Cuvée Vénus Brut – PN 50%, Ch 50%

Gosset (Ay)
NM, f. 1584, producing 200,000 bottles, claims to be oldest Champagne house, owns Philipponnat
Non-Vintage: 'mostly black grapes' (Av. bottle age 2–3 years)
Vintage: 'mostly black grapes'
Cuvée Prestige: Grand Millesime (vintage); 4me Centenaire more 2/3 black grapes
Rosé: 53% black grapes, 43% white

Paul Gobillard (Epernay)

Alfred Gratien (Epernay)
NM, f. 1864. Also own Gratien and Meyer, producers of Saumur Mousseux in the Loire. Very traditional
Vintage: (1976) PN 15%, PM 15%, Ch 70%
Rosé: (skin contact)

Georges Goulet (Reims)
NM. Also uses the brands, Saint-Marceaux and A. Lepitre. Has no vineyards. Produces 1,000,000 bottles
Crémant Blanc de Blancs

Cuvée de Prestige: Cuvée du Centenaire
Rosé

Roger Guy (Reims)

Emile Hamm (Ay)

Heidsieck & Co. Monopole (Reims)
NM, f. 1785, producing 2,000,000 bottles, 33% from 110 *ha*
Non-Vintage: PN and PM 66.6%, Ch 33.3% (Av. bottle age 3 years)
Vintage: PN 65%, Ch 35%
Cuvée Prestige: Diamant Bleu – PN and PM 50%, Ch 50%
Rosé: 65% PN and PM, Ch 35%

Charles Heidsieck (Reims)
F. 1851, own 120 *ha*
Non-Vintage: 85% PN and PM, 15% Ch (bottle age at least 3 years)
Vintage: PN and PM 75%, Ch 25%
Cuvée Prestige: Cuvée Champagne Charlie – PN and at least Ch 30%
Rosé: blend varies

Henriot
Family company, now part of same concern as Ch. Heidsieck
Luxury Brand: Réserve Baron Philippe de Rothschild

Bernard Ivernel (Ay)
NM, f. 1880, producing 190,000 bottles, 10% from own 2 *ha*
Non-Vintage: PN and PM 60%, Ch 40%
Vintage: PN and PM 50%, Ch 50%
Cuvée Prestige: PN and PM 50%, Ch 50%
Rosé: a blend

Jacquesson & Fils (Epernay)
NM, f. 1798, producing 350,000 bottles, 60% from own 22 *ha*
Non-Vintage: PN 30%, PM 50%, Ch 20% (Av. bottle age 2–2.5 years)
Vintage: PN 50%, PM 15%, Ch 35%
Cuvée Prestige: Signature – PN 50%, Ch 50%
Rosé: PN 55%, PM 10%, Ch 35% (very pale, 10% red wine added)

Jacquart (Reims)
Cooperative producing 7,000,000 bottles from 900 *ha*
Non-Vintage – Brut Tradition: PN 33%, PM 33%, Ch 33%
Non-Vintage – Brut Sélection: PN 40%, Ch 60% (Av. bottle age 3 years)
Vintage: PN 40%, Ch 60%

Jacquinot & Fils (Epernay)

Jamart & Co (Saint-Martin d'Ablois)

Jardin & Co (Le Mesnil-sur-Oger)

Krug (Reims)
NM, f. 1843, producing 20% from own 15 *ha*. Very traditional
Non-Vintage 'Grande Cuvée' blend varies (a high percentage of very mature wine goes into the blend)
Vintage: blend varies
Cuvée Prestige: Clos du Mesnil
Rosé: blend varies

Louis Kruger (Epernay)

Lang-Biémont (Oiry, Epernay)
NM, f. 1875, producing 500,000 bottles, 95% from own 50 *ha*
Non-Vintage: PN 10%, PM 10%, Ch 80% (Av.bottle age 3 years)
Vintage: 50% from vines in Cramant
Rosé: PN 20%, Ch 80%

Lanson Père & Fils (Reims)
NM, f. 1760, producing 10,000,000 bottles, 35% from own 200 *ha*
Non-Vintage: PN and PM 50%, Ch 50% (Av. bottle age 2.5 years)
Vintage: PN 55%, Ch 45%
Cuvée Prestige: Noble Cuvée – PN 40%, Ch 60%
Rosé: PN 70%, Ch 30%

Laurent Perrier (Tours-sur-Marne)
NM, f. 1812, producing 6,500,000 bottles, 10% from own 80 *ha*
Non-Vintage: PN 35%, PM 15%, Ch 50% (Av. bottle age 3 years)
Vintage: PN 45%, PM 5%, Ch 50%
Cuvée Prestige: Cuvée Grande Siècle – PN 45%, Ch 55%
Rosé: PN 100% (skin contact)

Albert Le Brun (Arize)
NM, f. 1860

Lecherre (Reims)
Supplies the 'House Champagne' to the Venice-Simplon Orient Express

R & L Legras (Chouilly)
NM

J. Lemoine (Rilly-la-Montagne)

Lenoble (Epernay)

Abel Lepître
Second name of Georges Goulet

Mailly-Champagne (Mailly)
Cooperative, f. 1923 producing 500,000 bottles from own 70 *ha*
Non-Vintage: PN 75%, Ch 25% (Av. bottle age 4 years)
Vintage: PN 75%, Ch 25%
Cuvée Prestige: Cuvée des Echansons – PN 75%, Ch 25%
Rosé: PN 100%

Mansard Baillet (Epernay)

G.H. Martel & Co

Marne & Champagne (Epernay)
NM. Little known by its own name, but holding a stock of over 75,000,000 bottles mostly to be sold under customers' labels. Best-known wines are A. de Rothschild and Réserve Grand Trianon.

Masse (Reims)
A subsidiary of Lanson.

Medot & Co (Reims)

Mercier (Epernay)
Belongs to Moët & Chandon/Hennessy. F. 1858. Produces 5,500,000 bottles, 20% from own vineyards.
Non-Vintage: PN 30/40%, PM 40/60%, Ch 10/20% (Av. bottle age 2–2.5 years)
Vintage: PN 30/40%, PM 40/50%, Ch 20/30%
Cuvée Prestige: Réserve de l'Empereur (only sold in France)
Rosé: at least 50/60% black grapes, (some skin contact)

Emile Michel (Verzenay)

Moët & Chandon (Epernay)
NM, f. 1743, the biggest producer, making nearly 26,500,000 bottles, 20% from own 876 *ha*
Non-Vintage: PN 40/60%, PM 30/50%, Ch 10/30% (Av. bottle age 2–3 years)
Vintage: PN 30/40%, PM 20/30%, Ch 10/30%
Cuvée Prestige: Dom Pérignon – PN 40/60%, Ch 40/60%
Rosé: At least 50/60% black grapes, (some skin contact)

Montaudon (Reims)
NM, f. 1891, producing 400,000 bottles, 30% from own 20 *ha*
Non-Vintage: PN 50%, PM 25%, Ch 25% (Av. bottle age 3 years)
Vintage: PN 50%, Ch 50%
Rosé: PN 75%, Ch 25% (some skin contact)

Montvilliers (Ay)

G. Morel (Reims)

G.H. Mumm (Reims)
Owned by Seagram, f. 1827, producing 7,000,000 bottles, 25% from own 220 *ha*
Non-Vintage: PN 50%, PM 25%, Ch 25%
Vintage: PN 66.6%, Ch 33.3% (but blend varies)
Cuvée Prestige: Cuvée President René Lalou – PN 50%, Ch 50%
Blanc de blancs: Cramant de Cramant
Rosé: PN 66.6%, Ch 33.3%

Oudinot-Jeanmaire (Epernay)
NM, producing 800,000 bottles, 90% from own 60 *ha*, including the Clos Saint-Rémi. Also uses the name A. Jeanmaire
Non-Vintage: PN 66.6%, Ch 33.3% (Av. bottle age 3 years)
Vintage: PN 66.6%, Ch 33.3%
Cuvée Prestige: Cuvée Particulière Brut – Ch 100%
Rosé: PN 100% (skin contact for 36 hours)

Bruno Paillard (Reims)
NM, f. 1981, producing 250,000 bottles.
Non-Vintage: PN 35%, PM 40%, Ch 25% (Av. bottle age 3 years)
Vintage: PN 40%, Ch 60%
Rosé: PN 90–95%, Ch 5–10% (skin contact)

Perrier-Jouët (Epernay)
NM, f. 1811, prodcuing 3,000,000 bottles, 40–45% from own 108 *ha*
Non-Vintage: PN 75–80%, Ch 20–25% (Av. bottle age 2–3 years)
Vintage: PN 70%, Ch 30%
Cuvée Prestige: Belle Epoque – PN 55–60%, Ch 40–45%
Rosé: Blason de France – PN 75–80%, Ch 20–25%
Rosé – Vintage: Belle Epoque – PN 55–60%, Ch 40–45%

Joseph Perrier Fils (Châlons-sur-Marne)
NM, f. 1825 producing 600,000 bottles, 35% from own 20 *ha*
Non-Vintage: PN and PM 66.6%, Ch 33.3% (Av. bottle age 3 years)
Vintage: PN and PM 50%, Ch 50%
Cuvée Prestige: Cuvée du Cent-Cinquantenaire – PN and PM 50%, Ch 50%
Rosé: PN 66.6%, Ch 33.3%

Philipponat (Ay)
NM, f. 1912, producing 600,000 bottles, 20% from own 12 *ha* including Clos de Goisses. See Gosset.
Non-Vintage: PN 50%, PM 20%, Ch 30% (Av. bottle age 2.5 years)
Vintage: Royale Réserve – PN 70%, Ch 30%
Cuvée Prestige: Clos des Goisses – PN 70%, Ch 30%
Rosé: PN 80%, Ch 20%

Jules Pierlot (Epernay)
NM, f. 1889, producing 120,000 bottles
Non-Vintage: (Av. bottle age 3 years)
Cuvée Prestige: Cuvée des Archers
Rosé

Marcel Pierre (Reims)

Piper Heidsieck (Reims)
F. 1785, producing 5,000,000 bottles
NV
Brut Sauvage 100% Chardonay, sans dosage
Cuvée Prestige: Florens Louis

Ployez-Jacquemart (Ludes)
NM, f. 1930, producing 100,000 bottles. 15% from own 2 *ha*
Non-Vintage: PN and PM 50%, Ch 50%, or Ch 100% in good years (Av. bottle age 2–3 years)
Vintage: PN and PM 50%, Ch 50% or Ch 100% in good years
Cuvée Prestige: Cuvée Liesse d'Harbonville – PN and PM 100%
Rosé: PN and PM 50%, Ch 50%

Pol Roger (Epernay)
NM, f. 1849, producing 1,300,000 bottles, 40% from own 70 *ha*
Non-Vintage: PN 33.3%, PM 33.3%, Ch 33.3% (Av. bottle age 3–4 years)
Vintage: PN 60%, Ch 40%
Cuvée Prestige: Sir Winston Churchill
Rosé: PN 60%, Ch 40%

Pommery & Greno (Reims)
NM, f. 1836, producing 6,850,000 bottles, 50% from own 300 *ha*
Non-Vintage: PN 33.3%, PM 33.3%, Ch 33.3% (Av. bottle age 3 years)
Vintage: PN 50%, Ch 50%
Cuvée Prestige: Louise Pommery
Rosé: PN 70%, Ch 30% (skin contact)

Eugène Ralle (Verzenay)

Ernest Rapeneau (Epernay)

Louis Roederer (Reims)
NM, f. 1760, producing 2,500,000 bottles, 80% from own 180 *ha*
Non-Vintage: PN 64%, Ch 36% (Av. bottle age 3.5–4 years)
Vintage: PN 66%, Ch 34%
Cuvée Prestige: Cristal – PN 55%, Ch 45%
Rosé: PN 70%, Ch 30% (skin contact)

> On 28 May 1984, in Stockholm, Dan Westerdehl and his team built a pyramid out of 3,654 Champagne glasses, filling them with 1,000 litres of Champagne.

Théophile Roederer (Reims)
NM, f. 1864.
Non-Vintage: PN 66.6%, Ch 33.3% (Av. bottle age 3 years)
Vintage: PN 66.6%, Ch 33.3%

Jean Rohrbacher (Epernay)

Ruinart Père & Fils (Reims)
NM, one of the oldest producers of Champagne. Like Mercier, belongs to Moët-Hennessy. F. 1729. Makes 1,000,000 bottles, 20% from company's 876 *ha*
Non-Vintage: PN 30–40%, PM 30–40%, Ch 25–30% (Av. bottle age 3 years)
Vintage: PN 35–45%, PM 20–30%, Ch 35–40%
Cuvée Prestige: Dom Ruinart Blanc de Blancs – Ch 100%
Rosé: Dom Ruinart Rosé de Luxe Cuvée – PN & PM 70%, Ch 30% (some skin contact)

Sacotte (Epernay)
NM, f. 1887, producing 250,000 bottles
Vintage: PN 66.6%, Ch 33.3%
Cuvée Prestige: Cuvée Prestige
Rosé

Sacy (Verzy)

Saint-Marceaux (See A. Lepitre)

Saint-Michel (See Union Champagne)

Salon (Avize)
NM, f. 1900, producing 150,000 bottles, 5% from own 1 *ha*. Very traditional
Cuvée Prestige: Salon le Mesmil – Ch 100% (from le Mesmil)

S.A.M.E. (Epernay)

Secondé Preroteau (Ambonnay)
NM, 12 *ha* Princesso de France – Brut
Fleuron de France – Blanc de Noirs

> Mr Bobby Acland of the 'Black Raven' tavern in Bishopsgate, City of London, drank 1,000 bottles of Champagne a year, i.e. nearly three bottles a day.

Société Générale de Champagne (Ay)

Société Remoise des Grands Vins de Champagne (Reims)

Société Vinicole Golden Roy (Epernay)

Marie Stuart (Reims)
NM, f. 1867, producing 960,000 bottles
Non-Vintage: PN 80%, Ch 20% (Av. bottle age 3 years)
Vintage: PN 40%, Ch 60%
Cuvée Prestige: Cuvée de la Reine – PN and Ch
Rosé: PN, PM and Ch

Taittinger (Reims)
NM, founded just after World War 1 producing 6,000,000 bottles, over 50% from own 250 *ha*
Non-Vintage: PN and PM 60%, Ch 40% (Av. bottle age 3 years)
Vintage: PN and PM 60%, Ch 40%
Cuvée Prestige: Comtes de Champagne – Ch 100%
Rosé: Comtes de Champagne – PN 100% (skin contact)

Léon de Tassigny (Reims)

Bernard Tassin (Celles-sur-Ource)

J. de Telmont (Damery)

Trouillard (Epernay)
Part of the Ch. Heidsieck-Henriot conglomerate, selling much of its production under customers' own labels.

Union Champagne (Avize)
1,000-member cooperative, selling 1,000,000 bottles itself and returning 4,000,000 to its member-growers for them to sell themselves. Uses the labels: St-Gall, St-Michel

Valentin (Epernay)

Pierre Vaudon (Avize)

Lucien Vazart (Chouilly)

De Venoge (Epernay)
NM, f. 1837, producing 2,500,000 bottles. With Trouillard, part of the Ch. Heidsieck-Henriot group.
Non-Vintage: Pinot 60%, Ch 40% (Av. bottle age 3 years)
Vintage: Pinot 40%, Ch 60%
Cuvée Prestige: Champagne des Princes – Ch 100%
Rosé: PN 100% (skin contact)

Veuve Clicquot-Ponsardin (Reims)
NM, f. 1772, producing 8.4 million bottles, 33% from own 265 *ha*

Non-vintage: PN 50%, PM 20%, Ch 30% (bottle age at least 3 years)
Vintage: PN 66.6%, Ch 33.3%
Cuvée Prestige: La Grand Dame – PN 66.6%, Ch 33.3%
Rosé: PN 52%, Ch 33% Bouzy Rouge 15%

Vollereaux (Epernay)
NM, f. 1933, producing 350,000 bottles, exclusively from own 40 *ha*
Non-Vintage: PN 33.3%, PM 33.3%, Ch 33.3% (Av. bottle age 3 years)
Vintage: PN 40%, PM 20%, Ch 40%
Rosé: PN 100% (skin contact)

Jean Warris (Avize)

Champagne Words

Assemblage the blending of Champagne.

B.O.B. (*Marque Acheteur*) literally 'Buyer's Own Brand', referring to a Champagne bought from a producer and labelled with a name of the buyer's choice. This would include the house-fizz of a restaurant, e.g. The Ritz Champagne, or a Champagne with an authentic-sounding producer's name which turns out to have come from a cooperative or merchant.

Brut dry.

Crémant champagne with less *mousse (qv)*.

Cuvée wine from the first pressing – the best, and better than *Premier* and *Deuxième Taille (qv)*.

Dégorgement the removal of the yeast and deposit from Champagne once it has finished its *remuage (qv.)*.

Dosage the sweetening of dry wine with *Liqueur d'expédition (qv)*.

Grandes Marques the 'big names' of Champagne, the syndicate of major Houses which are considered to produce top quality wine. Some equally good wine is nonetheless produced by producers who are not in this group, and there are non-members who call themselves Grandes Marques.

Gyropalettes machines which perform the *remuage (qv)*.

Liqueur d'expédition the sweetening syrup used for *dosage (qv)* which may include a little brandy.

Liqueur de tirage the yeast and sugar which is added to raw (still) Champagne to induce the secondary fermentation which will make it sparkle.

Mousse the bubbles in Champagne.

Négociant-Manipulant a merchant who blends and produces Champagne – in practice, this describes any Champagne house, and excludes only cooperatives.

Première Taille wine from the second pressing, with Deuxième Taille (third pressing) referred to as 'taille', in critical contrast to Cuvée *(qv)*.

Pupitre the wooden racks in which bottles go through their remuage *(qv)* when the process is performed by hand.

> Only 100 litres of Champagne are produced for every 150 kg of grapes, i.e. nearly 3 lb per bottle.

Récemment Dégorgé (RD) this describes a style of Champagne pioneered by Bollinger, which has been allowed to remain on its deposit for far longer than the minimum year (for non-vintage) or three (for vintage champagne). Bollinger's RD has usually spent seven to ten years on its deposit.

Récoltant-Manipulant a grower who sells wine produced exclusively from his own vines and made by him.

Remuage the daily turning of bottles to shift the deposit down to the cork, prior to *dégorgement*.

Sous-Marque a subsidiary brand name.

The Champagne Academy 12 major houses are responsible for the founding, in 1956, of the Academy which, each year, welcomes members of the trade, introducing them to the intricacies of Champagne, and awarding them a diploma. These houses were also the ones which, between 1958 and 1960, fought a case against the British Costa Brava Wine Company, preventing it from selling Perelada, a Spanish sparkling wine, as 'Champagne' in Britain.

The Current Grandes Marques

Ayala	Montebello
Billecart-Salmon	Mumm
Bollinger	Joseph Perrier
Canard-Duchêne	Laurent Perrier
Deutz & Geldermann	Perrier-Jouët
Charles Heidsieck Heidsieck	Pol Roger
Dry Monopole	Pommery & Greno
Henriot	Prieur
Krug	Louis Roederer
Lanson	Ruinart
Masse	Salon
Mercier	Taittinger/Irroy
Möet & Chandon	Veuve Clicquot

Eight good, less well-known Champagne houses

Albert Le Brun	Gosset
Joseph Perrier	F. Bonnet
Théopile Roederer	Bruno Prillard
Alfred Gratien	Secondé Prevoteau (Ambonnay)

Four good inexpensive Champagne houses

Lambert	Boizel	Duval Leroy	Massé

Good rosé Champagne houses

Veuve Clicquot	Besserat de Bellefon
Lanson	Bollinger
Piper Heidsieck	Perrier-Jouët
Louis Roederer	Philipponnet
Krug	Pol Roger
Laurent Perrier	

The Champagne Label

Every champagne label has, by law, to bear a code number allotted by the Comité Interprofessionel des Vins de Champagne. The number will permit the curious (and persistent) to trace any Champagne, whatever its name, back to its original producer. More simply, the letters prefixing the number reveal whether the wine was made by a grower, a co-op or a merchant, and whether or not the name is a sous-marque.

C.M. – A registered brand name used by a cooperative.

M.A. – A subsidiary brand name used by a Champagne house for one of its own wines, or a name used by a company on the label of wine produced by a grower or another *négociant*.

N.M. – The registered name of a wine produced by a single champagne house. (This is what you will find on the labels of all the Grandes Marques).

R.M. – The registered name of an individual winegrower which appears on the labels of wine he has produced himself.

Other label descriptions

Vintage Non-vintage Champagne is a blend of wines of different years. Vintage Champagne, on the other hand, has to be made of at least 80 per cent of wine of a designated, high-quality, year. Vintage champagnes are always Brut.

Cuvées de Prestige: Moët & Chandon were, with Dom Pérignon, the first to produce a 'top-of-the-range' Champagne. Others followed.

Bottle Sizes

Split		20.0 *cl*	6.5 *fl.oz.*
Pint		40.0 *cl*	13.0 *fl.oz.*
Bottle		75.0 *cl*	24.5 *fl.oz.*
Magnum	2 bottles	1.6 *l*	52.0 *fl.oz.*
Jereboam	4 bottles	3.2 *l*	104.0 *fl.oz.*
Rehoboam	6 bottles	4.8 *l*	156.0 *fl.oz.*
Methuselah/em	8 bottles	6.4 *l*	207.0 *fl.oz.*
Salmanazar	12 bottles	9.6 *l*	312.0 *fl.oz.*
Balthasar	16 bottles	12.8 *l*	416.0 *fl.oz.*
Nebuchadnezzar	20 bottles	16.0 *l*	520.0 *fl.oz.*

Sweetness

Almost all Champagne is sweetened, to a certain extent, but the labelling descriptions are confusing: 'Extra-Dry' is not really dry at all. The following list should make everything a little clearer.

French Name	English Name	Percentage of Sweetness	
Brut Zéro	Brut Zero	0%	(very popular amongst
Brut Intégral	Brut Integral		food and fitness faddists
Brut Sauvage	Brut Sauvage		in Paris and the USA)
Brut	Brut	1–2%	
Extra-Sec	Extra Dry	2–2.5%	
Sec	Dry	2.5–4%	
Demi-Sec	Semi-Dry	4–6%	
Doux	Sweet	over 6%	(very rare these days)

The Champagne Regions

There are four winegrowing regions:

La Côte des Blancs (as its name would imply, planted in Chardonnay)
La Montagne de Reims
La Vallée de la Marne and
l'Aube (least important in terms of quality)

In each region, villages have been denoted as growing grapes of a certain quality. These quality designations will determine the prices paid by the houses when they are buying for their blends.

The original quality designations were

COTE DES BLANCS

Catégorie Hors-Classe	Première Catégorie	Deuxième Catégorie
Avize	Le Mesnil-sur-Oger	Bergères-les-Vertus
Cramant	Oger	Chouilly
	Oiry	Vertus

LA MONTAGNE DE REIMS (Vins de la Montagne)

Ambonnay	Tauxières	Chigney-les-Roses
Beaumont-sur-Vesle	Verzy	Ludes
Bouzy		Rilly-La-Montagne
Louvois		Trépail
Mailly		Vaudemanges
Sillery		Villers-Allerand
Verzenay		Villers-Marmery

VALLÉE DE LA MARNE Vins de la Rivière)

Ay	Dizy	Avenay
	Mareuil-sur-Ay	Bisseuil
		Champillon
		Cumières
		Hautvillers
		Mutigny

Now the list of villages has been simplified into 12 Grands Crus (categorized as producing grapes of 100 per cent quality), 41 Premiers Crus (categorized at 90–99 per cent) and the rest, where the quality ranges from 77–89 per cent.

Avize	Mailly
Cramant	Puisieul
Ambonnay	Sillery
Ay	Tours-sur-Marne
Bouzy	Verzenay
Louvois	Vesle

Eastern France

JURA
The region
Right in the right hand side of the map of France, the Jura looks as if someone has tucked it out of the way. It does however, apart from an excellent rose (often sold as Vin Gris), have several wines which are quite unique.

The wines
ARBOIS
Principal Appellation for the region. Reds and whites tend to be less interesting than rosés.

MACVIN
An aperitif, likened to white port.

VIN JAUNE
Like good old Fino sherry, and benefiting from the same 'Flor'-induced effect.

VIN DE PAILLE
Rich dessert wine made from grapes which have been hung from the roof to ripen during the winter.

The Grapes
Poulsard
Trousseau
Pinot Noir

Chardonnay (also known as Gamay Blanc and Melon d'Arbois)
Savagnin

Recommended producers

Arbois Cooperative	l'Etoile
Ch. d'Arlay	Chateau Gréa
Château-Chalon & Cotes du	Henri Maire
Jura Coopérative	Désiré Pet & Fils
Caves Jean Bourdy	Domaine de la Pinte
Hubert Clavelin	Poligny, Caveau des Jacobins

Pupillon	Jacques Tissot
J. Reverchon & Fils	Vandelle Père & Fils

SAVOIE
Situated almost on the banks of Lake Geneva, and 'within easy reach' of the ski-slopes, Savoie produces pleasant white wines of some character, some fresh Gamay reds and an excellent sparkling wine, made by Varichon & Clerc. Wines are known by their village, or the grape from which they are made – or both.

The grapes:

Bergeron	Jaquère
Chasselas	Mondeuse
Roussette (also known as Altesse)	Gamay
Molette	Pinot Noir

The villages

*Abymes	Marestel
*Apremont	Marignan
Ayze	Marin
*Chignin	Monterminod
Chignin-Bergeron	Monthoux
Chautagne	*Montmelian
*Crepy	Ripaille
Cruet	*Seyssel
Frangy	

Recommended producers

Pierre Boniface	
Canelli-Suchet	
*Cave Coopérative de Chautagne	
*Cave Coopérative 'Le Vigneron Savoyard'	
*Cave Coopérative des Ventes des Vins Fins	
Château de Monterminod	*L. Mercier & Fils
Château de Ripaille	Dom Million-Rousseau
Claude Delalex	Dom Mollex
Marcel Fert	J, Neyroud & Fils
Dom Fichard	Jean-Claude Perret
J-F Girard-Madoux	J. Perrier & Fils
H. Jeandet	Dom Quenard
*Lucien Magnin	*Varichon & Clerc

LOIRE

IF full bodied red wines are what you want, look elsewhere. Everything else is available aplenty here: dry and semi-sweet whites, fresh, light, fruity reds, dry Méthode Champenoise sparklers, rosé, and even the occasional honeyed dessert wine.

Perhaps some of them are not really world-beaters, they're seldom unpalatable either. Taking it from the top, there are the bitingly crisp Sauvignons of Pouilly Blanc Fumé, the delicate raspberry'd Pinot Noir of Sancerre Rouge, and the Cabernet Franc of Chinon, the usually reliable sparkling Saumurs and the delicious sweet old Savennières, Quart de Chaumes and Vouvray. Better known than all of these, and perhaps consequently less reliably good, are Muscadet, Sancerre and Anjou Rosé.

Anjou rosé is sweet, pink and very undemanding, try Cabernet d'Anjou instead, or even the dry Rosé de la Loire, if you can find a bottle. One bottle you will find without too much difficulty is pink Sancerre. It is a very pleasant wine indeed; unfortunately like its red brother, it is usually overpriced. Bourgueil is better value than both.

White Sancerre is usually billed as the epitome of the Sauvignon, the wine to drink with oysters if you are not going to have Chablis. Sadly, all too often, like Chablis, its tangy edge seems to have been dulled by warm vintages and the desire to make a more 'commercial' product. As the wine marketeers say, people talk dry and drink sweet. Muscadet has suffered in the same way: its bone dry flavour is frequently as absent as the yeasty richness of its 'sur lie' bottling. Like Beaujolais, its red counterpart, Muscadet is often a shadow of its characterful self. As for Vouvray, in its semi-sweet guise, the least said the better – it is the Chenin Blanc at its most typically tedious.

But do not despair, help is on its way, in the form of the Touraine Sauvignon and the prettily named Vin de Pays du Jardin de la France, both of which are inexpensive, unambitious, and crisply delicious.

Bourgueil List

The longest-lived Loire red wine, that needs the warmer summers like 1976 and 1983 to show its true depth of raspberry-style fruit and tannin. Otherwise can be drunk young, in much the same way as Chinon. Good rosé is also made from the Cabernet Franc grape principally.

Audebert et Fils
Audebert, Georges. Domaine du Grand Clos
Billet, Jean-Yves
Boucard, Moise. Domaine de la Chanteleuserie
Bureau, Claud. Château d'Ingrandes
Caslot-Galbrun
Caslot-Jamet, Domaine de la Chevalerie
Delavente, Maurice
Druet, Pierre-Jacques
Fleury, Roland
GAEC de la Dime. Clos de l'Abbaye
Galteau, Raphael et Fils
Gambier, Jean. Domaine des Galluches
Gambier, Paul. Domaine des Ouches
Girault, Roland. Domaine de la Gardière
Grégoire, Pierre. Domaine du Geslets
Lamé-Delille-Boucard
Maître, P et Viémont R. Domaine des Raguenières
Meunier, G et M. Clos St André
Morin, Jacques. Clos Nouveau
Mureau, Marc
Nau, Jean
Renou, Georges
Richer, J-L
Rochereau Frères
Vincent-Chezé

Chinon List

Red wines that drink well when young, but which in the hotter summers can age for 8 to 10 years. Cabernet Franc based, they have a little less depth than the Bourgueils. Some rosé and interesting whites are also produced.

Aimé-Boucher
Allouin, Robert
Angélliaume, Gérard
Angélliaume, Léonce
Baudry, Jean. Domaine de la Perrière
Blandin, Père et Fils
de Bonnaventure, Jacques. Château de Coulaine
Bonnet, Georges. Château du Pin
Chauveau, G et D. Domaine de Pallus-Beauséjour
Couly, René. Clos de l'Echo
Couly-Dutheil SCA
Delalande J-C. Domaine de la Semellerie
Desbourdes, Raymond
Donabella, Annie. Domaine de Roncé
Dozon, Père et Fils. Close du Saut au Loup
Farget, Georges. Clos de la Lysardière

Farou, Louis. Clos du Parc de St Louans
Ferrand, Gatien. Château de Ligré
Fontaine, Michel. Domaine de l'Abbaye
Gasné, Michel. Domaine de la Tranchée
Gosset, Albert. Château de la Grille
Gouron, René et Fils
Guertin, Paul. Clos du Martinet
Haerty, Francis
Hérault, Bernard
Joguet, Charles
Jalladeau, Rémy
Jamet, Père et Fils
Lemaire, Guy
Loiseau, Mme Hélène et Fils
Loiseau, Yves. Domaine du Colombier
Manzagol, Pierre. Domaine de la Noblaie
Moreau, Yves. Domaine de la Bellonière
Olek, J-F. Domaine de la Chapellerie
Page, André
Plouzeau, et Fils. Domaine de la Garrelière
Raffault, Jean-Maurice
Raffault, Olga
Raffault, Raymond. Domaine du Raifault
Sourdais, Serge et Fils
Spelty, Mme Jean et Fils

Coteaux du Layon List

Underestimated and slow-developing wines made from the Chenin Blanc grape in the area south of Angers. The coteaux du Layon Villages, e.g. Rablay and Rochefort, are excellent value for money and can live for 20 years. The Quarts de Chaume and Bonnezeaux wines have a shade more depth but are several shades more expensive.

Beaulieu-sur-Layon

Les Caves de la Loire
Chéné, J-P. Domaine d'Ambinos
GAEC Bertrand
Maingot, Jules
Menard, René
Papin, C. Domaine de Pierre Bise

Faye d'Anjou

Leblanc, Jean-Claude
Leblanc, Philippe. Domaine des Saulaies
Leduc, Pierre. Château de Montbenault

Rablay-sur-Layon

Bidet, Alfred. Coteau de la Magdelaine
Dulong, Jean-Marie
GAEC Lecointre. Caves de la Pierre Blanche
Robin, Mme. Château de la Roche

Rochefort-sur-Loire

Baumard, Jean. Domaine des Baumard
Gaschet, J et A. Domaine des Martereaux
Grosset-Château, Raymond
Merlet-Dénéchau
Mingot, C. Clos du Moulin Sainte-Catherine
Papiau, A. Domaine de Pont Perrault
Sorin, André. Domaine de la Motte
Van der Hecht, Philippe. Château de Piegue

St Aubin-de-Luigné

Banchereau GAEC Paul

Davy, André. Domaine de la Roche Moreau
Jamain Frères. Domaine de Saulaie
Lequeux, Eugène

St Lambert-du-Lattay

Aubert Frères. Domaine des Hardières
Cailleau, Francis. Domaine du Sauveroy
Cailleau, GAEC Gérard. La Ducquerie
Morin, Albert. Domaine de la Grand Chauvière
Moron, Fernand. Domaine des Maurières
Petiteau, Paul. Celliers des Bonnes Blanches
Ogereau Fils SCA. Domaine de la Pierre Blanche

Chaume

Doucet, Michel. Château de la Guimonière
Jaudeau, D. Château de la Roulerie
Lalanne, Jacques. Château de Bellerive
Renou, Joseph
Rochais, H. Château de Plaisance
Tijou, Jean-Paul. Château de Bellevue
Tijou, Pierre-Yves. Domaine de la Soucherie

Bonnezeaux

Boivin, Jacques. Château de Fesles
Goizil, Vincent. Domaine du Petit-Val
Renou, René. Domaine de la Croix-de-Mission

Quarts-de-Chaume

Baumard, Jean
Chevalier-Lequeux, Yves
Chiron, Vve Jean-Jacques
Davy, André. Domaine de la Roche Moreau
Laffourcade, Mme Simone. Château de l'Echarderie
Lalanne, Jacques. Château Bellerive
Moron, Fernand
Renou, Joseph
Thomas, Mme

Various Communes

Douet, Louis et Jean. Château des Rochettes
Dhommé, Père et Fils
SCV Château de Breuil
Delhumeau. Domaine de Brizé
Chevalier-Dubray, Charlotte
Les Vins Touchais

Montlouis List

Chenin Blanc based white wines from near Tours. The dry wines start life with rasping acidity and need 5 or 6 years to soften. Sparkling and sweet versions are also made, being less wholesome than their more distinguished neighbour Vouvray (qv).

Berger Frères
Chevalier, Roger
Dardeau, René-Pierre
Délétang Père et Fils
Fradin, Georges
Gerbault, Gilles
Habert, Jean-Paul
Leblois, Jean-Pierre

Levasseur, Claude
Lucas, Roger
Martin, Christian
Martin-Lutun, André
Moyer, Dominique
Petibun, Jacky
Régnard, René
Roy-Leblois
Simier, James
Trouvé, Jean-Pierre

Muscadet List

Searchingly dry white wine made from Melon de Bourgogne grape in the area south and east of Nantes, near the mouth of the Loire. Excellent to drink before it is two years old with fresh

---

seafood. Smaller domaines at higher prices represent best value for money, since some very shoddy cheap Muscadet turns up in Britain.

Basse Goulaine

Chéreau, Bernard fils. Domaine du Bois Bruley

La Chapelle-Basse-Mer

de Berthenais, Serge
de Bascher, Mme Antony. Château de la Berrière
Martin-Jarry. Château de la Bigotière
Petard, Antoine. La Saulzaie

La Chapelle-Heulin

Bahuaud, Donatien. Château de la Cassemichère
Baron, Joseph
Beauquin, Jean
Bonneau. Château du Poyet
Bonnet, Félix
Bossard, Gilbert
Charpentier, Roger
Doucet, Jean-Paul
Dugast, Maurice
Fleurance, Benjamin et Fils. Domaine des Gautronnières

Clisson

Forget, Jean
Guérin, Georges
Héraud, Camille et Marcel
Herbreteau, Michel
Lesimple

Gorges

Aulanier, Jean. Château de L'Oiselinière
Barré Frères
Blanchard, Maurice et Claude
Bonhomme, Auguste. Domaine du Banchereau
Hervieau, Jean-Louis. Domaine du Pied de Garde

Haute-Goulaine

Babin, Joseph
Bureau, Félix
Gauthier, Alexandre
Gautier-Audas
de Goulaine, Marquis. Château de Goulaine

La Haye Fouassière

Bideau, Emile
Bonneteau-Guesselin
Brosseau, Louis
Brosseau, Robert. Domaine des Mortiers-Gobin
Landron, Julien et Pierre. Domaine de la Louvetrie
Nogue, Louis. Château des Gillières

Roy, Paul
de Saint-Sauveur, Mme. Château de Rochefort

Le Landreau

Audoin, Père et Fils
Bertin, Marcel
Bossard, Robert
Luneau, Pierre
Pellerin, André
Potineau, Jean

Maisdon-sur-Sèvre

Batard, André
Branger, Guy
de Camiran, Comte Michel. La Bidière
Cormerais, Roland
Dugast, Marcel
Poiron, Henri. Domaine des Quatre Routes

Monnières

Chereau, Etienne
Chereau, Henri
Dugast, R. Domaine des Moulins
Ménard-Gaborit, André
Puget, H. Château La Court des Mortiers

Mouzillon

Chiron, Michel. Clos des Roches Gaudinières
Guilbaud Frères
Hardy, Edmond. Domaine de la Grange
Martin, Marcel et Suzanne

Le Pallet

Bahuaud. J. Domaine de Poissonais
Durance, Louis
Lusseaud, Pierre. Château de la Galissonière
Potier, Joseph. Domaine de la Chantepie
Sautejeau, Marcel. Domaine de L'Hyvernière

Saint-Fiacre

Beauzombe
Bossis et Fils. Château de la Cantrie
Chéreau-Carré, Mme. Château de Chasseloir
Dabin, Jean. Domaine de Gras-Moutons
Futeuil Frères
Gadais Frères
Martin, Emile
Métaireau, Louis. Le Grand Mouton
Rigaud, Joseph
Thébaud, Gabriel. Domaine de la Hautière

Vallet

Aubert Frères
Aubron, Jean
Bahuaud, Henri
Beauquin, Loic
Boullault Père et Fils. Domaine des Dorices
Couillaud, M et F. Château de la Ragotière
Douillard, J et J-P. Domaine du Grand Ferré
Drouet Frères
Guillot, Victor
Hallereau, Joseph
Laure, Philippe
Luneau, Germain. Clos des Bois Gautier
Malestroit, Comte Jean. Château la Noë
Petiteau, Bernard. Domaine des Montys
Poiron, Joseph
Sauvion. Château du Cléray

Vertou

Bachelier, André
Formon, Joseph. Domaine de la Denillère
Luneau, Louis

Pouilly Fumé List

The most distinguished, classy Loire dry white wine, made from the Sauvignon grape grown north west of Nevers. Good firm gooseberry-lemon flavours which develop well after two or three years.

Bailly, Père et Fils
Baudin, Guy
Blondelet, Gaston
Boucher, Aimé
Cave Co-operative Les Moulins-à-Vent
Châtelain, Jean-Claude. Domaine de St Laurent l'Abbaye
Chollet, Roland
Crochet, Fernand
Dagueneau, Didier

Dagueneau, J.-C. Domaine des Berthiers
Denis, Père et Fils
de Ladoucette, Patrick. Château de Nozet
Figeat, Paul
Gaudry, Domaine
Gitton, Père et Fils
Guyot, Georges
Guyot, Jean-Claude
Landrat & Guyollot
Langoux, Marcel
Masson-Blondelet, J-M
Michot, René et Fils
Pesson, Robert. Domaine des Cassier
Redde, Michel et Fils. La Moynerie
Renaud-Bossuat. La Calvaire
Saget, G. Château de la Roche
Seguin, Père et Fils
Tracy, Château de

St Nicolas de Bourgueil List

Lighter wines, red and rosé, than Bourgueil, said to be so because the soil in this neighbouring vineyard has more sand. Emphasis on a bright, young fruity taste, but they are more expensive than some local reds of similar style – e.g. Sauvier Champigny.

Amirault, Claude et Thierry. Clos des Quarterons
Beaufils, Denis
Beaufils, Jean-Pierre
Bruneau, A et M
Brunhes, Jean
Cognard-Taluau, Max
David, Lucien
Delanoue, Jean
Godefroy, Gérard. Domaine des Croix
Jamet, Anselme. Clos Le Vigneau
Jamet, Pierre et Fils. Domaine du Fondis

Mabileau, Jacques
Mabileau, Jean-Claude
Mabileau, Jean-Paul. Domaine du Bourg
Mabileau-Coulom, Yves
Moreau, Daniel
Meslet, Philippe
Morin, Abel et Claude
Morisseau, James. Domaine de la Caillardière
Olivier, Bernard
Ory, Claude
Taluau, Joel

Sancerre List

Sauvignon-based dry white wine best drunk young when its racy, gooseberry-style fruit can be best appreciated. More zip, less elegance and depth of flavour, than neighbour Pouilly Fumé. Reasonable rosé and occasionally decent light red, both made from the Burgundian Pinot Noir grape.

Bué

Bailly, Sylvain et Fils
Bailly-Reverdy, Bernard et Fils
Balland, Chapuis, Joseph
Balland, Bernard et Fils
Clos de la Poussie
Crochet, Lucien
Girault, Pierre
Merlin, Thierry
Millet, Gérard
Picard, Lucien
Roger, Jean-Max

Chavignol

Bourgeois, Henri et Fils
Brochard et ses Fils
Cotat, Francis et Paul
Delaporte, Jean
Delaporte, Vincent
Denis, Père et Fils
Thomas, Claude

Sancerre

Chevreau, Robert
La Cave des Vins de Sancerre
Fouassier, Père et Fils
Gitton, Père et Fils
Marnier-Lapostolle
Mellot, Alphonse
Millériaux, Paul
Vacheron, Jean

Verdigny-en-Sancerre

Archambault, Pierre
Dezat, André et Fils
Fournier, Père et Fils
Fleuriet, Michel et Jacques

Girard, Michel
Neveu, Roger
Prieur, Paul et Fils
Reverdy, Bernard
Reverdy, Jean et Fils
Riffault, Pierre et Etienne
Vatan, Jean et André

Various Communes

de Benoist, Philippe. Château du Nozay
Dezat, Pierre et Alain. Maimbray
Lauverjat-Roblin et Fils. Sury-en-Vaux
Natter, Henry. Montigny
Raimbault-Pineau, Maurice. Sury-en-Vaux
Roblin, Georges et Fils. Sury-en-Vaux
Saget, Château de Thauvenay

Saumur List

Chiefly known for its sparkling white wines made from the Chenin Blanc grape. They are decent value for money, especially as a cut-rate Champagne substitute. Some good dry white wines are emerging, where the Chenin grape is softened by the addition of the Chardonnay from Burgundy.

Ackerman-Laurance, Ets
Amiot, Veuve
Aupy, Henri. Close de l'Abbaye
Besombes, Albert
Biguet, Marcel. Le-Puy-Notre-Dame
Bouvet-Ladubay
Cave Co-operative des Vignerons de Saumur. St-Cyr-en-Bourg
Collé, Gilles. Caves du Château de Parnay
Compagnie Française des Grands Vins
Effray, Pierre. Le-Puy-Notre-Dame
Gratien, Meyer, Seydoux et Cie
Guibert, Jean. Le Petit-Puy
Langlois-Château SA
Mainfray, Sylvain. Château d'Aubigné
Millerand, Mme. Distré
Moc-Baril, SA
de Neuville
Pérols, Gabriel. Le Coudray-Macouard
Reclu, Jean-Marie. Montreuil-Bellay

Rémy-Pannier, SA
de Thuy, Mme. Château de Montreuil-Bellay

Saumur Champigny List

Good, lightweight red wines made from Cabernet Franc (mostly) and Cabernet Sauvignon. Emphasis is on fruit and they are excellent to drink in the first three or four years. Good value for money.

Bourdin, J-C
Charuau, J-P. Domaine du Val Brun
Chevallier, Robert. Château de Villeneuve
Chevallier, Yves
Collée, Gilles
Daheuiller, Claude. Les Varinelles
Dézé, Gilbert
Drouineau, Gérard
Duveau, Denis. Domaines Des Roches Neuves
Filliatreau, Paul
Foulon, Gérard
Fourrier, André
Guillaud-Thevent. Clos de la Seignère
Hardouin, Maurice
Hospices de Saumur. Clos Cristal
Joseph, Robert. Domaine du Bourg Neuf
Mary-Coutant, Jean
Millon, André et Fils
Misandeau, Jean-Christophe
Neau, Robert et Régis. Domaine de Nerleux
Pasquier, J-P et J. Le Prieuré d'Aunis
Pisani-Ferry, Edouard. Château de Targé
Ratron Frères. Clos des Cordeliers
Rébeilleau, A et J-P. Domaine des Raynières
Rouiller, Alain. Domaine de la Perruche
Sanzay, Alain
Sanzay-Legrand
de Tigny, Bernard. Château de Chaintres
Vatan, Pascal. Domaine du Hureau

Savennières List

Vigorously dry, though occasionally slightly sweeter,

Chenin Blanc produced on the banks of the Loire. The Coulée-de-Serrant an exclusive domaine and the appellation's best, takes longer to mature; Savenniéres-Roches-Aux-Moines is another individual appellation within the appellation.

Baumard, Jean. Clos du Papillon
Bizard, A. Château d'Epiré
Jessey, Mme. Domaine du Closel
Joly, Nicolas. Clos de la Bergerie, Clos de La Coulée de Serrant
SCI de la Cour au Domaine de la Roche aux Moines. La Roche aux Moines
Plessis, André
Roussier, François. Clos de Coulaire
Soulez, Yves. Château de Chamboreau, Domaine de la Bizolière

Vouvray List

The leading Loire sparkling wine noted for its ageing powers: the Chenin grape allows a life of eight to ten years, and more for the still wines, especially the sweet ones. Acidity is high when young, so waiting is almost compulsory.

Allias, Daniel. La Caillerie
Audebert, Maurice. La Chateria
Besnard, Claude. Rochecorbon
Brédif, Marc. Rochecorbon
Bertrand, Jean. Rochecorbon
Cave Co-operative La Vallée Coquette
Champion, Gilles. Vernou-sur-Brenne
Couamais, Jean-Paul. Vernou-sur-Brenne
Courson, Bernard
Freslier, André
Hallay, Jacques. Vernou-sur-Brenne
Huet, Gaston. Domaine du Haut-Lieu
Mallein Héritiers. Domaine des Barguins
Marpault, Robert. Reugny
Métivier, Claude
Monmousseau, J-M SA. Château Gaudrelle
Montcontour, Château de
Poniatowski, Prince. Le Clos Baudoin, Clos de la Meslerie

Sauger, René, et Chevreau, Jacques
Vaudenuits, Château de

Vicard, Jacques. Rochecorbon
Vigneau et Chevrea. Chançay

RHONE

THE Grenache and Syrah grapes perform a fine double act in the Rhône, ably assisted by the Cinsault and a number of other less familiar names. The wine can vary between the easy-to-drink and undemanding Côtes du Rhône to the outrageously spicy, smoky, leathery, gamey (all right, come up with your own definitive adjective for the Syrah) wines of Hermitage and Côte-Rôtie.

Styles are even more diverse than ever now that a large number of producers have begun to use Macération Carbonique; it is increasingly difficult to say exactly what many of these wines really ought to taste like. What most of them do taste is good.

The Grape List

Northern
Syrah
Roussanne
Marsanne
Viognier

Southern
Grenache Noir
Syrah
Mourvèdre
Cinsault
Counoise
Vaccarèse
Terret Noir
Muscardin
Carignan
Clairette
Bourboulenc
Grenache Blanc
Rousanne
Picpoul
Picardan
Terret Blanc
Ugni Blanc

Rhône Négociants

Bellicard
Le Cellier des Dauphins
David et Foillard
A. Ogier et Fils
Société Nouvelle des Vins Fins Salavert
Abbaye de Bouchet
Barbier, Léon et Fils
Boissy et Delaygue
Brotte, Jean-Pierre
Du Peloux et Cie
Garnier, Camille
Malbec, Eugène
Meffre, Ets Gabriel
Revol, Léon
Delas Frères
Ets E. Guigal
Paul Jaboulet Aîné

Chapoutier et Cie
Père Anselme
Vidal-Fleury SA
Caves St-Pierre
Caves Eugène Bessac
Bérard Père et Fils

Note: some of these *négociants* are also vineyard owners – eg Guigal, Jaboulet, Delas, Bérard, Caves St-Pierre, Vidal-Fleury, Chapoutier, Meffre.

The Wine Regions

BEAUMES DE VENISE

Sweet wine made from the Muscat grape that is now very fashionable in Britain. Drunk in France as an apéritif, in Britain as a pudding wine. Strong grapey aromas, sometimes almonds are found in the flavour. Drink well chilled.

Leading Growers at Beaumes-de-Venise
Leydier, Bernard. Domaine Durban
Castaud-Maurin. Domaine des Bernardins
Co-opérative Intercommunale des Vins et Muscats
Nativelle, Yves. Domaine de Coyeux
Rey, Guy. Domaine St-Sauveur
Meffre, Jean-Paul. Château des Applanats. No VDN
Domaine de Cassan No VDN

CHÂTEAU GRILLET

Used to be France's smallest Appellation, and a wine that has been exported to England for over two centuries. Present owner has enlarged area under vines and increased average production. Very expensive white wine, worth trying as a curiosity rather than for its own merits.

Recommended producers

Neryret-Gachet. Château Grillet

CHATEAUNEUF-DU-PAPE

The major southern Rhône red wine, notable for a variety of fruit flavours and a bouquet that has herbs, spices and even cigar connotations. Full wine, winter drinking and make sure you're seated with food beside you. Emerging white wines, that drink well when young and fresh.

1 to 6 Years

Domaine de Beaurenard
Domaine de Nalys
Domaine de la Solitude
Domaine du Vieux Lazaret
Château de la Font du Loup
Clos de l'Oratoire des Papes
Domaine de Mont-Redon
Domaine Durieu

5 to 12 Years

Château Fortia
Domaine du Vieux Télégraphe
Les Cailloux
Les Clefs d'Or
Chante-Perdrix
Domaine Font-de-Michelle
Domaine de Cabrières
Le Clos des Papes
Château de la Gardine
Château des Fines Roches
Domaine de la Tour St Michel
Domaine du Grand Tinel
Domaine de Montpertuis
Château de Vaudieu
Domaine des Sénéchaux
Château Rayas
Domaine Roger Sabon
Domaine des Chanssaud
Domaine Chante-Cigale
Domaine de la Terre Ferme
Domaine du Haut des Terres
  Blanches
Domaine Lucien Barrot
Le Vieux Donjon
La Cuvée des Sommeliers
Les Cabanes
Père Anselme
La Cuvée du Vatican

8 to 20 Years

Domaine de Beaucastel
Château La Nerte
Clos du Mont-Olivet
Le Bosquet des Papes

CONDRIEU

Excellent, old-fashioned white wine made from the rarely found Viognier grape. Develops great peach and pear flavours within three odd years. Sit down wine, best with fish dishes, and just the job for a treat.

Leading growers at Condrieu

Multier, Jean-Yves. Château-du-Rozay
Vernay, Georges
Dumazet, Pierre
Cuilleron, Antoine
Corompt, Pierre
David, Emile
Delas Frères
Dézormeaux, André
Jurie-des Camiers, Robert
Lagnier, Georges
Perret, Pierre
Pinchon, Jean

CORNAS

Black coloured wine made in very traditional ways from the Syrah grape. The Rhône's answer to Guinness. Needs 6 to 12 years to soften. Scarce, worth a try when a few years old, otherwise is too tannic for most drinkers.

Leading growers at Cornas

Clape, Auguste
Michel, Robert
de Barjac, Guy
Juge, Marcel
Balthazar, René
Catalon, Roger
Delas Frères
Dumien, Henri
Fumat, André
Gilles Louis
Lionnet, Jean
Maurice, Marc
Teysseire, Jean
Verset, Louis
Verset, Noël
Voge, Alain

COTE ROTIE

Fine northern Rhône red wine. Develops tremendous fruit and floral bouquet after 6 to 12 years ageing. Can be rather rustic and odd ball when made by lesser growers, majestic when made by top half dozen men.

Leading growers at Côte-Rôtie

Barge, Gilles
Barge, Pierre
Bernard, Guy
Bonnefond, Claude

Brugaud, Roger et Bernard
Chambeyron, Marius
Champet, Emile
Chapoutier, M.
Chol et Fils
Clusel, Jean
Clusel, René
Delas, Frères
Dervieux, Albert
Dervieux-Thaize
De Vallouit, L.
Drevon, André

Gentaz-Dervieux, Marius
Gérard, François
Gerin, Alfred
Guigal, E.
Jamet, Joseph
Jasmin, Georges et Robert
Minot, Henri
Remiller, Louis
Rostaing, René
Vernay, Georges
Vidal-Fleury, SA

COTES-DU-RHONE

Ardèche

Recommended producers

Goossens Rodolphe. Domaine de l'Olivet, Bourg St Andéol

Herberigs, Gilbert. Château de Rochecolombe, Bourg St Andéol

Grangaud, Alain. Domaine des Fines Grunes, Vinsas

Sabatier, Jacques. Le Plan de Lage, St Marcel

Terrasse, R. Domaine du Roure, St Marcel

Thibon, J-P. Mas de Libian, St Marcel

Drôme

Recommended producers

Bérard, Père et Fils Domaine de la Berardière

Blanc, Robert. Les Asseyras, Tulette

Bourret, Pierre. Domaine de Roquevignan

Château la Borie. Suze-la-Rousse

Cave Jaume. Vinsobres

Couston et Monnier. Domaine de la Tour Couverte

Château de l'Estagnol. Suze-la-Rousse

Estève, Jean-Pierre. Domaine du Bois Noir

Feschet, R. et Fils. Domaine du Petit Barbaras, Bouchet

Gautier, Jean. Château de Lignane

Ginies, Gilbert

Domaine A. Mazurd et Fils. Tulette

Pinet, Joseph. Domaine Chastelle

Pradelle, R. et Fils. Domaine du Jas

Roux, Mme et Fils. Domaine de la Taurelle, Mirabel-aux-Baronnies

Domaine La Serre du Prieur

Le Terroir St-Rémy

Tourtin, Mme Louis. Domaine du Gourget

Domaine des Treilles. Montbrison-sur-Lez

Trutat, Bruno. Les Davids

Domaine Ste-Marie

GARD

Recommended producers

Allauzen. Château de Valpinson, St Alexandre

Arène, Augustin. Domaine le Haut Castel, Bagnols-sur-Cèze

Arnaud, J-P. Domaine des Roches d'Arnaud, Domazan

Castay et Johannet. Domaine de Signac, Bagnols sur Cèze

Charre, Daniel. Domaine du Sarrazin, Domazan

Chaudérac, Christian. Château de Domazan, Domazan

Chinieu, Jean-Claude. Domaine de Lindas, Bagnols sur Cèze

Coste, Pierre. Domaine de Laplagnol, Pont St-Esprit

De Serésin, Père et Fils. Domaine de Bruthel, Sabran

Fabre, René. Domaine des Coccinelles, Domazan

Gallon, Serge. Mas d'Eole, Domazan

Guigue, Père et Fils. Domaine de la Rouette, Rochefort-du-Gard

Herbouze, Claude. Mas Claulian, St Alexandre

Imbert, Père et Fils. Domaine de Lascamp, Cadignac

Juls, Joel. Château du Bresquet, St Nazaire

Klein, F. Domaine de la Réméjeanne, Cadignac

Malabre-Constant. Château de Boussargues, Colombier

Meger, Lucien. Domaine des Boumianes, Domazan

Pages, Urbain. Domaine de l'Amandier, Carmes

Payan, Achille. Domaine du Cabanon, Saze

Payan, André. Domaine des Moulins, Saze

Pons, Dominique. Domaine des Cèdres, St Nazaire

Poudevigne, André. Domaine de la Crompe, Domazan

Reynaud, Louis et Fils. Domazan

Riot Frères. Domaine des Riots, St-Michel-d'Euzet

Rique, Pierre. Domaine de Roquebrune, St Alexandre

Robert, Alain et Fils. Vieux Manoir de Frigoulas, St Alexandre

Sabatier, Roger. Domaine de l'Espéran, St Alexandre

Sabot, Jean-Paul. Domaine de Cocol, Domazan

Silvestre, Pierre. Château de Farel, Comps

Simon, Francis. Domaine du Moulin du Pourpré, Sabran

Tarsac, Jacques. Domaine St-Jacques, St-Michel-d'Euzet

Valat, André. Château St-Maurice-l'Ardoise, Laudun

Verda et Fils. Domaine Cantegril-Verda, Roquemaure

VAUCLUSE
Recommended producers

Alessandrini, Vincent. Domaine Bois Lauzon, Orange

d'Arnaudy J.-P. Château de la Serre, L'Isle-sur-la-Sorgue

Autard, Paul. Domaine Autard, Courthézon

Barbaud, Jean-Paul. Domaine des Favards, Violès

Biscarrat, François. Domaine de la Guicharde, Derboux

Biscarrat, Louis. Château du Grand-Prébois, Orange

Domaine du Bois des Dames. Violès

Ch. du Bois de la Garde. Châteauneuf-du-Pape

Bouche, J-C et Dominque. Domaine du Vieux Chêne, Camaret

Boussier, Marcel et Claude. Domaine de la Chapelle, Châteauneuf-de-Gadagne

Boyer et Fils. Domaine de Bel-Air, Violès

Brun Pierre. Domaine de la Cambuse, Villedieu

Charasse, Claude et Associés. Domaine de St-Claude, Vaison-la-Romaine

Combe, Pierre. Domaine des Richards, Violès

Combe Pierre. Domaine de Tenon, Violès

Coulon, Paul et Fils. La Ferme Pisan, Rasteau

Damoy, Julien. Domaine de la Renjarde, Sérignan

Daniel Guy, Domaine La Bastide St-Vincent, Violès

Daumas, Frédéric. Domaine Ste-Apollinaire, Puyméras

Daussant, Eric. Domaine de Grand Plantier, Vedène

Domaine Deforge. Châteauneuf-de-Gadagne

Fauque, Jean-Claude. Domaine St-Pierre, Violès

Farion, Albert. Les Grands Rois, Ste-Cécile les Vignes

Faurous, Henri et Fils Domaine le Grand Retour, Trevaillan

Français-Monier. Ch. de St Estève, Uchaux

Garagnon Paul. Domaine du Gros-Pata, Vaison-la-Romaine

Gargani, R. La Fauconnière, St Romain-de-Mallegarde

Girard, Louis. Domaine de la Girardière, Rasteau

Gleize, André. Vignoble Gleize, Violès

Gonnet, Cohendy et Fils. Domaine la Berthète, Camaret

Groiller, M. Domaine de Boilauzon, Travaillan

Jaume Alain. Domaine du Grand Veneur, Orange

Julien et Fils. Domaine de l'Aigaillons, Suzette

Latour, Edmond. Domaine de l'Espigouette, Jonquières

Lobreau, Jean-Marie. Plan Dei, Trevaillan

Martin, Hélène et Fils. Domaine de Grangeneuve, Jonquières

Martin, Jules et ses Fils. Domaine Martin, Travaillan

Maurizot, Charles. Domaine les Roures du Plan de Dieu, Travaillan

Meffre Gérard. Château la Courançonne, Violès

Domaine la Meynarde. Travaillan

Mitan, Frédéric. Domaine Mitan, Vedène

Nativelle, J-L. Ch. Malijay, Jonquières

Nicolas, Jean. Domaine St Michel, Uchaux

Perrin, Pierre. Coudoulet, Courthézon

Reynaud, Jacques. Ch. de Fonsalette, Lagarde-Paréol

Ch. de Ruth. Ste-Cécile-les-Vignes

Ryckwaert, M. Ch. de Grand Moulas, Mornas

Sahuc, Abel. Domaine de la Grand' Ribe, Ste Cécile-les-Vignes

Sanchez et Gauchet, Ch. de Gourdon, Bollène

Saurel, S. Domaine de la Combe Dieu, La Baumette

Serguier, Yves et Fils. Clos Simian, Uchaux

COTES DU RHONE VILLAGES
More gutsy, full bodied and longer lived red wines than the standard Côtes du Rhône. 17 Villages, the leading ones like Cairanne, Vaqueyras, Séguret and St Gervais make wines that should be drunk when 3 to 6 years old.

Recommended producers

Alary et ses Fils. L'Oratoire St Martin, Cairanne

Archimbaud-Vache. Clos des Cazaux, Vacqueyras

Arène, Luc. Domaine de la Marsane, Sablet

Arnoux et Fils. Le Vieux Clocher, Vacqueyras

Aubert. Max. Domaine de la Présidente, Cairanne

Beaumet, Père et Fils. Domaine de St-Andéol, Cairanne

Bernard, Albert et Lucien. Domaine de la Garrigue, Vacqueyras

Bernard, René. Sablet

Bonnefoy. Notre Dame de Vieille, Valréas

Brusset, André et Fils. Domaine des Travers, Cairanne

Bouchard, N. Domaine de la Bicarelle, Vinsobres

Bouchard, Romain. Le Val des Rois, Valréas

Domaine de Cassan. Beaumes-de-Venise

SCA Le Clos de Caveau. Vaqueyras

Chamfort, Louis et Fils. Sablet

Chassagne, F et Fils. Sablet

Chastan, A et Fils. Domaine de la Jaufrette, Vacqueyras

Chastan, Fernand. Les Garrigues, Séguret

Chauvin Frères. Domaine le Souverain, Sablet

Cave des Vignerons de Chusclan. Chusclan

Domaine de la Colline St Jean. Vacqueyras

La Cave des Coteaux de Cairanne. Cairanne

Cave des Coteaux de St Maurice-sur-Eygues, St Maurice-sur-Eygues

Combe, Roger et Fils. Domaine La Fourmone, Vacqueyras

Domaine de Costechaude. Visan

Davin, Henri. Domaine de la Prévosse, Valréas

Depèyre Frères. Clos du Père Clément, Visan

Durma, Fernand. Domaine St Vincent, Vinsobres

Dusser-Beraud, Edouard. Ch. des Roques, Vacqueyras

Dusserre-Audibert, Jean. Domaine de Montvac, Vacqueyras

Estournel, Rémy. Laudun

Ezingeard. Domaine les Aussellons, Vinsobres

Faraud, J.-P. Domaine du Pont du Rieu, Vacqueyras

Cave Co-opérative La Gaillarde. Valréas

Grangeon, M et Fils. Domaine du Parandou, Sablet

Cave Co-opérative de St Gervais. St Gervais

Gras, André. Domaine de St-Chetin, Valréas

Grignan, Raoul. Domaine du Grand-Jas, Cairanne

Co-opérative Intercommunale. Beaumes-de-Venise

Jullian-Gap. Domaine d'Aeria, Cairanne

Laget-Roux. Domaine de la Cantharide, Visan

Lambert, Florimond. Roaix

Lambert Frères. Domaine des Lambertins, Vacqueyras

Latour, Nadine. Domaine de Cabasse, Séguret

Liautaud, Jean. Domaine du Sommier, Séguret

Marseille, Pierre. Domaine de Chantegut, Vacqueyras

Mayre, Rémy. Le Mousquetaire, Vacqueyras

Meffre, Gérard. La Fiole du Chevalier d'Elbène, Séguret

Meffre, Jean-Paul. Ch. des Applanats, Beaumes-de-Venise

de Menthon, Etienne. Ch. Redortier Beaumes-de-Venise

Caves Co-opérative d'Orsan. Chusclan

Pascal Frères. Vacqueyras

Domaine St-Pierre. Laudun

Pierrefeu, Gérard et Fils. Domaine Le Plaisir, Cairanne

Pelaquié, Luc et Emmanuel. Laudun

La Cave du Prieuré Vins. Vinsobres

Union des Producteurs de St Pantaléon-les-Vignes et Rousset-les-Vignes. St Pantaléon-les-Vignes

Cave des Quatre Chemins 'Le Serre de Bernon'. Laudun

Rabasse-Charavin. Les Coteaux St Martin, Cairanne

Ricard, Jean. Vacqueyras

Ricard Père et Fils. Domaine du Couroulou, Vacqueyras

Richaud, Marcel. Le Bon Clos, Cairanne

Cave Co-opérative de Roaix-Séguret. Séguret

Cave Co-opérative Vinicole de Rochegude. Rochegude

Roumanille, Paul. Sablet

Rousseau, Alexis. Laudun

Roussin. Léo. Domaine de la Fuzière, Valréas

Roux, Charles et Fils. Ch. du Trignon, Sablet

Sayn, André. Cours de la Recluse, Valréas

Sinard, René. Domaine des Grands-Devers, Valréas

Steinmaier, Guy et Fils. Domaine Ste-Anne, St Gervais

Cave des Vignerons 'Le Troubadour'. Vacqueyras

Vallot, François. Domaine du Coriançon, Vinsobres

Vallot, Xavier. Domaine des Escoulaires, Vinsobres

Cave Co-opérative de St Victor-la-Coste. Laudun

Cave Co-opérative la Vinsobraise. Vinsobres

Vinson, Jean. Domaine du Moulin, Vinsobres

Cave Co-opérative Les Coteaux de Visan. Visan

Zanti-Cumino. Domaine de Banvin, Cairanne

CAVES CO-OPERATIVES OF THE COTES DU RHONE

Co-opérative Vinicole, 'Comtadine Dauphinoise'. Puyméras

Cave Co-opérative de Vénéjan, Vénéjan

Cave Co-opérative, 'La Vigneronne', Villedieu

Cave Co-opérative des Vignerons, Bagnols sur Cèze

Cave des Vignerons, Cavillargues

Cave des Vignerons du Duché de Gadagne, Châteauneuf-de-Gadagne

Cave Co-opérative des Coteaux, Fournes

Cave Co-opérative Vinicole, Morières

Cave Co-opérative Agricole du Nyonnais, Nyons

Les Vignerons du Castelas, Rochefort du Gard

Cave Coopérative de St-Hilaire-d'Ozilhan, St-Hilaire d'Ozilhan

Cave Co-opérative Vinicole Cécilia', Ste Cécile-les-Vignes

Cave des Vignerons Réunis, Ste-Cécile-les-Vignes

Co-opérative Vinicole Les Coteaux du Rhône, Sérignan du Comtat

Cave Co-opérative Vinicole La Suzienne, Suze la Rousse

Cave Co-opérative de Tresques, Tresques

Cave Co-opérative Costebelle, Tulette

Co-opérative Vinicole des Coteaux de Tulette, Tulette

Cave Co-opérative des Vignerons, Vaison la Romaine

CROZES-HERMITAGE

Very acceptable reds, Syrah grape-based, which drink well when young but which can age for 10 odd years. The Domaine de Thalabert is a star example. Quite good whites, some nutty flavours, but must be drunk young and fresh before they oxidise.

Leading Growers at Crozes-Hermitage

Borja. Domaine des Clairmonts, Beaumont-Monteux

Bégot, Albert. Serves sur Rhône

Bied, Bernard. Mercurol

Cave Co-opérative de Vins Fins. Tain-l'Hermitage

Chapoutier et Cie. Les Meysonniers, Tain-l'Hermitage

Chave, Bernard. Mercurol

Collonge, Marcel. Domaine la Négociale, Mercurol

Delas Frères. Tournon

Desmeure, Père et Fils. Mercurol

Fayolle, Jules et ses Fils. Gervans

Ferraton, Jean et Michel. Tain l'Hermitage

Jaboulet Aîné, Paul. Domaine de Thalabert, Tain-l'Hermitage

Margier, Charles. Mercurol

Martin, Michel. Crozes-Hermitage

Michelas, Robert. Domaine St-Jemms, Mercurol

Peichon, Pierre. Frôme

Pradelle, Jean-Louis. Domaine de la Pradelle, Chanos Curson

Roure, Raymond. Gervans

Rousset, Robert. Frôme

Tardy, Charles et Ange, Bernard. GAEC de la Syrah, Chanos-Curson

de Vallouit, L. St-Vallier

GIGONDAS

Full southern Rhône red wine, it has plenty of tannin when young and the big, almost earth taste that goes well with steaming stews and roast meats. Drink around 6 to 10 years old.

Leading growers at Gigondas

Amadieu, Pierre. Gigondas

Archimbaud, Maurice. Ch. de Montmirail, Gigondas

Ay, François. Domaine de Raspail-Ay, Gigondas

Barruol, Henri. Domaine St-Cosme, Gigondas

Bezert, Pierre. Domaine de la Tuilière, Gigondas

Boutière, Raymond et Fils. Domaine du Pesquier, Gigondas

Cartier, Jean-Pierre. Domaine les Goubert, Gigondas

Combe, Roger. L'Oustau Fauquet, Gigondas

Burle, Ed. Les Pallieroudas, Gigondas

Chapalain, Serge. Domaine de Longue-Toque, Gigondas

Chassagne, F. et Fils. Domaine du Pourras, Sablet

Chastan, André et Fils. Orange

Chastan, Fernand, Clos du Joncuas, Gigondas

Chauvet, Bernard. Le Grapillon d'Or, Gigondas

Chauvet, Edmond. Domaine le Péage, Gigondas

Domaine de Cassan. Lafare

Faraud, Jean-Pierre. Gigondas

Faravel, Antonin. Domaine la Bouissière, Gigondas

Fauque, Jean-Claude. Domaine St-Pierre, Violès

Gaudin, Roland. Domaine du Terme, Gigondas

Gorecki, J. Le Mas des Collines, Gigondas

Gras, André. Domaine St-François-Xavier, Gigondas

Lambert, Pierre. Domaine de la Mavette, Gigondas

Meffre, Gabriel. Domaine des Bosquets, Gigondas

Meffre, Roger. Domaine St Gayan, Gigondas

Meunier, Laurent. La Gardette, Gigondas

Pascal. Domaine de Grand Montmirail, Gigondas

Quiot Pierre. Domaine des Pradets, Gigondas

Richard Georges. Domaine la Tornade, Gigondas

Roux, Charles et ses Fils. Ch. du Trignon, Gigondas

Roux, Georges et Jean, Domaine les Chênes Blancs, Gigondas

Roux, Hilarion, les Fils de. Les Pallières, Gigondas

Veyrat Pierre, Ch. St-André, Gigondas

Cave des Vignerons de Gigondas. Gigondas

HERMITAGE

The top Rhône red, made from the Syrah grape which allows long life and eventually complex flavours. Classy stuff, spans the divide between Rhône and Burgundy well enough to upstage plenty of more expensive red Burgundies. Becoming a wine sought by international drinkers – and investors. Small quantities. Pretty sumptuous white, can live for 10 years.

Leading growers at Hermitage

Chapoutier, M. Tain-l'Hermitage

Chave, Jean-Louis. Mauves

Delas Frères. Tournon

Desmeure, Père et Fils. Mercurol

Faurie, B. Tournon

Faurie, P., et **Bouzige,** J. Mauves

Favolle, Jules et ses Fils. Gervans

Ferraton, Jean et Michel. Tain-l'Hermitage

Gray, Terence. Tain-l'Hermitage

Grippat, Jean-Louis. Tournon

Jaboulet Aîné, Paul. Tain-l'Hermitage

Michelas Robert. Mercurol

Sorrel, Tain-l'Hermitage

De Vallouit, L. St-Vallier

Cave Co-opérative de Vins Fins. Tain-l'Hermitage

LIRAC

Soft red wines from the southern Rhône, easy to drink and good accompanying poultry, veal etc. Very good rosés, similar to Tavel and keenly priced. Some decent white too.

Leading growers at Lirac

Amido, Christian, Tavel

Assémat, Jean-Claude. Les Garrigues, Roquemaure

Cappeau, Y. et C. Domaine du Sablon, Roquemaure

Cave Co-opérative de Roquemaure. Roquemaure

Cave Co-opérative des Vins de Cru Lirac. St-Laurent-des-Arbres

Cregut, E. et J. Domaine de Cantegril, Roquemaure

Degoul, R. Ch. de Bouchassy, Roquemaure

Duseigneur Jean. Domaine Duseigneur, St-Laurent-des-Arbres

Fuget, Robert. Ch. de Boucarut, Roquemaure

Granier, Achille. Domaine de la Croze, Roquemaure

Leperchois, Emile. Les Carabiniers, Roquemaure

Lombardo, J., Domaine du Devoy, St-Laurent-des-Arbes

Maby, Armand. La Fermade, Tavel

Mayer, Marius, Ch. de Clary, Roquemaure

Méjan, André. Domaine Méjan, Tavel

Nataf, Edmond. Domaine de Maillac, Roquemaure

Olivier, Société Jean. Ch. d'Aquéria, Tavel

Pons-Mure, Charles. Domaine de la Tour de Lirac, St-Laurent-des-Arbres

Pons-Mure, Marie. Domaine de Castel Oualou, Roquemaure

de Régis, François. Ch. de Ségriès, Lirac

Roudil, Gabriel et Fils, Tavel

Rousseau, Louis et Fils. Domaine Rousseau, Laudun

Rousseau, Pierre. Domaine de la Claretière, Roquemaure

Sabon, Roger. Domaine Sabon, Roquemaure

Testut, Philippe. Lirac

Verda, Antoine et Fils. Domaine du Ch. St-Roch, Roquemaure

RASTEAU

A fortified sweet wine from the southern Rhône, made from the Grenache grape which has been selected for maturity. It has what the French would call a 'special' taste, one that would probably suit Madeira and old sherry drinkers.

Recommended producers

Bressy-Masson. Domaine de la Grangeneuve, Rasteau

Cave des Vignerons, Rasteau

Chamfort Louis et Fils. Domaine de Verquière, Sablet

Charavin, Emile. Rasteau

Charavin, Maurice. Domaine de Char-à-vin, Rasteau

Charavin, Robert. Rasteau

Colombet, Philippe. Rasteau

Girard, Louis. Domaine de la Girardière, Rasteau

Gleize, André. Violès

Joyet Paul. Domaine des Girasols, Rasteau

Liautaud, Jean. Domaine du Sommier, Séguret

Martin, Yves. Travaillan

Meyer et Fils. Domaine des Nymphes, Rasteau

Nicolet-Leyraud, Rasteau

Richaud, Marcel. Cairanne

Roméro, André. Domaine la Soumade, Rasteau

Saurel S. Domaine de la Combe Dieu, La Baumette

Vache, Francis, Rasteau

ST-JOSEPH

Bouncy, fruity red Rhône made from Syrah and good to drink between 2 and 10 years old. Good value generally. Also a medium bodied white, to be drunk with summer food before it is four years old.

Leading growers at St-Joseph

Cave Co-opérative de St-Désirat-Champagne. St-Désirat

Chapoutier, M. Tain-l'Hermitage

Chave, Jean-Louis. Mauves

Courbis, Maurice. Châteaubourg

Coursodon, Pierre et Gustave. Mauves

Cuilleron, Antoine. Chavanay

De Boisseyt-Chol. Chavanay

Delas Frères. Tournon

Desbos, Jean. St-Jean-de-Muzols

De Vallouit, L. Saint-Vallier

Faurie, B. Tournon

Florentin, Emile. Mauves

Gonon, Pierre. Mauves

Gripa, Bernard. Mauves

Grippat, Jean-Louis. Tournon

Lagnier, Georges. Chavanay

Maisonneuve, Jean. Mauves

Marsanne, Jean. Mauves

Michelas, Robert. Mercurol

Paret, Alain. St-Pierre-de-Boeuf

Trollat, Raymond. St-Jean-de-Muzols

Vernay, Georges. Condrieu

ST-PÉRAY

Northern Rhône fizz made in the Champagne way. Has more guts and a bit more of a coarse flavour than The Real Thing, but in the £5 bracket would be worth a try. Also still white wine, decent quality.

Leading growers at St-Péray

Cave les Vignerons de St-Péray. St-Peray

Chaboud, Jean-François. St-Péray

Clape, Auguste. Cornas

Cotte-Vergne, R. St-Péray

Darona, Pierre. St-Péray

Fraisse, Robert. St-Péray

Gilles Père et Fils. St-Péray

Gripa, Bernard. Mauves

Juge, Marcel. Cornas

Mathon, Léon. St-Péray

Milliand, René. St-Péray

Maurice, Marc. Cornas

Teyssiere, Jean. St-Péray

Thiers, Jean-Louis, Toulaud

Vérilhac, Eugène. St-Péray

Voge, Alain. Cornas

TAVEL

France's leading dry rosé, Tavel has more guts and depth of flavour and colour than rosé is thought capable of possessing. Chill it down, get plenty of bottles in, head out for a picnic and forget about those summer drinks that need mixing up.

Leading growers at Tavel

Allauzen. Prieuré de Montézargues, Tavel

Amido, Christian. Tavel

Bernard, Vve Aimée, Domaine de la Genestière, Tavel

Charmasson-Plantevin. Les Trois Logis, Tavel

Demoulin, F. Ch. de Trinquevedel, Tavel

Fraissinet, Les Filles de. Tavel

Cave Co-opérative des Grands Crus de Tavel. Tavel

Lafond Jacques. Domaine Corne-Loup, Tavel

Lafond, Jean-Pierre et Fils. Domaine Roc-Epine, Tavel

de Lanzac. Tavel

Lefèvre, Edouard. Domaine de Tourtouil, Tavel

Lévêque. Seigneur de Vaucrose, Tavel

Maby Armand. Domaine de la Forcadière, Tavel

Château de Manissy. Tavel

Méjan-Taulier. Clos Canto-Perdrix, Tavel

Olivier, Société Jean. Ch. d'Aquéria, Tavel

Roudil, Gabriel et Fils. Le Vieux Moulin de Tavel, Tavel

SOUTHERN FRANCE

BANDOL

One of France's little-known, but certainly up-and-coming wines, Bandol has only had an appellation of its own since 1977. This is not just another southern French Provençal wine: Bandol is individual, and capable of competing with far pricier wines from the Rhône. Reds need time to mature and can be worth keeping for a decade or more.

The grapes

Red	White
Cinsault	Bourboulenc
Grenache	Sauvignon
Mourvèdre (at least 50%)	Ugni Blanc
	*Château Vannieres
	Coopérative Vins de Bandol
	Caves du Moulin de la Roque
	*Domaine Tempier
	*Mas de la Rouvière
	Moulin des Costes
	Pradel

BELLET

A tiny appellation, tucked away in the hills behind Nice. Red, white, rosé.

The grapes:
Cinsault
Folle Noir
Grenache

Recommended producers:
Château de Bellet
Château de Cremet

BLANQUETTE DE LIMOUX

All those non-Francophones who thought that 'blanquettes' were things you slept under, will be interested to learn that – in this instance at least – the word refers to the coating of white dust which is found on the leaves of the Mauzac Blanc grape. Other grapes used are the Chardonnay and Clairette. Wine can be both still and (methode Champenoise) sparkling, though outside France it is most familiar in the latter form. Young examples can be appley-fresh; older bottles like tiring, yeasty Champagne. Either way it's a good wine to slip into a blind bubbly tasting.

CASSIS

No, it doesn't taste of blackcurrant, and its best wines are white anyway. Grapes used are the Clairette, Grenache Blanc, Marsanne, Pascal Blanc, Sauvignon, Ugni Blanc, Carignan, Cinsault, Grenache, and Mourvèdre. The white is full-bodied and quite soft; the red and rosé variable.

*Clos Ste-Magdelaine
*Mas Calendal

CLAIRETTE DE BELLEGARD
Soft white wine made from the Clairette grape in the department of the Gard, close to Nimes. Drink it young – with age 'soft' becomes 'dull'.

Recommended producer:
Domaine de l'Amarine

COLLIOURE
Very full-bodied red wine, produced in the Pyrenees Orientales close to Spain, and with a softness of flavour which is slightly reminiscent of some Rioja – except that here, the grapes are still very much the varieties of southern France: primarily Grenache, plus Cinsault and Mourvèdre. Carignan is kept to a minimum. High tannin content calls for patience; limited production calls for exploration to even find a bottle.

Cave Coopérative 'l'Union des Producteurs'
Domaine du Mas Blanc

CORBIÈRES
This is one of the most variable of France's southern regions. There are over 75.000.000 bottles made every year – enough for a bottle and a half for every Frenchman, woman and child – and ranging from colossally dull, to full, fruity and delicious. Almost all of the wine is red.

The grapes:
Red

Carignan	Picpoul
Cinsault	Syrah
Grenache	Terret Noir
Mourvèdre	

White
Clairette
Bourboulenc

Recommended producers
Cave Coopérative 'L'Avenir'
Cave Coopérative 'Cap Leucate'
Cave Coopérative Cascastel
Cave Coopérative 'Château de Queribus'
Cave Coopérative 'La Corbière Bizanetoise'
Cave Coopérative Corbières
Cave Coopérative Durban
Cave Coopérative Embres & Castelmaure
Cave Coopérative Fitou
Cave Coopérative Fraisse les Corbières
Cave Coopérative Lagrasse
Cave Coopérative Paziols
Cave Coopérative 'Portel'
Cave Coopérative Monseret
Cave Coopérative Mont Tauch
Cave Coopérative 'St-Martin'
*Château de Nouvelles
*Château de Beauregard
Château de Bouquignan
Château des Ollieux
*Château Les Palais
Château de Quilhanet
Domaine Huc
Domaine de Montjoie
*Domaine de Villemajou

CORSICA
The Greeks made wine here, preceding the Romans and Gauls on the mainland. Nowadays, the wines which are made from several indigenous grapes tend to be something between herby and spicy, with a flavour not unlike some wines from northern Italy.

The grapes
Red

Carignan	Niellucio
Cinsault	Sciacarello
Grenache	Syrah
Mourvèdre	

White
Muscat
Ugni Blanc
Vermentino (Malvoisie de Corse)

The wines
*VIN DE CORSE
The name used for wine produced throughout the island. Good red, white and rosé and VDN comparable to the Rhône.

Domaine de Pratavone

VIN DE CORSE CALVI
Red, white and rosé including a semi-dry white. Good, characterful, fruity wines with – in the case of the red – the capacity to age.

Domaine de Pietralba

*VIN DE CORSE COTEAUX D'AJACCIO
Red, white and rosé not unlike good basic Rhônes, but with the character of the Corsican grapes. Little white is made, though what there is, is good.

Comte Peraldi

*VIN DE CORSE COTEAUX DU CAP CORSE
Red, white and rosé including an excellent Muscat VDN called 'Rappu' and good dry Vermentino.

*VIN DE CORSE FIGARI
Red, white and rosé with particularly good whites.

*VIN DE CORSE PATRIMONIO
Red, white and rosé and VDN grown on chalk. Steven Spurrier compares the red to Chateauneuf-du-Pape.

*VIN DE CORSE DE PORTO-VECCHIO
Red, white and rosé with fresh, crisp whites.

Domaine de Torraccia

*VIN DE CORSE SARTENE
Red, white and rosé grown on granite soil.

Domaine de San Michele

CÔTES DE PROVENCE

Proud of its newish (1977) Appellation status, this region is making great efforts to raise its standards. Once only known for rosé, it now produces growing amounts of white and red.

The grapes:

Cabernet Sauvignon	Syrah
Carignan	Sauvignon
Cinsault	Semillon
Grenache	Ugni Blanc
Mourvèdre	

Recommended producers:
*Jean Bagnis & Fils (L'Estandon)
*Commanderie de Peyrassol
*Dom de la Bernarde ('Cuvee St Bernard')
 Dom de la Croix
*Dom des Feraud
 Dom des Hauts de St Jean
*Domaine Ott (also owners of Château Romasson, Château de Selle and Clos Mireille.
 Dom des Planes

COTES DU ROUSSILON

Red, white and rosé from Carignan, Cinsault, Grenache, Mourvèdre, Maccabeo and local varieties. The white, made exclusively from the Maccabeo, are not unlike the Clairettes of southern france: soft, pale amber-coloured and dry. Drink it young before the dullness of age sets in. Rosé can be good and reds are improving, thanks to the efforts of the region's cooperatives, but these are still, with a few commendable exceptions, only up-and-coming country wines, rather than justifiable Appellation Contrôlée stuff. Spend the extra pennies on Côtes du Roussillon-Villages, for a far better red wine.

COTES DU ROUSSILLON-VILLAGES

Exclusively red, and made in very small quantities from an established set of communes (just like Beaujolais, or Côtes du Rhône, Villages), this is richer, fuller-bodied and fruitier than plain Côtes du Roussillon. It's worth ageing too.

Cave Coopérative d'Aigly	Château Cap de Fouste
Cave Coopérative de Baixas	Château de Corneilla
Cave Coopérative Caramany	Château de Cuxous
Cave Coopérative Cassagnes	*Château de l'Esparrou
Cave Coopérative Lamsac	*Château de Jau
Cave Coopérative Lesquerde	Château de Rey
Cave Coopérative Les Maîtres	Château de Villclare
Vignerons	Domaine Baillo
Cave Coopérative Maury	Domaine de Caladroy
Cave Coopérative	*Domaine de Canterrane
Montalba-le-Château	Domaine Jaubert-Noury
Cave Coopérative Montner	Domaine de Roquebrune
Cave Coopérative Planèzes	Domaine St-Luc
Cave Coopérative Rasiguères	Domaine de Sau
Cave Coopérative St Vincent	Le Moulin
Cave Coopérative Tarerac	*Mas de la Dona
Cave Coopérative Thuir	*Mas Balande
Cave Coopérative Terrats	*Mas Pechot
Cazes Frères	

FITOU

Often thought to be just 'up-market Corbières', this is an individual wine with a character of its own. For a start, it's just about the only appellation to give the Carignan – usually only a southern blending variety – the chance to show its own merits. Indeed, for chance, read obligation, because almost three quarters of the blend has to be Carignan. If you think you can taste wood, you're right there too: Fitou has to be wood aged for a year and a half, an requirement not

even forced onto Gevrey Chambertin. Good full-bodied wine which rewards keeping for five years or so. Most comes from cooperatives.

The grapes:

Carignan	Mourvèdre
Cinsault	Syrah
Grenache	

Domaine Cassignol
Cave Coopérative 'Cap Leucate'
Cave Coopérative de Cascastel
Cave Coopérative de Fitou
Cave Coopérative Mont Tauch
Cave Coopérative de Paziols
Cave Coopérative 'Pilote de Villeneuve les Corbières'
Château de Nouvelles

PALETTE

Red, white and rosé made from same grapes as Côtes de Provence, in very small quantities indeed. Peculiar chalky subsoil makes wines slow to mature, and characterful when they do.

Recommended producer:
*Château Simone (rosé)

SOUTH WEST FRANCE

BERGERAC

The region

Bergerac is situated on the River Dordogne, and produces red and dry white Bordeaux-type wines as well as a sweet white (Monbazillac q.v.) Cool fermentation is helping the dry whites and careful winemaking is improving the reds too. The Bordeaux negociant firm of Yvon Mau can claim much of the credit for promoting Bergerac and introducing it to foreign markets.

Appellations within Bergerac:

Bergerac (dry)
Côtes de Bergerac (semi-sweet)
Côtes de Montravel (dry)
Haut-Montravel (medium-sweet)
Côtes de Saussignac (sweet)
Monbazillac (sweet)
Pecharmant
Rossette

The Grapes – as Bordeaux. Recommended producers:

Ch. Belingard	*Ch. de Monbazillac (cooperative)
Ch. du Bloy	Ch. de Michel Montaigne
Ch. la Borderie	Ch. de Panisseau
Ch. le Caillou	Ch. Poulvere
Dom Constant	Ch. Thenac
Ch. Court-les-Muts	Dom Theylet Marsalet
Ch. Le Fage	Ch. Tiregand
*Dom du Haut Percharmant	Unidor (cooperative)
Dom de la Jaubertie	

CAHORS

'The thick black wine' they call it. On the other hand, there was a time when they called it Bordeaux (the port from which Cahors was shipped) and got away with it. It's not a wine for the impatient and is more suited to the palate of the Barolo lover than to most Beaujolais quaffers, but it's no longer the dark 'put-it-away-and-forget-about-it' stuff of its reputation, and there are some very attractive examples now being produced.

The grapes:

Auxerrois (Malbec)	Merlot
Dame Noire (Jurançon Noir)	Syrah
Gamay	Tannat

Recommended producers:

Jean Bernède	Colette Delfour
Henri Bessières	Durou & Fils
Andre Bouloumie	Dumeaux & Fils
Charles Burc	Jacques Jouves
Dom Burc & Fils	Roger Labruyère
*Dom Mas d'El Perrie	Mathieu Lescombes
Caves St-Antoine	Luc Reutenauer
*Château de Cayrou	SCEA de Quattre & Treilles
*Château de Chambert	M.J.C. Valière
*Chateau St Didier	Charles Vehaegue
*Clos Triguedina	Georges Vigouroux

Côtes de Buzet

Little-known, but increasingly popular, this is another Bordeaux substitute. The grapes are principally Merlot and the Cabernets, though some Malbec is used. From a good year, these wines will keep for 5 years or so. Whites and rosés are rare and of no enormous distinction. Most wines come from the Cooperative.

Recommended producers:
Caves Réunis des Côtes de Buzet
Château Pierron
Domaine Padere

Côtes de Duras

As Bergerac begins to move into the market for inexpensive Bordeaux, Côtes de Duras is hard on its heels. The grapes for the red are the same, and the winemaking is increasingly skilful and reliable. As for the whites, they vary between Ugni-Blanc-based bores and Sauvignon-fresh. The local Mauzac and Ondenc are also used.

Recommended producers:
Cave Coopérative des Vignerons des Coteaux de Duras

Côtes du Frontonnais

Using the same grapes as for red Bordeaux, plus the Syrah, Gamay, Cinsault and Mauzac, and most particularly, the local Negrette, the Frontonnais produce red and rosé wine which can be both full-bodied and fruitily characterful. Look out for labels which mention the commune of Villaudric.

Caves Coopérative 'Les Côtes du Fronton'
Cave Coopérative Villaudric
Château Bellevue-La-Foret

GAILLAC

Like Cahors, Gaillac used to be left for a decade or so before anyone dreamed of bottling, let alone drinking it. Nowadays, styles are lighter and the arrival of non-indigenous grapes such as the Gamay and Sauvignon is playing its role too. Drink the red within a couple of years, the white rather more quickly.

Grapes include:

White	**Red**
Loin d'Oeil (l'En de l'En)	Brocol
Mauzac	Cabernet Franc
Ondenc	Duras
Sauvignon	Ferservadou
	Gamay
	Merlot
	Syrah

It's quite tough when young, but develops into an attractive characterful style as it matures which recalls both Cahors and Bordeaux. Wines vary largely according to the particular blends of grapes a producer chooses to use.

The grape:

Cabernet Franc	Tannat
Cabernet Sauvignon	

Recommended producers:

Cave Coopérative de Tursan	Dom Bouschasse
Cave Coopérative Vic-Bilh	Dom Laplace
Château de Peyros	Dom Pichard
Dom Barrejat	Dom de Sitère

Jurançon Sec

To the few people outside France who may have heard of it, Jurançon is usually thought of as sweet white wine. In fact, though, by far the greater part (90%) of this appellation is made dry – which is a far easier process. At its best, this is a wine which can easily compete with dry Vouvray, as a dry, spicy accompaniment to fish.

Recommended producers:
Cave Coopérative de Gan-Jurançon
Clos Camcaillau
Cru Lamouroux
Domaine Guirouilh

MONBAZILLAC

(see Bergerac)
Made from the same grapes as sweet Bordeaux, and often an inexpensive alternative to those wines. Under the influence of the Cave Co-operative, quality is generally good and improving. Wines can be made alcoholic and more liquorous than many Sauternes, and only lacks the complexity of flavour of fine examples of those more illustrious wines.

*Ch. Peroudier
*Ch. de Monbazillac (cooperative)

PACHERENC

A white wine produced by Madiran makers from vines in the same region. Can be dry or fairly sweet. Clear bottles used for both, give little indication of the sugar content.

The grapes:

Courbu (Sarrat)	Sauvignon
Mansengs	Semillon
Pacherenc du Vic Bilh	

Recommended producers:
Dom Laplace
Vic Bilh-Madiran

LES VINS DOUX NATURELS/VINS DE LIQUEUR

Trust the people who establish French labelling law. 'Naturel' means 'fortified' ('liquoreux', which sounds as though it might have had liquor added, actually describes a wine which owes its sweetness and alcoholic strength to the ripeness of its grapes) and all Vins Doux Naturels – or VDNs – have had brandy added to them to stop the fermentation process. Vins de Liqueur, just to confuse you further, are the same as VDNs, but are easy to remember since the appellation only extends to Pineau de Charentes and Ratafia. And, if you thought you were just beginning to come to grips with the subject, despite the word 'doux' VDNs don't even have to be sweet at all – provided they have been sufficiently fortified and the alcoholic strength reaches the required minimum. White VDNs are all basically sweetly Muscatty in style while the red and rose are more like tawny port; wines which have been aged in cask (they do not develop in bottle) are described as 'Rancio' and take on a flavour reminiscent of Madeira.

Banyuls

Sweet red and tawny wines, made from the Grenache Noir, Blanc, Gris, Maccabeo, Malvoisie and Muscat. Much of the wine is bottled young, served on the rocks as an aperitif and rarely of first class quality. Better examples are oak aged, and Banyuls Grand Cru has to spend 2½ years in cask before bottling. It also has to be made from a higher proportion of Grenache grapes and to satisfy two tasting panels.

Banyuls Rancio

Made almost like Madeira – barrels are left to cook gently in the sun – this tawny-coloured style is much sought after.

Cave Coopérative 'Las Banyulencque'
Mas Blanc
Mas Saint-Louis
Le Moulin

Côtes d'Agly

Basically, these are like sweeter, cheaper versions of Banyuls. 'Rancio' and 'Vieux' styles are made too.

Cave Coopérative 'Aglya'

Grand Roussillon

Red, white and rosé styles at the top end of the VDN price range.

Maury

Red, white and rosé, similar to Côtes d'Agly.

Cave Coopérative de Maury

Muscat de Beaumes de Venise

This is the superstar, the wine which, almost single-handedly made sweet wine acceptable to people who thought it unsophisticated. The cooperative, with its (many reckon ugly) screw-topped bottle may seem to have the monopoly of the production of this wine, but this isn't the case. Try wines from some of the independent producers too. Drink young and well chilled.

Cave Coopérative
Dom des Bernardins
Dom Durban

Muscat de Frontignan

Thank goodness for wines which share their names with the grape variety from which they are made; the Muscat de Frontignan is the type of Muscat used for most of these VDNs. This one is one of the best, but many people find it a little too big, and too rich. If you like your Muscat delicate, Beaumes de Venise may be a better bet.

Cave Coopérative de Frontignan
Mas Neuf des Aresquiers

Muscat de Lunel

Tagging along on the coat-tails of the finer Muscats de Beaumes de Venise and Frontignan, this is nevertheless a basically good VDN.

Cave Coopérative Muscat de Lunel

Muscat de Mireval

Really an extension of the Muscat de Frontignan vineyards, producing similar, but less classy wine.

Cave Coopérative de Rabelais
Mas Neuf des Aresquiers

Muscat de Rivesaltes

Similar to Muscat de Frontignan, but seldom quite as good. Some independent estates are making good examples though.

Cave Coopérative de Baixas   *Cave Coopérative de Cassagnes*

Cave Coopérative de Montner	Château de Rey
Cave Coopérative de Rasiguères	Dom Baillou
Cave Coopérative Tauteval	Dom de Caladroy
'Les Maitres Vignerons'	Dom de Canterrane
Cave Coopérative de Terrats	Dom Jaubert-Noury
Cazes Frères	*Mas Pechot
Château de l'Esparrou	Le Moulin
Château de Jau	

Muscat de St-Jean-de-Minervois

From a high-situated plateau around Minerve which also produces the fullest-bodied Minervois.

Cave Coopérative de St-Jean-de-Minervois

Pineau de Charentes

Fortified with Cognac, this is the aperitif you'll be served when visiting any of the major Cognac houses.

Rasteau

Like Muscat de Beaumes de Venise, this is made in a village which also produces good red Côtes du Rhône. The VDN Rasteau can however come in 'red' or 'white', meaning gold or tawny and is made from the Grenache.

Cave Coopérative de Rasteau	Dom Martin
*Dom Bressey-Masson	*Dom de Verquière

Ratafia

Champagne's own Vin de Liqueur, made with Eau de Vie de Champagne, and produced by most Champagne houses.

Rivesaltes

Red, white and rosé similar to Cotes d'Agly.

Cave Coopérative d'Agly	Cazes Frères
Cave Coopérative de Baixas	Dom Baillou
Cave Coopérative de Cassagnes	Dom de Caladroy
Cave Coopérative de Lesquerde	Dom de Canterrane
Cave Coopérative de Montner	Chateau de l'Esparrou
Cave Coopérative de Rasiguères	Chateau de Rey
Cave Coopérative St Vincent	Dom de Roquebrune
Cave Coopérative Tauteval	Dom St Luc
les Maîtres Vignerons	Le Moulin
Cave Coopérative Terrats	Tresserre

VDQS LIST

The Vins Délimités de Qualité Supérieur of France stand midway between the humbler Vins de Pays and the more exhalted wines with their own regional Appellations Contrôlées. Some VDQS wines deserve no greater recognition; others are certainly as good as some Appellation Contrôlée wines.

Cabardes *Aude*
Red and rosé, made from Carignan, Cabernet Sauvignon, Cinsault, Cot, Fer, Grenache, Merlot, Mourvedre, Syrah.

*Cabrières *Herault*
Fine quality rosé, made from Carignan, Cinsault and Grenache. Cave Coopérative 'Les Coteaux de Cabrières'.

Châteaumeillant *Cher*
Red and rosé made from Gamay, and Pinots Gris and Noir.
*Rosé.

*Cheverny *Loire*
Red, white and rosé (some sparkling) made from Arbois (Menu-Pineau), Chardonnay, Chenin Blanc, Romorantin (an acid grape, now being phased out), Sauvignon, both Cabernets, Cot, Gamay, Pineau

d'Aunis, Pinots Gris and Noir. White grape names usually appear on the label.

La Clape *Hérault*
Hard to sell in Anglo-Saxon lands (imagine the question: 'do you remember where you got it from?') these are nonetheless good red, white and rosé wines of some character. They are made from Carignan, Cinsault, Grenache, Terret Noir; Clairette, Malvoisie (or Bourboulenc) and Picpoul. Both reds and white vary in style depending on the grape varieties used.

Château de Rouquette-sur-Mer   *Jean Ségura*
Château de Salles   *Societe Aupecle*
Domaine de Pech Redon

Costières du Gard *Gard*
Red, white and rosé made from Carignan, Cinsault, Counoise, Grenache, Mourvèdre, Syrah, Terret Noir; Clairette, Bourboulenc, Ugni Blanc. Good fruity red wine – the epitome of what inexpensive French wine should be about.

Cave Coopérative de Bellegarde   *Domaine La Perdrix*
Château Roubaud   *La Méridionale*
Château St-Vincent

Coteaux d'Aix-en-Provence *Bouches-du-Rhône*
Unjustly deprived of an appellation, making red, white and rosé from Cabernet Sauvignon, Carignan, Cinsault, Counoise, Grenache, Mourvèdre, and Grenache Blanc, Sémillon, Sauvignon and Ugni Blanc. From 1985 will bear an Appellation contrôlée.

Château de Fronscolombe   *Domaine de la Tour Campanets*
Château Vignelaure   *Les Vignerons Provençaux*
Domaine de la Cremade   *Marquis de Saporta*
Domaine de Paradis

Coteaux d'Ancenis *Loire*
Red, white and rosé, made from Cabernet Franc, Chenin Blanc, Gamay, Malvoisie Pineau de la Loire, Pinot Beurot. The grape variety used must appear on the label.

Coteaux des Baux-en-Provence *Provence*
Red, white and rosé, made from Carignan, Cinsault, Cabernet Sauvignon, Counoise, Grenache, Mourvèdre; Grenache Blanc, Sémillon, Ugni Blanc. This is one of France's overlooked regions, producing inexpensive, full, fruity wine.

Domaine de Trevallon

Coteaux du Giennois *Loire*
Red, white and rosé made from Gamay, Pinot Noir, Chenin Blanc, Sauvignon. Wines are light, pleasant and unambitious.

Coteaux du Lyonnais *Rhône*
Red, white and rosé made from Aligoté, Melon de Bourgogne, Chardonnay; and Gamay. The vineyards are only just to the south of the Beaujolais, and the reds can be a good alternative to that region's wines.

Coteaux de la Mejanelle *Hérault*
Red and white made from Carignan, Cinsault, Grenache. White almost impossible to find, but red, though hard and tannic when young, merits ageing and softens to be characterful wine.

Château de Flaugergues
Domaine de la Costière

Coteaux de Pierrevert *Provence*
Red, white and rosé made from Carignan, Cinsault, Grenache; Clairette, Marsanne, Roussanne. Particularly good rosé which competes easily with much Appellation Contrôlée wine from Provence.

Coteaux de Saint-Christol *Herault*
Red wine made from Carignan, Cinsault, Grenache. Cave Co-opérative les Coteaux de St-Christol.

Coteaux Varois *Provence*
Red, white and rosé, made from traditional Provence grapes: Carignan, Cinsault, Grenache, Mourvèdre, Alicante and Aramon, Clairette, Grenache Blanc, Malvoisie and Ugni Blanc. Some good Syrah and Cabernet too. Whites tend to be dull.

Claude Courtois
Compagnie des Salins du Midi
Domaine des Chabert

Coteaux de Verargues *Hérault*
Red and rosé made from Aramon, Carignan, Cinsault, Grenache, Good, simple, full-bodied wine.

Muscat de Lunel Cooperative

Coteaux du Languedoc *Hérault*
Blanket VDQS, including around a dozen individual VDQS's. Red and rosé made from Carignan, Cinsault, Counoise, Grenache, Mourvèdre, Syrah, Terret Noir. Reds are more distinguished than rosé. Good value.

Cave Coopérative de St Felix de Lodez
Cave Coopérative de St Jean-de-la-Blaquiere
Cave Coopérative de St-Saturnin

Coteaux du Vendômois *Loire*
Red, white and rosé made from Chardonnay, Chenin Bl, Gamay, Pineau d'Aunis (both for rosés), Cabernet, Pinot Noir. Mostly red and rosé.

Côte Roannaise *Loire*
Red and rosé made from Gamay. Comparable with Beaujolais, but styles vary – some producers making wine which improves with keeping.

Côtes d'Auvergne *Loire*
Red, white and rosé made from Gamay, Pinot Noir, Chardonnay. There is very little white, but reds can be a good alternative to Beaujolais or Bourgogne Passetoutgrain – at a far lower price. Some choice commune names appear on labels:

Côtes d'Auvergne-Boudes   *Côtes d'Auvergne-Corent*
Côtes d'Auvergne-Chanturgue   *Côtes d'Auvergne-Madargues*

Cotes du Forez *Loire*
Red and rosé made from Gamay. Good examples are like Beaujolais from better producers in unripe years: fruity but occasionally over-acidic.

Cave Coopérative des Côte du Forez

Cotes du Luberon *Rhône*
Red, white and rosé which were once sold as Côtes du Rhône, and use

the same grapes: Carignan, Cinsault, Counoise, Grenache, Mourvèdre, Muscardin, Syrah, Terret Noir, Vaccarese; Bourboulenc, Clairette, Grenache Blanc, Marsanne, Roussanne, and Ugni Blanc. Reds tend to be lighter than much Côtes du Rhône, but are pleasant and inexpensive.

Cellier du Marrenon
*La Vieille Ferme
Château de Canorgue

*Côtes de la Malepère *Aude*

Red and rosé made from Cinsault, Cot, Grenache, Merlot, both Cabernets, and Syrah. Good, full-bodied, characterful reds; Grenache/Cinsault rosés are comparable to Tavel. Quite rare outside France.

Côtes du Marmandais *South-West*

Red and white made from Abouriou, both Cabernets, Fer, Gamay, Malbec, Merlot, Syrah; Sauvignon, Semillon, Ugni Blanc. Light, easy-to drink wine; red better than white.

Cave Coopérative Intercommunale de Cocumont
Societe Coopérative Vinicole des Côtes du Marmandais

*Côtes de Saint-Mont *South West*

Red, white and rosé made from Tannat, both Cabernets, Merlot, Jurançon, Meslier, Picpoul, Sauvignon. Whites are made from wine much of which used to be distilled to produce Armagnac. They can be fruity and distinctive. Reds are quite tough, and comparable to Madiran.

*Union des Producteurs Plaimont

Côtes de Toul *Lorraine*

Red, white and rosé, but particularly light Vin Gris rosé, made from Gamay. Pinots Meunier and Noir are also grown.

Côtes du Vivarais *Rhône*

Red, white and rosé made from Carignan, Cinsault, Counoise, Gamay, Grenache Mourvedre, Muscardin, Syrah, Terret Noir, Vaccarese; Bourboulenc, Clairette, Grenache Blanc, Marsanne, Roussanne, and Ugni Blanc. Only the Gamay distinguishes the list of permitted grapes from that used for Côtes du Rhône. White is almost non-existent.

Fiefs Vendéens *Vendée*

Red, white and rosé, made from Gamay, Pinot Noir, both Cabernets, Negrette and Gamay Chaudenay, Chenin Blanc, Sauvignon, Chardonnay.

Bernard Babin
Rachel Davies
La Chargnée

*Gros Plant du Pays Nantais

White wine, made from the Gros Plant, elsewhere known as the Folle Blanche. Can be an inexpensive, dry altenative to Muscadet. Little known outside France.

Haut-Comtat *Rhône*

Grenache based red and rosé which is rare because it falls within the region for Appellation Contrôlee Côtes du Rhône.

Montpeyroux *Hérault*

Red and rosé made from Carignan, Cinsault, Grenache, Mourvedre, Syrah. Red can be kept for a few years, and when well made is of some interest.

Cave Coopérative Les Coteaux du Castellas

Picpoul de Pinet *Hérault*

White, made from the Clairette, Folle Blanche (known here as Picpoul), and Terret Blanc. Undistinguished.

Pic-Saint-Loup *Hérault*

Red, white and rosé made from Carignan, Cinsault, Counoise, Grenache, Mourvèdre, Syrah, Terret Noir; Clairette. Quite light, pleasant wines. White is very rare.

Cave Coopérative les Coteaux de Montferrand
Cave Coopérative les Coteaux de Valflaunes
Cave Coopérative les Coteaux de St-Gely-du-Fesc
Domaine de la Roque
Domaine de Villeneuve

*Quatorze *Hérault*

Red, white and rosé made from Carignan, Cinsault, Grenache, Mourvèdre, Terret Noir. Little found outside the region, but reportedly much used for their colour and strength in more northerly areas such as Burgundy, where such qualities are often lacking. Southern France's answer to Algeria.

Yvon Ortola

Saint-Drezery *Hérault*

Red wine mostly made from Carignan. More of a jumped-up Vin de Pays than a would-be Appellation Contrôlée.

Cave Coopérative des Coteaux de St-Drezery

*Saint-Georges-d'Orques *Herault*

Red wine made from Carignan, Cinsault, Grenache. Quite 'big' wines which can age.

Cave Coopérative de St-Georges-d'Orques
Château de l'Engarran

*Saint-Pourcain-sur-Sioule *Loire*

Red, white and rosé made from Aligoté, Chardonnay, Sacy (known here as Tressalier), Saint-Pierre-Doré, Sauvignon, Gamay, Pinot Noir. Good examples are competition for Beaujolais, Bourgogne Passetoutgrain and even Bourgogne Rouge.

*Cave Coopérative de Saint-Pourcain

*Saint-Saturnin *Hérault*

Red and rosé made from Carignan, Cinsault, Grenache, Mourvedre, Syrah. Good, full-flavoured wine.

Cave Coopérative de Saint-Saturnin
*Château de la Condamine Bertrand

*Sauvignon de Saint-Bris *Burgundy*

White made from Sauvignon. Good, crisp, wine this is as much of an alternative to a dull Chablis as it is to a Sancerre Sauvignon.

*Domaine Brocard   *Georges Verret*
Albert Pic   **Sorin-Defrance*

*Tursan *South West*

Red, white and rosé made from both Cabernets, Fer and (mainly Tannat); Baroque. Reds are comparable to Madiran; whites are less interesting than their grape name (specific to Tursan) might lead you to hope.

Coopérative de Tursan

Valencay *Loire*

Red, white and rosé made from Arbois (Menu-Pineau) – not less than 60%, Chardonnay, Pineau de la Loire, Romorantin, Sauvignon, both Cabernets, Cot, Gamay, Pineau d'Aunis. Very little white made.

*Vin du Bugey *Savoie*

Red, white and rosé (some petillant and sparkling) made from Gamay, Mondeuse, Poulsard; Aligoté, Altesse, Chardonnay, Jacquère, Mondeuse Blanche, Pinot Gris. Grape varieties sometimes appear on labels, as can the names of a number of *Cru* villages: Cerdon, Machuraz, Manicle, Montagnieu, Virieu-le-Grand. Whites have more character than reds and rosés, but all fresh, fruity and worth seeking out.

Cave Coopérative de Vente des Vins Fins
*Varichon & Clerc

Vins d'Entraygues et du Fel *South West*
Red, white and rosé made from both Cabernets, Fer, Gamay, Jurançon Noir, Merlot, Negrette, Chenin Blanc Mauzac.

Vins d'Estaing *South West*
Red, white and rosé made from both Cabernets, Fer, Gamay, Jurançon Noir, Merlot, Negrette, Chenin Blanc, Mauzac. Very little white.

Vins du Haut-Poitou *Loire*
Red, white and rosé (some sparkling) made from Chardonnay, Chenin Blanc, Pinot Blanc, Sauvignon, Cabernet Sauvignon, Cot, Gamay, Groslot, Pinot Noir. Generally good quality, particularly Sauvignon and Chardonnay.

Coopérative de Haut-Poitou

Vins de Lavilledieu *South West*
Red, white and rosé made from Fer, Gamay, Jurançon Noir, Mauzac Noir, Negrette, Picpoul. Good, simple wine. Very little white or rosé.

*Vins de l'Orléanais *Loire*
Red, white and rosé made from Chardonnay, Pinot Blanc, Cabernet, Pinots Noir and Meunier. The red can be light and fruity but the speciality is the Gris Meunier d'Orléans, a rosé which offers the rare opportunity to taste one of the three Champagne varieties in isolation.

*Vins de Marcillac *South West*
Red and rosé made from Cabernet, Fer (of which wine must contain 80%), Gamay, Jurançon Noir, Marcillac. Good, full-flavored wine.

Vins de Moselle *Lorraine*
Not what you might have thought, the French name for wine from across the Rhine, but light reds (made from Gamay and Pinots Gris and Noir) and whites made from Pinot Blanc and Sylvaner. Very rare.

*Vin Nobel du Minervois *Aude*
Sweet white, made from late-picked Grenache, Maccabeo, Malvoisie, Muscat. Excellent but very rare.

Vins du Thouarsais *Loire*
Red, white and rosé made from both Cabernets and Chenin Blanc. To be drunk young.

GAULT ET MILLAU WINE OLYMPIAD

COMPARATIVE TASTINGS of wines from a variety of different countries have a long-established tradition: as long ago as the late 19th century, producers from a number of unexpected countries were winning gold medals from Parisian judges who were probably quite unused to wines made outside France. Amongst the recent crop of international tastings, none has been more comprehensive, none more important than the 'Olympiades' held in 1979 by the French magazine, Gault et Millau, which set 330 wines from 34 different countries before 62 tasters who were themselves of 10 different nationalities.

CHARDONNAY

★ ★ ★ ★ ★

1st. U.S.A.
Chardonnay Trefethen, 1976

★ ★ ★ ★ ★

2nd. U.S.A.
Chardonnay
Robert Mondavi, 1977

★ ★ ★ ★ ★

3rd. Italy
Pinot Bianco del Collio
Mario Schiopetto (Frioul), 1978

★ ★ ★ ★ ★

4th. Australia
Tyrell's Chardonnay, 1977

★ ★ ★ ★ ★

5th. U.S.A.
Chardonnay
Spring Mountain, 1977

★ ★ ★ ★ ★

6th. U.S.A.
Chardonnay
Freemark Abbey, 1975

★ ★ ★ ★ ★

7th. France
Pouilly-Fuissé A.O.C.
Nicolas, 1976

★ ★ ★ ★ ★

8th. U.S.A.
Chardonnay
Sterling Vineyards, 1977

★ ★ ★ ★ ★

9th. U.S.A.
Chardonnay
Mayacamas, 1976

★ ★ ★ ★ ★

10th. Argentina
Andean Chardonnay
Peñaflor, 1977

★ ★ ★ ★ ★

11th. France
Puligny-Montrachet
Nicolas, 1978

★ ★ ★ ★ ★

12th. U.S.A.
Chardonnay Château
Montelena, 1976

★ ★ ★ ★ ★

12th. U.S.A.
Chardonnay Heitz Cellars, 1973

★ ★ ★ ★ ★

14th. Switzerland
Chardonnay Dupraz,
Lully, 1976

★ ★ ★ ★ ★

15th. France
Chablis 'Côte-de-Lechet',
1er Cru, Nicolas, 1978

★ ★ ★ ★ ★

16th. Argentina
Château Vieux Lopez, 1975

★ ★ ★ ★ ★

17th. France
Chablis A.O.C. Nicolas, 1978

★ ★ ★ ★ ★

18th. France
Chablis 'Blanchots' Grand Cru,
Nicolas, 1969

★ ★ ★ ★ ★

19th. South Africa
Spier Colombar, 1976

★ ★ ★ ★ ★

20th. Yugoslavia
Beli Burgundee Ljut. Ormoske
Gorice, 1971

★ ★ ★ ★ ★

RIESLING *(German style)*

★ ★ ★ ★ ★

1st. U.S.A.
Johannisberg Riesling
Smith-Madrone, 1977

★ ★ ★ ★ ★

2nd. Switzerland
Riesling 'Vendange
Laurencienne', Desfayes-
Crettenand, Leytron, 1976

★ ★ ★ ★ ★

3rd. Germany
Riesling, Kabinett Halbtröcken,
'Rheingau' Schloss
Vollrads, 1977

★ ★ ★ ★ ★

4th. Australia
'Yalumba Barossa'
Rhine Riesling, Pewsey Vale,
Smith & Son, 1972

★ ★ ★ ★ ★

5th. Belgium
'Clos Veuve Clypot', Michel
Mouehart, Neufvilles
(Hainaut), 1976

★ ★ ★ ★ ★

6th. Australia
Kaiser Stuhl Gold Ribbon Rhine
Riesling, cooperative
Barossa, 1977

★ ★ ★ ★ ★

7th. Austria
Burgstall, Rheinriesling
Coopérative Dinstlgut
Loiben, 1977

★ ★ ★ ★ ★

8th. Brazil
Kiedrich Riesling Cia
Monaco, 1976

★ ★ ★ ★ ★

RIESLING *(Alsace style)*

★ ★ ★ ★ ★

1st. New Zealand
Te Kauwhata Riesling,
Cooks, 1978

★ ★ ★ ★ ★

2nd. France
Riesling 'Cuvée particulière'
Léon Beyer, Eguisheim, 1977

★ ★ ★ ★ ★

3th. South Africa
De Wetsof, Riesling, 1978

★ ★ ★ ★ ★

4th. Luxembourg
Riesling 1er Cru 'Wormeldange
Wousselt' Mathes, 1977

★ ★ ★ ★ ★

5th. Austria
Welschreisling 'Römerstein',
Domaine Tscheppe, 1977

★ ★ ★ ★ ★

CABERNET MERLOT

★ ★ ★ ★ ★

1st. France
Saint-Estèphe A.O.C. Nicolas,
sans mill.

★ ★ ★ ★ ★

2nd. Italy
Sassicaia, Tenuta San Guido
Bolgheri, 1975

★ ★ ★ ★ ★

2nd. South Africa
Cabernet-Sauvignon
Rustenberg, 1973

★ ★ ★ ★ ★

4th. France
Château La-Tour-de-By
Cru Bourgeois, Médoc, 1970

★ ★ ★ ★ ★

5th. Australia
Tyrell's Cabernet 1975

★ ★ ★ ★ ★

6th. New Zealand
Cook's te Kauwhata Cabernet-
Sauvignon, 1975

★ ★ ★ ★ ★

7th. Romania
Merlot, Vinexport, Bucarest,
sans mill.

★ ★ ★ ★ ★

7th. Australia
McLaren Vale Cabernet-
Sauvignon, Private Bin
Hamilton Ewell, 1974

★ ★ ★ ★ ★

9th. Italy
Cabernet Trentino
Guerrero Gonzaga, 1973

★ ★ ★ ★ ★

9th. France
Château Larcis-Ducasse
Grand Cru Classé Saint-
Emilion, 1971

★ ★ ★ ★ ★

11th. Romania
Cabernet Vinexport, sans mill.

★ ★ ★ ★ ★

12th. Switzerland
Merlot del Ticino,
Selezzione d'Ottobre, Matasci
Fratelli, Tenero 1976

★ ★ ★ ★ ★

13th. France
Château Roland-La Garde
Côtes-de-Blaye A.O.C.
Nicolas, 1975

★ ★ ★ ★ ★

13th. Romania
Premiat Cabernet-Sauvignon,
Hemri, 1975

★ ★ ★ ★ ★

15th. Italy
Merlot, Collio D.O.C. Gradnik,
Cormons (Frioul) 1977

★ ★ ★ ★ ★

16th. France
Chinon A.O.C., Nicolas, 1978

★ ★ ★ ★ ★

RED WINES

★ ★ ★ ★ ★

1st. Spain
Gran Coronas Reserva Rioja,
Miguel Torres, Villafranca del
Penedes, 1970

★ ★ ★ ★ ★

2nd. France
Château-Latour, 1er Grand Cru
Classé, Pauillac, 1970

★ ★ ★ ★ ★

3rd. France
Château Pichon-Lalande
2e Grand Cru Classé,
Pauillac, 1964

★ ★ ★ ★ ★

4th. France
Château Mission Haut-Brion
Cru Classé, Graves, 1961

★ ★ ★ ★ ★

5th. Chile
Finissimo, Gran Viño José
Canapa, sans mill.

★ ★ ★ ★ ★

6th. France
Domaine de Mont-Redon
Châteauneuf-du-Pape, 1955

★ ★ ★ ★ ★

7th. Spain
Coronas, Rioja Miguel Torres,
Villafranca del Penedes, 1976

★ ★ ★ ★ ★

8th. France
Gevrey-Chambertin
Nicolas, 1976

★ ★ ★ ★

9th. Chile
Santa Rita, Casa Real
Viña Santa Rita, 1972.

★ ★ ★ ★ ★

10th. France
Château Branaire-Ducru
4e Grand Cru Classé, St-Julien
A.O.C., 1971

★ ★ ★ ★ ★

11th. Chile
Gato Negro (Cabernet) Wagner,
Stein, 1976

★ ★ ★ ★ ★

11th. Chile
Cabernet-Sauvignon
Viña Santa Carolina, 1974

★ ★ ★ ★ ★

13th. Spain
Tinto 'Las Campañas'
Castillo de Tiebas, Vinicola
Navarra, sans mill.

★ ★ ★ ★ ★

14th. Spain
Gran Viña Sol, Reserva, Miguel
Torres, Villafranca del Penedes,
1971

★ ★ ★ ★ ★

15th. Spain
Viña Salceda, Rioja Tinto 1974

★ ★ ★ ★ ★

16th. Chile
Antiguas Reservas
Cabernet-Sauvignon,
Cousiño Macul, 1971

★ ★ ★ ★ ★

17th. Chile
Gran Porton tinto Cabernet,
Viña Santa Carolina, 1976

★ ★ ★ ★ ★

17th. Spain
Marques de Caceres, Rioja
Union Vinicola, Cenicero, 1978

★ ★ ★ ★ ★

19th. Chile
San Pedro '71, Tinto, Cabernet-
Sauvignon, Wagner-Stein, 1971

★ ★ ★ ★ ★

20th. Chile
Casillero del Diablo
Special Reserva, Cabernet-
Sauvignon, Concha y Toro, 1972

★ ★ ★ ★ ★

21st. Spain
Imperial Cune, Rioja,
Compania del Norte, 1970

★ ★ ★ ★ ★

22nd. France
Château des Fines-Roches
Châteauneuf-du-Pape, 1976

★ ★ ★ ★ ★

SAUVIGNON BLANC

★ ★ ★ ★ ★

1st U.S.A.
Sauvignon
Sterling Vineyards, 1977

★ ★ ★ ★ ★

2nd. Italy
Sauvignon delle Venezie
Enofriulia 1978

★ ★ ★ ★ ★

3rd. U.S.A.
Sauvignon
Spring Mountains, 1976

★ ★ ★ ★ ★

4th. France
Sauvignon de Touraine A.O.C.
Nicolas, 1978

★ ★ ★ ★ ★

5th. Spain
Don Bertran, Saragossa, 1977

★ ★ ★ ★ ★

6th. Chile
Sauvignon Concha y Toro, 1977

★ ★ ★ ★ ★

6th. Mexico
Calafia, Pedro Domecq

★ ★ ★ ★ ★

8th. U.S.A.
Sauvignon E. & J. Gallo

★ ★ ★ ★ ★

9th. Chile
Gato Blanco, Viña San Pedro,
Wagner, Stein, 1977

★ ★ ★ ★ ★

10th. France
Sauvignon de Bordeaux
Nicolas, 1978

★ ★ ★ ★ ★

11th. France
Entre-Deux-Mers A.O.C.
Nicolas, 1978

★ ★ ★ ★ ★

12th. France
Graves A.O.C., Nicolas, 1977

★ ★ ★ ★ ★

13th. Israel
Sauvignon Blanc, Carmel Coop.
Zichon le Zion, 1976

★ ★ ★ ★ ★

14th. Chile
San Pedro '71
Wagner, Stein, 1971

★ ★ ★ ★ ★

15th. Chile
Sauvignon Blanc
Viña Santa Carolina, 1974

★ ★ ★ ★ ★

16th. Italy
Alghero Vermentino, Sella &
Mosca (Sardinia), 1978

★ ★ ★ ★ ★

PINOT NOIR

★ ★ ★ ★ ★

1st. Australia
Tyrell's Pinot noir, 1976

★ ★ ★ ★ ★

2nd. France
Clos-de-Vougeot, Nicolas, 1969

★ ★ ★ ★ ★

3rd. U.S.A.
Pinot noir, Hoffman Mountain
Ranch, 1975

4th. Switzerland
Pinot noir du Valais
'Chevaliers', Mathier-Kuchler,
Salquenen, 1977

★ ★ ★ ★ ★

5th. France
Côtes-de-Beaune-Villages
Nicolas, 1976

★ ★ ★ ★ ★

5th. France
Gevrey-Chambertin
Nicolas, 1976

★ ★ ★ ★ ★

7th. Switzerland
Pinot noir Sang de l'Enfer
Nouveau Salquenen,
Adrien Mathier, Valais, 1978

★ ★ ★ ★ ★

8th. Romania
Pinot noir Valea Calugareasca,
sans mill.

★ ★ ★ ★ ★

9th. Greece
Naoussa (cépage local
xynomavro) Boutaris &
Fils, 1976

★ ★ ★ ★ ★

10th. U.S.A.
Pinot noir
The Eyrie Vineyards, 1975

★ ★ ★ ★ ★

11th. France
Mercurey, 1973

★ ★ ★ ★ ★

Germany's wines are very underpriced indeed. So what does the German producer do? He uproots his Riesling and plants a more tolerant, higher-yielding variety, and goes for quantity rather than quality. And since the world seems to be full of people ready to buy cheap, anonymous-tasting, sweet white wine, he has little reason to do otherwise.

German law scarcely encourages him to concentrate on quality: a Burgundian cannot swap his Pinot Noir for another easier-to-grow variety and still call his wine Burgundy, yet the German grower can take his pick from a wide variety of newly-developed grapes without losing his right to use the same wine name as his great grandfather. Unlike most other appellation systems, the Germans categorize their wines according to the natural sweetness of the grapes rather than the particular variety grown, or indeed the established quality of the piece of land in which they are planted. So, in theory at least, the finest level of German wine, a Trockenbeerenauslese could be legally produced from the dull Müller-Thurgau grape on a flat piece of poorly situated soil, whilst the less ripe Riesling planted in a prime site might only reach 'QbA' status.

And what about all those names and quality designations? They seem terribly authoritative and informative, but what exactly do they mean? Well, a full explanation appears in the following pages but, in basic terms, it is worth remembering that what the Germans call a 'Qualitätswein bestimmter Anbaugebiete' (QbA), or in other words a 'quality wine from a designated region', invariably has to be sweetened up with grape juice to reach its required sugar and alcohol levels. So the cheapest, nastiest Liebfraumilch is deemed a 'quality wine'. It is a little like giving anyone whose feet reach the pedals a driving licence. It is a strange paradox that the country which has proved so unwilling to compromise on the quality of its motorcars has been eager to jettison any possible pride in the standard of its basic wine. Perhaps one answer would be to hand over the running of some of Germany's larger wine merchants to BMW or Volkswagen: a Liebfraumilch of the quality of a Volkswagen Beetle would be very welcome indeed.

In the meantime, we would suggest that you concentrate your attention on the higher quality QmPs and the humbler, and thus often overlooked Tafelweins and Landweins. For the price of two utterly forgettable bottles of Piesporter, you could have a truly delicious taste of what German wine producers can make when they want to.

This section being called 'Germany', we have deliberately excluded 'EEC Tafelwein', the bottled Italo-German wine lake which masquerades as hock or Moselle (watch out for the small print referring to 'different countries of the EEC'). We have, for the same reason excluded Sekt, the 'German' fizz which is usually a cocktail mix including a generous measure of poor white wine from south-west France and a more generous measure from Italy.

GERMANY

G ERMANY produces some of the very finest white wines in the world. Honeyed, rich spicy-appley Rieslings, wines of a perfumed delicacy unmatched by any other wine country. It also produces an ocean of some of the most mediocre sugar-water ever to call itself wine.

The problem with German wine is easily explained. Germany is situated too far north for the great Riesling grape (its traditional variety) to ripen with any reliability at all. Even in the years when it does, and is attacked by noble rot, developing into the glorious Auslesen, Beerenauslesen and Trockenbeerenauslesen on which Germany's vinous reputation was founded, too few wine drinkers are prepared to pay enough money to make it worth the growers' while. Make no mistake about it, at the top end of the scale, given their quality and the effort required for their limited production,

The Wine Regions

Anbaugebiete

AHR
Germany's northernmost wine region, and, paradoxically, the source of almost all its home-grown red wine. Vineyards are sheltered by the steep sides of the valley in the upper reaches of the river, and it is here only that the wines are produced. Most of the red wine is light (and often sweetish), more suited to German taste than destined for export markets.

MOSEL-SAAR-RUWER
Although lumped together into one area, the wines from the three rivers in the region's name can be very different in style. One factor unites the greatest examples: the Riesling grape. In the Mosel it can

make delicate, appley, honeyed wines, in the Saar the slaty soil gives it a steely firmness, and on the Ruwer it shares the delicacy of the Mosel wines, without their pronounced flowery character. Wines made from other grapes are generally poor reflections of the fine Rieslings.

MITTELRHEIN

This is castle country. These are memorable, the wines less so. Although planted mainly with Riesling, the vineyards of the Mittelrhein seem incapable of producing wines of the quality of the neighbouring regions. Drunk in wine cellars and restaurants on a 'schloss-crawl', however, they slake the thirst in an agreeably rustic way.

RHEINGAU

Probably Germany's finest wine region. Overwhelmingly planted in Riesling, the Rheingau produces wines that combine the delicacy of the Mosel-Saar-Ruwer with steely power. Best wines are grown, matured and bottled on individual estates, often small. Famous names are expensive, but most estate-bottled Rheingau from reliable growers is worth the asking price.

NAHE

An under-rated area. Some of Germany's best winemakers have estates here, and their wines are worthy of more general acclaim. Nahe wines are said to combine the characteristics of the Mosel and the Rhine, delicacy and full-bodied power. However described, they are usually good value for money.

RHEINHESSEN

The largest of the German regions. It deserves better than to be remembered as the historical home of Liebfraumilch, but that is the fate of most of its crop. Away from the riverfront, the land is flat and the wines lifeless. Around Nierstein and Bingen, however, great estates can produce superb wines, soft and gentle in character.

RHEINPFALZ

A sunny climate and fertile soil make the Rheinpfalz one of Germany's most productive regions. Although linked in the popular imagination with the other two Rhine areas, the Rheingau and Rheinhessen, Rheinpfalz wines display an indisputably 'southern'character – riper and spicier, as if the sun draws the very

essence of the soil into the grapes. Helped by conditions like these, output is enormous. Much of the less distinguished wine disappears into the lake of Liebfraumilch also known as Palahate wines..

HESSISCHE BERGSTRASSE

Smallest region, dominated by hundreds of small-holders. Most wine is made by the area's two co-operatives, and seldom travels outside the region, let alone the country. The best of the wines have the generosity of the Rheingau without its pedigree.

FRANKEN

It is sad to reflect that Franconia's most famous contribution to the outside world has been the Mateus Rosé bottle. The squat, flagon-shaped 'Bocksbeutel' is traditional in Franken, and its contents particularly prized throughout southern Germany. This makes Franken wines verymuch more expensive than wines of comparable quality from other regions, although the classic Silvaner wines have an earthy stylishness.

WÜRTTEMBERG

Another region whose wines rarely reach the outside world. Production of red wine makes up a quarter of Württemberg's total. The best of the wines, both red and white, are drunk by the natives of the region, who have the reputation of being the thirstiest wine-drinkers in all Germany.

BADEN

As the Baden region stretches for 250 miles, it is not surprising that it produces many very different types of wine along its length. Apart from the famous, spicy wines grown on the volcanic soil of the Kaiserstuhl and Tuniberg mountains, there are two distinct styles. The southerly position of Baden enables it to produce full-bodied, even alcoholic wines (in German terms), but the modern tendency is towards lightness and freshness. The co-ops, particularly the giant ZBW, lead in producing this type of wine.

The Grape List

Bacchus. A crossing of the Müller-Thurgau with a Riesling/Silvaner cross. It can be pleasantly flowery when ripe, but has a slightly dirty flavour when coming from a bad vintage, vineyard or cellar.

Huxelrebe. A cross of the Weisser Gutedel with the Courtillé Musqué, giving pleasantly peachy, grapy wines.

Kerner. A cross of the Riesling with the Trollinger vine, producing elegant, very Riesling-like wines.

Morio Muscat. The name and fragrance of this grape belie its actual origins. It's a cross between the Weissburgunder (Pinot Blanc) and the humble Silvaner, and the sweet, intensely perfumed, muscatty flavour is pure chance.

Müller-Thurgau. Germany's most widely planted grape. It's prolific, ripens early, and *can* make good wine, if not overcropped. No-one knows quite which vines were crossed to create it about 100 years ago. In its best examples, it can make sound, rarely exciting wine, tasting of flowering currant, and, believe it or not, quite pleasantly of cats' pee.

Optima. Another cross of Silvaner/Riesling with Müller-Thurgau, easy to ripen, so much so that it sometimes lacks bite.

Ortega. A crossing of the Müller-Thurgau with the Siegerrebe (itself a crossing of the Madeleine Angevine with the spicy Gewürztraminer) making full, peachy wines, though it can be bitter in poor years.

Portugieser. (or **Blauer Portugieser**) Probably imported from Portugal into Austria in the 18th century, and thence to Germany. No-one is quite sure what it is. It makes a light *red* wine with a fresh acidity.

Reichensteiner. These crosses are hard to bear after a bit. This one's of the good old Müller-Thurgau and an unnamed crossing of the Madeleine Angevine and the Calabreser Fröhlich (happy broccoli?). Fairly neutral flavoured wine, vaguely resembling the Pinot Blanc.

Riesling. At last, the noble original whence so many of these crossings have sprung. Pronounced 'ree-zling', *not* 'rye-zling'. When young, it makes crisp, fruity, flowery wines, sometimes honeyed. Good examples age for several years, becoming increasingly complex and strangely petrol-flavoured. Sounds disgusting, tastes delicious.

Ruländer. The Pinot Gris or Tokay of France. A full, lightly spicy wine, often with a honey flavour.

Scheurebe. Pronounced 'shoy-rayber'. A Silvaner/Riesling crossing distinctive for its grapefruit-skin-like smell and flavour. Nice, fresh acidity. One of the best of the 'new' German varieties.

Silvaner. A fairly neutrally flavoured grape, often used in blends. At its best, it can have a spicy, earthy, sometimes slightly vegetal character.

Spätburgunder. Otherwise known as the Blauer Burgunder or the Blauburgunder. A variation on the Pinot Noir of Burgundy that makes, here in Germany, light, fragrant, sweetish pinky-reds.

A List Of Recent German Vintages

1983
A good year. The best since 1979, in fact, with some excellent Rieslings made. Look out for the Kabinett quality wines, which are reasonably priced. Most wines above this quality level will repay keeping.

★ ★ ★ ★ ★

1982
Some examples are perfectly satisfactory, but many are flabby and low in acidity. There were problems during the vintage of rain and enormous quantities of grapes. Some wine lost concentration of flavour because of the rain, and some actually became tainted because of fermentations at over-high temperatures.

★ ★ ★ ★ ★

1981
Reasonable vintage, with balanced, pleasant wines. Good acidity levels have ensured survival of wines in the higher quality levels, where they are to be found.

★ ★ ★ ★ ★

1980
An undistinguished year. Not many wines still around.

★ ★ ★ ★ ★

1979
A good vintage, with balanced wines. Quite a lot of Spätlese wines made, and some Auslese. Not a vintage to keep much longer, though.

★ ★ ★ ★ ★

1976
Excellent vintage from a long, hot summer. A high proportion of wines in the highest quality levels. Some less well made wines lack the acidity necessary to age successfully, but the best examples are still going strong. A vintage to enjoy for years to come.

★ ★ ★ ★ ★

1971
Another excellent vintage. Increasingly rare, but worthwhile for the German wine enthusiast. The wines have an incredible balance and tenacity. Stick to Rieslings from reputable producers, however, to avoid disappointment.

★ ★ ★ ★ ★

German Wine Words

Abfüllung Bottling (as in 'bottled by')

Amtliche Prüfungsnummer officially awarded number relating to quality control. Indication of chemical analysis and tasting tests carried out by government testing centres on all QbA and QmP wines.

Anbaugebiet one of 11 designated wine regions (e.g. Rheingau).

Anreichern To enrich. Addition of sugar to grape-must to boost the alcohol content. Allowed only for QbA and Tafelwein, not QmP wines.

Auslese selected. Third rung on the QmP ladder, relating to wines made from very ripe grapes in good years only. Wines have to have attained a certain, stipulated specific gravity (measured in degrees Oechsle), in other words, a certain sweetness, to qualify. This varies from region to region.

Beeren grapes.

Beerenauslese selected grapes. Theoretically, wine made in very good vintages, out of selected, super-ripe grapes. In practice, all depends, as in auslese, on the Oechsle reading. The natural sugar is very often concentrated in these wines by Edelfäule, or noble rot. Fourth stage on the QmP scale.

Bereich sub-district within a region (Anbaugebiet). Seen on a label as a wine name (i.e. Bereich Schloss Böckelhein) usually applied to relatively undistinguished QbA wines.

Bocksbeutel distinctive squat flagon used for wines from Franken and a few from Baden. Same shape as Mateus Rosé.

Burg fortress or stronghold. Sometimes used in wine names, relating to wine from a particular castle's estate.

Deutsche Sekt Not necessarily, as you might expect, sparkling German wine, but usually sparkling wine which has had the sparkle put in in Germany. A misleading definition, as the actual wine is almost always imported from France or Italy.

Deutsche Tafelwein This really *does* come from Germany. Wine of the quality level below QbA and QmP wines, table wine. The 'Deutsche' is added to distinguish it from the 'Germanised' EEC Tafelwein.

Diabetikerwein very dry wine suitable for drinking by diabetics. Bottles carry a yellow seal.

Edelfäule noble rot. Fungus (*botrytis cinerea*) that affects very ripe grapes, causing them to shrivel and lose their water content, thus concentrating the natural sugars.

Einzellage single vineyard site. Follows the name of the village on QbA and QmP labels (i.e. Bernkasteler *Doktor*).

Eiswein wine made from frozen grapes. Grapes are left on the vine through November and into December or even January, and picked and pressed early in the morning, while still frozen. The frozen water crystals remain in the press, and the resulting juice is concentrated in both sugar and acidity. The pressed juice must reach Beerenauslese Oechsle level, but, because of the concentration reached through the elimination of the water crystals, a wine of very high quality can be made in years when the grapes would not otherwise reach levels higher than auslese.

Erzeugerabfüllung bottled at the estate.

Flurbereinigung Government-sponsored remodelling of vineyards. Construction of new roads to hitherto hard-to-reach vineyards, and rationalisation of holdings of scattered parcels of vines, making the land easier and more profitable to work.

Gebiet region.

Glühwein mulled wine, popular on the ski slopes. Usually made from red wine, sugar, water, lemon and spices.

Grosslage district within a Bereich producing wines of similar style, made up of many Einzellagen. Many well-known wine names are of wines from Grosslagen, rather than specific Einzellagen (i.e. Piesporter *Michelsberg*).

Halbtrocken half dry. Wine at the halfway house between trocken (dry) and ordinary German wines, containing no more than 18gm/litre of unfermented sugar.

Herb dry. Often seen in German restaurants to describe the drier wines on the list.

Hock term used to describe wines from the Rhine, said to have originated either as a corruption of Hochheim, or of 'hoch' (high), referring to quality. Now can also be used of QbA wines from the Ahr, Hessische Bergstrasse or Nahe, in addition, of course, to those from regions on the Rhine.

Kabinett lowest of the QmP categories. Because no QmP wines may contain added sugar, these are amongst the lightest and most delicate of quality German wines, usually less sweet than the 'enriched' QbA wines.

Kellerei wine cellar.

Landwein one step up from Deutsche Tafelwin. Wine from one of 15 designated areas which has a natural alcohol content $\frac{1}{4}$% higher than the minimum for Deutsche Tafelwein. It must also be no drier than halbtrocken.

Most must, or grape juice.

Oechsle the Oechsle scale is that by which the specific gravity, and hence the sweetness, of a must is measured.

Ortsteil section of a town, or community (i.e. Eitelsbach is an Ortsteil of the city of Trier). Another use in German wine law is to describe an estate so well-known that it is considered to be a community in its own right, separate from the village in which it is situated (i.e. Steinberg).

Perlwein slightly sparkling wine. Usually of a lesser quality than Sekt.

QbA Qualitätswein bestimmter Anbaugebieter: quality wine from one of the 11 specified wine regions. It must be made from permitted grape varieties, have a certain specified natural sugar content, and pass the analytical and tasting test to gain an A.P. number.

QmP Qualitätswein mit Prädikat quality wine with distinction. Into this quality bracket come all the great German wines. The six categories are kabinett, spätlese, auslese, beerenauslese, eiswein and trockenbeerenauslese, which all have to attain certain officially prescribed must weights on the Oechsle scale, depending upon grape variety and area.

Rebe grape.

Rotling light red wine made from a mixture of red and white grapes.

Rotwein red wine

Schaumwein basic sparkling wine. Higher quality sparklers are called sekt.

Schillerwein Rotling (*see above*) QbA or QmP produced in Württemberg.

Schloss castle.

Sekt quality sparkling wine.

Spätlese late harvested. Second of the categories in the QmP scale.

Spritzig slightly fizzy.

Steinwein archaic name for any Würzburg wine sold in a bocksbeutel. Now reserved for wine from the Stein Einzellage.

Süssreserve sweet reserve. Unfermented grape juice to add to a fully fermented wine in a process called back-blending to enhance the natural fruitiness of the wine. Widely used for Tafelwein and QbA wines.

Tafelwein table wine. Humbler quality level than QbA, and without the Deutsche prefix can come from anywhere within the EEC. It is rare to find a pleasant EEC Tafelwein.

Trocken dry. Wine that has less than 4 gm/litre of unfermented sugar, or 9 gm/litre if the acidity is not less than 2 gm/litre under that of the unfermented sugar (i.e. 9 gm/litre unfermented sugar to 7 gm/litre acidity). Trocken wines often seem curiously emasculated compared with slightly sweeter ones.

Trockenbeerenauslese wine made from selected dried grapes. Very rare and extremely expensive, the Oechsle levels required for this quality category can only be achieved in the very best years. To reach a sufficiently high concentration of sugar, the grapes used will usually have been affected by Edelfäule (noble rot).

Weinberg literally, a wine hill, but often used of flat vineyards.

Weinbrand brandy made from wine.

Weingut wine estate. May only be used on wines made exclusively from grapes grown on the particular estate.

Weinstrasse wine road. Route through wine producing country, often with specially designed signs.

Weissherbst rosé QbA wine made from a single grape variety, usually encountered in the Ahr, Baden and Württemberg regions.

Winzergenossenschaft cooperative cellar, taking in grapes on behalf of its grower members, and then vinifying and selling the resulting wines.

Winzerverein another word for a cooperative cellar.

Zentralkellerei central cellar of a group of cooperatives, taking in either grapes or wine. There are six such in Germany, in the Baden, Franken, Nahe, M-S-R, Rheinhessen and Württemberg regions. They are enormous operations.

A List of Recommended German Wine Villages and Vineyards

● Indicates a particularly recommended vineyard.

Alsheim, Rhsn. Village lying well back from prime river sites, which can nevertheless produce some good Rieslings.

●*Alsheimer Frühmesse*

Altenahr, Ahr. Castles ruined and standing dominate this little town at the end of the Ahr valley. Most wine is drunk by the locals and tourists.

Alzey, Rhsn. Little known outside the Rheinhessen, but locally famed for its viticultural research station.

Assmannshausen, Rhg. Best known for its red, or reddish, wine. Not really the stuff for those weaned on claret and Burgundy, but pleasant in a sweetish way.
●*Assmannshausener Höllenberg*

Ayl, M-S-R. One of the most distinguished wine-growing villages of the river Saar. In good years, the wines have a steeliness tempered with sweetness.
●*Ayler Herrenberger*
●*Ayler Kupp*

Bacharach, Mrh. More a stopping place for the river cruisers that constantly ply up and down this stretch of the Rhine than a great wine village. Some good Rieslings.

Bad Dürkheim, Rhpf. The home of the annual Dürkheimer Wurstmarkt (Sausage Market) in September. In fact, this is Germany's biggest *wine* fair, comparable to the Munich Beer Festival. Some of the finest wines in the Rheinpfalz, as well.
●*Dürkheimer Fuchsmantel*
●*Dürkheimer Spielberg*

Bad Kreuznach, Nahe. The most important town in the Nahe, both for its attractions as a spa and tourist resort, and its position as a centre of commerce. Many of the top vineyards in the region surround the town.
●*Kreuznacher Brückes*
●*Kreuznacher Krötenpfuhl*
●*Kreuznacher Narrenkappe*

Bensheim, HsBg. The Hessisches Bergstrasse's only town of any size, with its own municipally-owned vineyards.

Bernkastel-Kues, M-S-R. One of the great names of the Mosel. Not only the source of many of the finest wines of the Mittelmosel, but also a magically pretty town, in the best Disney tradition.
●*Bernkasteler Bratenhöfchen*
●*Bernkasteler Doktor*
●*Bernkasteler Graben*
●*Bernkasteler Lay*
●*Bernkasteler Matheisbildchen*
●*Bernkasteler Schlossberg*

Bingen, Rhsn. A town at the meeting of the rivers Nahe and Rhine. The Scharlachberg (scarlet mountain) behind the town, overlooking the Nahe, produces some elegant and complex wines.
●*Binger Scharlachberg*

Brauneberg, M-S-R. A village known principally for one vineyard: Juffer. This lies just the other side of the river from Brauneberg itself, and ranks with the top names of the Middle Mosel.
●*Brauneberger Juffer*

Castell, Frkn. One of the most reliable wine villages in Franken. Local wine-making is dominated by one large estate, the Fürstlich Castell'sches Domänenamt.
●*Casteller Kirchberg*

Cochem, M-S-R. Another example of the Mosel's seemingly endless capacity to delight with its small towns. As well as Riesling wines of style, Cochem boasts a castle, town fortifications and plenty of attractive, timber-framed houses.

Deidesheim, Rhpf. One of the two great wine towns of the enormous area of the Rheinpfalz. Not only a beautiful town, with distinguished Riesling-planted vineyards clustering round it, but also has an annual *goat* auction.
●*Deidesheimer Grainhübel*
●*Deidesheimer Herrgottsacke*
●*Deidesheimer Hohenmorgen*
●*Diedesheimer Kieselberg*
●*Deidesheimer Langenmorgen*
●*Deidesheimer Leinhöhle*

Dhron, M-S-R. Middle Mosel village lying between the two better known names of Piesport and Trittenheim. Some good Riesling wines from the steeper slopes.
●*Dhroner Goldtröpfchen*

Dorsheim, Nahe. Peaceful Nahe village above Laubenheim. The best vineyards are on the steep slopes of Burg Layen.
●*Dorsheimer Goldloch*
●*Dorsheimer Burgberg*

Durbach, Bdn. Durbach makes a speciality of unusual names for familiar grape varieties: Riesling becomes Klingelberger in local parlance, and Traminer, Clevner.

Eitelsbach, M-S-R. One of the two really top-class villages on the river Ruwer, and famous because of one particular estate, the Karthäuserhofberg.

Eltville, Rhg. Town which houses the State of Hessen Wine Estate headquarters. One of the most important wine estates in the whole of Germany, incorporating as it does the German Wine Academy. The wines themselves, though, are the main attraction, Rheingau Rieslings with backbone.

Enkirch, M-S-R. Not seen outside Germany a great deal, but Rieslings from the pretty town of Enkirch are attractively spicy.
●*Enkircher Steffensberg*

Erbach, Rhg. Rheingau village noted for the weight of the wines from its top vineyard, Marcobrunn. Unusually, this is not on the steep slopes, but right down by the river.
●*Erbacher Marcobrunn*
●*Erbacher Michelmark*
●*Erbacher Rheinhell*
●*Erbacher Siegelsberg*

Erden, M-S-R. The last of the truly fine villages of the Mittelmosel, as it meanders its way northwards towards Koblenz. Prälat is the top vineyard, and correspondingly expensive.
●*Erdener Prälat*
●*Erdener Treppchen*

Escherndorf, Frkn. Franconian village with one unforgettable and

renowned vineyard, Lump, which produces powerful Silvaners.
- *Escherndorfer Lump*

Forst, Rhpf. The other great Palatinate wine town. The Riesling vines planted in the Jesuitengarten and Ungeheuer vineyards are some of the best and most concentrated in the Pfalz.
- *Forster Jesuitengarten*
- *Forster Musenhang*
- *Forster Pechstein*
- *Forster Ungeheuer*

Freiburg, Bdn. Old university city with many historical buildings, and some good vineyards, especially those administered by the State Viticultural Institute.

Geisenheim, Rhg. A famous Rheingau village whose vinous renown has almost been overshadowed by that of its Research Institute. The Geisenheim Institute has pioneered many successful new grape varieties, and is one of the world's leading schools for winemakers.
- *Geisenheimer Kläuserweg*
- *Geisenheimer Mäuerchen*
- *Geisenheimer Rothenberg*

Graach, M-S-R. Although the best known vineyard is the evocatively named Himmelreich (kingdom of heaven), fine wines are produced in all the single vineyards of this Mittelmosel village.
- *Graacher Abstberg*
- *Graacher Domprobst*
- *Graacher Himmelreich*
- *Graacher Josephshöfer*

Guntersblum, Rhsn. A Rheingau village in the shadow of the nearby Oppenheim. Even some of the good individual estates turn to the better-known Oppenheimer Krotenbrunnen name to facilitate the selling of their wines. The name of Guntersblum should be recommendation enough.

Hallgarten, Rhg. High-lying Rheingau village, which, by virtue of its altitude, is protected from the mists and frosts that can afflict estates down by the river. It can make fine Rieslings.
- *Hallgartener Schönhell*

Hammelburg, Frkn. In the northern part of Franconia, on the river Saale, not far from the famous spa town of Bad Kissingen. The best vineyards are on limestone, and make firm, acidic wines.

Hattenheim, Rhg. One of the finest of the pedigree wine villages of the Rheingau, and that means in all Germany. The supreme estate within its boundaries is that of Steinberg.
- *Hattenheimer Nussbrunnen*
- *Hattenheimer Wisselbrunnen*
- *Steinberg*

Heidelberg, Bdn. Better known for its university and warring students perhaps than its wines, Heidelberg can make reliable wines from a variety of grapes.

Hochheim, Rhg. The village that is said to have given its name to the English nickname for Rhine wine, hock. It was certainly appreciated by Queen Victoria, after whom one of the finest vineyards is named.
- *Hochheimer Domdechaney*
- *Hochheimer Hölle*
- *Hochheimer Kirchenstück*
- *Hochheimer Königin Victoria Berg*

Ihringen, Bdn. One of the villages in Baden to make a passable red wine, as well as wine from the white Silvaner grape.

Iphofen, Frkn. Quality village to the east of the bend in the river Main round Würzburg and Kitzingen.
- *Iphofener Julius-Echter-Berg*
- *Iphofener Kalb*

Johannisberg, Rhg. A village so identified with wine made from the Riesling grape that 'Johannisberg' is actually used to differentiate between the true Riesling and its lesser cousins in some parts of the world. The village derives its own name from Schloss Johannisberg, one of Germany's most famous wine estates.
- *Johannisberger Hölle*
- *Schloss Johannisberg*

Kallstadt, Rhpf. The village in which the best-known single vineyard in the Palatinate is situated. Annaberg used to be referred to by this name alone. Now the rules have changed, and the village name is added.
- *Kallstadter Annaberg*
- *Kallstadter Steinacker*

Kanzem, M-S-R. One of a small clutch of quality Saar winemaking villages. Known for its Riesling wines.
- *Kanzemer Altenberg*

Kasel, M-S-R. The charm of the Ruwer, as opposed to the steel of the Saar, is personified by this small village.
- *Kaseler Hitzlay*
- *Kaseler Kehrnagel*
- *Kaseler Nieschen*

Kiedrich, Rhg. Small Rheingau village in the hills above Erbach and Eltville. Fine Riesling wines, particularly in good years.
- *Kiedricher Gräfenberg*
- *Kiedricher Sangrub*

Lieser, M-S-R. Just up-river from Bernkastel, Lieser is the family seat of the von Schorlemers. The Riesling wines are elegant and delicate.

Longuich, M-S-R. One of the first villages of quality on the Middle Mosel, below its confluence with the Ruwer above Trier. Gentle, flowery Mosels, rather than top quality wines.

Maximin-Grünhaus, M-S-R. One of the most famous of Ruwer wine names. Entirely owned by the C. von Schubert Gutsverwaltung, this tiny village produces classic if pricy Rieslings.

Meersburg, Bdn. Lovely old town on the shores of Germany's largest lake, the Bodensee. Although the vineyards, overlooking the lake, are at quite a high altitude, the Bodensee acts as a huge storage heater, and enjoys a very temperate climate.

Mittelheim, Rhg. Small town sandwiched between the famous Rheingau names of Winkel and Oestrich. Many of its wines are sold under the Oestrich label, and wines which actually bear the Mittelheim name are hard to find, but excellent value.

Mülheim, M-S-R: Another village less well known than its more illustrious neighbours, in this case Bernkastel and Bra. Mülheim can make well-balanced, racy Rieslings.

Münster-Sarmsheim, Nahe. Too much of a mouthful in its entirety, especially in conjunction with its best Einzellage, Dautenpflänzer, this village drops its Sarmsheim on the labels of bottles. Full-bodied, opulent Rieslings from the best sites.
- *Münsterer Dautenpflänzer*
- *Münsterer Pittersberg*

Nackenheim, Rhsn. The most northerly of the great villages on the stretch of the Rheinhessen between Mainz and Guntersblum. Total vineyard area is not extensive, and is planted upon red sandstone.

Niederhausen, Nahe. Not a familiar name in the UK wine market, perhaps, but source of some of the finest pedigree Riesling wines of the under-rated Nahe area. Home of the famous Nahe State Wine Cellars.
- *Niederhauser Hermannsberg*

Nierstein, Rhsn. The best-known of the Rheinhessen wine villages, although all too often for its least reputable product, Niersteiner Gutes Domtal. Top wines from Nierstein can really carry the torch for the region, and the local growers' assocation is fighting to disallow the linking of their village's good name with the inferior wines from the Gutes Domtal grosslage.

● *Niersteiner Bildstock*
● *Niersteiner Findling*
● *Niersteiner Hipping*
● *Niersteiner Ölberg*
● *Niersteiner Orbel*
● *Niersteiner Paterberg*
● *Niersteiner Pettenthal*

> The German term 'Kabinett' was originally used to describe those wines selected by the Duke of Nassau for his cellars.

Norheim, Nahe. Another distinguished village between Bad Kreuznach and Schloss Böckelheim on the best stretch of the Nahe. Good Rieslings, Silvaners and Müller-Thurgaus to be found.

● *Norheimer Dellchen*

Oberemmel, M-S-R. Tucked away up a valley a couple of kilometres from the great Scharzhofberg estate, Oberemmel is capable of producing fine, steely Saar Rieslings.

Oberwesel, Mrh. One of the very few villages in this region in which really good wine can be made. Steeply sloping vineyards, planted in Riesling, produce firm-bodied, vigorous wines.

Ockfen, M-S-R. It is villages like Ockfen which make the German wine enthusiast wonder why the fine, individual wines of the Saar and Ruwer were lumped in with the enormous lake of wine from the Mosel. One of the most distinguished sources in a classy region.

● *Ockfener Bockstein*
● *Ockfener Herrenberg*

Oestrich, Rhg. Smack in the middle of the priciest stretch of the Rheingau, Oestrich is the home of many fine estates and growers. Perhaps its wines do not scale the dizzy heights of some more illustrious neighbours, but they are uniformly reliable, and can be great in good years.

● *Oestricher Doosberg*
● *Oestricher Lenchen*
● *Schloss Reichhartshausen*

Oppenheim, Rhsn. The other Rheinhessen village (together with Nierstein) known more for the wine from one of its grosslagen, Krötenbrunnen, than its finer offerings. But finer wines there are in plenty, soft but concentrated.

● *Oppenheimer Kreuz*
● *Oppenheimer Sackträger*

Piesport, M-S-R. Together with Liebfraumilch and Niersteiner Gutes Domtal, probably the most widely known name in German wine – for all the wrong reasons. Piesporter Michelsberg, the wine from the surrounding grosslage, is rarely better than drinkable, and usually a lot worse than that. A pity, because some of the einzellage Rieslings are very good.

● *Piesporter Goldtröpfchen*
● *Piesporter Gunterslay*
● *Piesporter Treppchen*

Randersacker, Frkn. Reliable producer of powerful, earthy Silvaners and some slaty Rieslings. Like most Franken wine villages, however, its wares are expensive – even from the excellent local co-operative.

● *Randersackerer Teufelskeller*

Rauenthal, Rhg. High in the hills above the Rheinfront at Eltville, Rauenthal boasts individual Rieslings with a good acidity, particularly successful in really ripe vintages.

● *Rauenthaler Baiken*

Rödelsee, Frkn. One of the far-flung eastern outposts of good wine in this most diverse of German wine regions. The history of wine-making in Rödelsee reaches way back, although the village has been at the forefront of modernisation in the area.

● *Rödelseer Küchenmeister*

Rüdesheim, Rhg. This famous tourist town just above Bingen *does* have some splendid wines. You're unlikely to meet many of them in the Drosselgasse (the pedestrianised wine-tavern alley), but you'll have a thigh-slapping good time. Best Rieslings are rich and powerful. Rüdesheimer Rosengarten does *not* come from here, but from a much less distinguished village in the Nahe.

● *Rüdesheimer Berg Roseneck*
● *Rüdesheimer Berg Rottland*
● *Rüdesheimer Berg Schlossberg*

Ruppertsberg, Rhpf. Up with the top-ranking wine villages of the Rheinpfalz. Some of the fine, small individual sites make Ruppertsberger wine worth looking out for, Rieslings in particular.

● *Ruppertsberger Linsenbusch*
● *Ruppertsberger Reiterpfad*

Saarburg, M-S-R. Old and picturesque town upriver from Ockfen, Ayl and Wiltingen. Castle ruins dominate the vineyards, from which come some fine, steely Rieslings.

Schlossböckelheim, Nahe. Name given both to a single wine village and half the entire Nahe region (Bereich Schlossböckelheim). Wines from the village are elegant and balanced, especially those from the Kupfergrube vineyard, named after an old copper mine.

● *Schlossböckelheimer Felsenberg*
● *Schlossböckelheimer Kupfergrube*

Serrig, M-S-R. Situated right up the valley of the Saar, the wines of Serrig have an acidity which makes them almost unapproachable in mediocre years, but excellently suited for the manufacture of quality Riesling sparklers. In good years, however, the combination of steel and ripeness is memorable.

● *Serriger Schloss Saarfelser Schlossberg*

Steeg, Mrh. Perched high above Bacharach on the Mittelrhein is Schloss Stahleck, which gives its name to the surrounding Grosslage. Even further away, up a narrow tributary, is the village of Steeg, which can make the finest Rieslings in the area.

Traben-Trarbach, M-S-R. Thriving town divided by the Mosel in one of its tightest loops. Most of the best sites are on the Trarbach side, in the steeper vineyards.

Traisen, Nahe. Small village lying some way back from the river on one of the most exciting sections of the Nahe. The best sites produce lively, spicy Rieslings.

● *Traisener Bastei*
● *Traisener Rotenfels*

Trier, M-S-R. West Germany's oldest city has been growing vines since Roman times, and now houses the headquarters of the most prestigious estates of the surrounding area. Trier is rich in attractions for tourists, and the Ruwer wines are delicate but distinguished.

Trittenheim, M-S-R. Allegedly, the first vineyards planted with Germany's noblest grape, the Riesling, were here. Still the source of honeyed, soft Mittelmosel wines.

● *Trittenheimer Altärchen*
● *Trittenheimer Apotheke*

Ungstein, Rhpf. Bad Dürkheim's next-door neighbour down in the Mittelhaardt. Its vineyards are divided between three different Grosslagen, of which the sites in Honigsäckel, peculiar to Ungstein, are the best.

Ürzig, M-S-R. Best known for its Würzgarten (spice garden)

Einzellage, and producer of good, characterful Mittelmosel Rieslings.
● *Ürziger Würzgarten*

Volkach, Frkn. Attractive town with plenty of old buildings and art treasures on a curve of the Main north-east of Würzburg. Pleasant Silvaners and Müller-Thurgaus.

Wachenheim, Rhpf. A village which seems to typify all ever said about the superior richness and ripeness of the Palatinate wines. Full, unctuous Rieslings in any year which rises above mediocre.
● *Wachenheimer Böhlig*
● *Wachenheimer Gerümpel*
● *Wachenheimer Goldbächel*

Walporzheim, Ahr. A wine-making town for at least six centuries. Now producer of light Spätburgunder wines, mainly consumed by locals and the tourists who flock to the region.

Wawern, M-S-R. Steep slopes overlooking a sharp bend in the Saar river ensure typically firm, bracing Riesling wines.

Wehlen, M-S-R. One of the best of the Mittelmosel villages, its top wines paragons of honeyed sweetness. Most of these come from the vineyard across the river, Sonnenuhr, complete with eponymous sundial.
● *Wehlener Sonnenuhr*

Weinsberg, Wtbg. Home of the oldest wine academy in Germany, which also happens to be the largest wine estate in Württemberg. Several new grape varieties were first bred here, most notably the Kerner, and the wines are mostly dry and well-flavoured.

Wiltingen, M-S-R. Arguably the noblest of the several distinguished Saar wine villages, Wiltingen can make wines which are full of slaty elegance. Many top estates have fine vineyards here.
● *Scharzhofberg*
● *Wiltinger Braunfels*
● *Wiltinger Kupp*
● *Wiltinger Schlangengraben*

Winkel, Rhg. Another pedigree Rheingau village, whose top Rieslings are complex and delicious. Schloss Vollrads, one of the very few single estates allowed to use its own name without a qualifying village name on the label, lies at the back of the little town.
● *Schloss Vollrads*
● *Winkeler Hasensprung*
● *Winkeler Jesuitengarten*

Worms, Rhsn. Much Liebfraumilch has flowed down the throats of thirsty thousands since the vineyards surrounding the Liebfrauenkirche in Worms first gave their name to the world's most popular German wine. Wine from that original vineyard isn't anything wildly special, either.

Würzburg, Frkn. Such is the popularity of Franken wines in Germany that they are expensive compared to wines of similar

quality from other areas. Würzburg still has some exquisite 18th century corners, however, and wonderful old cellars in which to enjoy the local offerings.
● *Würzburger Innere Leiste*
● *Würzburger Stein*

Zell, M-S-R. The wine from Zell's grosslage, Schwartze Katz (black cat), has so captured the imagination of the main overseas markets, especially the USA, that even humble wines bearing this label command surprising prices. Zell *can* make light, flowery Rieslings, but they seldom reach top-quality level.

Zeltingen-Rachtig, M-S-R. Wines from these linked wine villages can enjoy all the charm and attraction of classy Mosel Riesling. As is so often the case, however, the more widely available Grosslage wine, Zeltinger Münzlay, is but a pale shadow of the fine single vineyard wines.
● *Zeltinger Himmelreich*
● *Zeltinger Schlossberg*
● *Zeltinger Sonnenuhr*

Key to Wine Regions

Ahr **Ahr**
Bdn. **Baden**
Frkn. **Franken**
HsBg. **Hessische Bergstrasse**
M-S-R **Mosel Saar Ruwer**
Nahe **Nahe**
Rhg. **Rheingau**
Rhsn. **Rheinhessen**
Rhpf. **Rheinpfalz**
Wtbg. **Württemberg**

Reliable Estates and Growers

Abteihof, Weingut	*M-S-R*
Adelmann, Weingut Graf	*Wtbg*
Adeneuer, Weingut-Weinkellerei	*Ahr*
Affaltrach, Weingut Schlosskellerei	*Wtbg*
Allendorf, Weingut Fritz	*Rhg*
Altenkirch, Weingut Friedrich	*Rhg*
Alzey, Weingut der Stadt	*Rhsn*
Anheuser, Weingut konomierat August E.	*Nahe*
Anheuser, Weingut Paul	*Nahe*
Annaberg Stumpf-Fitz'sches Weingut	*Rhpf*
Arnet, Wilhelm	*Rhg*
Aschrott'sche Erben, Geheimrat	*Rhg*
Bad Kreuznach, Staatsweingut Weinbaulehranstalt	*Nahe*
Balbach Erben, Bürgermeister Anton, Weingut	*Rhsn*
Basserman-Jordan, Weingut Geheimer Rat Dr von	*Rhpf*
Basting-Gimbel, Weingut	*Rhg*
Baumann, Weingut Friedrich	*Rhsn*
Becker, J.B. Weingut Weinkellerei	*Rhg*
Belz Erben, Weingut C.	*Rhg*
Bensheim, Weingut der Stadt	*HsBg*
Bentzel-Sturmfeder'sches Weingut, Gräflich von	*Wtbg*
Bergdolt, F. & G.	*Rhpf*
Bergstrasse, Staatsweingut	*HsBg*
Bergstrasse Gebiets Winzergenossenschaft eG	*HsBg*
Bergweiler-Prüm Erben, Zach	*M-S-R*
Biffar, Weingut Josef	*Rhpf*
Bischöfliche Weingüter, Verwaltung der	*M-S-R*
Blankenhorn K.G., Weingut Fritz	*Bdn*
Brenner'sches Weingut	*Rhsn*

Brentano'sche Gutsverwaltung, Baron von	*Rhg*	Hövel, Weingut von	*M-S-R*
Breuer, Weingut G.	*Rhg*	Hupfeld Erben, Weingut	*Rhg*
Buhl, Weingut Reichsrat von	*Rhpf*	Immich-Batterieberg, Carl Aug.	*M-S-R*
Burg Hornberg, Weingut	*Bdn*	Johannisberger Rosenhof, Weingut	*Rhg*
Bürgerspital zum Heiigen Geist	*Frkn*	Johannishof, Weingut	*Rhg*
Bürklin-Wolf, Weingut Dr	*Rhpf*	Josefinengrund, Weingut	*M-S-R*
Castell'sches Domänenamt, Fürstlich	*Frkn*	Josephshof, Weingut der	*M-S-R*
Christoffel Jr, Jos.	*M-S-R*	Jost, Weingut Toni	*Mrh/Rhg*
Crusius, Weingut Hans	*Nahe*	Juliusspital-Weingut	*Frkn*
Dahlem Erben, Weingutsverwaltung Sanitätsrat Dr	*Rhsn*	Kaiserstühler Winzergenossenschaft, Ihringen eG	*Bdn*
Dahlem		Kallstadt eG, Winzergenossenschaft	*Rhpf*
Deidesheim eG, Winzerverein	*Rhpf*	Kanitz, Weingut Graf von	*Rhg*
Deinhard & Co. KgaA	*M-S-R/Rhg/*	Kanzemer Berg, Weingut	*M-S-R*
	Rhpf	Karp-Schreiber, Weingut Chr.	*M-S-R*
Deutsches Weintor, Gebiets-Winzergenossenschaft eG	*Rhpf*	Karst & Söhne Weingut Weinkellerei, Joh.	*Rhpf*
Diefenhardt'sches Weingut	*Rhg*	Karthäuserhof, Gutsverwaltung Werner Tyrell	*M-S-R*
Diel auf Burg Layen, Schlossgut	*Nahe*	Kaseler St.Irminenhof, Weingut	*M-S-R*
Domklausenhof, Weingut	*M-S-R*	Kern, Weingut Dr	*Rhpf*
Drathen KG, Ewald Theod.	*M-S-R*	Kesselstatt, Weingut Reichsgraf von	*M-S-R*
Duhr Nachf., Weingut Franz	*M-S-R*	Kies-Kieren, Weingut	*M-S-R*
Dünweg, Weingut Otto	*M-S-R*	Knebel, Weingut Erwin	*M-S-R*
Ehses-Berres, Weingut Geschwister	*M-S-R*	Knoll & Reinhart, Weinbau-Weinkellerei	*Frkn*
Ehses-Geller-Erben, Weingut	*M-S-R*	Knyphausen, Weingut zu	*Rhg*
Eltville, Verwaltung der Staatsweingüter	*Rhg*	Koch, Weingut Apollinar Josef	*M-S-R*
Engelmann, Weingut Karl Fr.	*Rhg*	Koch Erben, Weingut Bürgermeister Carl	*Rhsn*
Eser, Weingut August	*Rhg*	Koeler-Ruprecht, Weingut	*Rhpf*
Finkenauer, Weingut Carl	*Nahe*	Koeler-Weidmann, Weingut	*Rhsn*
Fischer, Weingut Dr	*M-S-R*	Königin Victoria Berg, Weingut	*Rhg*
Fischer Erben, Weingut konomierat J.	*Rhg*	Köster-Wolf, Weingut	*Rhns*
Fitz-Ritter, Weingut K.	*Rhpf*	Krebs-Grode, Vereinigte Weingüter	*Rhsn*
Forster Winzerverein eG	*Rhpf*	Kühn Weinbau Heinrich	*Rhg*
Franken eG, Gebietswinzergenossenschaft	*Frkn*	Kurfürstenhof, Weingut	*Rhsn*
Frankensteiner Hof	*Rhg*	Laible, Weingut Andreas	*Bdn*
Frankfurt am Main, Weingut der Stadt	*Rhg*	Lamm-Jung, Weingut	*Rhg*
Freiberger, OHG, Weingut H.	*HsBg*	Landenberg, Weingut Schlosskellerei Freiherr von	*M-S-R*
Freiberg, Staatliches Weinbauinstitut	*Bdn*	Lang, Weingut Hans	*Rhg*
Friedelsheim eG, Winzergenossenschaft	*Rhpf*	Langehof, Weingut	*Rhg*
Friedrich-Wilhelm-Gymnasium, Stiftung Staatliches	*M-S-R*	Lauerberg, Weingut J.	*M-S-R*
Gallais, Weingut le	*M-S-R*	Licht-Bergweiler Erben, Weingut P.	*M-S-R*
Gebhardt, Ernst, Weingut Weingrosskellerei	*Frkn*	Liebfrauenberg, Winzerverein	*Rhpf*
Geisenheim, Institut	*Rhg*	Loewen, Weingut Karl	*M-S-R*
Geltz Erben, Weingut Forstmeister	*M-S-R*	Loosen-Erben, Weingut Benedict	*M-S-R*
Gemmingen-Hornberg'sches Weingut, Freiherrl.von	*Bdn*	Löwenstein-Wertheim-Rosenberg'sches Weingut,	
Gleichenstein, Weingut Freiherr von	*Bdn*	Fürstlich	*Frkn*
Göler'sches Rentamt, Freiherr von	*Bdn*	Männle, Weingut Andreas	*Bdn*
Gunderloch-Usinger, Weingut	*Rhsn*	Marienhof, Weingut	*M-S-R*
Guntrum-Weinkellerei GmbH, Louis	*Rhsn*	Marienthal, Staatliche Weinbaudomäne	*Ahr*
Haag, Weingut Fritz	*M-S-R*	Matheus-Lehnert, Weingut J.	*M-S-R*
Haart, Weingut Johann	*M-S-R*	Meersburg, Staatsweingut	*Bdn*
Hahnhof GmbH, Die Weinbau	*Rhpf*	Meyerhof, Weingut	*M-S-R*
Hain, Weingut Dr J.B.	*M-S-R*	Milz, Weingut	*M-S-R*
Hallgarten/Rhg eG, Winzergenossenschaft	*Rhg*	Minges, Weingut Ernst	*Rhpf*
Hammel & Cie Weingut Weinkellerei, Emil	*Rhpf*	Minges, Rudolf	*Rhpf*
Hammelburg, Stadt. Weingut	*Frkn*	Mosbacher, Weingut Georg	*Rhpf*
Heddesdorf, Weingut Freiherr von	*M-S-R*	Mosel-Saar-Ruwer eG, Zentralkellerei	*M-S-R*
Heilsbruck, Kloster	*Rhpf*	Müller, Weingut Felix	*M-S-R*
Herpfer, Weinbau-Weinkellerei Christoph Hs.	*Frkn*	Müller GmbH & Co, Rudolf	*M-S-R*
Hessische Forschungsanstalt	*Rhg*	Müller, Weingut	*Frkn*
Hessisches Weingut, Landgräflich	*Rhg*	Müller-Dr Becker, Weingut	*Rhsn*
Heyl zu Herrnsheim, Weingut Freiherr	*Rhsn*	Müller-Scharzhof, Weingut Egon	*M-S-R*
Hoensbroech, Weingut Reichsgraf & Marquis zu	*Bdn*	Mumm'sches Weingut, G.H.von	*Rhg*
Hof Sonneck, Weingut	*Rhg*	Nägler, Weingut Dr Heinrich	*Rhg*
Höfer, Weingut Dr Josef	*Nahe*	Nahewinzer eG, Zentralkellerei der	*Nahe*
Hohenlohe Langenburgsche Weingüter, Fürstlich	*Wtbg/Frkn*	Neckarauer, Weingut K.	*Rhpf*
Hohenlohe-Ohringen'sche, Fürst zu	*Wtbg*	Neipperg, Weingüter & Schlosskellerei Graf von	*Wtbg*
Holschier, Weingut Nikolaus Jacob	*Rhg*	Nell, Georg-Fritz von	*M-S-R*

Neus, Weingut J.	*Rhsn*
Neveu, Weingut Freiherr von	*Bdn*
Nicolay'sche Weinguts-Verwaltung C.H. Berres Erben	*M-S-R*
Niederhausen-Schlossböckelheim, Verwaltung der Staatlichen Weinbaudomäne	*Nahe*
Niederkirchner Winzerverein	*Rhpf*
Nikolai, Weingut Heinz	*Rhg*
Oberemmeler Abteihof, Weingut	*M-S-R*
Ohler'sches Weingut, Kommerzienrat P.A.	*Rhsn*
Oetinger'sches Weingut, Robert von	*Rhg*
Offenburg, Weingut der Stadt	*Bdn*
Oppenheim, Staatsweingut der Landes-, Lehr- und Versuchsanstalt	*Rhsn*
Ortenaukreises, Weinbauversuchsgut des	*Bdn*
Pallhuber Weingut & Weinkellerei GmbH, Maximilian	*Nahe*
Pauly KG, Weingut Otto	*M-S-R*
Perll, August	*Mrh*
Pfarrkirche, Weingut der	*M-S-R*
Pfeffingen, Weingut	*Rhpf*
Piedmont, Weingut konomierat Max-G.	*M-S-R*
Plettenberg'sche Verwaltung, Reichsgräflich von	*Nahe*
Popp KG, Weingut Ernst	*Frkn*
Prüm, Weingut Joh. Jos.	*M-S-R*
Prüm Erben, Weingut S.A.	*M-S-R*
Randersacker eG, Winzergenossenschaft	*Frkn*
Rappenhof, Weingut	*Rhsn*
Rebholz, Weingut konomierat	*Rhpf*
Reh & Sohn GmbH & Co. KG, Franz	*M-S-R*
Ress KG, Balthasar	*Rhg*
Reverchon, Weingut Edmund	*M-S-R*
Rheinart Erben, Weingut Adolf	*M-S-R*
Rheinfront eG, Bezirks-Winzergenossenschaft	*Rhsn*
Rheingau eG, GebietsWinzergenossenschaft	*Rhg*
Rheingräfenberg eG, Winzergenossenschaft & Weinkellerei	*Nahe*
Richter, Weingut Max Ferd.	*M-S-R*
Richter-Boltendahl, Weingut	*Rhg*
Riedel, Weingut Jakob	*Rhg*
Ronde, Weingut Sanitätsrat Dr	*M-S-R*
Ruppertsberger Winzerverein 'Hoheburg' eG	*Rhpf*
St Johannishof, Weingut	*M-S-R*
St Nikolaus Hospital	*M-S-R*
Schaefer, Weingut Karl	*Rhpf*
Schales, Weingut	*Rhsn*
Schlangengraben, Weingut	*M-S-R*
Schleinitz'sche Weingutsverwaltung, Freiherr von	*M-S-R*
Schlink-Herf-Gutleuthof, Vereinigte Weingüter	*Nahe*
Schloss Groenesteyn, Weingut des Reichsfreiherrn von Ritter zu Groenesteyn	*Rhg*
Schloss Johannisberg, Fürst von Metternich-Winneburg'sches Domäne Rentamt	*Rhg*
Schloss Lieser, Weingut	*M-S-R*
Schloss Rheinhartshausen, Prinz Friedrich von Preussen	*Rhg*
Schloss Saarstein, Weingut	*M-S-R*
Schloss Salem	*Bdn*
Schloss Schönborn, Domänenweingut	*Rhg*
Schloss Staufenberg, Markgräflich Badis'ches Weingut	*Bdn*
Schloss Vollrads, Graf Matuschka-Greiffenclau'sche Gutverwaltung	*Rhg*
Schlotter, Weingut Valentin	*Rhg*
Schlumberger, Weingut Hartmut	*Bdn*
Schmitt, Weingut Hermann Franz	*Rhsn*
Schmitt-Dr Ohnacker, Weingut	*Rhsn*
Schmitt'sches Weingut, Gustav Adolf	*Rhsn*
Schneider, Weingut Georg Albrecht	*Rhsn*
Schneider, Weingut Jakob	*Nahe*
Schneider Nachf., Michel	*M-S-R*
Schneider GmbH, Weingut Weinkellerei L.	*Rhpf*
Schorlemer GmbH, Hermann Freiherr von	*M-S-R*
Schubert'sche Gutsverwaltung, C.von	*M-S-R*
Schuch, Weingut Geschwister	*Rhsn*
Schultz-Werner, Weingut Oberst	*Rhsn*
Schumann-Nägler, Weingut	*Rhg*
Schuster, Weingut Eduard	*Rhg*
Schweinhardt Nachf., Weingut Bürgermeister Willi	*Nahe*
Sebastian Nachf., Jakob	*Ahr*
Selbach-Oster, Weingut Geschwister	*M-S-R*
Simmern'sches Rentamt, Freiherrlich Langwerth von	*Rhg*
Simon, Bert	*M-S-R*
Sittman, Weingut Carl	*Rhsn*
Sohlbach, Weingut Georg	*Rhg*
Solemacher, Weingut Freiherr von	*M-S-R*
Sonnenhof, Weingut	*Wtbg*
Spiess, Kommerzienrat Georg Fr.	*Rhpf*
Spindler, Weingut Eugen	*Rhpf*
Stauch, Alfred & Hartmut	*Rhpf*
Stodden, Weingut Jean	*Ahr*
Strub, Weingut J. & H.A.	*Rhsn*
Studert-Prüm, Stephan	*M-S-R*
Sturm & Sohn, Weingut	*Rhg*
Tesch, Weingut Erbhof	*Nahe*
Tanisch, Weingut Wwe. Dr H.	*M-S-R*
Thüngersheim eG, Winzergenossenschaft	*Frkn*
Tillmanns Erben Weinsgutverwaltung, H.	*Rhg*
Tobias, Weingut Oskar	*M-S-R*
Trier, Verwaltung der Staatlichen Weinbaudomänen	*M-S-R*
Vereinigte Hospitien, Güterverwaltung	*M-S-R*
Vereinigte Weingutsbesitze Hallgarten eG	*Rhg*
Vier Jahreszeiten-Kloster Limburg, Winzergenossenschaft	*Rhpf*
Villa Sachsen, Weingut	*Rhsn*
Vollmer, Weingut Adam	*Rhg*
Volxem, Weingut Bernd van	*M-S-R*
Volxem, Weingut Staatsminister a.d.Otto von	*M-S-R*
Wachtenburg-Luginsland eG, Winzergenossenschaft	*Rhpf*
Wagner, Weingut-Weinhaus	*Mrh*
Wagner-Weritz, Weingut	*Rhg*
Wegeler Erben, Gutsverwaltung Geheimrat J.	*Rhg*
Wehrheim, Weingut Eugen	*Rhsn*
Weil, Weingut Dr R.	*Rhg*
Weiler, Weingut Heinrich	*Mrh*
Weinsberg, Staatliche Lehr- und Versuchanstalt	*Wtbg*
Weins-Prüm Erben, Weingut Dr F.	*M-S-R*
Werner'sches Weingut, Domdechant	*Rhg*
Winkels-Herding, Weingut	*Rhpf*
Winzerkeller Südliche Bergstrasse	*Bdn*
Wirsching, Weingut Hans	*Frkn*
Wolf Erben, Weingut J.L.	*Rhpf*
Wolff-Metternich'sches Weingut, Gräflich	*Bdn*
Württembergische Hofkammer-Kellerei	*Wtbg*
Würzburg Staatliche Hofkeller	*Frkn*
Zentralkellerei Badischer Winzergenossenschaft eG,	*Bdn*
Zentralkellerei Mosel-Saar-Ruwer	*M-S-R*
Zentralkellerei Rheinischer Winzergenossenschaft	*Rhsn*
Zwierlein, Weingut Freiherr von	*Rhg*

List of Recommended German Wines
(And Wines to Avoid)

CHEAP WINES TO LAY DOWN

There are none. Inexpensive German wine is made to be drunk young.

Occasionally, in a very good year, a Riesling of mere QbA quality from the Rheingau, from a very good grower, might last for several years. But by the time these various conditions had been met, it would not be a particularly cheap bottle.

★ ★ ★ ★ ★

CHEAP WINES FOR IMMEDIATE DRINKING

In all these recommendations, the wine should be from the most recent acceptable vintage.

Landwein der Mosel
Landwein der Saar
Rheinpfalz Morio Muscat
Gebietswinzergenossenschaft Franken Silvaner
Winzergenossenschaft Thüngersheim Müller-Thurgau
Any wine from the Gebietswinzergenossenschaft Rheingau
Kröver Nacktarsch – for the silly label

★ ★ ★ ★ ★

MORE EXPENSIVE WINES TO LAY DOWN

1983 Nahe auslesen
1983 Maximin-Grünhaus wines
1983 Schloss Reinhartshausen wines
1983 Rheingau from Balthasar Ress
1983 Kallstadter Annaberg, Stumpf-Fitz'sches Weingut
1983 Ayler Herrenberg, Bischöfliche Weingüter
1983 Schlossböckelheimer Kupfergrube, Niederhausen-
Schlossböckelheim Staatliche Weinbaudomäne
1983 Scharzhofberg, Reichsgraf von Kesselstatt
1983 Winkeler Hasensprung, Basting-Gimbel
1983 Forster Jesuitengarten, Basserman-Jordan

★ ★ ★ ★ ★

MORE EXPENSIVE WINES FOR IMMEDIATE DRINKING

1971 M-S-R auslesen and trockenbeerenauslesen
1976 Wachenheimer Böhlig, Bürklin-Wolf
1976 Deidesheimer Herrgottsacker, von Buhl
1976 Niersteiner Hipping, A. Balbach
1979 Wehlener Sonnenuhr, J. -J. Prum
1979 Binger Scharlachberg Eiswein, Villa Sachsen
1979 Bernkasteler Doktor, Deinhard
1981 Serriger Schloss Saarfleser Schlossberg, Vereinigte Hospitien
1981 Kaseler Kehrnagel, B. Simon
1981 Kiedricher Sandgrub, Dr. R. Weil

★ ★ ★ ★ ★

WINES TO AVOID

Liebfraumilch
Piesporter Michelsberg
Niersteiner Gutes Domtal
Oppenheimer Krötenbrunnen
Zeller Schwartze Katz
All EEC Tafelwein

> **The longest wine name:**
> '**Hochheimer Koenigin Victoria Berg Riesling Trockenbeerenauslese QmP**'
> **has 61 characters.**

GOOD PINOT NOIRS

(other than Burgundy)

The Pinot Noir is hard enough to grow in Burgundy, its native soil. No-one has truly succeeded in producing Pinot Noir of the quality of great red Burgundy elsewhere, but the following wineries are having a pretty fair shot at it.

Acacia St Clair Vineyard
California

★ ★ ★ ★ ★

Almaden
California

★ ★ ★ ★ ★

Babich
New Zealand

★ ★ ★ ★ ★

Buena Vista – Special Selection
California

★ ★ ★ ★ ★

Calera – Selleck
California

★ ★ ★ ★ ★

Carneros Creek
California

★ ★ ★ ★ ★

Chalone
California

★ ★ ★ ★ ★

Clos du Bois
California

★ ★ ★ ★ ★

Clos du Val
California

★ ★ ★ ★ ★

Columbia
Washington, U.S.A.

★ ★ ★ ★ ★

Edmeades
California

★ ★ ★ ★ ★

Eyrie
Oregon

★ ★ ★ ★ ★

Frick
California
a good wine despite its label.
See p.000

★ ★ ★ ★ ★

Mihaly
California

★ ★ ★ ★ ★

Mondavi
California

★ ★ ★ ★ ★

Moss Wood
Western Australia

★ ★ ★ ★ ★

Nobilo
New Zealand

★ ★ ★ ★ ★

Saintsbury – Garnet
California

★ ★ ★ ★ ★

Sanford
California

★ ★ ★ ★ ★

Sebastiani
California

★ ★ ★ ★ ★

Robert Stemmler
California

★ ★ ★ ★ ★

Tualatin
Oregon, U.S.A.

★ ★ ★ ★ ★

Tyrrells – Ashmans
Hunter Valley, Australia

★ ★ ★ ★ ★

Wantirna Estate
Victoria, Australia

★ ★ ★ ★ ★

Hermann Wiemer
Finger Lakes, New York, USA.

★ ★ ★ ★ ★

GREAT CHARDONNAY PRODUCERS

apart from Burgundy

Unlike the Pinot Noir, its Burgundian neighbour, the Chardonnay has proven successful in almost every country which has planted it. The following is a list of great white, non-Burgundian, Chardonnays.

Brown Brothers Milawa Estate
Australia

★ ★ ★ ★ ★

Buena Vista
California

★ ★ ★ ★ ★

Carneros Creek
California

★ ★ ★ ★ ★

Chalone
California

★ ★ ★ ★ ★

Chappellet
California, USA

★ ★ ★ ★ ★

Château des Charmes
New Zealand

★ ★ ★ ★ ★

Château Grand Traverse
Michigan, USA

★ ★ ★ ★ ★

Château Ste Michelle *Washington, USA*	**Orlando-Riverland** *Barossa Valley, Australia*
★ ★ ★ ★ ★	★ ★ ★ ★ ★
Clos du Bois *California*	**Parducci** *California*
★ ★ ★ ★ ★	★ ★ ★ ★ ★
Jean Léon *Spain*	**Petaluma** *Australia*
★ ★ ★ ★ ★	★ ★ ★ ★ ★
Domaine Laurier *California*	**Rosemount Show Reserve** *Hunter Valley, Australia*
★ ★ ★ ★ ★	★ ★ ★ ★ ★
Gold Seal *Finger Lakes, New York, USA*	**Rothbury** *Australia*
★ ★ ★ ★ ★	★ ★ ★ ★ ★
Hargreave *Long Island, New York, USA*	**Seppelt** *Adelaide, Australia*
★ ★ ★ ★ ★	★ ★ ★ ★ ★
Lake's Folly *New South Wales, Australia*	**Shafer** *Oregon, USA*
★ ★ ★ ★ ★	★ ★ ★ ★ ★
Leeuwin *Western Austrlia*	**Tisdall-Mount Helen** *Victoria, Australia*
★ ★ ★ ★ ★	★ ★ ★ ★ ★
Mondavi *California*	**Wente Brothers** *California*
★ ★ ★ ★ ★	★ ★ ★ ★ ★
Montana-Gisbourne *New Zealand*	**Wynn's** *Australia*
★ ★ ★ ★ ★	★ ★ ★ ★ ★

The Great Grape List

The Red List

Alicante Bouschet
An early (19th century) cross between the Grenache and the Petit Bouschet which yields generous amounts of very deeply coloured wine. So what's wrong with that? Nothing, except that the colour fades very rapidly indeed, and the wine tastes watery and dull. The North Africans, on whom a large acreage of these vine was foisted by French colonists, are uprooting them as fast as they can. *Grown in: S. France, Uruguay, Algeria, Morocco, California.*

Barbera
Of all Italy's black grapes, the Barbera is arguably the one best suited to the fruit-obsessed palate of the Anglo-Saxon wine drinker. Which probably explains why this Piedmont variety is beginning to make a home for itself in California. Another reason though lies in the high levels of acidity which mark its wines: acidity – or a shortage of it – can be a major problem in the warm vineyards of western USA. Either way, American or Italian, these spicily fruity wines can be amongst the most characterful reds. *Grown in: Argentina, Brazil, California, Chile, Italy (Piedmont), Uruguay.*

Cabernet Franc
Grassy is the note here – that and summer berry fruit. It is reminiscent of the more illustrious Cabernet Sauvignon, but in the way of a young and slightly abrasive cousin with a great deal to learn. The Cabernet Franc plays its part in the blend of great claret, and stands firmly on its own two feet in the Loire and in northern Italy, producing fresh, fruity red wines to be drunk young. It is also pretty good at making rosé. *Grown in: France, Argentina, Australia, Algeria, California, Bulgaria, Chile, Tunisia, Greece, Romania, Yugoslavia.*

Carignan
The Carignan is a very important grape indeed. Because there is, as they say, a lot of it around. Unfortunately, there's not a great deal to commend the wine which it produces. When it isn't plain dull, it can be bitter and clumsy tasting, making for red wines which really have to be drunk chilled on hot summer days. *Grown in: Algeria, California, France, Israel, Lebanon, Mexico, Morocco, Spain, Tunisia, Turkey, Uruguay.*

Cinsault
A 'component' grape which has sufficient fruit and acidity to stand alongside the Grenache in red and more particularly rosé wines. In South Africa and New Zealand it has been crossed with the Pinot Noir to produce Pinotage. *Grown in: Algeria, France – Midi, Provence, Loire – Greece, Lebanon, Morocco, Spain, S. Africa, Tunisia, Turkey, Uruguay.*

Concord
'Delusions of adequacy': that's one way to describe this traditional American east-coast variety. Its wines taste obvious, earthy and almost totally lacking in any subtlety or complexity. They're the kind of wines you think were somehow sidetracked into your glass on their way to the saucepan or the distillery. Kosher, sweet versions, are perhaps the best use for the Concord. Canadian wine writer Tony Aspler's comment says it all: 'Concord grapes make awful wine. As grape juice, or when its "foxy" taste is camouflaged as "sherry" or "port", its OK but as wine I'd rather drink the gum they used to stick on the label'. *Grown in: Brazil, Japan, USA.*

Gamay
Like its more illustrious neighbour, the Pinot Noir, the Gamay is very fussy about where it will and will not do its thing. In the Beaujolais, the only really successful region so far, it produces gloriously mouth-watering wine which can make you think of boiled sweets, cherries, plums . . . above all, of fresh, fruity flavours. One confusing factor is the way in which the wine is made. Macération Beaujolaise, used for Nouveau for example emphasises that fresh youthfulness to the full, but tends to blur the precise details of the Gamay flavour. For pure Gamay, look at one of the ten *Cru* villages, Fleurie or St Amour for example. As they mature, these wines can lose the character of the Gamay altogether, mimicking the Pinot to such an extent that the rare Beaujolais that survives for a couple of decades without dying or being drunk en route, can taste just like a mature Burgundy. *Grown in: Algeria, Austria, Bulgaria, England, Egypt, France – Beaujolais, Jura, Loire, Rhône – Hungary, South Africa, Switzerland, USA, California and East Coast Yugoslavia.*

Grenache
Tap a Rhône vine on the shoulder and ask its name, and the odds are that the answer will be 'Grenache'. It is this sweetly fruity, but also dustily peppery grape which gives most Côtes du Rhône and Côtes de Provence roses their characteristic flavours. In Spain, as the Garnacha, it features in Rioja and a wide range of other wines. Wherever it is grown, though, pepper is probably the taste which will give the Grenache away. *Grown in: Australia, California, France, Greece, Israel, Mexico, New Zealand, North Africa, Spain, South America.*

Kadarka

Kadarka's great claim to fame lies in the stories which surround Bull's Blood, the best known red wine in Eastern Europe – at least the best known to wine drinkers in the west. As the story goes, it was only draughts of this wine which gave the Hungarian defenders of Eger the strength to fend off attacking hoards of Turks. Unfortunately, closer examination of Bull's Blood today would reveal that, at least according to Hugh Johnson, Bordeaux grapes are used to 'fortify' the Kadarka, and to give the wine 'colour, substance and strength'. *Grown in: Hungary, Yugoslavia.*

Malbec

One of the two less well known cast members in Bordeaux. It's quite light in flavour, produces a fairly generous amount of wine and helps to moderate the powerful fruit and tannin of the Cabernet Sauvignon. The Malbec's days may be numbered in Bordeaux because it has proved vulnerable to disease, but Cahors, where it is called Cot o' Auxerrois (but not Malbec) could not really exist without it. *Grown in: Argentina, Australia, California, France, Italy, New Zealand, USSR.*

Merlot

Mellow. There are not many grapes which really match the copywriter's description for his ideal commercial red wine, but the Merlot makes a very good attempt at it. Used to soften tannic Cabernet Sauvignon in the great red wines of Bordeaux, and increasingly taking on the same role elsewhere, the Merlot makes relatively few solo appearances. When it does – as in Italy or California or Bulgaria – look out for the smell and taste of toffee, honey and sometimes mint. *Grown in: Australia, Brazil, Bulgaria, California, Chile, France, Greece, Hungary, Japan, Lebanon, New Zealand, Romania, South Africa, Switzerland, USSR, Yugoslavia.*

Mourvèdre

Some grapes can work solo; others need a straight-man to play off in a blend; others exist simply to take on the role of the straight man. The Mourvèdre does just this in Bandol where there are nine permitted varieties, and more importantly in Châteauneuf-du-Pape, where there are 13. *Grown in: Algeria, France, Tunisia.*

Nebbiolo

If you think red wine should taste overtly 'fruity' this isn't your kind of grape. It's like one of those hard-eyed, aggressive-looking, macho actors who feature in artier Italian movies. There's no way of knowing what they're thinking (since they rarely open their mouths) if anything, until the film is almost over. By which time you might have given up through boredom. Most Barolos and Barbarescos for instance take a tremendously long time to 'come round', to lose their harshness and to develop into a mixture of prune and southern herbs. Some never do. But it is worth remembering that these wines are made to enjoy with plates of flavoursome Italian food. *Grown in: California, Italy, Uruguay.*

Pinot Noir

Great – and sad to say, more often disappointing – in Burgundy its home, and in Champagne, this sulky beast rarely obliges elsewhere. Look for the smell and flavour of wild raspberries in young Burgundy and in rosé made from this grape, for an almost animal, undergrowthy character in good mature examples. Anthony Hanson, in *Burgundy* upset the Burgundians by saying that good old Burgundy 'smells of shit'. He was right. In the hotter areas of the world though, the aroma, young or old, is more likely to be that of rubber. Rosé Champagne, freshly uncorked, can be one of the best sources of real pure Pinot aroma; Blanc de Noirs bubbly on the other hand often displays an aroma and even a slight flavour of bitter chocolate which can be another mark of the Pinot. So far, the only non-Burgundian vineyards which are turning out even half-way successful Pinot Noir, are in New Zealand, Australia and the north west of America. *Grown in: Algeria, Australia, Austria, Bulgaria, Canada, Chile, Czechoslovakia,*

England, Egypt, France, Germany, Hungary, Italy (NE) Lebanon, Lichtenstein, Mexico, New Zealand, Romania, South Africa, Spain – Navarria, Torres – Switzerland, Tunisia, USA, USSR, Yugoslavia.

> The record distance at which a grape thrown from the ground has been caught in the mouth is 270ft 4ins, by Paul Tavilla, Massachusetts. He also successfully caught a grape dropped from the top of a 31 storey building in Fort Lauderdale, (321ft 5ins).

Pinotage (Pinot Noir & Cinsault)

This can be a very interesting mixture of flavours – gamey and fruity – but one which palls very quickly. It's rather like a comedian who becomes boring after a couple of stories. The connection with the Pinot Noir tastes slight. *Grown in: New Zealand, South Africa.*

Sangiovese

The Sangiovese is not one of the world's greatest grapes – but it *is* very adaptable. In far too many Chiantis, the Sangiovese can reach its nadir of boring flavourlessness; but then again, used properly, both in good Chianti, and in such wines as Brunello di Montalcino and Vino Nobile di Montepulciano, it can provide the perfect embodiment of good Italian wine. *Grown in: Brazil, Italy.*

Syrah

Whether or not its origins really do lie in the Persian town of Shiraz, the thoughts of mysterious oriental smells and flavours which are evoked by the Middle East are entirely appropriate. 'Sweaty saddle' in Australia, 'smoky spice' in the Rhône: either way, this gamey, wayward grape is one of the most existing of all. It is perhaps the Australians who have been the most inventive with their use of this variety, blending the Shiraz (as they call it) with the Cabernet Sauvignon in varying proportions to produce wines which owe nothing to either Rhône or Bordeaux. *Grown in: Algeria, Australia, California, France, Greece, Iran, Lebanon, New Zealand, S. Africa.*

Tempranillo

Usually the fruit flavour of this grape is overlaid by that of vanilla imparted by ageing in oak barrels (or possibly contact with oak chips or even – illegally – oak essence). *Grown in: Spain.*

Zinfandel

There are so many styles, ranging from 'Nouveau' to 'port', that no general description can ever apply. Even so, imagine a blend of leather, rubber and liquorice, mixed up with a good dollop of dark fruit jam, and you're probably heading in the right direction. Incidentally, the Italians are now beginning to doubt that the Zinfandel is related to their *Primitivo* as was previously thought; some people might feel Hungary (the other possibility) to be a more likely origin. *Grown in: California (Napa), Italy, Hungary, S. Africa, Yugoslavia.*

The White List

Alvarinho

Ask most Vinho Verde producers what grapes they use to make Portugal's best known white wine and, like as not, they will scratch their heads for a moment or two before listing a succession of varieties whose names are as unfamiliar as they are unpronounceable. Ask the makers of the finest wine in the region, and there will be no hesitation at all: there's only one grape involved and its name is on the label. The wine it produces has been compared to good dry Mosel, with a little more alcohol. Unfortunately, as yet, less than 5% of Vinho Verde is made with this variety. *Grown in: Spain, Portugal.*

Aligoté
If you want bone-dry, possibly acidic, white wine, this is for you. In Burgundy, at its best, it can be an inexpensive alternative to a characterless Chardonnay. *Grown in: Bulgaria, France, New Zealand, Romania, USSR.*

Bual
Anyone casually acquainted with Madeira will tell you exactly what Bual tastes like: nutty, tangily spicy and sweetly delicious. And he or she will be quite right. The only problem is that the wine they are describing may well have contained little if any fruit of the Bual grape. Most inexpensive Madeira is made from the Tinta Negra Mole (said to be a variant of the Pinot Noir) and owes its flavour to the height at which *that* grape is grown. Still, put the real thing and the mimic side by side, and you don't need any great expertise to spot the depth and complexity of the Bual. *Grown in: Madeira, Spain.*

Chardonnay
Did it start its days in Burgundy? Or in Lebanon? And will it really reach its apogee in California, Australia, New Zealand, Canada, or ...? The Chardonnay can produce gloriously buttery, hazelnutty-rich wines in Burgundian villages such as Meursault and Chassagne, it can be steely dry in Chablis, creamily yeasty in Blanc de Blancs Champagne, pineapply fresh in Mâcon, and all kinds of other flavours in Spain, Italy and everywhere else. *Grown in: Australia, Bulgaria, France – Burgundy, Champagne, Mâcon – Canada, China, Czechoslovakia, Italy, Japan, Lebanon, Mexico, New Zealand, Romania, Spain, USA, USSR.*

Chasselas
Steven Spurrier in his book *French Country Wines* divides *Cépages Nobles* from *Secondary Grapes*. The Chasselas, which is also a table grape, is to be found amongst the second of these groups. Its wine can be quite fruity and light, both in France and in Switzerland where it is widely grown. *Grown in: Alsace, Switzerland, Geneva Switzerland, Germany, Languedoc, Savoie, Australia, Lebanon, Egypt, England, New Zealand.*

Chenin Blanc
There is one main reason why this is so popular with producers of sparkling wine in the Loire: it has both the characteristics they look for in a grape. It is neutral-tasting and acidic. It is often used to make bone-dry and semi-sweet wines which are often unexceptional. Perhaps the most appealing characteristic flavour of these wines is that of honey. Outside France, there are signs that the Chenin can make attractively fresh young wines, but back home its one forte is, on occasion, to attract noble rot and consequently to produce some really first class sweet wine with a capacity to improve for decades. *Grown in: France – Loire, – S. Africa, Australia, S. America, Canada.*

Colombard
When wine is distilled to make brandy, it does not so much matter what it tastes like – not many people bother to take a bite out of the cooking apples before they make a pie. If you drink a lot of Armagnac, you will have consumed a fair amount of Colombard. Nowadays, with the Gascon winegrowers becoming more ambitious and with winemakers elsewhere trying every grape under the sun, you'll begin to find some rather attractive, simply fruity pure Colombard wines. Drink young. *Grown in: Bordeaux, Dauphines, Charente, California, S. Africa, Zimbabwe.*

Elbling
Grown in Germany, but really rather atypical of that country, the Elbling may have been introduced by the Romans. Its acidity makes it ideally suited for making sparkling wine. *Grown in: Alsace, Luxembourg, Germany, Liechtenstein, England.*

Folle Blanche
Evocatively named, this is France's third most widely grown variety. Most of the wine it produces is distilled or drunk unnoticed. The only place where its name does appear on a label is in the Loire, where it calls itself the Gros Plant. Recently the Louis Martini winery in California has managed to make a wine described by Leon Adams in his *Wines of America* as 'lovely, dry, crisp . . . resembling Chablis'. Even so, the experts at the University of California do not recommend growing the Folle Blanche anywhere in their state. *Grown in: Armagnac, Loire, California.*

Furmint
In its Yugoslavian guise, this is actually more of an appley-fresh gulper than a wine to sip, but good, sweet, Hungarian Tokay, made from the Furmint is for lingering over. Unfortunately, much of the Hungarian Tokay which is exported seems rather disappointing. *Grown in: Hungary, Savoie, Yugoslavia, Romania, Spain, New Zealand.*

Gewürztraminer
This is possibly the most curious of all the world's great white grapes. Born – it is said – in the village of Tramin in the Italian Sud Tyrol at least four centuries ago, neither white nor red, but pale pink, it helpfully lets you know what to expect with its name: 'Gewürz' – 'spicy'. But what kind of spice? Some Gewürztraminer can be so intensely aromatic that the Alsatians themselves call it 'pommade'; tasters' attempts to convey its character tend to include lychees, Muscat grapes and Parma Violet sweets. As the wine matures, its fleshiness increases and it becomes strangely oily in texture, coating the inside of the mouth with pungent flavour. In Italy they still call it the Traminer and, appropriately enough, make a less spicy version. *Grown in: Austria, Australia, Chile, France, Italy, Luxembourg, Germany, New Zealand, Spain, South Africa, Switzerland, Yugoslavia, USA.*

> The largest recorded vine was planted in Carpinteria, California in 1842, and by 1900 was yielding up to nine tons of grapes. It died in 1920. The largest surviving vine in the UK is the Great Vine at (Hampton Court), with a girth of 85ins (219.9cm), which yields an average 703lb (318.8kg) each year. In 1983 Mr. L. Stringer's vine, in Dartford, Kent, yielded 1015½lb (460.6kg) of grapes.

Grüner Veltliner
In Austria they like to drink their white wine young – often within months of the harvest. The Grüner Veltliner is ideally suited to produce that kind of wine: fresh, light and aromatic. It's not for pondering over, but for quaffing with smoked fish. *Grown in: Austria, Italy – Sud Tyrol, California, Czechoslovakia, Hungary.*

Kerner
The Kerner, produced from crossing the (white) Riesling with the (red) Trollinger, ripens early – a prime consideration for Germany with its short Summer – and makes for good quantities of reasonably fruity wine. With the help of the Müller-Thurgau, and a little luck, it should have ousted the Riesling from many of Germany's best vineyards completely by the turn of the century and no-one will have to struggle to grow that tediously late-ripening, low-yield, high-quality variety. *Grown in: England, Germany, Luxembourg.*

Malvasia
The Malvasia, which has its origins in Ancient Greece, would really like to be the Muscat. It would love to be able to produce good, dry white wine as well as sumptuous sweeties. There are some pretty creditable examples of dry and semi-dry Malvasias in Italy, and the unique quality of genuine Malmsey Madeira is enough to place the grape in the Hall of Fame, but it cannot really claim all-round success. *Grown in: Madeira, France, Brazil, Argentina, Greece, Canaries, Yugoslavia, Portugal, Italy, Spain, S. Africa, Crete.*

Müller-Thurgau

This (supposedly) Riesling/Sylvaner cross has cut a swathe through the vineyards of Austria and Germany, ousting the Riesling, before gathering its strength for the onslaught on England. Switzerland, once thanked and blamed for filling the world with cuckoo clocks and chocolate can, with this invention, now add an all-conquering grape to the tally. It ripens early and produces (quite) flowery wine. Who could ask for anything more from the vineyards of the Mosel? Who would want the really fine wine they used to make there from the great Riesling? *Grown in: Luxembourg, New Zealand, Germany, Austria, Yugoslavia, Italy – Friuli, Trentino, Sud Tyrol – Australia, Czechoslovakia, Japan, England, Hungary.*

Muscat

Here is a table grape whose name is used to describe an enormous number of closely – and distantly – related varieties. Almost all the wines produced (except Muscat d'Alsace) are sweet; some sparkle, others are fortified. *Grown in: Bulgaria, Chile, Cyprus, Czechoslovakia, France – Alsace, Anjou, Bordeaux, Loire – Germany, Greece, Italy, Lebanon, Malta, Portugal, Romania, Sicily, Africa, Tunisia, USSR, Yugoslavia, USA.*

Palomino

A horse of a different colour? This is *the* sherry grape, and one which, without the benefit of flor and fortification produces some rather dull white wine elsewhere in Spain. *Grown in: Spain, S. America, S. Africa, New Zealand, Australia.*

Pedro Ximenez

Observers at professional sherry tastings are sometimes surprised to hear comments like 'typical PX', and presumably spend the next few moments trying to establish a link between army stores and sweet brown wine. What the grape stands for is the flavour of currants; indeed the Pedro Ximenez is often allowed to dry in the sun before being used. *Grown in: Spain, Argentina, Tunisia, Australia, Morocco, New Zealand.*

Pinot Blanc

Now that the purists have (correctly) stopped calling Burgundy's great white grape the Pinot Chardonnay, maybe this, the variety it has completely supplanted there, will attract a little more attention. It is believed to be a mutation of the Pinot Noir, and whilst not as intrinsically interesting as either that grape or the Chardonnay, it does have a touch of their class. Its wines can be fresh and occasionally, as in Italy and Alsace, quite nuttily rich. It is also quite good for making sparkling wine and the Austrians even succeed in picking it late and turning it into Beerenauslese. *Grown in: France – Alsace, Burgundy – Italy – Sud Tyrol – Germany –Baden – Czechoslovakia, Yugoslavia, Hungary, Argentina, Australia, Chile, Luxembourg, Uruguay, Egypt, Canada, California.*

Pinot Gris

Another 'natural mutation of the Pinot Noir'? Perhaps, but it is another variety you will not find very easily in Burgundy. No-one is very certain whether or not this was brought back to Alsace from Hungary after a war in the mistaken belief that it was the Furmint (hence calling it the Tokay); nor whether it was taken to Hungary from Burgundy in the first place. Nowadays, Alsace is still where it produces its most impressive, most long-lived, spicy wine, but as Tocai and Pinot Grigio, it can be used to make some excellent, almost almondy dry wines. *Grown in: France – Alsace, Burgundy – Germany, Czechoslovakia, Luxembourg, Romania, Italy, Hungary, USSR, Switzerland, Yugoslavia.*

Riesling

A brief glance at the shelves of any wine merchant will reveal 'Italian', 'Laski', 'Lutomer', 'Californian' and 'Hunter Valley' Rieslings, none of which are even remotely Riesling-like. Some – the Eastern Europeans – try to be vaguely *like* Riesling, and merely achieve watery sweetness; others are clearly different (the Australian 'Hunter Valley' which is really Sémillon). The real thing, as grown in Germany, Alsace and California (to name but three) is one of the two greatest white grapes in the world. Its wine is essentially flowery, but there's also often a smell and flavour of cooked apple pie (yes, complete with cloves). Given time, and the Riesling is a grape that makes wine you can keep, these wines can take on a curious characteristic which some tasters call 'petrolly'. What they are referring to is the pungency of the aroma. Try it sweet in Germany, dry in Alsace, or under the name of Johannisberg or Rhine Riesling, in America, Australia or New Zealand. *Grown in: Australia, Austria, Bulgaria, Canada, England, France – Alsace – Germany, Italy, Korea, Luxembourg, New Zealand, South Africa, Switzerland, Spain, USA.*

Sauvignon Blanc

Like its cousin the Cabernet Sauvignon, this is one of those grapes professional tasters kick themselves for not identifying. It can smell of gooseberry (particularly in the Loire) of blackcurrant, of freshly cut grass and of all manner of other green, mouth-watering fruit, but it's usually reliably distinctive. The one aroma it rarely has – except in the village of Pouilly in the Loire, and then not always – is of smoke. Even so, it is the Blanc-Fumé name which has been adopted by the Californians to describe their wines made from this grape (sweet versions are labelled Sauvignon). In Bordeaux, apart from its overt role in the dry whites of Graves and Entre-Deux-Mers, the Sauvignon also provides the essential acidity to balance the Sémillon in the great sweet wines of Sauternes and Barsac. *Grown in: France – Loire, Bordeaux, S. W. France – California, South Africa, Australia, Italy – Sud Tyrol – England (rare), Greece, Israel. New York State, Bulgaria, Czechoslovakia, USSR, Yugoslavia, Romania, Tunisia, Lebanon.*

Sémillon

Not very long ago, if one asked even an experienced wine taster what wine made from the Sémillon tasted like, he would have answered 'honeyed and sweet'. That is because the only use he would have known for this grape was in the great dessert wines of south-western France. When it is made 'straight' and dry, the result is either soft and dull, or soft and slow to evolve. In both cases a bit of Sauvignon in the blend to perk things up seldom does any harm. In Australia, however, where Sémillon is put into new oak barrels and called Hunter Valley Riesling, you can find some deliciously fat, savoury-buttery wines which would have many tasters thinking them to be Chardonnay. *Grown in: Bordeaux, Argentina, Chile, Japan, Uruguay, USSR, Tunisia, Israel, Turkey, Yugoslavia, California, Australia, S. Africa.*

Sylvaner

An original native of Austria, the Sylvaner is now generally thought of as a typically Alsatian style grape. With the Pinot Blanc, it fills the useful role of yielding plentiful enough amounts of reasonably priced wine. It is rarely exciting, but is usually an easy enough wine to quaff. 'Drink it young', is probably the best advice. *Grown in: France – Alsace, Jura – California, Germany, Italy –Sud Tyrol – Spain, Australia, Czechoslovakia, USSR, Yugoslavia, Romania, Luxembourg.*

Trebbiano
A Frenchman will readily accept that the Ugni Blanc is one of his country's most undistinguished grape varieties; an Italian will probably not agree that the Trebbiano is anything less than noble. Both are talking about the same grape, and most people who have tasted the wine it produces anywhere it is grown, will echo the Frenchman in dubbing it dull. *Grown in: Italy, France – Rhône, South and South-West – Corsica, Bulgaria, Algeria, Tunisia, Lebanon.*

Verdelho
It is very difficult to say what this grape's wines really taste like when the only ones we tend to see are all fortified, but in its port and Madeira guises it is one of the world's great dry aperitif styles. *Grown in: Portugal, Spain, Australia.*

GREAT RIESLINGS

Generally associated with the cool vineyards of Alsace and Germany, the Riesling has proven willing to produce fine wine elsewhere, both in its dry and its sweet, late harvest, styles.

Amity
Oregon, USA.

★ ★ ★ ★

Buena Vista
California

★ ★ ★ ★ ★

Casa Larga
Finger Lakes, New York, USA.

★ ★ ★ ★ ★

Château Benoit
Oregon, USA.

★ ★ ★ ★ ★

Château St Jean
California

★ ★ ★ ★ ★

Château Ste Michelle
Washington, USA.

★ ★ ★ ★ ★

Clos du Bois
California

★ ★ ★ ★ ★

Columbia 'Cellarmaster's Reserve'
Washington, USA.

★ ★ ★ ★ ★

Cullen's Willyabrup
Western Australia

★ ★ ★ ★ ★

Facelli
Idaho, USA.

★ ★ ★ ★ ★

Felton Empire
California

★ ★ ★ ★ ★

Fern Hill Estate
South Australia

★ ★ ★ ★ ★

Firestone
California

★ ★ ★ ★ ★

Franciscan
California

★ ★ ★ ★ ★

Glenora
Finger Lakes, New York, USA.

★ ★ ★ ★ ★

Thomas Hardy 'Old Castle'
South Australia

★ ★ ★ ★ ★

Haywood
California, USA.

★ ★ ★ ★ ★

Heron Hill-Ingle Vineyard
Finger Lakes, New York, USA.

★ ★ ★ ★ ★

Hogue-Markin Vineyard
Washington, USA.

★ ★ ★ ★ ★

> The world grape eating record is held by Jim Ellis of Montrose, Michigan, who on 30 May 1976 ate 3lb 1 oz grapes in 34.6 seconds.

Hood River Vineyard
Oregon, USA.

★ ★ ★ ★ ★

Katnook Estate
South Australia

★ ★ ★ ★ ★

Knusden Erath
Oregon, USA.

★ ★ ★ ★ ★

Milano
California

★ ★ ★ ★ ★

Penfolds
South Australia

★ ★ ★ ★ ★

Petaluma
South Australia

★ ★ ★ ★ ★

Phelps
Oregon, USA.

★ ★ ★ ★ ★

Pipers Brook ·
Tasmania, Australia

★ ★ ★ ★ ★

Plantagenet Wines
South Australia

★ ★ ★ ★ ★

Quelltaler
South Australia

★ ★ ★ ★ ★

Rosemount
New South Wales, Australia

★ ★ ★ ★ ★

Ste Chapelle
Idaho, USA.

★ ★ ★ ★ ★

St Hubert's
Victoria, Australia

★ ★ ★ ★ ★

Seppelt 'Black Label'
South Australia

★ ★ ★ ★ ★

Smith's Yalumba
South Australia

★ ★ ★ ★ ★

Stag's Leap
California

★ ★ ★ ★ ★

Hermann Wiemer
Finger Lakes, New York, USA.

★ ★ ★ ★ ★

Wirra Wirra
South Australia

★ ★ ★ ★ ★

Wrights
Western Australia

★ ★ ★ ★ ★

THE GREATEST WINE THEFT OF ALL TIME

Author Richard Condon may have to take some responsibility for the spate of fine Bordeaux thefts which took place during 1981. Some years earlier, in his thriller *Arrigato*, he had described just such a crime. The real-life thefts took place over weekends, and were all carried out by a gang who simply drove up to the château, broke into the cellars and helped themselves to the most saleable vintages they could find – using the château's own fork-lift trucks for the loading operation. At one stage, the police believed that the thieves would be unable to sell the wine which, coming directly from the cellars, did not bear the obligatory taxed 'capsules'. This problem was swiftly solved when a large load of capsules was stolen. The supposed gang leader, a Monsieur Varona was captured after a hold-up, and half the capsules discovered at his mistress's home. But despite his incarceration, the thefts continued. The police had two strokes of luck when the thieves had to abandon one hijacked truck which, though full of wine, proved to be empty of petrol, and another following a hit-and-run accident outside

Rouen. On neither occasion however was the driver caught. At one point during the series of thefts, the robbers evidently tired of claret and moved north-west, removing the cellar doors from the Domaine de la Romanée-Conti before relieving Burgundy's most prestigious estate of 150 magnums of its prize wine. The final tally of unrecovered goods was of some 50,000 bottles and 250,000 capsules, all of which were valued at around half a million dollars.

List of stolen wine and capsules

1,500 bottles Mouton-Rothschild 1975 and 1978.
1,300 bottles Château La Gombeaud and Lascombes.
519,000 lead capsules.
1,680 bottles Château l'Evangile.
1,620 bottles Château Mazeyres.
1,176 bottles Château d'Yquem 1976.
1,000 various selected bottles from the cellars of the merchants Cruse.
1,600 various selected bottles from the cellars of the merchants de Luze.
3,000 various selected bottles from the cellars of the merchants Consortium Vinicole (including Haut-Brion, Batailley and Cheval-Blanc).
3,820 various selected bottles from the cellars of the merchants firm of UTV (including Margaux 1980, d'Yquem, Mouton-Rothschild 1978).
150 Magnums of Romanée-Conti 1969.
1,200 bottles Château Cormeil-Figeac 1978.
14,000 assorted wines from merchants, Barton & Guestier.

List of recovered wine and capsules

1,200 bottles Château Cormeil-Figeac 1978.
14,000 assorted wines from merchants, Barton & Guestier.
270,000 capsules.

GREECE

THE PROBLEM WITH GREEK WINES can be expressed in two words: low expectations. Few foreigners have every had a really good bottle of Greek wine; few Greeks see anything wrong with the stale, oxidised, stuff they are served in their tavernas - indeed, in the words of one good producer, 'if you served them a crisp, fresh young wine, they'd probably send it back complaining that there's something wrong with it'. So why should anyone bother to try to make something that little bit better?

In fact there are a few winemakers who are trying to break the mould, planting different varieties of grapes and installing modern equipment into their wineries. Their wines are more than promising, but these pioneers are still just that. Their future progress, and that of those who might follow their example, depends on us *not* accepting the next bottle of flabby old Retsina we are offered with our Greek meal; and of our looking out for some of the good examples listed below. It was just this kind of encouragement which helped to revolutionise Spanish wines not so

The Grape List

Red
Agiorgitiko
Cabernet Franc
Cabernet Sauvignon
Cinsault
Fokiano
Grenache
Limnio
Mandilaria
Mavroudi
Merlot
Romeiko
Syrah
Vertzani
Xynomavro

White
Aidani
Amorgiano
Assyrtiko
Athiri
Debina
Monemvasia
Moschofilero
Muscat
Rhoditis
Sauvignon Blanc
Savatiano

The Wine Regions

PELOPONNESE

An important region in terms of acreage and production 110,000 *ha*; 1 million *hl*) and in that it also contains six of Greece's 26 appellations. Achaia Clauss and Andrew P. Cambas both have their headquarters here. Monemvasia, a grape known elsewhere as the Malvasia, or Malmsey, takes its name from a town on the Southern Coast of the Peloponnese which originally shipped wine from Crete and the Cyclades. The Mavrodaphne ('black laurel') grape was discovered here by the Bavarian viticulturalist Gustav Clauss, who founded the firm of Achaia Clauss.

Grape varieties
Mavrodaphne
Agiorgitiko
Fileri
Moschofileri
Muscat
Rhoditis
Savatiano
Wines with 'appellation of origin of superior quality'

Nemea
Red, known as the 'blood of Hercules' (who slew the Nemean lion). A dry full-bodied wine which ages well and is made from the Agiorgitiko grape.

Mantinea
White, dry, light and fruity, made from the Moschofilero grape.

Patras
White, from the Rhoditis grape, grown on the site of Julius Caesar's vineyards.

Wines with 'controlled appellation of origin'

Mavrodaphne of Patras
Rich, red, from the Mavrodaphne grape, needs aging. 15–20% alcohol.

Muscat of Patras

Muscat of Rion
Both Muscats are sweet, heavy, aromatic, topaz-coloured wines.

Porto Carras
Financial backing from a shipping magnate and expert advice from world famous oenologist Prof. Emile Peynaud have been combined in Carras's modern, fully automated winery to produce a range of Greece's newest, most exciting wines. Cabernet Sauvignon, Cabernet Franc, Cinsault, Grenache, Merlot and Sauvignon Blanc are used along with the best and most prolific Greek varieties. The wines are:

Blanc de blancs
Grand Vin Blanc (light, smooth, very dry)
Château Carras
Grand Vin Rouge (fine dry red)
Côtes de Méliton (light, dry, perfumed rosé)

AEGEAN ISLANDS

Samos
Muscat of Samos, the 'wine of the Gods', golden, sweet fragrant, beloved of Byron and recommended by the physician Hippocrates, is produced under strict appellation laws by the two wineries of the Union des Coopératives Vinicoles de Samos. It is made from the White

Muscat grape in two forms: Vin Naturellement Doux de Samos ('Nectar') and 'Vin Liqueur de Samos'. The Muscat grape is also used to make Samena, a dry white wine.

The other major producer is George Karelas, making Ambelina (a dry white from the Rhoditis grape), Esperia, a blended white, and two reds, Aeolos and Orpheus.

Rhodes

The appellation of origin Muscat of Rhodes is a naturally sweet, fragrant wine made from a mixture of the White and Trani Muscat grapes. The major producer is the Compagnie Agricole et Industrielle de Rhodes (CAIR), who also produce Ilios, a fresh, fruity, dry white from the Athiri grape, Chevalier de Rhodes, a deep red from the Amorgiano grape, and a gold medal winning Méthode Champenoise wine.

Lemnos

Makes an appellation of origin Muscat, which also comes in dry and fortified styles. Some red wine is also produced.

Santorini

An appellation exists for Santorini sparkling wines. These, as well as dry and sweet whites, are made from the Assyrtiko and Aidani grapes.

Cyclades

These islands are said to be 'the cradle of Greek wine'. Paros has an appellation for its red wines, of which Botrys is the chief producer. White wines with high alcohol and relatively good acidity are made on Thera and Naxos.

CRETE

The chief grapes are:
Romeika
Kotisfali
Liatiko
Mandilaria

This island has four appellations of superior quality, all for dark, heavy, red wines in a very traditional style:
Daphnes
Sitia
Peza
Archanes.

The latter two coming from the Heraklion area. Botrys make a recommended Peza, and Stratos Koniordos make a non-demarcated white wine, Mira Bello.

IONIAN ISLANDS

There are three appellations of origin:
Robola of Cephalonia (white)
Muscat of Cephalonia
Mavrodaphne of Cephalonia

From Zakinthos comes the non-appellation white, Verdea, and red, Byzantis.

EPIRUS

Has one appellation, Sitsa, a white wine made from the Debina grape in dry and sparkling styles.

Some Cabernet Sauvignon is being produced in the Metsovo area.

THESSALY

Has two appellations:
Anchialos (white)
Rapsani (red)

CENTRAL GREECE

Eighty per cent of wine produced here is Retsina, predominantly from the Savatiano grape. The Rhoditis grape is used to produce rosé (Kokkineli) wines. Central Greece contains the three areas which have the 'Traditional appellation of designation of origin' for Retsina – Attica, Viotia and Evia. There is only one wine with the appellation of origin of superior quality – Kantza (an amber-coloured fruity dry white from the Savatiano grape). Light reds are made from the Mandilaria and Mavroudi grapes, the best from around Delphi. Hymettis is a dry white wine from Athens which needs ageing.

Recommended producers

Andrew P. Cambas S.A.
Retsina Attica
Cava Cambas (blended white)

Cambas Blanc (amber, fruity, Savatiano grape)
Cambas Rouge
Cambas Kokkineli
Domaine de Kantza

Stratos Koniordos
Bella Rosa (pale, dry rosé)

Kourtakis
Retsina Attica
Apelia (red: Xynomavro and Agiorgitiko grapes; white: Debina and Savatiano grapes)
Apollo (red: Agiorgitiko, Grenache and Syrah; white: Debina and Savatiano)

Agricultural and Technical S.A.
Semeli (red and white, produced using advanced technology)

MACEDONIA AND THRACE

Attracting the most attention from the outside world, with two companies dominating production of some of the best wines in Greece.

Wines with appellation of origin of superior quality

Naoussa

Rich, dry red from the Xynomavro grape

Amynteon

A deep, astringent red from vineyards near the Albanian border.

Producers

Tsintalis

Methods are some of the most progressive and advanced in Greece. Cabernet Sauvignon, Cabernet Franc and Sauvignon Blanc have been planted together with the best Greek varieties. When the new Greek appellation laws came into force, George Tsintalis introduced a modern winery with automated bottling lines in record speed to produce his wood-aged reds and cold-fermented whites. Grapes for their Athos range of wines are grown in monastery vineyards where even now no woman is allowed to set foot. The wines are:

Retsina
Naoussa
Cava Tsintalis (red)
Athos Tsintalis (red, white and rose)
Agiorgitikos
Imiglykos
Makedonikos

Branded and non-demarcated wines

Demestica
Red and white. Popular both in Greece and abroad, production of

bottled Demestica has increased fifteenfold in the last ten years.

Kleoni
Red, white and Retsina. St George, Rhoditis and Savatiano grapes.

Othello
Own label red from
Mavrodaphne grape.

Castel Danielis
Cambas red, recommended, dry,
from the Agiorgitiko grape.

Cambas rosé
Dry, fruity from Agiorgitiko and
Fileri grape.

Verdea
A greenish wine.

Santa Laura

Santa Helena
Both dry whites

Santa Rosa

Tegea
Both rosés

Recommended producers
Achaia Clauss
Mavrodaphne
Muscat
Nemea
Demestica
Retsina
Castel Danielis
Santa Helena
Santa Rosa

Andrew P. Cambas S.A.
Mavrodaphne
Nemea
Mantinea

Botrys
Mavrodaphne
Nemea

P. Lafkiotis & Co.
'St George' Nemea
Kleoni
Tsantalis
Mavrodaphne

HEALTH

The Wine Remedy List

Acne: an Austrian face mask
1 raw carrot
2 tablespoons of plain yoghurt
*1 tablespoon rosé wine, blended
together*

Arthritis: 'Hungary water' once
extremely popular at Court
1oz lavender
1oz rosemary
½oz myrtle
1 quart brandy
¼ cup red wine
Steep together for two weeks,
then rub into the affected area.

Athlete's foot:
1oz sage
1oz agrimony
2 cups white wine
Heat together for 20 mins, then
soak feet in it.

Cellulite: a French massage oil
1oz lemon oil
½oz lime oil
3oz almond oil
3oz vodka
3oz red wine

Cold sores/chapped lips:
apply apple slices soaked in
white wine for an hour.

Common cold (1): Swiss;
immerse half an onion in a cup
of warm water for a few seconds,
remove and add 2 tablespoons of
white wine drink.

Common cold (2): to a strong
cup of horehound tea add a
teaspoon of honey and a
tablespoon of Burgundy.

Common cold (3): drink a cup of
hot catnip tea, then a glass of
warm water to which has been
added three tablespoons of
Rhine wine.

Complexion (1): a mask for oily
skin
1 cup minced dandelion leaves
1½ cups cold water
¼ cup white wine
Simmer together and apply on
cottonwool pads.

Complexion (2): a mask for dry
skin
½ teaspoon honey
1 egg yolk
1 tablespoon white wine
*1-2 tablespoons skimmed milk
powder*
Mix and apply.

Corns: for four days apply a
corn pad soaked in red wine and
a 10% solution of salicylic acid.

Fallen arches: an Italian
remedy
1½oz talcum powder
1 pint strong red wine
½ pint rum
Let stand for a week, then rub
into feet.

Falling hair(1):
3oz rosemary leaves
1 teaspoon baking soda
½ teaspoon camphor
1 teaspoon red wine
1 quart mineral water
Bring to boil, strain and add 4oz
rum. Rub in daily.

Falling hair(2):
1 cup olive oil
1 teaspoon dried marjoram
1 teaspoon rosemary oil
1 teaspoon red wine.
Rub in daily.

Falling hair(3):
1oz olive oil
1oz rosemary oil
½oz nutmeg oil
½oz red wine
Rub in daily.

Fat: Scandinavian herbal fat
soak
1oz thyme
1oz seaweed
1oz jaborandi
2 cups white wine
Add to bath.

Halitosis: a Russian remedy
1 cup 100° proof vodka
¼ cup strong red wine
2oz powdered myrrh
oil of cloves
Let stand for two weeks.
(Kills you and the halitosis).

Hiccups:
2 teaspoons red or white wine
2 teaspoons cider vinegar.
Mix together.

Impetigo: a Swiss remedy;
combine equal parts of acidic red
wine and cider vinegar, add a
teaspoon of sugar. Let stand and
apply to affected area.

Itching: a remedy from
Denmark
3 tablespoons white wine
1 teaspoon fresh horseradish
1 cup yoghurt
Combine and refrigerate.

Laryngitis: Italian
1 teaspoon dry white wine
1 teaspoon vinegar
2 drops honey
Mix in warm water.

Longevity: 'Pontius Pilate
water' is very popular in the
Rhône Valley, where it is said to
impart longevity and vitality;
Pulverise 1 teaspoon each of
mace, fennel seeds, dried mint,
cloves, anise seeds, ginger,

caraway seeds, cinnamon,
nutmeg, thyme. Add to one
gallon of Côtes du Rhône, leave
to stand for 2 weeks, then distil.

Smoking: a tonic for those
giving up
1 pint gentian root
1 cup Burgundy
1 cup water
Leave to stand for two weeks;
take 1 teaspoon four times a day.

Wrinkles: an anti-wrinkle
lotion from the Loire;
blend a cucumber with a cup of
rosé wine, beat in a melted
tablespoon of anhydrous lanolin,
2oz comfrey water and the
contents of two vitamin E
capsules.

*(With thanks to Marjorie
Michaels, Stay Healthy With
Wine, Dial Press, New York)*

HOLLAND

DUTCH vineyards have been
reported, but not discovered.
Nonetheless the Dutch are a
keen wine drinking nation,
consuming over 14 litres per
head – half as much again as the
British. Wine is now Holland's
second favourite beverage after
beer, replacing gin.

Ten per cent of Holland's wine
is imported from Belgium. The
Belgians (and Luxembourgers)
for their part, import some of the
wine *they* drink from Holland.
Which must keep the custom
officials busy. Other imports:

France	39% of the market
Germany	18.5%
Italy	10%
Portugal	5%
Spain	2% (mostly sherry)

Favourite wines
Keller Geist (German
 Liebfraumilch)
Perlwein (German
 semi-sparkling)
Chianti
Rioja
Red and White Bordeaux

HUNGARY

LIKE Bulgaria, Hungary has proved that Eastern Europe can be
very good at exporting wine to the west. Unlike Bulgaria,
however, Hungary has achieved its success with styles of wine which
are at least based on indigenous flavours and grapes. Tokay, arguably
Hungary's finest wine, is still quite unique. Its history stretches back
a very long way indeed, as do the legends which surround it. Made

from the local Furmint grape at Tokay and close to Lake Balaton, the wine owes part of its character to the effects of noble rot, and part to the addition of variable doses of sweetening syrup. Although there are 108 farms which grow Furmint for Tokay (on 77,000 acres) all the wine is produced in the stately cellars of Tokajhegyaljai and Satoraljaujhely.

Much the same could be said about Hungary's most famous red wine: Bull's Blood, or Egri Bikavér. Once renowned for its fullness and body and its longevity, it has sold its soul to become the Eastern European vin de table.

Olasz Riesling – at least the versions which have been exported to Britain – is, like the Czechoslovakian cars of the 1960s, a product which would put many otherwise left-thinking people off socialism for life.

Hungary's vines were first planted as a means of reclaiming sandy-soiled land. This, in turn, has meant that the vines have suffered less from phylloxera than elsewhere. The State Monimpex has a monopoly of wine exports, which now represent around 20 per cent of the total production, most of which is controlled by seven large State-owned 'combinats' such as those at Kecksemét (62,000 acres) and Szeged (28,000 acres). Hungarovin owns some 3,000 acres and acts in much the same way as a négociant might in France.

The Grape List

Reds
Cabernet
Medon Noir (Merlot)
Bourgignon
Pinot Noir
Blau Portugieser
Ezerjé
Kekfrankos (Gamay)
Kadarka

Whites
Sylvaner
Rhine Riesling
Traminer
Furmint
Pinot Gris
Italian Riesling
Sargomuskataly (Yellow Muscat)
Leányka ('Young Girl')
Muskotaly
Müller-Thurgau
Pinot Blanc
Chardonnay
Zierfandler
Grüner Veltliner
Hajos
Juhfark ('Lambs Tail')
Siklos
Meźesfeher ('White Honey')
Härsevelü ('Lime Leaf')
Kéknyelü ('Blue Stalk')

The Wine Regions

TRANSDANUBE
Badacsonyi
White wines, mostly, though Badacsonyi Burgunder is good. The best wines are from the Szürkebarát (Pinot Gris) and Kéknyelü grapes.
Others from Furmint and Yellow Muscat and Italian Riesling, widely planted after phylloxera.

Balaton
Generic name 'Balaton', for wines produced from the Italian Riesling.
Sylvaner, Ejerzó, Mezesfeher, Hajos and Cabernet grapes.
Sparkling wine – Csabagöngye.
State farm of Balatonboglár produces wines from Sylvaner, Leányka, Traminer and Muskotaly grapes.

Somló
Furmint, Italian Riesling, Traminer, Ezerjó.
Somló wines are supposed to impart virility and longevity.

Mor
Sandy soil resistant to phylloxera.
Morí Ezerjó a good red.
Chief wines are from the Barsönyös-Csaszar district.

Balatonfured-Csopak
Italian Riesling, Sylvaner, Furmint, Müller-Thurgau

Mecsek
White wines, and some reds in south.
Italian Riesling, Furmint, Müller-Thurgau, Pinot Blanc, Chardonnay, Zierfandler.
Pecs Olaszriesling, one of best known names outside Hungary, comes from this region.

Villanyi-Siklos
Red and some white.
Villanyi Burgundi is the best wine (Pinot Noir), also Siklos Kadarka, Blau Portugieser, Italian Riesling and Hársevelü.

Szekszárd
Voros Kadarka and Szekszárdi reds from the state farm at Nemes Kadar.

NORTHERN MASSIF
Matra
Italian Riesling, Leányka, Mezesfeher, Kadarka, Harsevelu.
Debro and Gyongyos and the main wine centres.
Debroi Harsevelu is the best known wine.

Bukk
The Leányka grape predominates, with Italian Riesling, Mezeseeher, Muskotaly. (Also varietal Kadarkás and rosés.)
Eger is the home of Egri Bikavér – the famous Bull's Blood.

Hegyalja
Furmint, Hársevelü and Yellow Muskotaly grapes predominate.

Districts producing quality white wine:

1. Tokaj-Hegyalga	Northern Massif	5,900 ha
2. Badacsony	Transdanubia	1,800 ha
3. Balatonfured-Csopak	Transdanubia	1,400 ha
4. Somló	Transdanubia	400 ha
5. Bukkalja	Northern Massif	3,200 ha
6. Mor-Csaszar	Transdanubia	2,600 ha
7. Balaton	Transdanubia	3,250 ha
8. Mecsek	Transdanubia	1,500 ha
9. Matraalja	Northern Massif	11,700 ha

Districts producing quality red wine

1. Sopron	Kisalfold (Small Plain)	1,100 ha
2. Villany-Siklos	Transdanubia	2,000 ha
3. Szekszard	Transdanubia	1,900 ha
4. Eger	Transdanubia	3,400 ha
5. Alfold	Northern Massif	115,000 ha

INDIA

WINE has been made in India for more than 2,000 years. The grape was introduced by the Greeks, and was first grown on the southern slopes of the Himalayas. It was enjoyed during the era of the Mogul Empire, and in 1628 the Emperor Jehangir is pictured on a gold coin with a wine goblet in his hand.

In 1888 wines from Kashmir were shown at the Calcutta Exhibition and met with some success. However, phylloxera put paid to them, and the few vines which survived are now grown to produce table grapes. The only reports we have of Indian winemaking today concern vineyards near Delhi and Madras where, in the case of the latter, sweet red wine is made.

In 1931 a vineyard was planted in Pimpali, southeast of Bombay with the Baramati ('twelve soils') grape, and is still in production. The present winery is of Italian design and its operation complies with international specifications. The winery is supervised by a famous Italian oenologist, who makes frequent visits to ensure standards are maintained in the production of wines which include a varietal Riesling and Cabernet, described by their importers as 'a stimulating experience'.

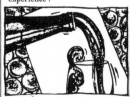

INGREDIENTS

86 per cent water	**Potassium**
★★★★★	good for kidneys, nervous system
12 per cent ethyl alcohol	★★★★★
★★★★★	**Sodium**
2 per cent mineral and vegetable substances	the relatively low quantities in wine is healthy
★★★★★	★★★★★
300–500 mg acetic acid per litre	**Copper**
★★★★★	★★★★★
600–700 Kcal. per litre (red)	**Vitamins trace substances:**
★★★★★	**BI**
600–1000 Kcal. per litre (white)	★★★★★
★★★★★	**B2** riboflavine
Phosphorus good for healthy bone tissue	★★★★★
★★★★★	**C** tiny
Sulphur good for the liver	★★★★★
★★★★★	**C2** lowers blood pressure
Fluoride good for teeth and bone	★★★★★
★★★★★	**Pyridoxine**
Calcium good for teeth and bone	★★★★★
★★★★★	**Pantothenic acid**
Iron combats anaemia. Sherry, Port, Bordeaux, and Burgundy best	★★★★★
★★★★★	**Nicotinic acid**
	★★★★★

Other Ingredients (all illegal)
Synthetic aroma
Synthetic flavour
Glycol

Wine Investment List

The people who invest in wine are very similar to those who put their money into stamps, art and first edition novels: they are generally very conservative in their tastes. They know that wines from renowned Bordeaux châteaux, produced in 'good' vintages go up in value pretty reliably. So that is what they buy – even though wines made by less well-known properties, in less-celebrated years can be just as enjoyable to drink, and are often patently undervalued by comparison. Wine investors are rarely gamblers: given a choice between trusting their own taste buds and slavishly trusting proven reputations, they will do the latter. Since these are the people to whom you will have to resell any wine you have bought, you would be well advised to play by their rules. Buy the underrated wines for your own pleasure – paying for them with the profits from selling the big names.

Fine German wine (Beerenauslese etc.)
There is so little of this quality made, and Germany has so few great vintages, that this ought to be an area for growth. Perhaps this will come if and when the world swings away from dry white wine. In the foreseeable future however, this is an unwise area in which to look for a good return.

Sweet White Bordeaux
As above. 'Great' names like d'Yquem, Coutet and Climens have a following; the rest are a far less reliable bet than their red Bordeaux neighbours.

Burgundy
On the up-and-up, but very tricky. There are so many variables, particularly the number of different merchants and growers whose names can feature on bottles of wine from the same commune. It should also be noted that, at present, buyers for fine Burgundy are possibly easier to find on the European mainland and the USA than in Britain. Nonetheless, the following producers and communes will be amongst the safer bets:

Producers	
Hospices de Beaune	Dom. Leflaive
Dom. Gouges	Dom. de la Pousse d'Or
Louis Jadot	Dom. Ramonet-Prudhon
Comtes Lafon	Dom. de la Romanée-Conti
Louis Latour	Dom. Sauzet
	Comte de Vogüé

Communes/Appellations	
Bâtard-Montrachet	Corton Charlemagne
Beaune Greves	Echézeaux
Beaune Theurons	Grand Echézeaux
Bienvenue-Bâtard Montrachet	Meursault Charmes
	Meursault Perrières
Le Chambertin	Le Montrachet
Chevalier-Montrachet	Musigny
Close de la Roche	Romanée-Conti
Clos Vougeot	La Tâche
Corton	Volnay Santenots

Red Bordeaux

Classed clarets from fine vintages. Stick to these, and you should not go far wrong. Even so, some will be more successful each vintage than others. Amongst the high fliers:

Ch. Beychevelle	Ch. Léoville-Las-Cases
Ch. Cheval-Blanc	Ch. Margaux
Ch. Ducru-Beaucaillou	Ch. La Mission-Haut-Brion
Ch. Gruaud-Larose	Ch. Mouton-Rothschild
Ch. Haut-Brion	Ch. Palmer
Ch. Lafite	Ch. Pétrus
Ch. Latour	Ch. Pichon, Lalande

Madeira

Madeira does come up at auction – usually old vintages. There are many who believe that since, as a consequence of Portugal's entry into the EEC, Madeira will have to be made of the grapes whose names it bears, Madeira prices may be set to rise dramatically.

Vintage Port

The classic investment wine. It generally takes a reasonably long time to mature, is made in small quantities, is only 'released' in vintages which are considered to be well above average quality. It is not quite as simple as that, because different houses can produce more successful wines in particular vintages than others. Read the tasting reports in wine magazines and newsletters and go for the following houses rather than some of the more obscure Portuguese houses which may not ring quite so many bells with the casual auction-goer. Key producers:

Cockburn	Fonseca	Sandeman
Croft	Graham	Taylor
Dow	Quinta do Noval	Warre

IRAN

JUST the stuff to enjoy with a decent book of verse, and a friend, beneath a handy tree – or so Omar Khayam apparently thought, singing the praises of Persian wine. Appropriately enough, local legend has it that wine was first 'discovered' by a concubine of the Shah Jamsheed who, despairing of her chances of every rising to Number One Wife decided to do away with herself. Finding a jar full of fermenting grapes which had been deemed poisonous, she drank the liquid and prepared to meet her maker. The Persian word for 'wine' is 'Zeher-e-Koosh' – 'the delightful poison'. As you will have guessed, the only person she met was the Shah who, seeing how cheerful the girl was, followed her example and, at a stroke, turned Persia into a winegrowing nation.

Most famous of all Persian winemaking centres was Shiraz which gave its name to the grape which now grows with such success in the Rhône (where it is called Syrah) and Australia. Marco Polo mentions the vineyards here in the account of his journey to the east. Nowadays however, the principal grape variety is the Thompson Seedless, the table grape which is responsible for so much dull Californian jug wine.

The average Iranian drinks only half a litre a year. Or at least that was the figure recorded before the fall of the Shah. Consumption is believed to have dropped somewhat since then.

Main Iranian winemaking regions
Khorasan
Teheran
Fars
Hamadan
Lorestan
Zanjan

Wineries were in or near
Teheran
Shiraz
Hamadan
Malayer
Shiravan
Sharooh
Abedeh

ISRAEL

'THE children of Israel sit each beneath his vine and his fig'. In 1500 BC the gardens of Canaan were said to produce wine as copiously as water – which might be thought to render at least one miracle a trifle unnecessary.

Noah is reputed to have been the first winegrower, but drinkers of today's wines have Edmond de Rothschild to thank, for it was he who, in the 1880s, planted some 1,000 hectares of vine. At around the same time, German monks planted Rhineland cuttings at Carmel.

During the following decade cellars were built at Richon-le-Zion (north of Tel Aviv) and at Zichron-Jacob (Mt Carmel) and given by Rothschild to Zionist cellars. Now trading as The Carmel Wine Company, these cellars account for over 75 per cent of Israel's wine. In 1957 the Israeli Wine Institute at Rehovat was established for the quality control of exports.

There are 7,000 hectares of vines producing around 430,000 hectolitres of wine; in 1970 Israel was making five times as much wine from a tenth of the vineyard area, as Syria, Lebanon and Jordan combined. Fifteen per cent of Israel's wine (all kosher) is exported, 70 per cent of which goes to the USA, much of the rest to Britain. The Israelis themselves each drink around five bottles of wine per year, much of which is consumed during religious festivities.

If your taste is for 'dessert red wine' made in the desert, some of these will suit you very well

indeed. As for one of the dry whites, the editor of this book and one of the editorial advisors have both tasted the Carmel Sauvignon Blanc 'blind' on three occasions. On each of these, they agreed that it was one of the very nastiest wines they had ever tasted. A recent tasting has however shown a remarkable improvement.

The Grape List

Red
Cabernet Sauvignon
Carignan
Grenache

White
Clairette
Muscat d'Alexandrie
Sauvignon
Sémillon

The Wine List

White
Almog
Ashod
Caesarea
Carmel Hock
Carmel Topaz
Château de la Montagne
Golden Cream
Hadar
Maagal

Muscatel
Partom
Porath
Poria
Sauvignon Blanc

Red/White
Askalon
Avdad
Avdat (dry)
Binyamina (and rosé)
Château Richon (sweet)
Mikveh-Israel (and rosé)

Red
Adom Atic
Cabernet Sauvignon (sold under SCV label)
Carignan (sold under SCV label)
Château Windsor
Independence (dessert red)
Petite Syrah (sold under SCV label)

Sparkling
Sambatyon
Méthode Champenoise ('The President')

The Wine Regions

SOUTH
Negev Desert.
Vineyards at Beersheba and Ascalon.
Jerusalem is renowned for its dessert wines.

NORTH
Mt Carmel, Haifa, Galilee.

ITALY

ITALY'S wines are a curate's egg: very good – in parts. The irony is that very few of the good parts are in the well-known wine areas. A novice wine drinker will be far less disappointed with his Beaujolais and Muscadet than he might be with Barbaresco and Soave. There are many reasons for these disappointments, but most important amongst them are probably the frequent inability of producers to agree amongst themselves, and the ease with which the better-known wines have sold overseas. For Italy's most exciting wines you really have to look for the names which appear in few of the older wine books. It is a little like a Hollywood film in which Redford, Newman, Fonda and Hepburn all fluff their lines whilst the supporting actors steal the show. On the one hand there are the revolutionaries scattered throughout the country busily and successfully planting grape varieties of which few Italian traditionalists had even heard; on the other, there are some of those traditionalists themselves who are conscientiously trying to make wines worthy of their great old Italian names.

New regulations and quality designations may play their part too (though not if the meddlesome and bureaucratic way in which the previous ones worked is anything to go by) in tightening up the loose strands of Italian wine production. There are already a few young examples of Chianti conforming to the new DOCG regulations which give hope for the future. Italy has to learn, as Spain already has, that quality control is essential. Far too often, the good bottle is followed by another, far less good one, bearing the same name and vintage. Much of this stems from the way in which the wine has often been bottled batch by batch rather than barrel by barrel. Which in practise means that too much wine languishes in half-full casks, oxidizing gently.

Italian Wine Words

Abboccato Semi-Dry.

Amabile Semi-sweet.

Amaro Bitter-flavoured.

Annata Vintage.

Asciutto Dry.

Azienda Estate.

Bianco White.

Botte Barrel.

Bottiglia Bottle.

Cantina Cellar.

Cantina Cooperativa Growers' cooperative.

Cantina Sociale Growers' cooperative.

Casa Vinicola The producer – usually indicating a merchant.

Cascina Estate.

Chiaretto Rose or pale red. Means the same as 'Clairet' in France.

Classico (as in Chianti Classico) means that the wine comes from a specified section within the denominated region.

Colle Hill.

Consorzio Consortium (of growers, e.g. Chianti Putto).

DOC (Denominazione di Origine Controllata) The Italian version of Appellation Controlée, indicating the wine's provenance.

DOCG (Denominazione di Origine Controllata e Garantita) Newly established (1982/3) set of denominations 'guaranteeing' the quality of a select number of DOC's, and setting certain strict standards for them.

Dolce Sweet.

Enoteca (as in Enoteca Italica Permanente) – literally a 'wine library' where wines of different vintages and denominations are stored.

Etichetta Label.

Fattoria Estate (in Tuscany).

Fermentazione Naturale Cuve Close (tank) method of making sparkling wine.

Fiasco Straw-covered, round-bottomed, Chianti bottle.

Frizzante Pétillant, slightly sparkling.

Gradazione alcoolica Alcohol content.

Imbottigliato nel'origine Estate-bottled.

Liquoroso Strong, (though not always) sweet wine.

Marchio Depositato Trademark.

Metodo Champenois Méthode Champenoise.

Moscato Sweet sparkling wine, made from the Muscat grape.

Nero Red (for heavier wines than 'Rosso').

Passito Sweet, raisiny wine made from (usually) sun-dried grapes.

Pastosto Medium-dry.

Podere Estate.

Putto (as in Chianti Putto) – literally 'cherub' – and means that the wine has been produced by a member of the Chianti Putto consortium.

Recioto Sweet wine, made from semi-dried grapes. (See also *Passito*).

Riserva Wine which has been allowed to spend a specified length of time in barrel – which can mean that, to non-Italians it will taste stale.

Riserva Speciale As above, but aged for longer.

Rosato Rosé.

Rosso Red.

Secco Dry.

Semisecco Semi-sweet.

Spumante Sparkling.

Stravecchio Very old.

Superiore Usually indicates prolonged ageing (See *Riserva*).

Tenementi Estate.

Tenuta Estate.

Vecchio Old.

Vendemmia Vintage.

Vigna Vineyard.

Vigneto Vineyard.

Vin Santo Sweet wine made from grapes which have been allowed to dry during the winter months.

Vino da Pasto Table wine (of basic quality).

Vino da Taglio Strong wine used for blending.

Vino da Tavola Table wine.

Vite Vine.

Vitigno Variety of vine.

The Grape List

Red
Aglianico
Aleatico
Barbera
Bombino Nero
Bonarda
Brachetto
Brunello di Montalcino
Cabernet
Calabrese
Cannonau
Carignano
Cesanese
Chiavennasca
Corvina Veronese
Croatina
Dolcetto
Freisa
Gaglioppo
Grignolino
Garnaccia
Lagrein
Lambrusco
Malbec
Malvasia Nera
Marzemino
Merlot
Monica
Montepulciano
Nebbiolo (or Spanna)
Negroamaro
Nerello Mascalese
Petit Rouge
Piedirosso (Per'e Palummo)
Pinot Nero
Primitivo
Raboso
Refosco
Rossesse
Sangiovese
Schiava

Teroldego
Tocai Nero (or Rosso)
Uva di Troia
Vespolina

White
Albana
Arneis
Biancolella
Blanc de Valdigne
Bombino Bianco (or Trebbiano
   d'Abruzzo)
Bosco
Carricante
Catarratto
Chardonnay
Cortese
Fiano
Forastera
Garganega
Greco
Grillo
Inzolia
Malvasia
Moscato
Müller-Thurgau
Nuragus
Picolit
Pigato
Pinot Bianco
Pinot Grigio
Prosecco
Riesling (or Riesling Italico)
Riesling Renana (or
   Rheinriesling)
Sauvignon
Tocai Friulano
Traminer (or Gewürztraminer)
Verdeca
Verdicchio
Verduzzo
Vermentino
Vernaccia di Oristano
Vernaccia di San Gimignano

The Wine Regions

ABRUZZO

This region, midway down the eastern coast of Italy is the source of an up-and-coming red and a dullish white. The former, made from the Montepulciano grape (with a little Sangiovese) is now benefitting from modern, cooler, methods of fermentation and a reduction of the time spent in barrel. The latter, made from the Trebbiano can occasionally be worth trying too. Drink youngish, or may be aged.

Montepulciano d'Abruzzo

C.S. Di Tollo
Emidio Pepe
Edoardo Illuminati
Paolo Mezzanotte

Rubino

Very similar to Montepulciano d'Abruzzo with a little more Sangiovese. Drink youngish.

Tenuta S. Agnese

Trebbiano d'Abruzzo
Edoardo Valentini
Dino Illuminati
Emidio Pepe

BASILICATA

Right in Italy's instep, and a region which is almost completely devoid of interest for the tourist or wine lover, Basilicata has often been overlooked. Which is a pity for one great traditional wine.

Aglianico del Vulture

The name comes from the mountain on the slopes of which the Aglianico grape is grown. As for the grape itself, its origins are Greek – which should indicate the wine's history. Sold young, fizzy and sweet, this is simply another Lambrusco lookalike; cellared until it is at least five years old, the wine becomes more complex and softer than many of Italy's better known reds.

Fratelli d'Angelo

CALABRIA

The toe-tip of Italy, Calabria produces what the locals claim to be the world's oldest wine, the forebear of which was supposedly served to Olympic athletes. Ciro comes in both red and rosé, is made from the Gaglioppo grape, and needs about five years to develop. Greco di Bianco, made from the grape of the same name, is a powerful and honeyed dessert wine. It can be enjoyed young or mature.

Cirò (Rosso)

Antonio Librandi.

Greco di Bianco

Umberto Ceratti.

CAMPANIA

This is the region around Naples, producing numerous wines of which few people have heard, and one – Lacryma Christi – which is known to millions of people who have probably never tasted it.

Falerno

The red, made from the Aglianico, needs around five years; the white should be drunk as young as possible.

Villa Matilde
Michele Moio

Fiano di Avellino

White wine with, Burton Anderson says, a bouquet of 'pears and toasted hazelnuts', made from a grape grown by the ancient Romans.

Mastroberardino.

Greco di Tufo

A dry, slightly almondy, white, made from the ancient Greco grape, grown in Campania before Christ was born. Drink youngish.

Mastroberardino.

Lacryma Christi del Vesuvio

There are countless different versions of this beautifully named wine, but only the red white and rosé of Vesuvio have a DOC. The red and rosé are made from the Piedirosso, Olivella and Aglianico grapes; the white, from the Coda di Volpe, Verdeca, Falanghina and Greco. The red is quite 'rustic' in style; the white can be attractive and light.

Mastroberardino.

Taurasi

Mostly made from the Aglianico grape, planted in volcanic soil, this is quite a big red wine which needs around eight years to soften.

Mastroberardino.

EMILIA ROMAGNA

Lambrusco

The region which, every year, produces a large proportion of Italy's most anonymous bulk wine has produced one name which is known the world over: Lambrusco. It is easy to sneer at the sweet pink froth which goes out under this name, but it has one great advantage over the seemingly 'respectable' wines of Valpolicella, Frascati and Chianti. At least it makes no claims to be anything more than it is – fun wine. Besides, the purist can always seek out a bottle or two of the traditional-style dry version, which still does exist in Italy. He may have to hurry though: the Italians are beginning to develop their own taste for 'American-sweet' Lambrusco. Incidentially, the varieties of Lambrusco grape used for the wine could form a lengthy list in themselves. But rather a boring and useless one.

The best Lambruschi are:

Lambrusco di Sorbara
Lambrusco Grasparossa di Castelvetro
Lambrusco Reggiano
Lambrusco Salamino di S. Croce
Albana di Romagna
Sangiovese di Romagna
Trebbiano di Romagna

Romagna has three wines, Albana di Romagna, made from the Albana grape, can be sweet, dry, sparkling or still and could become a workaday competitor to Frascati and Soave. Trebbiano di Romagna will fill a similar role, though it can be quite pleasantly fruity on occasion; and Sangiovese di Romagna is this region's answer to Chianti. Drink Albana Secco young; Amabile, youngish. Sangiovese Crus can be aged, but most of this wine and all the Trebbiano should be drunk young.

Fattoria Paradiso
Ferrucci
Fratelli Vallunga
Ronco (esp. Sangiovese Crus)

Barbarossa di Bertinoro and Pagadebit

At his Fattoria Paradiso, Mario Pezzi has achieved something quite remarkable: given the multitude of grapes which are known to flourish in Italy, he has gone out and discovered a couple of new (or rather, forgotten) ones. The Pagadebit means literally 'pay debt' and produces a sippable dessert wine of great delicacy, whilst the Barbarossa – named after the emperor – is appropriately enough a muscular wine which could go a few rounds with quite a few Australian Shirazs and still be able to stand up to the flavour of a well-hung pheasant. Barbarossa can be matured; Pagadebit should be drunk young.

Colli Bolognesi Vino da Tavola

Enrico Vallania believes that much of Italy is better suited to the Cabernet Sauvignon than Bordeaux. His success extends to other French varieties. Drink youngish.

Terre Rosse (Vallania)

Rosso Armentano

Burton Anderson compares the Rosso del Armentano, made by the Fratelli Vallunga, to 'the finest crus of Pommard and Volnay' in its 'flowery softness'. Needs five years.

FRIULI-VENEZIA GIULA

Just as the Sud Tirol is confusingly German for a region which is technically Italian, Friuli-Venezia-Giula has its own identity problems. There are parts which have been Yugoslavian, and some which are half way to being Austrian. Over the last 20 years however, the region has begun to make an impact with newly planted vineyards.

Colli Orientali del Friuli

This is one of Italy's most interesting places to seek out examples from a long list of local and imported grape varieties, including the Tocai, Malvasia, Pinot Bianco and Grigio, Müller-Thurgau, Rhine Riesling and Riesling Italico, Traminer, Cabernet Franc, Merlot, Pinot Noir, Ribolla Gialla, Refosco, Verduzzo and Picolit. Of these the most interesting are perhaps the Verduzzo which produces a fine Amabile style, and the Picolit, a traditional grape which, like the region, is making something of a comeback. Drink whites young; reds youngish.

Giovanni Dri
Livio Felluga
Valle
Volpe Pasini
Abbazia di Rosazzo
Ronchi di Fornaz
G. B. Comelli

Collio

Using most of the same grapes as in Colli Orientali, Collio produces a range of excellent reds and whites for drinking young, although some well made reds may stand ageing.

Attems
Borgo Conventi
Livio Felluga
Marco Felluga
Gradimir Gradnik
Francesco Gravner
Jermann
Doro Princic
Mario Schiopetto
Enofriulia
Villa Russiz

Grave del Friuli

LIke many areas within the region, Grave suffered heavily from the earthquakes of 1976. Its wines are varied in quality but there are some which are worth watching out for – if only for the fact that they can offer exceptional value for money. The permitted grapes are Merlot (the most widely grown), Cabernet, Refosco, Pinot Bianco and Grigio, Tocai and Verduzzo. Drink whites young; reds youngish.

Germano Filiputti
Plozner
La Delizia (C.S. Casarsa)

Vintage Tunina

Burton Anderson suggests that, if Italy has any wine which might compete with a white Burgundy, this is it. Made from an eccentric blend of Chardonnay, Pinot Bianco, Sauvignon and Picolit, it is rich and complex, gaining much from the fact that unlike most other Italian white wines it undergoes a malolactic fermentation – just like a Burgundy. Drink fairly young.

Jermann

LAZIO

Frascati

If Tuscany is Chianti and the Veneto, Soave, then Lazio is Frascati. This occasionally almondy wine is another victim of its own popularity. Buy it if you must, but Soave's a cheaper dull wine and Marino produced in smallish quantities next door to Frascati, offers a cleaner, drier, more enjoyable wine at a lower price. The only kind of Frascati worth spending time on is one not found easily outside Italy. The sweet Cannellino is golden, honeyed and glorious and no match commercially for its better known cousin.

Marino

Cantine Sociale Cooperativa di Marino.

Torre Ercolana

Another of Italy's exalted – and pricy – Bordeaux-style reds, this one includes the traditional Roman Cesanese grape. Maturation varies from vintage to vintage.

Cantina Colacicchi

Fiorano

Using Cabernet Sauvignon, and Merlot (in a blend), for the red, and the Malvasia di Candia and Sémillon, for his whites Ludovisi proves that it is possible to make great wines within a lion's growl of the Coliseum. Unfortunately there's not enough to go round, and what there is proves very costly. Red needs five years; white – drink youngish.

Boncompagni Ludovisi

LOMBARDIA

Milan's vineyard, Lombardy makes prodigious amounts of sparkling wine and two red wines in particular which are beginning to become more familiar outside Italy.

Clastidium

Mix the Pinot Nero and the Pinot Grigio, and use a system of vinification which you cannot reveal to outsiders, and you could – just possibly – like Angelo Ballabio, make a white wine which needs several years ageing to develop into something really quite exciting.

Angelo Ballabio

Fraciacorta Pinot

One of Italy's most prestigious sparkling wines, produced from Pinot Nero, Grigio and Chardonnay.

Ca' del Bosco.

Franciacorta Rosso

This is possibly one of the most interesting examples of the marriage of traditionally French and Italian flavours. The grape mix involves, on the one hand, Cabernet Franc and Merlot; Nebbiolo and Barbera on the other. Drink youngish.

Ca' del Bosco
Longhi – de Carli

Oltrepò Pavese

One of the difficulties for this DOC lies in the number of different grape varieties from which it can be made, and thus the range of flavours it can encompass. Amongst the permitted reds:

Barbera and Bonarda

Can be enjoyed both young and mature.

M & G Fugazza (Castello di Luzzano)

Oltrepò Pavese Pinot Spumante

Much of the sparkling wine produced in Piedmont is actually made from grapes grown in Lombardy. There are, however, several excellent Spumantes which are made within Lombardy itself, from locally grown Pinot grapes.

Ballabio
Bassi Giuseppe
Contratto

Valtellina Superiore

Made from the Nebbiolo, this is a DOC which, like so many, promises variable quality. Better vintages – 70, 71, 78, 82, 83 – need at least five years to soften.

Enologica Valtellinese
Nera
Rainoldi

MARCHES

Verdicchio dei Castelli di Jesi

The grape after which the wine is named gives Verdicchio at least a basic level of dry fruitiness which Frascati would love to have. It is no great wine, but certainly one of which the Italians have little reason to feel ashamed. Drink young.

Garofoli & Cru
Don Antonio Marinoni
Monte Schiavo & Cru

Rosso Cònero

Made from the Montepulciano grape (sometimes with a dash of Sangiovese) this is another of those big Italian reds with a hint of bitterness lurking amidst the herbiness of its flavour. Fortunately for the impatient though, this is one you can enjoy within five years of the harvest.

Marchetti
Don Antonio Marinoni

MOLISE

Ramitello

This is one for the pioneers: a wine from a wine region the Italians hardly know themselves. A number of different grapes are grown, including the Moscato, Sangiovese, Montepulciano, Trebbiano, Bombino Bianco and Barbera. Drink youngish.

Masseria di Majo Norante

PIEMONTE

Piedmont is known principally for its two 'great' reds, Barolo and Barbaresco, and the river of sweet white froth which bears the label of Asti Spumante and Moscato. Each of these is discussed beneath its own heading.

Arneis

This traditional grape is little known, even in Italy. It has no DOC – yet – but can be used to make dry white wine with complex mixtures of soft fruity flavours.

Cornarea
Bruno Giacosa
Vietti

Asti Spumante

Like sweet Lambrusco this is unashamedly 'pop wine'. It is for people who like drinking wine with a strong taste of grapes (it is also one of the only wines which goes well with Chinese food). Almost all Asti is made by the Cuve Close or Charmat method. Drink young.

Fontanafredda
Cinzano

Martini
Santero

Barbaresco and Barolo

The unsophisticated admit to finding Russian films boring and Barbaresco and Barolo hard, fruitless and no fun to drink. Lovers of these traditional Piedmontese wines will look at you condescendingly and suggest that perhaps you have never tasted one that is really mature. The problem, whatever the traditionalists may say, lies less in the palate than in the way in which these wines are being produced. Made from the Nebbiolo, a grape with a natural propensity for producing hard, acidic and dry red wines, they are all too often left to dry out still further in large barrels. Particularly in less ripe years the little fruit which the grape had in the first place disappears altogether. Despite what the reactionaries may say, wine, like language, evolves with time. Thankfully, there are a few good producers in both these denominations who are giving evolution a hand with new styles of vinification, and shorter periods spent in barrel. Producers making both Barolo and Barbaresco have been listed here under the DOC for which they have greater repute. Most also produce Dolcetto, Barbera etc., varying from reliable to excellent.

Barbaresco

Castello di Neive	La Spinona
Giuseppe Cortese	Marchese di Grese
Gaja	Prodottori di Barbaresco
Bruno Giacosa	Roagna – I Paglieri

Barbera

There are three types of Piedmontese Barbera, the Barbera d'Alba and the Barbera d'Asti, both of which are made exclusively from the grape from which they take their name, and the Barbera del Monferrato which may be made with a little help from one or two other friendly local varieties. Barbera d'Asti is reputedly best of the three, but all should, when well made, offer wines which are at once really muscular, but without the harshness so often found in Barolo. Needs at least 5 years, except for Barbera del Monferrato which can be drunk younger.

Gaja	Giacosa
Pio Cesare	Vietti

Barolo

Giacomo Borgogno	Podere Rocche dei Manzoni –
Giulio Mascarello Cavallotto	Valentino
Aldo Conterno	Prunotto
Contratto	*Renato Ratti
Cordero	Terre del Barolo
Fontanafredda (Crus only)	Vietti
*Pio Cesare	Vinarte

Bricco-Manzoni

A non-DOC blend of Barbera and Nebbiolo grapes of high quality. Drink youngish, or with some age.

Podere Rocche dei Manzoni-Valentino.

Carema and Donnaz

Like Barolo and Barbaresco, Carema and Donnaz are made from the Nebbiolo grape but at an altitude of as much as 2,000 feet above sea level. Far less well known than their two exalted neighbours, both wines prove that the Nebbiolo can produce wine with a delicacy of fruit which doesn't take a decade to break through the barrier of tannin.

Luigi Ferrando

Cortese di Gavi

Most straw yellow wine turns out to be old and dry or younger and sweet. This one however, made from the Cortese grape, is described by Cyril Ray as 'undoubtedly the cleanest, crispest, most refreshing white wine I have come across for many a long day'.

La Scolca
Soldati ('Gavi dei Gavi')

Dolcetto

You will be forgiven for thinking that any wine with a name like this had to be sweet. Actually it was once, but nowadays most of us like

our red wines dry. Well made Dolcetto, drunk young, has some of the fruit of a Côtes du Rhône or Beaujolais, with the toffee'd nose of a wine made from the Merlot. It is hard to find outside Italy, and the Piedmontese cannot get enough of it.

Giuseppe Poggio

Erbaluce di Caluso
Caluso Passito

Erbaluce has been translated as 'sunlight grass'. The grape can produce good, light dry wine or, in its semi-shrivelled state, a luscious and long-lived sweet one.

Vittorio Boratto
Corrado Gnavi

Gattinara

If reputation and price were sufficient to guarantee quality, this Nebbiolo would be one of Italy's finest reds. As it is, it can vary enormously, depending on the producer, from fine and delicate to dull and disappointing.

Luigi Dessilani

Moscato Naturale d'Asti

Most Moscato is used to make sparkling Asti, but the little which escapes is sold under this denomination. Drink as young as possible.

Vietti
I Vignaioli di Santo Stefano

Spanna

Another name for the Nebbiolo, this wine is yet another of those which the authorities consider unfit to bear a DOC. Those unimpressed by the authorities' infallibility in such matters should seek out an old bottle and compare it to a Gattinara or a Barolo.

Antonio Vallana

PUGLIA

This is Italy's stiletto heel, an area which was once only known as a source of basic plonk, but which is now making efforts to stem its contribution to the wine lake.

Favonio

At his Favonio estate, Signor Simonini has planted not only Pinot Noir and Blanc, but also Cabernet Franc, Chardonnay and a Pinot-Riesling cross only grown in Italy, and which would have the Alsatian growers of both grapes spluttering into their beer. Drink youngish.

Simonini

Torre Quarto

The Torre Quarto estate was founded by the Ducs de la Rochefoucauld, and now makes its long-maturing red from the Malbec (principally), and Uva di Troia grapes. Needs time.

Cirillo – Farrusi

Il Falcone
The Falcon in question here belonged to Friedrich 11 of Hohenstaufen, the 13th century emperor whose Castel del Monte has given its name to the wines of Puglia's most productive DOC. Il Falcone, made in tiny quantities, is made from the Uva di Troia, Bombino Nero, Montepulciano and Sangiovese grapes, takes a very long time – at least eight years – to develop.

Rivera

Alezia/Rosa del Golfo
A great number of fine winemakers prefer not to consider making rosé – for them it is a little like Escoffier turning his hand to cup cakes. Giuseppe Calo, however, uses the 'teardrop system' of lightly crushed Malvasia Nera and Negroamaro grapes, to make a rosé that Burton Anderson considers 'a match for elite Tavels'. Drink young.

Guiseppe Calo

SARDEGNA
'Sardinia? Oh yes, of course it *is* Italian . . . but I'd never thought of it as a fine wine producing region.' Well if that was your impression, don't feel too guilty, you're in plentiful company. But one firm, Sella & Mosca are now making several wines which are attracting a great deal of complimentary attention.

Anghelu Ruju
Spicy, powerful (18%) fruity red wine made from partly dried Cannonau grapes and which needs to be matured for a few years.

Sella & Mosca

Vermentino di Alghero
White wine made from the grape of the same name.

Sella & Mosca.

Vernaccia di Oristano
Sardinia's answer to sherry, made from overripe Vernaccia grapes, and matured in a kind of solera for two years. Unfortified, it is around 15% alcohol and needs at least five years before it is ready to drink.

Sella & Mosca

SICILIA
If Sicily were to stop making wine, the surface level of the European wine lake would go down visibly. And it is not just non-Italians who are failing to drink the stuff quickly enough: the Sicilians themselves consume less *per capita* than their neighbours on the mainland. Sicily is of course best known for Marsala, but there are several other wines worth looking out for.

Malvasia delle Lipari
The Malvasia is made in Passito and Liquoroso styles, as well as the semi-dry Delle Lipari which Burton Anderson describes as having 'seductive scents of apricots and citrus'.

Carlo Hauner

Marsala
Standing alongside Madeira port and sherry as one of the world's great English-influenced fortified wines (it was first sold in 1733 by John Woodhouse, whose name still appears on bottles of Marsala). Styles vary from house to house, but it is worth explaining the following terms:

Marsala Fine – wine of 17% alcohol. Basic Marsala.
Marsala Speciale – (including such terms as Marsala all'Uovo) describes wine flavoured with egg, nuts etc. Thin Zabaglione in a bottle.
Marsala Superiore – wine of 18% and a higher quality.
Marsala Vergine – like 'virgin olive oil', the finest level of quality. Drier tasting, it is often produced in a solera system and must be at least five years old.

Marco de Bartoli
Diego Rallo & Figli

Moscato di Pantelleria
Take your pick from the liquoroso (fortified), spumante naturale (sparkling) naturalmente dolce (very sweet) or naturale (sweet) styles. Or then again, you could try a passito . . .

Tanit – AG. AS. Di Pantelleria

Solicchiato Bianco di Villa Fontane

Sun-dried grapes are used to make a dessert wine which is left to age for ten years or longer, but which can be drunk young.

Giuseppe Coria

Stravecchio Siciliano di Villa Fontane
A solera-system dry wine made from sun-dried grapes.

Vecchio Samperi, Inzolia di Samperi, Josephine Dore
Marco de Bartoli has established an enviable reputation for his skill at making Sicily's finest sweet wines as here using the Grillo and Inzolia grapes, but not fortifying the end-result, putting it through a solera-type system instead.

Marco de Bartoli

Vino da Tavola
Apart from the above-listed, Sicily is now producing a growing number of excellent table wines.

Red table wines
Regaleali – Rosso del Conte (needs five years).

White table wines

Corvo
Although often thought to be a DOC, Corvo is in fact a brand name for a range of reasonable quality wines produced by Duca di Salapurata.

Corvo Colomba Platino (drink as young as possible)
Regaleali Bianco (drink as young as possible)
Rapitalà (drink as young as possible)

TOSCANA
Tuscany is Chianti – well that is the traditional view. And what is there to say about Chianti? Of all the great traditional wines, this is now possibly in the sorriest state. As an adventurous wine drinker you could do a great deal worse than look at some of Tuscany's other newer style Cabernet-influenced wines.

Chianti Classico
On the one hand there is plain Chianti, which could be good, bad or apalling. On the other there are the two consortia: the producers of Chianti Classico and Chianti Putto. Both groups' wines can be identified by their insignia. The former, the black cockerels, claim the excellence of the 'the original Chianti vineyards', whilst the latter, the cherubs, simply claim to make good wine.

The average bottle of Chianti is either pale and thin, thanks to the fact that up to a third of its content is made with easy-to-grow white grapes, or thick, dark and tasteless – in which case there will probably be about a sixth or seventh of bodybuilding wine shipped up from further south. Both of these tricks are quite legal in Italy and both represent a considerable saving for the uncaring winemaker.

As a general rule, the Classico cockerel is a guarantee of absolutely nothing at all; the Putto cherub may promise greater quality. Our advice is to take no notice of whether or not a producer is a member of either consortium (some of the best belong to neither) and to look for one of the names on the following list. They are divided into three quality levels.

Matters may improve with the introduction of the stricter and quite controversial DOCG legislation but no-one is yet certain of how dramatic the effect of these rules (which came into force with the 1984 vintage) will be.

Excellent
Antinori
Badia a Coltibuono
Castellare
Castell'in Villa
Castello di Querceto
Castello di Rampolla

Castello di San Polo in Rosso
Castello di Volpaia
Fontodi
Monte Vertini
Ruffino

Very good
Castello di Vicchiomaggio
Fossi
Il Grigio di San Felice
Lamole
Le Pici

Lilliano
Montagliari/La Quercia
Riecine
Rignana
San Cosma

Good
Cafaggio
Castelli di Grevepesa
Fattoria di Ama
Fonterutoli

Pagliarese
Rocca delle Macie
San Vito in Beradegna
Uzzano

Chianti Non-Classico
Artimino
Capezzana
Castello di Poppiano
Frescobaldi
Il Corno
La Querce

Montenidoli
Montellori
Pasolini dall'Onda Borghese
Spalletti
Uggiano
Villa di Vetrice

Variations on a Chianti Theme
But why go for Chianti anyway? Be as adventurous as some of the region's better producers who have begun to produce their own styles of wine. Some, like Antinori's excellent Tignanello, simply bear their name and the humble designation of 'Vino da Tavola' on their labels, others boast unfamiliar DOC's such as Carmignano, one of Italy's most interesting up-and-coming red wines. They all need ageing.

Coltassala
(Volpaia)
I Sodi di San Niccolò
(Castellare)
Le Pergole Torte
(Monte Vertine)

Sassicaia (needs five years)
(Antinori)
Tignanello
(Antinori)
Solaia
(Antinori)

Carmignano
The legal way to make Chianti with a welcome bit of Cabernet flavour, this is one of Italy's most promising DOC's. Drink youngish, or mature.

Villa di Capezzana (Contini Bonacossi)

Ghiaie della Furba
Made from both Cabernets and the Merlot, this is an uncompromising effort to see what a claret blend will achieve in Tuscany.

Contini Bonacossi

Brunello di Montalcino
Brunello di Montalcino is Italy's most prestigious – and, in the case of Biondi Santi, expensive – wine these days, having emerged from almost total obscurity less than two decades ago. Made from the Brunello grape, it is extraordinarily tough, tannic and dry when young, calling for at least eight years to mature, and as long as a day to 'breathe' in its bottle before serving. Its supporters claim that the disappointment often claimed by those who have bought bottles, stems from the wine having been drunk too young. Some need eight years others, such as Villa Banfi, can be drunk young.

Altesino
Argiano
Biondi Santi
Caparzo

Lisini
Poggio alla Mura
Tenuta Il Poggione
Villa Banfi

Moscadello di Montalcino
The great American sweet tooth has bitten deeply into Tuscany with this sweet, muscaty fizz, produced by Villa Banfi. Drink it in its infancy.

Villa Banfi

Vernaccia di San Gimignano
Made from the Vernaccia grape, this is one of Italy's most traditional white wines, with a history stretching back over three centuries. It used to be allowed to mature and to turn gold – nowadays new styles of winemaking have turned it into a lighter, fresher wine to drink young.

Teruzzi & Puthod

Vino Nobile di Montepulciano
Unlike the Brunello, this is made from more or less the same grapes as Chianti. Its name derives from the fact that the aristocracy used to use this wine for sacrimental purposes. The First of Italy's DOCF though possibly underservedly of this honour. Needs ageing.

Avignonesi
Casella
Fassati
Fattoria di Fognano

Montenero
Poderi Boscarelli
Poliziano

Vin Santo
Vin Santo is usually sweet. Montalcino, unusually, produces a dry one.

TRENTINO – SUD TIROL (ALTO ADIGE)
Despite the fact that it cannot make up its mind whether to call itself the Alto Adige, the Sud Tirol or, in English, the South Tyrol, this is the most exciting wine growing area in the whole of Italy. There must be some people who have failed to notice its arrival on the scene or who, seeing the Germanic style of its labels and the lederhosen-clad winegrowers who rejoice in names like Tiefenbrunner, Walch and Hofstätter, fail to realise that this province has anything to do with Italian wine at all.

The wines it produces are generally made from varieties of grapes more usually found in France and Germany, and the cooler climate and modern styles of winemaking help to make wines unlike any others produced in Italy. Look for deliciously fresh Chardonnays and Pinot Biancos and the characterful fruity red Vernatsch and the Lagrein, both indigenous to the region.

The following produce good to outstanding wine from several varietals in one or more wine zones. The speed at which they mature depends on the variety of grape and the producer's style.

Arunda (Méthode Champenoise)
  sparkling wine)
Foradori
Gorgio Grai
Hofstätter
Lageder
Muri-Gries

Niedermayr
Rottensteiner
Santa Maddalena (Vernatsch)
Schloss Rametz
Schloss Schwanburg
Tapfer (Goldenmuskateller)
Tiefenbrunner

TRENTINO
The Trentino, as its name indicates, is Italian through and through. The wines are softer than those of the Sud Tirol, but there is still some excellent winemaking going on, with quite a wide variety of grapes. Here too, the Chardonnay is on form, and there is some very nice Cabernet. The Schiava by the way is exactly the same grape as the Vernatsch – but the wine is rather less fun. The following produce good to outstanding wine from several varietals in one or more wine zones. The speed at which they mature depends on the variety of grape, the producer's style, and origin.

Barone de Cles
Castel San Michele
Conti Martini
De Tarczal

Foradori
Letrari
Pojer & Sandri
Zendi

UMBRIA
Most people outside Italy know of only one wine from Umbria: Orvieto. Which is a shame, because other wines, particularly those made by Lungarotti are a far worthier advertisement for this region.

Orvieto
Here is another of those familiar, inexpensive Italian whites which it would be pleasant to be able to praise – but in all conscience this really is impossible to do. For Frascati, read Orvieto, and all the same criticisms apply; as does the exception we would make for the sweet, golden Abboccato style they used to make. Perhaps Antinori will shake things up and instil a sense of pride into the growers here. We have to hope. Drink young.

Barberani	Cotti
Bigi	Decugnano dei Barbi
Castello della Sala (Antinori)	

Sagrantino di Montefalco, Montefalco Rosso
Sagrantino is, like Valpolicella Amarone, made from partially dried grapes. Made from the local black grape of the same name, it can be sweet or dry. Montefalco, on the other hand, is a light, easy-to-drink, Sangiovese, Malvasia and Trebbiano blend of no great pretention.

Adanti

Spumante
Lamborghini

Torgiano
Giorgio Lungarotti is one of the band of winemakers who, whilst refusing to compromise on standards, are gradually carving a new path for Italian wine.

Torgiano Riserva (Monticchio) – needs five years.
Torgiano San Giorgio – needs five years.
Torgiano Chardonnay di Miralduoldo – drink youngish.
Torgiano Cabernet Sauvignon di Miralduoldo – needs five years.

Lungarotti

Recioto di Soave
Like Valpolicella, Soave thankfully has one type of wine which protects its reputation from really hitting rock-bottom. This sweet white wine is that wonderful combination, rarer than it should be in Italy: traditional and good. Drink youngish or mature.

Anselmi

Campo Fiorin
Made by Masi by macerating valpolicella on the skins of Recioto.

Tocai di Lison
Unlike Hungarian Tokay this wine is bone dry. This is made from the Tocai Friulano grape and tastes nutty and peachy with a slightly bitter tang.

La Fattoria

Torcolato
This is a sweet white Breganze, made from the Tocai. Drink youngish or mature.

Maculan

Valpolicella
Hemingway described Valpolicella as 'like the house of a brother with whom one gets on well'. Maybe the house needs a spring clean since Ernest last visited it: like Bardolino whose mixture of grapes is the same, this can be extremely dull wine. Red wine's answer to Soave.

Good but untypical	Good, typical
Serègo Alighieri	Fabiano
Quintarelli	Guerrieri-Rizzardi
	Le Ragose
	Santa Sofia

Recioto della Valpolicella (Amarone)
Some of the money you save by not buying Valpolicella and Soave should be spent on an experimental bottle or two of Recioto della Valpolicella Amarone, one of Tuscany's better kept secrets. It is where one can find all the fruit which they forgot to put in, or dried out of, those other reds. Rare, sweet and expensive. Needs five years.

Allegrini	Quintarelli
Masi (especially Crus)	Tedeschi
Serègo Alighieri Vaio Armaron	Domenico Vantini (Tramanal)

Venegazzù – Cabernet/della Sala
The Cabernet Sauvignon continues in its gradual takeover of Italy. This is one to compare with Tuscan examples such as Sassicaia and Tignanello. Despite not having any kind of DOC, this is one of Italy's finest red wines. Needs 5 years.

Conte Loredan Gasparini

Villa dal Ferro
Making wine from both Cabernets, the Pinot Noir, Merlot, Tocai and Riesling, Villa dal Ferro, like Venegazzù, is proof of just how well traditional French varieties can flourish in the Veneto. Drink young or youngish, depending on varietal.

Lazzarini

ITALIAN 'CLARETS'

Anyone who criticizes the state of Italian wine today and describes much of it as flavourless, stands the risk of being thought 'unsympathetic'. No one wants to force, or seduce, the Italians into replacing the traditional flavour of their wines with a 'fruity international style'; equally there is no reason to make allowances for wines which many of this generation of winemakers' grandparents would have found as poor as we do. What we want is the best of what Italy can produce, rather than the worst. Besides, wine evolves. Wines which used to be sweet, are now dry; who is to say what they will, or should taste like a century from now. The following list includes the best of both worlds: the finest traditionalists, and the ever-growing number of exciting innovators.

Many of the most exciting wines now being produced in Italy contain a sizeable proportion of Cabernet Sauvignon – you could call them Italian Clarets.

★ ★ ★ ★ ★

Carmignano
Tenuta di Capezzana Tuscany

★ ★ ★ ★ ★

Castel San Michele
Istituto Agrario Provinciale San Michele all'Adige

★ ★ ★ ★ ★

Castello di Roncade
Vincenzo Ciani Bassetti, Veneto

★ ★ ★ ★ ★

Col Sandago
Orlandi, Veneto

★ ★ ★ ★ ★

Costozza Cabernet
Alvise da Schio, Veneto

★ ★ ★ ★ ★

Eno Friulia
Vittorio Puiatti, Friuli, Venezia Giulia

★ ★ ★ ★ ★

Fiorano Rosso
Fiorano, Latium

★ ★ ★ ★ ★

Foianeghe Rosso
Conti Bossi Fedrigotti, Trentino

★ ★ ★ ★ ★

Morio-Vecio
Lagariavini, Trentino

★ ★ ★ ★ ★

Pomino
Frescobaldi, Tuscany

★ ★ ★ ★ ★

Rosso Armentano
Fratelli Vallunga, Emilia-Romagna

★ ★ ★ ★ ★

San Leonardo
Tenuta San Leonardo, Trentino

★ ★ ★ ★ ★

Sassicaia
Marchese Incisa della Rocchetta, Tuscany

★ ★ ★ ★ ★

Tignanello
Antinori, Tuscany

★ ★ ★ ★ ★

Torre Ercolano
Bruno Colacicchi, Latium

★ ★ ★ ★ ★

Venegazzù
Venegazzù
Conte Loredan-Gasparini, Veneto

JAPAN

THE Japanese are now taking wine increasingly seriously, both as producers and as drinkers. It has to be said however that there has been a lack of a certain seriousness in the past: the nation which could unblushingly rename a village 'Scotland' so as to be able to print 'bottled in . . .' on the labels of Japanese whiskey had equally little compunction in the way in which it used expressions such as 'Mis en Bouteilles au Château'.

Luxury drinking comes from high-quality imported wines – the Japanese are eager buyers at the Hospices de Beaune auction. For more basic use wines and grapes must are imported from Chile and Australia often for blending before being sold to consumers.

There are, at present, some 30,000 hectares under vine, a figure which is increasing at the rate of 1,000 hectares per annum. Current annual production is 200,000 hectolitres. The majority of vines planted are of the native Japanese vinifera variety, the Koshu, and of imported American hybrids. However the 10 per cent of European varieties first imported by Japanese students in the 19th century are rapidly growing in importance.

The Wine Regions

Honshu – The Yamamashi prefecture south west of Tokyo has 6,000 *ha* of vineyards. Yamagata district has 3,500 *ha*. The major vineyards are in Nagano and Okayama

Kyushu – The major vineyards are in Fukuoka.

Hokkaido – The major vineyards are in Sapporo.

The Grape List

White
Campbells Early
Chardonnay
Delaware
Koshu (a native vinifera)
Muscat Bailey
Müller-Thurgau
Neo-Muscat
Riesling
Sémillon

Red
Cabernet Sauvignon
Concord
Merlot

The main producers

Godu Shusei
Manns Wine
Sanraku Ocean
Suntory

The principal wines

Château Mercian (Sanraku Ocean)
Concord
Delaware
Hachi Canon Vin Blanc

JORDAN

MOST of the grapes grown are eaten. What little wine is made is expensive, and few outside Jordan are ever likely to acquire a taste for it.

KOREA

SURPRISINGLY rumoured to have one vineyard, which produces a medium-dry white wine from the Riesling grape, Korea heads our list of the world's least likely wine producing regions.

KOSHER WINES

KOSHER wine from the grape is required in the strict observance of many Jewish festivals, for example, the Arba Kossot – the statutory four glasses of wine drunk, by young and old, at Passover.

All wine exported from Israel is Kosher, and many countries with Jewish populations also have wineries where certain controls are scrupulously observed. Traditionally, kosher wines are sweet and heavy, often fortified, and expensive; a result of the constant supervision needed to ensure that the laws are being adhered to. Exported wines have long been known by numbers, rather than names, to make life easier for non-English speaking immigrants. However, Israeli winemakers, notably Carmel and Palwin, are diversifying in their wine-styles. The 'kosher-ness' of the wines is treated more as a matter of course, rather than as their raison d'etre. It is in the new cepages and the more 'sophisticated' styles that the appeal to a wider, non-Jewish market is hoped to lie.

The Kosher Laws

1. Orlah. The injunction which prevents the use of a crop for the first three years of planting.
2. No other crops may be planted with, or amongst, the vines.
3. All substances used must be kosher, e.g. the use of isinglass as a fining agent is prohibited as it derives from a non-kosher fish.
4. Everybody involved in the making of the wine must observe the precepts of orthodoxy; this is written into the contracts of Carmel employees.
5. Schmittah. As with all crops, the fields must lie fallow every seventh year, when the vines are untended and the grapes unpicked. Exported wine must bear documentation certifying that it has not been made from a Schmittah vintage.
6. Rabbinical authority requires the 'Boreh Pri Hagofen' ('who created the fruit of the vine') blessing to be said over the wine.

Countries producing kosher wine

Canada	Italy
France	Spain
Israel	USA

LEBANON

JUST as there are men and women who persist in trying to scale Everest, a small group of winemakers have endeavoured to continue making wine in the Lebanon of the last few troubled years. Best known of these producers is Serge Hochar, whose Château Musar has achieved remarkable success in blind tastings around the world. But Hochar is not the only winemaker in Lebanon nor, though it may occasionally seem otherwise, was he the first person to make Lebanese wine.

As Hochar himself points out, Lebanon's wine-making history stretches back to the days of the Bible. Unfortunately, continuity has never really been the keynote here. No sooner had the Crusaders returned whence they came, the edicts of Islam put a pretty firm halt to any vinous proceedings; although the arrival of French colonists got the process moving again, the internal conflicts of recent years have prevented the development of a flourishing wine industry.

It is perhaps for this reason that the wine that is being made is often of such a high standard. Grape varieties are, in the majority, classic and French (though there are those who claim that the Chardonnay started here and was taken to

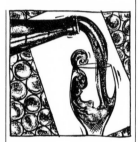

Burgundy, rather than vice versa) and winemaking generally benefits from modern expertise.

The main vineyard area is the Bekaa Valley, a long strip of land with good climate and soil, and focus of much of the recent conflict: several vintages have been picked literally beneath the gunfire. Even peace has proved difficult for winemaking. In 1984, a rare year without hostilities, Israeli roadblocks prevented Serge Hochar from getting his grapes back to the winery in time before they oxidized on the trucks.

The Grape List

Red
Aramon
Cabernet Sauvignon
Carignan
Cinsault
Merlot
Pinot Noir
Syrah

White
Chardonnay
Chasselas
Muscat
Sauvignon
Ugni Blanc

The main producers

Pierre Brun
Makes a good wine called Domaine des Tourelles.

Domaine de Kefraya
Red, white and rosé of reasonable quality.

Ksara
Caves Musar
Serge Hochar trained in France and uses Bordeaux style winemaking and barrels for his Château Musar which is a blend of Cabernet Sauvignon, Cinsault and Syrah. Proportions vary with each harvest. Hochar also produces a white (25 per cent of his production but little seen outside Lebanon) and a basic Cuvée Musar.

J. Nakad & Fils
A small company with a winery at Jdita in the Bekaa Valley and which still ferments and stores its wines in amphorae similar to the Tinajas of Montilla.

LIBYA

THE same quantity of wine is produced here as in the Lebanon, but here all resemblance ceases: Libyan wine is generally mediocre, at best.

Perhaps General Gadaffi's Green Revolution will produce some 'Green Wines' to compete with Vinho Verde. Some day.

LIECHTENSTEIN

UNTIL the nineteenth century, the vineyards of Liechtenstein were all tended by monks. Nowadays, however, this tiny country (which boasts the largest production of false teeth in the world) has a more secular wine industry, two thirds of which is grown in Vaduzer, the region around Vaduz, the Liechtenstein capital. Half of this wine is made by a single independent domaine, the Bockingwert. Vaduzer is a very pale red wine – almost rosé – made from the Blauburgunder (Pinot Noir) grape. As for the remaining third of Liechtenstein's wine, it is produced in Balzers, Schaan and Triesen, and is helpfully known as Balzner, Schaaner and Triesner. The small growers have formed into a cooperative. Several non-indigenous wine companies are believed to have bases in Liechtenstein, though possibly for venal rather than vinous reasons. In 1970 Liechtenstein produced some 800 hectolitres.

LUXEMBOURG

OF all the world's confusing sets of vinous quality designations, the Luxembourgois may well have established the most sensible. Each year wines are analysed and blind-tasted by a panel of experts nominated by the Minister of Agriculture and Viticulture; they are marked out of 20, and graded as follows:

Non-Admis (below 12°)	Premier Cru (16°–17.9°)
Marque Nationale (12°–13.9°)	Grand Premier Cru (18°–20°)
Vin Classé (14°–15.9°)	

The wine's status appears on a neck label issued by the Marque Nationale, the state control organization set up in 1935. Winegrowers have to declare precisely how much wine they have made, and are allocated an equally precise number of labels. One bottle of each wine is kept in the Marque Nationale cellars 'for future reference'.

Domaine sizes tend to be small – there are around 1,500 growers working only 2,000 *ha* of vines. Two-thirds of the wine is therefore made by cooperatives which are helped and overseen by the governmental controls of production and quality based at the Remich Viticultural Station. The wines, of which 75 per cent go for home consumption, are predominantly white and sparkling.

The Grape List

Rivaner *(Müller-Thurgau)*
Traminer

Ruländer *(Pinot Gris)*
Auxerrois *(increasing)*
Sylvaner
Elbling *(in decline)*
Pinot Blanc *(increasing)*

Gewürztraminer
Riesling
Pinot Noir
Muscat Ottonel

The Wine Regions

GREVENMACHER
Ahn
Bochsberg
Fels
Gollebour
Ongkaf
Palmberg
Rosenberg
Troerd
Syrberg
Wormeldange
Elderberg
Nussbaum
Keopp

LUXEMBOURG (CITY)
Bech-Kleinmacher
Foussach
Greiveldange
Herrenberg
Huette
Jongerberg
Kreitzberg
Roelschelt

REMICH
Hopertsberg
Wellenstein

STADTBREMINUS
Dreffert

WINTRANGE
Felsberg
Letschenberg
Remerschen
Schwebsinger
Hommelsberg

List of Leading Producers

Caves Bernard-Massard
  (Grevenmacher)
Vins moselles S.C. (Stadt-
  breminus Cooperative)
Caves Gales & Cie (Bech-
  Kleinmacher)
Caves St Martin (Remich)
Caves St Rémy (Remich)
Caves Krier Fréres (Remich)
Feipel Staar (Wellenstein)
Thill-Fréres (Schlengen)

MACAU

THIS tiny area on the Chinese mainland produces its own wine, a legacy from the days when it was a Portuguese colony.

MADAGASCAR

A SMALL amount of 'exotic-ally flavoured' wine is made mainly, it is said, influenced by French styles. Exactly which exotic French wines they have in mind is not entirely clear.

MALTA

WITH an industry which has concentrated its attention on satisfying the needs of tourists and the local popula-tion, Malta has never really seen much wine leave its shores. Which is just as well, since there are those who say that a George Cross was fully deserved by any-one capable of drinking regular draughts of some of the rough, full-bodied local reds. There have been recent improvements however, particularly with sweet wines made from the Muscat.

The Grape List

Dun Tumas
Gannaru
Gellewza
Insola
Muscat
Nigruwa

The Wine Regions

2,000 ha of vines are planted on a southern strip of the island around Rabat and Siggiewi and on neighbouring Gozo.
There are 10,000 individual growers supplying private and cooperative wineries which tend to produce branded wines. Best of these is possibly Verdala Rosé, produced in one of the island's most modern wineries.

MEXICO

EVER since Miguel Hidalgo, 'the Father of Mexican independence', planted vines in defiance of Spanish rule, and was shot, Mexican wine-makers have always suffered for their art. Their industry has reeled under a succession of entrepreneurial invaders, first the Spanish, then, in the 1890s, the Irish-American Concannon brothers, who brought millions of cuttings from California. Since the Second World War, the big producers have arrived – Domecq, Martell, Seagram, Osborne – setting up shop in Mexico to avoid the crippling import duties on wines and, more particularly brandies. But on the rare occasions when the Mexicans have been left to their own devices, the wine industry has nearly always suffered a decline.

The population is really not very interested in wine, drinking on average only a pint each per year. Government indifference to domestic consumption is reflected in the very high taxes levied, and the difficulty with which a licence to sell wine is obtained. However, Mexican winemakers are thriving under the impetus of outside interest. Old-established bodegas are now producing some of their best wines ever which will surely become better known if the industry succeeds in broadening the export market it relies on so heavily.

The Grape List

Red
Cabernet Sauvignon
Pinot Noir
Barbera
Carignan
Valdepenas
Grenache
Ruby Cabernet
Gamay
Zinfandel
Merlot
Malbec

Rosé
Mission
Rosa del Peru

White
Riesling
Chenin Blanc
Chardonnay
Palomino
Colombard
Ugni Blanc
Pinot Blanc
Pinot Gris

Recommended Producers

BAJA CALIFORNIA (GUADALUPE & SANTA TOMAS)

Vides del Guadalupe (Pedro Domecq)
Red and white table wines, 'Los Reyes' brand. Domecq also have an ageing cellar, 'Bodegas de la Mission' in the 'Calafia' Valley.

Bodegas de Santa Tomas (est. 1888)
Use a wide range of grape varieties; many of their vines brought from the Napa Valley. Make an excellent aged Barbera, a 'San Emilion' blended red, and a sparkling wine, 'Banda Azul', amongst others.

Formex-Ybarra (Productos Vinicola)
Make the 'Terrasola', 'Urbinova', 'Trevere' and 'Oncala' brands.

Vinícola de la Cetto
Produce the 'F. Chauvenet' brand.

Perez
'El Mirador' brand. The owner, Humberto Perez, is a bio-chemistry lecturer.

COAHUILA (PARRAS, SALTILLA)

Hacienda Alamo
The HQ of Nazario Ortiz Garza, Mexico's leading producer. Cabernets, bottle-fermented sparkling wines, 'Naturel' and 'Brut'.

Bodegas de San Lorenzo (est. 1626)
Pinot Blanc, Cabernet, Ruby Cabernet, Merlot and Zinfandel are amongst their predomi-nantly red varieties. Also produce 'Panache', which is similar to Pineau des Charentes.

Vinícola del Vergel (controlled by Cia Vinicola de Aguascalientes)
Make wines from Ruby Caber-net, Colombard and Ugni Blanc, amongst others.

Marqués del Aguayo
The oldest winery in Mexico. Some still and sparkling wine still made, but mostly brandy.

Casa Madero
Make the 'San Lorenzo' Brand.

Bodegas de San Ignacio

Bodegas de Monte Casino
Industrias de la Fermantación
Bodegas del Delfin
Bodegas del Rosario
Bodegas Ferrino
Bodegas del Vesubio

AGUASCALIENTES

**Cia. Vinícola de
Aguascalientes** (Garza)
Make the 'San Marcos' and
'Alamo' brands, and 'Champ
d'Or', a sparkling wine. 'Tinto
Nobleja', 'Blanco Verdizo' and
'Tinto Vina Santiaga' are Vergel
wines made here.

**Productos del Uva de
Aguascalientes** (Cetto)
The 'F. Chauvenet' brand is
again made here, along with
'Valle Redondo' and 'Calafia'.

RIO DE SAN JUAN

Caves de San Juan
Use the classic varieties of
Cabernet Sauvignon, Char-
donnay, Pinot Noir, Gamay and
Pinot Gris among their grapes.

Brands include:
'Carte Blanche' (Charmat
sparkling)
'Hidalgo'
'Blanco Seco'.
'Blanco Amabile'
'Rosado Seco'
'Clarete'
'Tinto'
'Cepa Cabernet Sauvignon'
'Cepa Pinot Noir'
'Blanc de Blanc' (Chenin/Ugni
Blanc)

Martell
Cabernet Sauvignon, Merlot,

Sauvignon Blanc, Grenache.
The 'Clos San Jean Tinto' and
'Châtillon' brands produced
here.

Madrileña
Makes 'Vinalta', a Cabernet/
Merlot blend, and a 'sherry',
'Tres Coronas'.

Bodegas de San Luis Rey
Here one can still find stocks of a
1912 sacramental Muscat wine.

ZACATEAS (OJOS CALIENTES & FRESNILLO)

Viñedos don Luis
Vergel vineyards.

Bodegas de Altiplena

MEXICO CITY

Seagram, Martini and Cinzano
all have bottling plants in
Mexico City.

Domecq's plant produces the
brands
'Los Reyes' (red, white and rose)
'Calafia' (red and white)
'Padre Kino' (red and white, 'low
alcohol-8')
'Val des Reyes' (red).

Bobadillo of Spain own the
Bodegas Santa Maria.

Cavas Bach
Produce varietal wines, notably
Nebbiolo, sparkling 'Champ-
brulé' and a variant of the
Canadian 'Cold Duck'-type
wine.

Garza
Bottling plant and ageing cellar,
from which they release a six-
year-old red wine, and the 'Jerez
Solera Alamo' 'sherry'.

MOROCCO

IN the 'Revised 1974' edition of his *Encyclopaedia of Wines and
Spirits,* Alexis Lichine stated that 'the future of the industry in
Morocco lies in supplying Europe with huge quantities of cheap wine
for blending'. Thankfully – for those who like their Burgundy to taste
French rather than North African – the Moroccan authorities decided
instead to concentrate on making far less, far better wine.

Between the mid 1970s and the mid 1980s the acreage of vines fell
from around 73,000 *ha* to around 20,000 *ha,* and the quality of the
wines has risen to compete with some from southern France. The reds
still tend to be a little beefy in style but some of the dry rosés and rich
Muscats in particular are delicious.

The industry was established in the 1820s by French settlers, with
much plantation of modern vineyards following the Second World
War. The central production organization, the SODEVI, includes a
cooperative union of Meknès which is linked to a Moroccan company
in Brussels which, in turn, bottles and sells a large proportion of its
wine. Due to the proscription of wine by the Muslim faith, the annual

production is more or less equally divided between tourists and lovers
of full-flavoured wines living outside Morocco. Export wine must
reach an alcoholic degree of 11%, but in practice, most of it easily
exceeds that figure and weighs in at 13% or 14%.

> **AOG** – *Appellation
> d'Origine Garantie (few
> wines)*
> **VOS** – *Vin de Qualité
> Supérieur*
> **VS** – *Vin Sélectioné*

The Wine Regions

MEKNES/FEZ
One private company, Meknès Vins accounts for 25 per cent of the
national production. SODEVI at Meknès makes the widespread but
non-AOG Ain Souala.

Gerrouana AOG Beni M'Tir sold abroad as Tarik.

Gerrouana Les Trois Domaines came first in its class (of 18 red
wines) at the 1979 Gault Millau wine Olympiade.

The Grape List

Red
Alicante-Bouschet
Carignan
Cabernet-Sauvignon
Cinsault
Grenache (used for 'vin gris'
rosé)
Mourvèdre
Syrah.

White
Clairette

Muscat d'Alexandrie
Pedro Ximénez
Rafsai
Ugni Blanc
Beni-Sadden
Sais
Zerkhoun

Principal grape varieties

Carignan
Cinsault
Grenache

The Wine Regions

COASTAL PLAIN (NORTH)
This is divided into three zones:
Dar bel Amri (north of Rabat)
Roumi (east of Rabat)
Sidi Larbi (south of Rabat)

All of which produce big, tough, sugary reds, mostly made from the
Alicante-Bouschet grape. Here, as in many regions, brand names are
being abandoned in favour of regional names, presumably as a first
step towards gaining appellation status, e.g. Chellah, Gharb, Zaer,
Zemmour.

COASTAL PLAIN (SOUTH)
This is divided into three zones:
Doukkala
Sahel
Zennata

Twelve per cent of the red is produced in Zennata, and is known as
Ourika. The firm of Sincomar makes Gris de Boulaoulane, a quality
rosé. Other good rosés are produced at El Jadida and Demnate, near
Marrakesh.

NORTH-EAST
Dry rosés from Taza, Oujda, Berkane, plus rich dessert wine from
Berka.

NEPAL

IN 1935 a Mr Denman described Nepal as 'an independent country of Northern Hindustan ... furnishing much useful wine'. Recent vintages have been furnished a trifle less readily.

NEW ZEALAND

IT is very easy to upset New Zealanders – just ask them whether they are from Perth or Sydney. After decades of being over-shadowed by their Australian neighbours, the New Zealanders are finally beginning to make their mark overseas. Climatically, there are enormous differences: whilst the Australians swelter, the Kiwis enjoy a very European-style climate. Amongst the success stories are some excellent Chardonnays, cool minty Cabernets and even some creditable attempts at that unattainable holy grail, the good non-Burgundian Pinot Noir. The closest parallel elsewhere is probably in the northwest of America, in states like Oregon and Washington where, almost unnoticed, many of the most exciting developments in the USA are to be found. Those who enjoy annoying their friends by saying 'I told you so' should hasten to try a bottle or two of New Zealand wine before those friends discover the quality for themselves.

Vineyard Area
hectares

Region	1970	1975	1980	1981	1982	1983
Northland	16	22	18	18	18	14
Auckland/Franklin	658	750	603	545	455	802
Waikato	182	247	326	336	336	204
Poverty Bay/Gisborne	278	612	1572	1772	1922	1782
Hawke's Bay	327	537	1490	1670	1891	1870
Nelson	3	6	39	39	39	42
Marlborough	–	175	777	1009	1175	1188
Bay of Plenty	–	–	9	9	9	11
Taranaki/Wellington	4	2	7	7	7	18
Canterbury	–	–	12	12	49	40

The Wine Varieties
as at 31 October 1983

	hectares
Unknown	121.6
Breidecker	51.4
Cabernet Sauvignon	414.5
Chardonnay	402.0
Chasselas	236.9
Chenin Blanc	372.2
Flora	70.5
Gamay Beaujolais	158.0
Gewürztraminer	284.8
Grey Riesling	44.1
Merlot	43.6
Müller-Thurgau	1873.7
Muscat varieties	331.0
Palomino	408.5
Pinot Gris	26.5
Pinot Meunier	8.6
Pinot Noir	139.1
Pinotage	100.0
Rhine Riesling	148.3
Sauvignon Blanc	200.6
Sémillon	86.5
Red Hybrids	151.0
White Hybrids	105.2
Other reds	16.4
Other whites	203.1

The Wine Regions

WEST AUCKLAND
Until the 1970s, this area was known for fortified or sweet table wines, produced by second and third generation Lebanese and Yugoslav families mainly from hybrid grape varieties. The vineyards are rapidly being replaced with classic European varieties, with an emphasis on the reds. The soil is a heavy clay, and the climate warm but fairly humid.

Main producers

Abel and Co.	Montana Wines Ltd
B. Henderson	Mazuran's Vineyards Ltd
Babich Wines Ltd	Nobilo Vintners Ltd
Balic Estate Wines Ltd	Nova Wines
Coopers Creek Vineyards Ltd	Pacific Vineyards Ltd
Collard Brothers Ltd	Penfolds Wines (NZ) Ltd
Corbans Wines Ltd	Panorama Vineyards
Delegat's Vineyard Ltd	Pleasant Valley Wines Ltd
Fairhaven Wines	Robard & Butler Ltd
K V Wines Ltd	San Marino Vineyards Ltd
Lincoln Vineyards Ltd	Selaks Wines Ltd
Matua Valley Wines Ltd	Soljans Wines
	Windy Hill Winery

SOUTH AUCKLAND
Although only about 20 miles south of Henderson, the area of Ihumatao is drier and has freer-draining volcanic ash soil. About 30 hectares have been planted since the 1970s with a range of classic varieties.

Main properties
Villa Maria Wines Ltd
Morton Estate Winery Ltd

THE WAIKATO
This area lies about 45 miles south of Auckland. The soil is a mixture of heavy clays and lighter silts and loams, and the climate warm and dry.

Main properties

Cooks New Zealand Wine Co. Ltd	Totara Vineyards Syc Ltd
De Redcliffe Estates Ltd	Vilagrad Wines
Karamea Wines	

GISBOURNE
The region has been growing grapes since the 1920s, but has seen a considerable expansion of plantings since the late 1970s. The soil is a deep fertile silt, and the climate can be slightly cooler and wetter than other parts of the North Island. Mainly white varieties are grown.

Main properties
Matawhero Wines
Montana Wines Ltd

HAWKE'S BAY
Gisbourne and Hawke's Bay between them produce about two-thirds of the wines in New Zealand. Hawke's Bay has a drier climate and a wider range of soil types than Gisbourne.

Main properties

Brookfields Vineyards (1977) Ltd	Mission Vineyards
Eskdale Winegrowers Co. Ltd	Ngatarawa Wines
Glenvale Vineyards Ltd	Te Mata Estate Winery Ltd
Lombardi Wines Ltd	Vidal Wine Producers Ltd
McWilliam's Wines (NZ) Ltd	

SOUTHERN NORTH ISLAND
There are very few estates to be found in this area, just a few that have found a suitable micro-climate for the making of wine. The most important are:

Holly Lodge Estate Winery
Pierre Wines

NELSON
This area of small properties only really started in the 1970s. The climate is cool and frosty in winter with long warm summers and has

the highest sunshine hours in New Zealand. The soil varies from silt loams to heavier clays on the hills.

Main properties

Korepo Wines	Victory Grape Wines
Neudorf Vineyards	Weingut Seifried Ltd
Ranzau Wines	

MARLBOROUGH

Though the newest of New Zealand's wine producing areas, Marlborough has grown rapidly to become the third most important area. The soil is mainly gravelly silt or stony, and the climate is moderate with long dry summers and cool autumns.

Main properties

Corbans Wines Ltd	Penfolds Wines (NZ) Ltd
Hunter's Wines Ltd	Te Whare Ra Wines
Montana Wines Ltd	

NEW ZEALAND PRIZE WINNERS

★ ★ ★ ★ ★

Cooks New Zealand Wine Co Ltd

★ ★ ★ ★ ★

Delegat's Vineyard Ltd

★ ★ ★ ★ ★

Glenvale Vineyards Ltd

★ ★ ★ ★ ★

Babich Wines Ltd

★ ★ ★ ★ ★

Pacific Vineyards Ltd

★ ★ ★ ★ ★

Montana Wines Ltd

★ ★ ★ ★ ★

Nobilo Vintners Ltd

★ ★ ★ ★ ★

Selaks Wines Ltd

★ ★ ★ ★ ★

Matua Valley Wines Ltd

NORWAY

PETER USTINOV gives an evocative description of Norwegian drinking habits: 'Alcohol rationing is all run by the state *Vinmonopol*; people buy their whole ration at the beginning of the month and finish it that afternoon. The first Saturday of any month produces scenes worthy of Hogarth, with people addressing imaginary crowds, rolling in the gutter, throwing up and all the rest of it. For the rest of the month they're very gloomy.'

Perhaps, in the circumstances, it is not surprising that Norway can proudly boast the lowest wine consumption, per capita, in Europe.

PERSONALITY CHOICE

*When asked by Marx's daughter what was his 'idea of happiness', Engels replied 'Château Margaux 1848'.

★ ★ ★ ★ ★

*Peter The Great had wines from Cahors in his cellars.

★ ★ ★ ★ ★

*The wine of Château Palmer, then called Château de Gasq, was beloved of both Louis XV and Cardinal de Richelieu.

★ ★ ★ ★ ★

*Napoleon's favourite Champagnes were Moët and Chandon and Jacquesson (Josephine preferred Ruinart, but blotted her copybook by failing to pay her Imperial bubbly bills). His favourite non-sparkler was Gevrey-Chambertin – which he preferred watered.

★ ★ ★ ★ ★

*President Nixon flew 13 cases of Schramsberg, his favourite sparkling wine to Peking, to be served at a televised banquet with premier Chou-en-Lai.

★ ★ ★ ★ ★

*Château d'Yquem was drunk and enjoyed by both Jefferson and Washington. It was also highly valued at the Russian court; in 1850 the Grand Duke Constantine, brother of the Tsar, visited Yquem and bought a tonneau of the 1847 vintage for 20,000 gold francs.

★ ★ ★ ★ ★

*Toulouse-Lautrec's favourite drink was of his own invention, called 'Tremblement' – it was a mixture of the dregs from all the bottles left after an evening's drinking.

★ ★ ★ ★ ★

*Sir Winston Churchill's favourite champagne was Pol Roger – and he named his horse after it.

★ ★ ★ ★ ★

*André Simon's favourite champagne: Pommery.

★ ★ ★ ★ ★

*Ruskin liked Aleatico wine from Tuscany. He was also trained in his father's sherry distributing business.

★ ★ ★ ★ ★

*W.G. Grace, supposedly teetotal, drank champagne and sherry.

★ ★ ★ ★ ★

*Longfellow was a supporter of indigenous North American wines, singling out Catawba and Delaware wines in particular.

★ ★ ★ ★ ★

*Oscar Wilde drank 'Hock and Seltzer', a Victorian equivalent of the present-day 'Spritzer', a glass of which he was reputedly sipping when arrested.

★ ★ ★ ★ ★

*Bismarck favoured Pottelsdorfer Rötwein.

★ ★ ★ ★ ★

*Wellington and Pitt were both addicted to port.

★ ★ ★ ★ ★

*Rabelais liked wines of Anjou and Saumur, and is still revered by La Confrérie des Sacavins d'Anjou.

★ ★ ★ ★ ★

*Liszt liked the Hungarian wines of Szekzardi and Voros.

★ ★ ★ ★ ★

*George Washington's favourite drink was Madeira, at one time immensely popular in the USA.

★ ★ ★ ★ ★

*US President Taft's favourite drink was Champagne, preferably Veuve Clicquot or Moët and Chandon.

★ ★ ★ ★ ★

*Harry Waugh's favourite Bordeaux vintage: 1929, especially Châteaux Léoville-Poyferré and Rausan-Ségla.

★ ★ ★ ★ ★

*One of Louis XIII's favourite wines, recommended to him by Richelieu, was Château Pouget.

★ ★ ★ ★ ★

*Edward VII's favourite Champagne was Duminy extra sec, 1889.

★ ★ ★ ★ ★

*Queen Victoria liked to 'strengthen' her claret with whisky.

★ ★ ★ ★ ★

*George V preferred to drink whisky with dinner, rather than wine.

★ ★ ★ ★ ★

*Her Majesty, Queen Elizabeth II, prefers sweet Moselles, Sauternes and Champagne.

★ ★ ★ ★ ★

*Sir Robert Walpole, as Prime Minister, served Lafite and Margaux on diplomatic occasions.

★ ★ ★ ★ ★

*Queen Victoria drank white Somlo wines from Hungary, sharing the belief with the ancient Hapsburg nobility, who were by tradition required to drink a bottle on their wedding nights, that it possessed both restorative and aphrodisiac qualities.

PERU

PERU'S first vines were planted at Ica in 1566 by Francisco de Carabantes. Since then, very little, wine-wise, has been heard.

Vines are rumoured to be grown at:

Ica	Moqueqa
Lima	Chincha
Cuzco	Tacana
Arequipa	Lacumba

Rather ordinary whites, very tannic reds and sherry and Madeira-style fortified wines are reportedly produced. The Peruvians evade further judgment being passed on their wines by the outside world by cleverly drinking it all themselves.

POLAND

IN the 12th century Cracow was described as 'a great and beautiful city with many houses and inhabitants, markets, vineyards and gardens'. Remnants survive, including town names such as Winiary.

Wine was produced at the Polish court for the visit of the Emperor Otto III who was known to prefer it to beer. At the time Polish wine was both expensive and rare. Queen Bona tried to revive winemaking but was defeated by the cold climate and her subjects took to importing wine from Hungary, Italy, France, Spain and Crete.

In 1791 J.E. Biester wrote in his *Letters on Poland* that 'there are three excellent important products in Poland: bread, wine and coffee . . . Good strong coffee is called Polish coffee and bad coffee is called German. Similarly, old strong Hungarian wine is called Polish wine, and heavy sweet wine, German'. Today, although wine is still made in Poland, only the most tough-palated patriot would choose to drink it rather than a bottle imported from Hungary. As one Pole joked, 'our wine is one of the only products I'd never queue for'.

PORTUGAL

UNTIL quite recently, as far as the outside world was concerned, Portugal had three wines: port, Madeira and rosé. The world taste for white wine opened the door for a fourth, Vinho Verde, which has achieved its own remarkable success, but the style the Portuguese enjoy drinking themselves found few fans overseas – apart from in those countries which were once colonies.

Most of Portugal's wine is red, ranging from acid young red Vinho Verde (which, to many non-Portuguese, tastes as much of a contradiction in terms as it sounds) to the thick, hard, tannic wines of Dão and the Douro. The non-Vinho Verde whites, Dão in particular, have been similarly slow to find an export market. Their deep mellow-yellow style is out of step with a world whose tastebuds are marching to the beat of the crisp Sauvignon grape.

Most of these old-fashioned wines can be highly palatable when drunk with traditional Portuguese dishes; unfortunately, few people outside that country enjoy a regular diet of salt cod and suckling pig. Portugal is changing fast however. As rosé sales slump worldwide, and port remains something of a minority taste, the Portuguese are revolutionizing the way in which they make some of those 'traditional' wines. Suddenly, there are cool-fermented, lemony-almondy white Dãos to be had; red Dãos are beginning to have more fruit and, most important of all, previously unfamilar wines are arriving on the export market. Look out for red Bairrada, which, when well made, can be a deliciously characterful wine that can shame many a complacent Italian producer.

Wine Words

Adega – Winery.

Clarete – light red wine.

Colheita – vintage.

Engarrafado – bottled (by).

Garrafeira – a wine selected by a merchant as being amongst his best, and which has benefitted from ageing.

Quinta – estate.

Região Demarcada – demarcated region. Sort of Portuguese Appellation Controlée.

Reserva – a merchant's or grower's first-quality wine.

Velho/Velhas – old.

Vinho Branco – white wine.

Vinho Consumo – basic table wine.

Vinho Doce – sweet wine.

Vinho Espumante – sparkling wine.

Vinho Generoso – strong, usually dessert wine.

Vinho Maduro – mature table wine. Maturity, in this case, means anything with any age at all. Young wine is Vinho Verde.

Vinho Rosado – rosé.

Vinho Seco – dry wine.

Vinho Tinto – red wine.

Vinho Verde – literally 'green wine', but describing red and white wine made from a demarcated region of north-western Portugal, and drunk within a year of the harvest.

The Grape List

Reds
Água Santa (Bairrada)
Alvarelhão (Dão, Port, Trás-os-Montes, Mateus Rosé)
Azal (red Vinho Verde)
Baga de Louro (Dão)
Bastardo (Dão, Port, Trás-os-Montes, Mateus Rosé)
Borracal (Bairrada)
Cabernet Sauvignon (only at Quinta da Bacalhoa)
Castelão (Bairrada)
Donzelinho Tinto (Port)
Jaen (Dão)
João de Santarém (Bairrada)
Moreto (Trás-os-Montes)
Mourisco Semente (Port, some other northern Portuguese wines)
Periquita (Periquita)
Preto Martinho (Ribatejo)
Ramisco (Colares)
Souzão (Port)
Tinta Amarela (Port, Trás-os-Montes)
Tinta Barroca (Port)
Tinta Carvalha (Dão, Trás-os-Montes)
Tinta da Barca (red Vinho Verde)
Tinta Francisca (Port)
Tinta Pinheira (Dão, Bairrada,

Mateus Rosé)
Tinta Roriz (Port)
Tinto-Cão (Port)
Trincadeira (Ribatejo)
Tourigo (Tràs-os-Montes)
Touriga Francesa (Port, Mateus Rosé)
Touriga Nacional (Dão, Port)
Vinhão (red Vinho Verde)

Whites
Alvarinho (Vindo Verde)
Arinto (Bucelas, Carcavelos, white Dão, Bairrada, Moscatel de Setúbal, Mateus White)
Barcelo (white Dão)
Bical (white Bairrada)
Bual/Boal (Madeira, Tràs-os-Montes)
Cerceal (white Dão, Mateus White)
Codega (Douro, Tràs-os-Montes)
Dona Branca (white Dão)
Donzelinho (Douro)
Esgana-Cao (Bucelas, Douro,

Mateus White)
Fernão Pires (white Dão, Ribatejo)
Folgazão (Douro)
Galego Dourado (Carcavelos)
Gouveio (white Port, Tràs-os-Montes)
Loureiro (Vinho Verde)
Maria Gomes (white Bairrada)
Malvasia (Madeira, Malmsey, Moscatel de Setúbal, Mateus White)
Malvasia Fina (white Port)
Moscatel Branco
Moscatel Roxo (in fact pink) (Setúbal)
Muscat (used for dry João Pires)
Rabigato (Douro)
Sercial (Madeira)
Tamarez (Moscatel de Setúbal)
Tarrantez (Tràs-os-Montes, Ribatejo)
Trajadura (Vinho Verde)
Verdelho (Madeira, white Dão)
Viosinho (Douro)

The Wine Regions

DEMARCATED AREAS

Algarve
The southern coast of Portugal, demarcated for politico/touristic reasons rather than for the quality of the wine. Some rosé, strong red and dull whites.

Bairrada
On the western coast, south of Oporto, producing red and white wines on clay soil. Almost 'clarety' reds are likely to overtake Daô in the international market.

Carcavelos
Between Lisbon and Estoril, it has only one small vineyard, Quinta do Barão, producing excellent dessert and aperitif wine of 19% alcohol. Drink chilled.

Colares
Western tip of Portugal. Produces nutty, soft whites, and very tannic reds from pre-phylloxera vines grown on sandy soil. The reds require great patience.

Dão
Possibly the best-known red Portuguese wines outside Portugal. From mountainous vineyards in the north of the country, taking its name from the river which crosses it. All the wines, except that of one estate – the Conde de Santar – are blended and sold by merchants and cooperatives. Reds tend to be hard and fruitless when young, soft and fruitless when mature. Whites are often dull, nutty and earthy. More modern styles of winemaking are beginning to yield fruitier, more interesting wines.

Douro
Situated in north-east Portugal, extending to the Spanish frontier. Although less than half this region's wine is fortified and sold as port, this is the product for which it is best known. Dullish dry whites and variable reds.

Madeira
Island to the south-west of Portugal. Produces Madeira (Buoal, Malmsey, Sercial, Verdeilho) and table wines which are not exported

for reasons which anyone who has tasted them will readily understand.

Moscatel de Setúbal
South of Lisbon on the Setúbal peninsula. Produces honeyed dessert wine which seems to age indefinitely, but is usually sold in six and 25-year-old versions.

Vinho Verde
In the north-west corner of Portugal, and the country's largest single demarcated region. It is itself divided into six sub-regions, Monção, Lima, Amarente, Basto, Braga and Panafiel. Far more red is produced than white, but this slightly fizzy, acidic wine has found few fans overseas. The white however is a major success story. Vines are grown 'in the air', trained between trees, concrete and wooden supports, to permit other crops to be grown at ground level. The very best wine is produced exclusively from the Alvarinho grape.

NON-DEMARCATED AREAS

Alentejo
Stretching from south of Lisbon to the Algarve, this region was, until recently, used for growing cereal and sunflowers. Wine growing is now proving successful.

Beiras
Upper and Lower Beira, in the east of Portugal, produce both red and white wines of which only those of Pinhel and the Moimenta de Beira, an acidic base for sparkling wines, are worthy of note.

Estremadura(also called the Oeste)
North-west of Lisbon, this is Portugal's most prolific region, and produces red and white wine.

Lafões
Small region, between Dão and Vinho Verde, producing only around 10,000 cases of wine per year, of which 90 per cent is light, acidic and red.

Pinhel
Another small area in the north, close to Spain, and making heavy, dry white wines.

Ribatejo
Unusually, for a wine region, situated in the rich alluvial soil of the Tagus Valley, this is the source of many of Portugal's best Garrafeira wines.

Setúbal
Apart from the Moscatel, this region, close to Lisbon, also produces good non-demarcated wines, most notably Periquita.

Tràs-os-Montes
In the north-eastern corner of the country, this is the birthplace of Portuguese rosé, which though now produced throughout Portugal, is still associated with this region.

The Best Producers

A.G.R.E.L.A.
Dom Ferraz and Verdegar Vinho Verde.

Adega Regional de Colares (Colares)
The exclusive producer of Colares, selling much of its wine to other merchants.

Arealva Limitada (Lisbon)
Tagus and Arealva rosé.

Barrocão
Produce Diamante Verde Vinho Verde, Quinta de Povoia rosé, fine old

Bairrada and good Dão, as well as huge quantities of sparkling Méthode Champenoise.

Borges & Irmão
A port house which also produces Trovador Rosé, Gatao and Gamba Vinho Verde, and Meia Encosta Dão.

Campo Velho
Campo Velho white.

Cantanhede
Vinho Verde, good quality Dão, and excellent Bairrada.

Carvalho, Ribeiro & Ferreira (Lisbon)
Produces excellent Garrafeira wines of unknown geographic origin, Ravel Vinho Verde, Serradayres red and white from Ribantejo, and sells the Conde de Santar Dão.

Caves Aliança (Sangalhos)
Best known for Méthode Champenoise sparklers of little distinction, this firm also produces Vinho Verde (Casal Mendes), Dão and good Bairrada (Alianca Tinto Velho).

Caves de Casalinho (Oporto)
Family-owned, this firm produces good Vinho Verde under its own name, as well as a good commercial rosé. Other names include Montemar, Cidades and Três Marias. The Alexandre Magno Dão is disappointing.

Caves de Raposeira (Lamego)
Belong to Canadian whisky giant, Seagrams, and produce Méthode Champenoise sparkling wines.

Caves Velhas (Lisbon)
Producers of a passable Dão, Romeira from the Ribatejo and exclusively, Bucelas.

Conde de Santar
The only single-estate Dão, sold by Carvalho, Ribeiro & Ferreira.

Dom Teodósio (Lisbon)
Cardeal Dão, Casalheiro, Teobar and Topazio dry white wines.

Ferreira
Port house, producing Barca Velha a good red from Trás-os-Montes.

Raúl Ferreira & Filho Lda (Carcavelos)
Exclusive producer of Carcavelos, making less than 40,000 bottles per year.

Abel Pereira da Fonseca (Lisbon)
Make 'Viriatus' Dão.

J.M. da Fonseca
One of the two most important wine companies in Portugal, producing Lancers rosé and white wines for the US market, (almost exclusively),

Moscatel de Setúbal, Dão Terras Altas, Faisca rosé and a range of excellent non-demarcated wines. Best-known of these, are Periquita, Tinto da Anfora, Pasmados and the pure Cabernet Quinta da Bacalhoa and Camarate, a Cabernet, Periquita and Merlot blend. A new white dry Muscat, called João Pires, after the winery at which it is made also shows great promise.

Gonçalves, Monteiro & Filhos (Vila Nova de Gaia)
Make Catedral Dão, Cavaleiros rosé, and Magrico Vinho Verde.

A. Henriques
Pascal white wine.

Império
Reasonable Dão. Dom Dias rosé and Império Vinho Verde.

Montanha
Trofeu white wine.

Moura Basto
Moura Basto Vinho Verde.

Palace Hotel do Buçaco (Mealhada)
A genuinely palatial hotel which also produces red and white wine from its own vineyards near Luso, using the same grapes as the neighbouring producers of Bairrada. The winemaking is as charmingly traditional (or old-fashioned) as the hotel, and vintages go back to the 1920s.

Palácio de Brejoiera (Monção)
Fine Alvarinho white.

Primavera
Primavera white and (very good) red Bairrada.

Quinta da Aveleda (Oporto)
Once linked to Mateus via the common ownership of the Guedes family, now wholly separate, this winery produces a commercial (Aveleda) and an excellent traditional (Quinta da Aveleda) Vinho Verde.

Quinta de Bacalhoa
Excellent American-owned Cabernet-planted estate. Wines are made by a young Australian, Peter Bright, and sold by J.M. da Fonseca.

Quinta da S. Claudio
Small estate producing excellent Vinho Verde.

Real Vinícola (Vila Nova da Gaia)
A well-known port house which also produces Lagosta rosé and Vinho Verde, Cabido Dãos, Colares and a red (Evel) and sweet white (Grandjo) from nearby Douro vineyards.

Restolo
Producers of 'own-brand' red and white wines.

Ribeiro & Irmão
Ribeiros Vinho Verde.

S. João
Bairrada producers, making good Porta dos Cavalheiros red.

J. Serra
Producers of Dão. Belong to Arealva.

C. da Silva
A port house which also makes D. Crespo and Dom Silvano Vinho Verde, Isabel Rosé and Dalva Dão.

Sociedade Vinícola Sul de Portugal
Southern producer, belonging to Arealva.

Solar de S. Domingues
Maduro rosé.

SOGRAPE

First and foremost, family-owned makers of Mateus rosé (and less successfully, white). This company, Portugal's largest winemaker, now sells over 40,000,000 bottles of wine each year. Other wines include Casal Garcia and Gazela Vinho Verde, Grão Vasco Dãos, and a red Douro Garrafeira.

Tavares & Rodrigues

Excellent Colares and Colares Reservas.

Vinexport

Excellent Alvarinho Vinho Verde, almost equally good Cepas do Minho, and (less exciting) Cepalima, Vinho Verde.

Vinhos de Monção (Moncao)

Cepa Velha, One of the very finest pure Alvarinho as well as good quality Vinho Verde.

Vinhos Messias

Good Santola Vinho Verde

Vinícola do Vale do Dão

Produce Grao Vasco Dão. Belongs to SOGRAPE.

Vinícola Ribalonga

Vinho Verde and Dão under their own name.

MADEIRA

INEXPENSIVE Madeira is generally disappointing, made as it is from the Tinta Negra Mole, rather than the noble grapes whose names appear on its label. The arrival of Portugal in the EEC will have corrected this confusing lassitude over labelling, and prices of genuine Madeira will rise.

Madeira Wine Words

Estufa – The process of making Madeira involves heating the wine in concrete vats or 'ovens' (*estufas*).

Solera – Much Madeira is still sold with a Solera vintage rather than a year of harvest. The Solera year refers to the age of the oldest casks.

Bual – Rich sweet, nutty wine. Often drunk with cheese.

Malmsey – The Malvasia of Greece and Italy, here the sweetest of Madeiras. It has a drier finish than port.

Rainwater – Named – it is said – after a consignment of well-liked Madeira diluted by a sudden storm whilst standing on the quay, this is a fairly dry style best known in the USA.

Sercial – Driest of all Madeiras, and supposedly made from a

relation of the Riesling. Excellent as an aperitif.

Tinta Negra Mole – The grape – possibly a relation of the Pinot Noir – used to make the majority of Madeira, even much of that sold under the names of the other grapes whose character it seems to mimic when grown at the same altitude.

Verdeho – Tangy, and standing between the bone dry Sercial and warmly sweet Bual, this is the Madeira which used to be enjoyed with Madeira cake.

The Best Producers

Barbeito
Family shipper run by a world expert on Columbus. Some fine old wine and 'Island Dry'.

Blandy
Still belonging to the family of the British seaman who started the Madeira trade. The most famous blend is 'Duke of Clarence'. Part of the Madeira Wine Company.

Cossart Gordon
Founded in 1745, and part of the Madeira Wine Company.

Henriques & Henriques
'Ribeiro Seco'.

Leacock
'Penny Black Malmsey'. Part of the Madeira Wine Company.

Madeira Wine Company

Rutherford & Miles
'Old Trinity House' Bual. Part of the Madeira Wine Company.

Tarquinio Lomelino
Have a large stock of old Madeira. 'Dom Henriques'.

BEST MADEIRAS

★ ★ ★ ★ ★

Blandy's Ten-Year-Old Malmsey

★ ★ ★ ★ ★

Henriques & Henriques Verdelho

★ ★ ★ ★ ★

Leacock's Sercial

★ ★ ★ ★ ★

Rutherford & Miles 'Old Trinity House' Bual

★ ★ ★ ★ ★

Leacock's 1951 Verdelho Vintage

★ ★ ★ ★ ★

Rutherford & Miles 1950 Sercial

★ ★ ★ ★ ★

Cossart & Gordon's 1920 Bual

★ ★ ★ ★ ★

Port

Confusing descriptions and names surround port, serving as a reminder that this is a drink which gentlemen used to enjoy from a decanter without worrying overmuch about any more than the name of the shipper and the vintage. Butlers and wine merchants could be left to ponder over the niceties of 'Fine Old Ruby' and plain 'Ruby' port. Nowadays, in a more democratic drinking age, 'ordinary' people have muscled in on the act and are just as likely to be seen buying port of every kind as the gentlemen of yesteryear.

Port Words

Wood Ports All shippers produce a range, including all or most of the following styles of port, which has been aged in wood:

Vintage As in Champagne, vintages are only declared in exceptionally fine years, and then only after the wine has been allowed 18 months or so to show its promise. It is bottled during the year following the decision, and will then require around 20 years or so before it is ready to drink. During that time its tannic flavour will soften and a deposit will be 'thrown' in the bottle, hence the need to decant. Unfortunately the idea of 'exceptionally fine' has been getting more frequent as the demand has increased in recent years.

Single Quinta Quinta is Portuguese for 'estate' and particular estate names are used on the labels of vintage ports from years not otherwise declared by the shippers, e.g. Graham's Malvedos 1968 and Taylor's Quinta de Vargellas 1974.

Vintage Character Blends of more than one vintage which are supposed to taste 'like vintage port'.

Late-Bottled Vintage (LBV) Can be one of two things: either an 'old style' LBV which is bottled four years after a specified vintage, or a 'new style' LBV, bottled as much as six years after the harvest. All LBVs are drinkable younger than vintage ports of the same age, having softened in barrel. New style LBV however is often little better than a good Ruby.

Crusted (or Crusting) Hard to find these days, but a good inexpensive alternative to vintage port, crusted ports are blends of different years bottled young and throwing the same kind of deposit as would a vintage.

Ruby Quite young port, bottled after a minimum of three years in oak.

Tawny Ruby that has been allowed to mature in the barrel, losing its rich red colour and gradually mellowing to an autumnal hue, as well as concentrating its flavour. Or at least, that's the theory. In practice, most inexpensive, commercial Tawny is simply a blend of ruby and white port.

Fine Old Tawny 10, 20, 30 and even 40 year-old-Tawny. This is the real thing, matured in barrel. But beware of those ages – the figure given is an *average* not, as in whisky, that of the youngest component. There is no such thing as 'Vintage Tawny' bearing a harvest year, but a Tawny label can include a year, following the word 'Reserve'.

White Port Made from white grapes, a dry or medium dry aperitif very popular in Portugal.

Port Vintage List

Vintages are only declared in years when the shippers consider the quality to be sufficiently high. So there are no 'bad' years, only a hierarchy of 'good' ones and vintages which soften up more quickly than others.

1982 and 83 have both been declared. It is too early to judge their potential.

1980
Should be ready for drinking between 1990-97.

1977
Really great. The one to drink on New Year's Eve 1999. And a few years later too.

1975
A light wine and a rapid ripener, and the least impressive vintage since 1960. Will probably all have been drunk by 1990.

1970
Not overpraised, this is very fine port, for drinking between 1985-1995.

1966
Port can be difficult to judge when it is young. This is a vintage which seemed to be on the light side, like 1975, and has gained in stature with age. Probably readier after 20 years than 1963.

1963
Another Great Year. And one which could see in the year 2,000.

1960
Neither in the first division, nor amongst the duffers, this is a port to drink whilst waiting for the 1963s and 1966s.

1955
A great vintage which proves how this remarkable wine can go on improving for 40 years.

Feurheerd
The Douro Wine Shippers
Vieira de Sousa

Grand Metropolitan, UK
Croft
Delaforce
Morgan

La Martiniquaise (France)
Gran Cruz
Productores Associados
  de Vinhos Progresso do Douro
Taylor

Independent Portuguese
Guimaraens (Fonseca)
Rozes
Vinicola
A.A. Ferreira
Constantino

St Raphäel (France) and Martini & Rossi (Italy)
Offley
Rodrigues Pinto Diez
Hermanos

SMALL

Independent French
Vasconcellos
Butler & Nephew
Pocas

Rumasa now Spanish Government (Spain)
C de Silva
Dalva
Presidential
Player's

Independent Portuguese
Messias
Albento Custro Lanca
Poças
Borges
Wiese & Krohn
Adriano Ramos Pinto
J Carvalho Macedo
Quinta do Noval
Osborne
Andresen

A.P. Santos
Pinto Pereira
Mackenzie
Alto Corgo

TINY

Independent Portuguese/Dutch
Niepoort

Independent Portuguese
Burmester
Gilberts

Vintage Port

The following shippers' vintage ports have the greatest prestige attached to them. This is reflected in their prices.

Taylor
Graham
Warre
Dow (=Silva & Cosens)
Fonseca
Croft
Cockburn

The following shippers are serious about producing vintage port but have never attained the prestige of the 'big seven'.

Sandeman
Noval
Ferreira
Delaforce

The Port Owners

There are 55 companies shipping port from Vila Nova da Gaia. All of these fall into 22 groups, as listed below.

LARGE

Independent Portuguese
Compania Velha
Real Vinícola

Independent British
Warre

Silva & Cosens (Dow)
W & J Graham
Smith Woodhouse
Quarles Harris

Allied Breweries UK
Cockburn
Martinez – Harveys of Bristol

MEDIUM

Independent Portuguese
Barros
Feist
Hutchinson
Kopke

Brown Bastard
This tastefully-named table wine was off the market for 250 years until Mr Patrick Simon, a wine merchant and Master of Wine, intrigued by the many references in Shakespeare to pints of Bastard, brown and white, decided to track it down. His researches took him from the cellars of Oriel College, Oxford, where cases of the stuff were known to have lurked in 1499, via a passing reference in Lorna Doone, to Portugal, where Barros Almeida, the Port shippers, were using it for blending purposes. Amidst much media attention, Mr Simon relaunched Brown Bastard on an unsuspecting UK. Commercially it was a complete failure, due, he surmises, to people being too embarrassed to ask for it by name.

Smith-Woodhouse
Quarles Harris
Gould Campbell
Offley
Martinez
Calem

They have recently been joined by

Churchill Graham

Most other shippers do produce a minute quantity of vintage port, but it is insignificant.

ROMANIA

The Grapes List

Until recently, most of Romania's wine was produced from traditional Eastern European varieties, but as in neighbouring countries, much progress is now being made with such western varietals as Chardonnay and Cabernet Sauvignon, particularly at the State research centres of Murfatlar and Valea Calugareasca (The Valley of the Monks).

Red
Cabernet Franc
  (Experimental plantations)
Cabernet Sauvignon
Pinot Noir
Merlot
Cadarka (de Banat.
Negru Virtos
Babeasca Neagra
Frincusa
Tamiiosa Romaesca
Feteasca Neagra

White
Riesling
Walsch Riesling
Sauvignon
Feteasca Alba
Feteascǎ Regala
Rulander
Aligoté
Chardonnay
Traminer
Muscat
Muscat Ottonel
Sylvaner
Grasa (or Furmint)
Neuberger
Majorca

The Wine Regions

The state produces 25 per cent of Romania's wine, most of the remainder being made by cooperatives, widely spread around the country. The few small-holdings which exist, make wine for local, domestic consumption.

MOLDAVIA
Cotnari
The town is famous for its sweet and Tokay-like wine. It also produces Perle de la Moldavie, a wine which was highly popular in the Paris of the late 19th century.

Focsani
Eastern wine region. Principal towns/wines.

Cotseti
Red (Pinot Noir, Cabernet Sauvignon, Merlot).

Recommended Romania Vineyards

Red
Nicoresti (Moldavia)
Halinga (Oltinia)
Corcova
Segarcea
Minis (Banat)

Ploesti
Rosé
Sadova

White (Including dessert wines)
Alba Iulia
Pietroasa
Ploesti
Iassy
Odobesti (Moldavia)

Pancio
Husi
Prut (Dealul Mare)
Tirnav
Simleul Silvaniei

The de Rothschild Label List

The arguably first person to associate great wine and great art was Baron Philippe de Rothschild, whose decision to ask prominent international artists to produce paintings for the labels of his Château Mouton Rothschild, gave at least some sections of the Bordeaux establishment apoplexy. To some of the more conservative châtelains, the association of Andy Warhol and fine claret (1975) was little short of blasphemy. Following the 1924 label there was a gap until the series really began in 1945; the labels for 1953 and 1977 respectively celebrated Mouton's centenary and offered a tribute to H.M. Queen Elizabeth the Queen Mother.

1924 **Jean Carlu**
1945 **Philippe Julian**
1946 **Jean Hugo**
1947 **Jean Cocteau**
1948 **Marie Laurencin**
1949 **Dignimont**
1950 **Arnulf**
1951 **Marcel Vertes**
1952 **Leonor Fini**
1954 **Jean Carzou**
1955 **Georges Braque**
1956 **Pavel Tchelitchew**
1957 **André Masson**
1958 **Salvador Dali**
1959 **Richard Lippold**
1960 **Jacques Villon**
1961 **George Mathieu**
1962 **Matta**
1963 **Bernard Dufour**
1964 **Henry Moore**
1965 **Dorothea Tanning**
1966 **Pierre Alechinsky**
1967 **César**
1968 **Bona**
1969 **Jean Miró**
1970 **Marc Chagall**
1971 **Wassily Kandinsky**
1972 **Serge Poliakoff**
1973 **Pablo Picasso**
1974 **Robert Motherwell**
1975 **Andy Warhol**
1976 **Pierre Soulages**
1978 **Jean-Paul Riopelle**
1979 **Hisao Domoto**
1980 **Hans Hartung**
1981 **Arman**
1982 **John Huston**

Silly Wine Names List

Le Pis (Beaujolais)
Les Blotters (Anjou, France)
Adom Atic (Israel)
Babeasca (Romania)
Backenacker (Rheingau, Germany)
Brown Bastard (Portugal)
Boos (Nahe, Germany)
Bunken (Rheingau, Germany)
Buzbag (Turkey)
La Clape (France)
Château le Crock (Bordeaux, France)
Far Niente (California)
Ficklin (California)
Château Grand Canyon (Bordeaux, France)
Gratallops (Tarragona, Spain)
Grgich Hills (California)
Grk (Yugoslavia)
Gyongyos (Hungary)
Hello Holz (Palatinate, Germany)
Knusden Erath (Oregon, USA)
Krk (Yugoslavia)
Luke Lunievich's Golden Vineyard Wines (New Zealand)
Lump (Franconia, Germany)
Mascara (Algeria)
Mia Mia (Victoria, Australia)
Les Migraines (Burgundy)
Dr Peste (Burgundy)
Philosophe (Switzerland)
Posip (Yugoslavia)
Ptuj (Yugoslavia)
Rittergut-Bangert (Palatinate, Germany)
Rouge Homme (Australia)
St Etheldreda (England)
Sipon (Yugoslavia)
Sokol Blosser (Oregon, USA)
Squinzano (Apulia, Italy)
1066 (England)
Thunderbird (USA)
Tiger Milk (Yugoslavia)
Vieux Télégraphe (France)
Vigne-du-Diable (Switzerland)
Wirra Wirra (Australia)

SOUTH AFRICA

IF a multi-national winemaking company were looking at a map of the world and wondering where to plant a few thousand acres of vines, South Africa ought to be up there amongst the handful of ideal countries. Climate, soil and technical know-how are all readily available. Unfortunately, the moment political considerations were taken into account, Australia might suddenly become a far more attractive prospect. The problem is that high-quality South African wines are not easy to sell outside the country. So importers restrict themselves to the budget-end of the scale, consumers are rarely dazzled and the vicious circle continues . . .

In South Africa some truly first-class Cabernets and Shiraz are being made; closer contact with winemakers and wine buyers from other countries – as is enjoyed by the Australians – would certainly lead to even finer quality. Sadly, politics and wine are inevitably enmeshed and the day when the wine drinkers of London and Los Angeles are as ready to enjoy bottles of wine from the Cape as ones from Bulgaria has not yet dawned.

In the meantime, if you are interested to know what South Africa's wines taste like, avoid many of the less expensive branded wines – they can taste heavy and curiously rubbery – and go for the estate wines we have recommended here. They may cost more, but are worth the difference.

The Vineyards

	hectares
Stellenbosch	18,574
Paarl	19,431
Worcester	13,868
Robertson	8,968
Malmesbury	15,534
Ceres & Tulbagh	13,660
Montagu	4,578
Olifants River	7,689

The Grape List

Alicante Bouschet (found in most areas)

Bukettrraube (Paarl, Tulbagh and Stellenbosch)

Cabernet Franc (found in most areas)

Cabernet Sauvignon (mainly in Stellenbosch and Paarl)

Carignan (mainly in Stellenbosch and Paarl)

Chardonnay (mainly experimental)

Chenel (cross between Steen and Trebbiano)

Chenin Blanc ('Steen' the most common variety)

Cinsault ('Hermitage' the most common red)

Clairette blanche (blending wine, grown in all areas)

Colombard (most popular in hotter areas)

Fernao Pires (experimental only)

Furmint (experimental only)

Gamay Noir (an experiment in Stellenbosch)

Gewürztraminer (scattered plantings in cooler areas)

Grenache Noir (small quantities in most areas)

Harslevelu (experimental only)

Heroldrebe (experimental only)

Canaan (early variety, used for distillation)

Kerner (mainly in Stellenbosch and Paarl)

Malbec (mostly in Olifants river area)

Merlot noir (mainly in Paarl)

Morio Muscat (experimental only)

Muscat d'Alexandrie (multi-purpose variety – Hanepoot)

Muscat Ottonel (experimental only)

Muskadel White (mostly in Robertson and Montagu)

Palomino (found everywhere, mainly for distillation)

False Pedro (sherry production, mainly in Paarl)

Pinot Noir (mainly in Stellenbosch)

Pinotage (crossing of Pinot noir and Cinsault)

Pontac (an original grape variety in S.A.)

Raisin Blanc (wine production in newer areas)

Riesling (mainly in Paarl and Stellenbosch)

Sauvignon Blanc (mainly in Paarl and Stellenbosch)

Sémillon-Greengrape (a traditional Cape grape variety)

Shiraz (mainly in Stellenbosch and Paarl)

Souzao (used for blending and fortified wine)

Sultanina (Thompson's Seedless, mainly distillation)

Tinta Barocca (new variety, red or fortified wine)

Trebbiano (mostly in Robertson)

Weisser Riesling (Rhine Riesling – various areas)

Weldra (experimental crossing as Chenel)

Zinfandel (mainly in Stellenbosch)

Muskadel red (component of Constantia)

The Wine Regions

CONSTANTIA AND DURBANVILLE
The cradle of the South African wine industry, this area is now chiefly famous for the *Groot Constantia* estate which is owned by the government and produces a range of high-quality red and some white wines. The main varieties are Cabernet Sauvignon, Shiraz, Pinotage, Chenin Blanc, Kerner and Riesling.

STELLENBOSCH
This area is the heart of the S. African wine trade, where most of the largest wine companies are to be found. The climate is the most moderate in the country, and the soil ranges from granitic close to the mountains to broken-down sandstone by the coast. The greatest number of estates are situated around the town of Stellenbosch.

The Stellenbosch Farmers' Wineries
The largest company in S. Africa, it presses more than 12,000 tonnes a year and also purchases a great deal of wine, more than one million hectolitres. The main brands sold are as follows:—
'Zonnebloem' – Cabernet Sauvignon, Pinotage, Riesling.
'Oude Libertas' – Pinotage and Dry Steen.
'Château Libertas' – A famous wine with a history stretching back at least fifty years, it is usually a blend of Cabernet Sauvignon, Shiraz and Cinsault.

The Oude Meester Group
The group includes the Distillers' Corporation, Castle Wine, E.K. Green and the Bergkelder and Drostdy Cellars. It has been one of the innovators in marketing estate wines, and is the biggest producer of brandy in S. Africa. The main brands are:
'Fleur du Cap' – Riesling, Pinotage, Cabernet Sauvignon, and Shiraz.
'Gruneberg Stein'

Gilbey's Distillers and Vintners Ltd
This, the third largest company in the province, has built a particular reputation for medium and high-quality wines. The main estates owned are Bertrams and Devonvale.

Delheim Estate
One of the earliest estates to carry out their own bottling, Delheim is situated on the slopes of the Simonsberg and is particularly known for its white wines.

Muratie Estate
Well-known for its red wines, this estate is the oldest in the region, and is situated very close to Delheim.

Blaauwklippen Estate
This property is on the lower-lying ground near Stellenbosch, and is rapidly gaining a reputation for itself.

Other Estates

Vergenoegd Estate	Overgaauw Estate
Kanonkop Estate	Alto Estate
Simonsig Estate	Spier Estate
Uitkyk Estate	Middelvei Estate
Rustenburg and Schoongezicht	Neetlingshof Estate

Koopmanskloof Estate	Bonfoi Estate
Meerlust Estate	Goede Hoop Estate
Uiterwyk Estate	Hazendal Estate
Verdun Estate	Jacobsdal Estate
Mooiplaas Estate	Montagne Estate
Vredenheim Estate	Oude Weltevreden Estate
Audacia Estate	

Co-operatives
Bottelary Cooperative Winery Ltd
Eersterivier-Valleise Cooperative Wine Cellar Ltd
De Heiderberg Cooperative Winery Ltd
Koelenhof Cooperative Co. Ltd
Vlottenburg Wine Cellar Cooperative Ltd
Welmoed Cooperative Wine Cellars Ltd

PAARL
Situated around the town of Paarl, this region is essentially the valley of the river Berg. The soil varies from weathered granite near the mountains to light sandy soils in the valleys, with the odd pocket of slate. The climate is much warmer than Stellenbosch but with a higher rainfall as well. The town of Paarl is the headquarters of the K.W.V. (Kooperative Wijnbouwers' Vereniging).

Nederburg
Part of the Stellenbosch Farmers' Wineries Group, this estate is one of the most famous in export markets, and produces a range of excellent quality varietal wines with a particular reputation for its whites. Their most famous wine is perhaps the Edelkeur which is made from Chenin Blanc grapes infected by the noble rot (Botrytis Cinerea).

K.W.V.
In Paarl can be found the centre of production for the K.W.V. sherry-style wines, which include a top quality range marketed under the Cape Cavendish label.

Monis
This cellar produces and matures the fortified wines sold by the Stellenbosch Farmers' Wineries Group.

Backsberg Estate
One of the earliest estates to market its own wines, it is well-known in South Africa for the quality of its Chenin Blanc, Cabernet Sauvignon and Pinotage.

Other Estates

Fairview Estate	Landskroon Estate
De Zoete Inval Estate	Boschendal Estate

Co-operatives
Bergrivierse Wine Cooperative Ltd
Bolandse Cooperative Wine Cellar Ltd
The Bovlei Cooperative Wine Cellar Ltd
Drakenstein Cooperative Wine Cellar Ltd
Franschhoekse Wine Cellars Cooperative Co. Ltd
Perdebergwynboere Cooperative Co. Ltd
Perelse Wine Cellars Cooperative Agricultural Co. Ltd
Simonsvlei Cooperative Wine Cellar Ltd
Wamakersvlei Cooperative Winery Ltd
The Wellington Wine Farmers' Cooperative Co. Ltd
Windmeul Cooperative Ltd

WORCESTER
Situated to the east of Paarl, and lying in the rain-shadow of the Du Toitskloo mountains, this region produces not only table wines but a great deal of fortified and dessert wines. The soil is very fertile, and the climate hot with irrigation necessary in the drier areas. There are very few estate bottlings in the area, most wines being produced in cooperatives.

ROBERTSON
Going further east one comes to the region of Robertson, which is becoming increasingly well-known for the quality of its table-wine production. The vineyards are situated close to water and are frequently irrigated since the climate is extreme, being hot in summer and with the danger of frost in winter. The soils vary from a rich alluvium to weathered shale known locally as Karoo type. The area is also known for its dessert wines and for the production of wine used for brandy distillation. There are nine cooperatives in the region as well as the following estates:

Dewetshof	Excelsior
Goedverwacht	Rietvallei
Weltevrede	Zandvleit

KLEIN KAROO
The Klein Karoo lies about 100 miles east of Cape Town and is situated between two ranges of mountains stretching east-west. The vineyards are mainly to be found around the town of Montagu in the west, where the soil is rich alluvial and the climate so hot and dry that the vineyards require irrigation. The area is best known for its dessert wines made with the Muscadel grape, though it also produces fairly ordinary table wines and wines for distillation.

SWELLENDAM
Lying south-east of Robertson, this region is very similar in all respects.

TULBAGH
Situated north-west of Worcester, the region has two distinct areas, the one being contiguous to Worcester and producing wines that are very similar in character, and the other based around the town of Tulbagh. This latter area has an excellent reputation for the quality of its white wines, many of which are grown high up on the slopes of the surrounding mountains. The three estates in the area are all very well-known throughout South Africa, and they are:

Montpellier
Twee Jonge Gezellen
Theuniskraal

MALMESBURY, PIQUETBERG, the OLIFANT, ORANGE
All better known for the production of the cheaper table wines, dessert and fortified wines, wines for distillation and raisins.

Best Wine List

BLENDED REDS	**Kanonkop Cabernet**
Meerlust Rubicon	**Sauvignon**
★ ★ ★ ★ ★	★ ★ ★ ★ ★
Nederburg Private Bin R103	**Meerlust Cabernet Sauvignon**
★ ★ ★ ★ ★	★ ★ ★ ★ ★
Rustenberg Dry Red	**Overgaauw Cabernet Sauvignon**
★ ★ ★ ★ ★	★ ★ ★ ★ ★
CABERNET SAUVIGNON	**Vergenoegd Cabernet Sauvignon**
Backsberg Cabernet Sauvignon	
★ ★ ★ ★ ★	★ ★ ★ ★ ★
Blaauwklippen Cabernet Sauvignon	**SHIRAZ**
	Uitkyk Shiraz
★ ★ ★ ★ ★	★ ★ ★ ★ ★

BLENDED WHITES
Nederburg Private Bins S312
and S333

★ ★ ★ ★ ★

LATE HARVEST
Blaauwklippen Noble Late
Vintage

★ ★ ★ ★ ★

Delheim Edelspatz Late
Harvest

★ ★ ★ ★ ★

Nederburg Edelkeur

★ ★ ★ ★ ★

Nederburg Steen Late
Harvest

★ ★ ★ ★ ★

Spier Colombard Special
Late Harvest

★ ★ ★ ★ ★

FORTIFIED MUSCAT
Rietvallei Red Muscadel

★ ★ ★ ★ ★

> The KWV cellars at Paarl, S.
> Africa, are the largest in the
> world, covering 25 acres (10
> ha) and with a capacity to
> hold 30 million gallons of
> wine (136 hl).

SPAIN

EUROPE'S great success story. It is true that there may have been a few non-Spanish Rioja afficionados 20 or 30 years ago, but they were probably as thinly scattered as non-Spanish bullfight fans today. For other wine drinkers, Spain simply meant cheap, thick, dull red wine and cheap, oxidized, yellow-coloured white wine. The quiet revolution which has transformed Spanish wines can be likened to the way in which Spain itself has adapted to democracy. Just as the new hotels and office blocks which line some of the busiest streets in Madrid and Barcelona are indistinguishable from their counterparts in a dozen other major cities around the world, Spain is now making white wines which could be thought to come from the most modern wineries of France, Italy or California.

The word 'modern' is key. As recently as the mid 1960s, the very idea of temperature control for a fermentation vat was as foreign to most producers as space travel. When the first innovators began to modernize their wineries, all the equipment had to be imported from France and Germany, the instruction manuals translated into Spanish. Today, new equipment gleams throughout Spain. And that word 'throughout' is important too. Suddenly those wine drinkers who

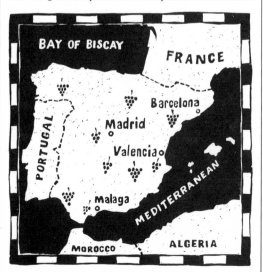

had only just learned to pronounce 'Rioja' have had to learn about areas of which they had never heard. And these are just the places to look for some of Spain's most interesting wines. The Chardonnay and Cabernet Sauvignon have arrived here too (inevitably) and with (equally inevitably) exciting results.

Tradition has not been jettisoned completely however. Those who want to find them will have no difficulty in discovering wines made the way they used to be made. Barrel-ageing – the factor which gave Spanish wine its recognizable vanilla flavour – is still the norm; the difference today is in the way in which those barrels are looked after.

For the first time, an adventurous wine drinker sentenced to a year of drinking exclusively Spanish wine could look forward to an enormous variety of flavours. Much the same would be said of Italy of course, but a diet of Italian wine would entail far more disappointment.

Wine Words

Abocado Medium sweet (table wine).

Aguardiente Brandy distilled from vegetable substances.

Almacenista Old unblended sherry.

Amontillado Literally, 'like Montilla'. Now applied to a type of sherry, made by ageing Fino sherry.

Amoroso A sweet Oloroso sherry.

Añada Sherry of one particular year.

Arroba A measure of liquid.

Arrope Must boiled down until thick, black and sweet: used for sweetening and colouring wine.

Blanco White.

Bodega A wine cellar.

Bodeguero The owner of a wine cellar.

Brut, Brut natur Extra dry (sparkling wine).

Cava A cellar for making sparkling wine, or the sparkling wine itself if made by the Champagne method.

Cepa A vine.

Clarete Light red table wine.

Con crianza Aged in oak. The phrase usually appears on the back label of a bottle.

Copita Small wine glass.

Cosecha Vintage.

Denominación de Origen Guarantee that the wine comes from a named demarcated wine area controlled by the Consejo Regulador.

Dulce Sweet.

Dulce color Dark and sweet Málaga.

Elaborado por Blended or matured by.

Embotellado por Bottled by.

Espumoso Sparkling.

Fino The lightest and most delicate of sherries.

Fino-Amontillado A fino that is maturing into an amontillado.

Flor Yeast that grows on sherry and sherry-type wines.

Generoso Aperitif or dessert wine.

Gran Reserva For the red wines of Rioja, a wine of seven years old (at least) which has had at least four years in cask or twice as long in bottle. For reds from other regions, a wine which has had at least two years in oak cask and three in bottle. Whites must have had four years' ageing, including at least six months in cask.

Gran Vas Cuve close method sparkling wine.

Lágrime The finest type of Málaga, made with juice pressed out of the grapes by their weight alone.

Manzanilla Sherry matured in the town of Sanlucar de Barrameda, which acquires a salty tang from the atmosphere.

Oloroso A full-bodied sherry.

Pajarete Dry or semi-dry Málaga.

Palo Cortado A rare sherry which has the character of both fino and oloroso.

Pasado, pasada Term for old and good fino and amontillado sherries.

Ranclo The taste of an old maderized white wine.

Raya A secondary-quality oloroso type sherry.

Reserva A red Rioja at least five years old, including two and a half years' ageing in cask; a white Rioja with at least six months in oak. From other regions, reds with three years' ageing including one year in cask, or whites with two years' ageing, including six months in cask.

Rosado Pink, rosé.

Sangría Mixture of red wine and fruit juice.

Seco Dry.

Semi-seco Medium dry.

Solera A system by which wines are aged in a series of butts, each containing older wine than the previous. The older wine is 'refreshed' with the younger.

Tinto red wine, darker than clarete.

Tinaja Large earthenware or concrete vat in which wine is kept and fermented.

Vendimia Vintage.

Vino Wine.

The Grape List

White
Airén (L'Airen): Almansa, Cañamero, Jumilla, Montilla-Moriles, La Mancha, Valdepeñas.
Albariño: Condado de Tea, El Rosal, Val de Salnes (Albariño).
Albillo: Cebreros, Cigales, Tierra de Madrid.
Alarije: Cañamero.
Cayetana: Tierra de Barros.
Bomita: Cañamero.
Chardonnay: Conca de Barberá, Penedès.
Dona Branca: Monterrey.
Forcallat: Almansa.
Garrido Fino: Huelva.
Garnacha Blanca: Alella, Ampurdan-Costa Brave, Cariñena, Navarra, Priorato, Terra Alta, Tarragona, Rioja.
Gewürztraminer: Penedès.
Gemariz: Ribeiro.
Jaén: Ribera del Duero, Tierra de Madrid.
Listán Blanca: Fuencaliente, La Geria, Icod.

Loureiro: El Rosal, Ribeiro.
Macabeo (Viura in Rioja): Ampurdan-Costa Brava, Cariñena, Conca de Barberá, Navarra, Somontano, Priorato, Penedès, Rioja, Ribeiro, Tarragona, Terra Alta.
Malvar: Tierra de Madrid.
Mantua: Huelva.
Marfil: Cañamero.
Merseguera: Jumilla, Valencia.
Moscato: Málaga.
Moscatel: Alicante, Jerez, Navarra, Montilla-Moriles, Valencia.
Muscat d'Alsace: Penedès.
Palomino (Xerez in Monterrey and Valdeorras): Cigales, El Bierzo, Huelva, Jerez, Monterrey, Rueda, Valdeorras.
Pansa Rosada: Alella.
Pansé: Conca de Barberá, Tarragona.
Parellada (or Montonec): Conca de Barberá, Penedès, Tarragona.
Pedro Luis: Huelva.
Pedro Ximenez: Canaries, Huelva, Jerez, Jumilla, Málaga, Montilla-Moriles, Prioarto, Terra Alta, Valencia.
Picapoll: Terra Alta.
Planta de Pedralba: Valencia.
Riesling: Penedès.
Sauvignon Blanc: Penedès.
Sémillon: Penedès, Felanitx.
Subirat-Parent: Penedès.
Treixadura: Condado de Tea, El Rosal, Ribeiro.
Torrentes: Ribeiro.
Verdejo: Cigales, Rueda.
Verdil: Alicante.
Vinate Blanc: Felanitx.
Xarel-lo (Pansa Blanca in Alella, and Caruxa in Tarragona): Alella, Ampurdan-Costa-Brava, Penedès, Tarragona.
Red
Alicante Negro: Monterrey, Condado de Tea, El Bierzo.
Beade: Ribeiro.
Bobal: Alicante, Campo de Borja, Cariñena.
Brancellao: Condado de Tea.
Cabernet Franc: Penedès.
Cabernet Sauvignon: Conca de Barberá, Penedès, Ribeira del Duera.
Caiño: Condado de Tea.
Callet: Binisalem, Felanitx.
Cariñena: Ampurdan-Costa Brava, Cariñena, Penedès, Priorato, Tarragona, Terra Alta.
Costeira: Ribeiro.
Espadeiro: Condado de Tea.
Fogoneu: Felanitx, Manacor.
Garnacha de Alicante: Valdeorras.
Garnacha Peluda: Alicante, Campo de Borja, Cariñena, Utiel-Requena.

Garnacha Tinta: Alella, Ampurdan-Costa Brava, Almansa, Alicante, Canamero, Campo de Borja, Cariñena, Cebreros, Cigales, Comarca de Toro, Jumilla, Monterrey, Méntrida, Penedès, Priorato, Ribeira del Duero, Rioja, Somontano, Tarragona, Tierra de Madrid, Utiel-Requena, Valdejalon, Valdepeñas, Valencia.
Graciano: Navarra, Rioja.
Juan Ibañez: Cariñena.
Listán Negra: Fuencaliente.
Malbec: Ribeira del Duero.
Mazuelo: Navarra, Somontano, Rioja.
Manto Negro: Binisalem.
Mencía: El Bierzo.
Merlot: Ribera del Duero, Penedès.
Monastrell: Alicante, Almansa, Jumilla, Penedès, Valencia, Yecla.
Monstelo: Monterrey.
Morisca: Cañamero.
Negramoll: Fuencaliente.
Palomino Negro: Cañamero.
Petit Syrah: Penedès.
Pinot Noir: Conca de Barberá, Penedès.
Regada: Ribeiro.
Samsó: Penedès.
Sonsón: Ribeiro.
Sumoll: Conca de Barberá, Penedès, Terra Alta.
Tempranillo (Ull de Llebre or Ojo de Liebre in Catalonia, Cencibel in Valdepeñas): Alella, Conca de Barberá, Jumilla, Méntrida, Navarra, Penedès, Rioja, Tarragona, Ribera del Duero, Tierra de Madrid, Valdepeñas, Utiel-Requena.
Trepat: Conca de Barberá, Tarragona.
Vijiriego: Fuencaliente.

The Wine Regions

ALICANTE
Light rosados, and very dark vino de doble pasta, made with a double ration of black grape skins to deepen the colour, plus some quite alcoholic reds.

Main producers
Bodega Alfonso
Bodega Divina Aurora
Bodega Cooperativa Ntra. Sra. de las Virtudes
HL Garcia Poveda SA
Bodegas Salvador Poveda Luz
Primitivo Quiles, SA

ALELLA *(Denominación de Origen)*
The suburbs of Barcelona have already engulfed part of this region, where the majority of the wine is made by the local cooperative. The whites are generally better than the reds.

Main producers
Alta Alella SA
Bodega Cooperativa Alella Vinícola (brand: Marfil)

ALMANSA *(Denominación de Origen)*
Most of the vines in this Castilian region are ungrafted – that is, unaffected by phylloxera. The wines they produce are generally red like those of the DO region to the north, Manchuela, and like much of the produce from this part of Spain, make up in alcohol what they lack in acidity.

Main producers
Hijos de Miguel Carrión
Bodegas Piqueras – Mario Boneta García

AMPURDAN-COSTA BRAVA *(Denominación de Origen)*
This area is not a million miles from the beaches of the same name, and makes rosado, whites, and some *primeur*-style red called Vi Novello.

Main producers
Cavas del Ampurdan SA (still wines and some sparkling, the latter the subject of the 'Spanish Champagne' case brought in 1960 by the Champagne companies in the UK)
Cellers Santamaría

BINISALEM
One of the Majorcan wine producing areas (now smaller than in the past). It is non-demarcated, like the rest of the island's vineyards, and produces fairly hefty reds.

Main producer
Bodegas José L Ferrer

EL BIERZO
This area is certainly a candidate for a *Denominación de Origen*, although perhaps its small size might count against it. The claretes, whites and rosés are of good quality.

Main producers
Bodegas Los Arcos
Bodegas Palacio de Arganza
Bodegas Valdeobispo

CAMPO DE BORJA *(Denominación de Origen)*
This small region is a recent promotion to DO status and makes a tough, alcoholic red that is happiest blended with the lighter growths of other areas.

Main producer
Bodegas La Magallonera

CAÑAMERO
Flor-growing whites come from this small town just south of Guadalupe.

Main producer
Félipe Ruiz Parralejo

CARIÑENA *(Denominación de Origen)*
This is the most important wine-growing area in Aragon, producing highly alcoholic rustic red wines that smooth out with a couple of years' cask ageing. There is also white wine made in the area, and a fortified dessert wine.

Main producers
Bodega Cooperativa San José de Aguaron
Bodega Cooperativa San Valero
Bodegas Joaquin Soria
Suso y Perez Viceate SA
Bodegas Enrique Lopez Pelay

CEBREROS
A region of heavy reds that are popular in nearby Madrid.

Main producer
Grupo Sindical de Colonización No. 795 (brand: El Galayo)

CIGALES
Some good clarets, otherwise the wines are often blended with wines from other regions.

Main producers
Vicente Conde Camazón
Hijos de Frutos Villar
Pablo Barrigón Tovar
Bodegas Rodríguez Sanz

CONCA DE BARBERÀ *(Denominación de Origen)*
A recent addition to the DO list, this region makes mostly white wine. Torres have also planted some Cabernet Sauvignon and Pinot Noir.

The locals believe that some of the best wine from the region comes from here and El Rosal, another Galician undemarcated region. But little is bottled commercially.

Main producers
Unió Agrària Cooperativa de Reus (brand: La Conca de Barberà)
Condado de Tea (Salvatierra)

CONIUSA
A bit of Catalonia notable for the presence of the firm of Raimat, who grow classic French vines as well as local varieties.

Main producer
Raimat

FELANITX
Majorca again, and the largest wine-producing area on the island making a lot of rosado.

Main producer
Bodega Cooperativa de Felanitx

FUENCALIENTE
There are many ungrafted vines – that is, unaffected by the dread disease phylloxera – growing in this part of the Canaries.

Main producer
Bodegas Teneguia

LA GERIA
Dark, alcoholic whites (produced by vines that have to be protected from the prevailing strong winds) are the local wine in this part of Lanzarote. Other, smaller, wine-producing parts of the Canaries are Icod and Tacoronte, the former producing mostly white wines and the latter spicey reds.

Main producers
Bodegas El Grifo
Bodegas Mozaga

HUELVA *(Denominación de Origen)*
Huelva is somewhat overshadowed by its eastern neighbours, Jerez and Montilla, but it makes white table wines and good generosos in sherry styles which used to be sent to Jerez for blending until demarcation in 1964. On the whole they lack the finesse of sherry.

Main producers
Bodegas Miguel Salas Acosta
Bodega Cooperativa Vinícola del Condado
Hijos de Francisco Vallejo

JEREZ *(Denominación de Origen)*
Real sherry comes only from the Jerez region, the Spanish would say, and they would be right: Cyprus sherries and the like are sherry-type wines but seldom if ever reach the heights of quality of the best of the real thing.

You will not find any vintage sherries. All, young or old, is matured in solera systems, with the young wine refreshing the old, so all sherry is a blend of different years. But it can vary tremendously in taste according to the type you choose. Fino and Manzanilla are dry, and Amontillados and Olorosos can be dry as well, although they are often sweetened. And cream sherry is very sweet.

Main producers
Antonio Barbadillo SA
Croft Jerez SA (owned by International Distillers & Vintners)
Duff Gordon y Cia SA (brands: Fino Feria, Club Dry, El Cid, Santa Maria Cream)
Garvey SA (brands: San Patricio, Tio Guillermo, Ochavico, Long Life, Bicentary Pale Cream)
Gonzalez Byass & Co Ltd (brands: Tio Pepe, Elegante, La Concha, Alfonso, San Domingo, Nectar. Also old olorosos)

John Harvey & Sons (España) Ltd (brands: Bristol Cream, Luncheon Dry, Isabelita, Bristol Milk, Copper Beech, Tico)
La Riva SA (subsidiary of Pedro Domecq. Brands: Tres Palmas)
Emilio Lustau SA (almacenista sherries)
Osborne y Cia SA (brands: Fino Quinta, Coquinero, Janna, Bailen, Osborne Cream)
Pedro Domecq SA (Don José Ignacio Domecq, who heads this firm, is one of the world's most respected sherry authorities. Brands: La Ina, Rio Viejo, Double Century, Celebration Cream)
Hijos de Rainera Perez Marin (brands: La Guita, Hermonsilla, Fino Bandera)
Sandeman Hnos y Cia (now owned by Seagrams. Brands: Dry Don, Don Fino, Armada Cream, Imperial Corregido)
Valdespino SA (brands: Matador, Tio Diego)
Williams & Humbert (brands: Dry Sack, Canasta Cream, Walnut Brown, Pando)
Wisdom & Warter Ltd (brands: Fino Oliva, Manzanilla la Guapa, Amontillado Royal Palace, Oloroso Merecedos, Widsom's Choice Cream, Pedro Ximenez Wisdom)
Zoilo Ruiz Mateos

JUMILLA
There are some ungrafted vines growing here, unaffected by phylloxera, and the wines are mostly red, and high in alcohol. But things are changing, and efforts are being made to reduce the alcohol levels and thus improve the wines by picking the grapes earlier, and by blending the reds with lighter white wines.

Main producers
Antonio Bleda García
Ascensio Carcelén NCR
Bodegas García Carrion
Cooperativa de San Isidiro
Señorio de Condesable SA

MÁLAGA
This wine was immensely popular in the last century, especially in North America, though these days it tends to be overshadowed by other more famous fortified wines. It is matured in solera systems, and often sweetened by an *arrope* of boiled down unfermented must.

Main producers
Hijos de Antonio Barcelo SA
Luis Barcelos SA
Larios SA
Perez Texeira SA
Scholtz Hermanos SA
La Mancha DO

LA MANCHA
Don Quixote country, La Mancha covers the greater part of the vast central plain, and with its 1.2m acres of vines, it is by far the largest wine-growing area in the country. But not the best, although improvements are coming.

Main producers
Adelaido Rodriquez Escobar
Ayuso
Cooperativa de Campo La Daimielana
Ecusa
Eduardo Izquierdo
Cooperativa Nuestro Padre Jesús del Perdón
Bodega Pinilla Peco
Bodegas San Roque
Bodegas Familia Saviron
Cooperativa Virgen de las Viñas

MÉNTRIDA *(Denominación de Origen)*
Reds with high alcohol and low acid come from Garnacha in this part

of Spain's central plateau. Much of the wine is used for blending.

Main producer
Bodegas La Cerca SA

MONTÁNCHEZ
The speciality of this region is a red flor-growing wine, which generally emerges more orange than red in colour. It is usually drunk as an aperitif.

Main producers
Bodegas Calan (brand: Trampal)
Isidora Sánchez Pintado
Ramón Cañamero Cañamero

MONTERREY *(Denominación de Origen)*
There are few private bottlers in this region which makes mostly red wines. They are the strongest wines in Galicia reaching unusually 14% alc/vol.

Main producer
Cooperativa de Monterrey

MONTILLA-MORILES
The sherry-type wines are made on the solera system, but unlike sherry are fermented in earthenware *tinajas*, which are also found in Malaga and La Mancha. They are often so high in alcohol that fortification is not necessary. The types are the same as for sherry, but for the UK must be labelled simply Fine Dry, Medium and Cream.

Main producers
Alvear SA (makes about 12 styles)
Gracia Hermanos SA (brands: Kiki Pale Dry; Montiole Medium Dry; Ben Hur Rich Cream)
Monte Cristo SA
Bodegas Montulia SA
Bodegas Navarro SA
Perez Parquero SA
Juan de Pozo Baena
Carbonell y Cia

NAVARRA *(Denominación de Origen)*
Although bordering Rioja, only its best wines can rival those of its neighbour. Most of the wines are somewhat heavy reds, and the area can be subdivided into the *comarcas* (sub-regions) of Baja Montana, Valdizarbe, Tierra de Estella, Ribera Alta and Ribera Baja.

Main producers
Bodegas Cajo Simon
Bodegas Carricas SA
Bodegas Julián Chivite (largest private company in the area)
Bodegas Irache
Bodegas Perez Iahera
Vinicola Navarra
Cooperativa Vinicola Navarra
Bodegas Ocloa
Bodegas Señorio de Sarría SA
Bodega Herederos de Camilo Caatilla SA

PRIORATO *(Denominación de Origen)*
Another region whose wines tend to be of the heavy red variety often blended. Priorato is a DO region within the larger DO of Tarragona, and as well as the reds it makes some deliberately oxidized whites.

Main producers
Cellers de Scala Dei
De Muller

RIBEIRO *(Denominación de Origen)*
Galicia is immediately north of the Portuguese border, and the wines that come from the province are low in strength and often pétillant, like their neighbour Vinho Verde. Some of the grape varieties are the same, but if you want consistency of winemaking, go for Vinho Verde.

Main producers
Bodegas Alanis
Bodegas Eloy Lorenzo
Bodegas Cooperitiva de Ribeiro
Bodegas Rivera
Bodegas Rofemar
Cosecheros del Vino del Ribeiro
Marqués de Ulloa

RIBERA DEL DUERO
A source of stylish reds which are sometimes said to be the best Spain makes, after those of Rioja and Catalonia.

Main producers
Alejandro Fernández
Bodegas Peñalba López
Bodega Cooperativa Ribera de Duero
Bodegas Vega Sicilia SA (grows both French and native vines, and the wines are in great demand).

RIOJA *(Denominación de Origen)*
Apart from its famous oaky reds and whites, Rioja also makes a newer-style of wine which is fruity, with no wood ageing and generally meant to be drunk young. The first Spanish region to be demarcated, in 1926, Rioja can be sub-divided into La Rioja Alta, La Rioja Alavesa and La Rioja Baja, the wines of the first two being the more delicate. However, French winemaking has always been evident in the Riojan bodegas: many French winemakers moved here after phylloxera had devastated the French vineyards in the late 1900s.

Main producers
Bodegas Unidas AGE SA (Marqués de Romeral, Fuenmayor Siglo reservas)
Bodegas Alavesas SA
Bodegas Berberana SA (brands: Carta de Oro, Carta de Plata)
Bodegas Berceo
Bodegas Beronia (Very modern winemaking)
Bodegas Bilbainas (Brands: Vina Pomal, Vina Paceta, Cepa de Oro, Vina Zaco)
Bodegas Campo Viejo SA (brands: San Asensio)
Bodegas Carlos Serras SA
Compania Vinìcola del Norte de España (CVNE) (brands: Cune, Imperial, Viña Real, Monopole)
Bodega Corral SA (brand: Don Jacobo)
Bodegas El Coto
Bodegas Granja Remélluri
Bodegas Faustino Martinez (brands: Faustino I, V and VII)
Bodegas Franco Españolas
Cooperativa Vinicola de Labastida
Bodegas Lagunilla (brand: Viña Herminia)
Bodegas Lan SA
Bodegas R. Lopez de Heredia Viña Tonia SA (brands: Cubillo, Tondonia, Bosconia)
Bodegas Marqués de Cáceres (Bordeaux influence particularly strong here)
Bodegas Marqués de Murrieta SA (brand: Castillo de Ygay)
Herederos de Marqués de Riscal
Martinez Lacuesta Hnos Ltda
Bodegas Montecillo SA
Bodegas Muga SA (brand: Prado Enea)
Bodegas Olarra (Brand: Cerro Anon, white)
Federico Paternina SA (brands: Banda Azul, Banda Dorada, Viña Vial)
Bodegas La Rioja Alta (brands: Viña Alberdi, Viña Ardanza, Viña Arana, 904, 890, Metropol, Leonora)
Bodegas Riojanas SA (brand: Viña Albina)
Sociedad General de Viños SA (built by Pedro Domecq. brands: Domecq Domain, Viña Eguia)

RUEDA *(Denominación de Origen)*
Clean whites from this region in Old Castille-León and, in addition, the bodegas make a traditional flor-growing white wine.

Main producers
Sociedad Cooperativa Agricola Castellana 'La Seca'
Bodega Los Curros
Bodegas de Crianza Castilla la Vieja
Hijos de Alberto Gutierrez
Vinos Blancos de Castilla SA (wines sold under the label of the firm of Marqués de Riscal)
Vinos Sanz

SOMONTANO *(Denominación de Origen)*
Light, quite acid red wines from this little-known DO region.

Main producer
Bodega Cooperativa Comarcal del Somontano

TARRAGONA *(Denominación de Origen)*
This warmest part of the Catalan coast makes big, highly alcoholic wines that are often better blended than drunk on their own, and some good solera dessert wines that are not unlike Málaga or oloroso sherry.

Main producers
Amigó Germans y Cía
Lopez Beltrán y Cía SA
Cochs SA
Dalman Germans y Cía
De Muller (fortified dessert wines. A prestigious family company that also makes altar wines.)
José Oliver SA
Ramon Mestre Serra
Vinos Padró SL
Joan Solé Bargallo (Cellers Catalano-Aragonesas)
Cellers Tapias SA
Pedro Rovira (Has a branch in Vilafranca del Penedès, as well.
La Vinícola Iberica
Union Agraria Cooperativa

TIERRA DE BARROS *(Denominación de Origen)*
Most of the wines here are neutral whites, low in acidity and often sent to other regions for blending. Of the rest, some are drunk in the area and some are distilled.

Main producers
Bodegas Cevisur
Bodegas Coloma
Industrias Vinícolas de Oeste SA (Inviosa)

TIERRA DE MADRID
This undemarcated region is the main wine area in New Castile-La Mancha, apart from the DO areas. It can be divided into the sub regions of Arganda-Colmenar de Oreja, Navalcarnero, and San Martin de Valdeiglesias.

Main producer
Bodegas Hijos de Jesús Diaz

UTIEL-REQUENA *(Denominación de Origen)*
Rosados are made here as a by-product so to speak, of the vino de doble pasta, very dark red wine, that is shipped elsewhere in Spain for blending.

Main producers
Cooperativa Agricola de Utiel
Casa de Calderon

VALDEORRAS *(Denominación de Origen)*
Another Galician region where the cooperatives reign supreme.

Main producers
Cooperativa de Larouco
Cooperativa de la Rúa
Cooperativa del Barco de Valdeorras

VALDEPEÑAS
The most widely grown grape here is the white Airén, but the black grapes are dark enough to redden a wine made of the two together; the result is called Aloque.

Main producers
Bodegas Delgado Cámara
Bodegas Espinosa SA
Bodegas La Gloria SA
Bodegas Sanchez Rustarazo
Félix Solis
Vda. de Rafael Galan
Videva SA
Visan SA
Cooperativa La Invincible (clarete)
Bodegas Lopez Tello
Bodegas Miguel Martin
Bodegas Morenito
Luis Megia SA
Bodegas Pintado
Carmelo Madrid SA

VAL DE SALNÉS *(Albariño)*
White Albariño (the wine is called after the grape) is among the best that Galicia has to offer: pale and flowery, like the Alvarinho from northern Portugal across the border.

Main producers
Palacio de Fefiñanes
Albariño del Palacio
Bodegas Chaves
Asociación de Cosecheros de Albariño
Pazo de Bayon SA

VALENCIA *(Denominación de Origen)*
This area produces more white wine than red, and most of it is high in alcohol and low in acidity.

Main producers
Bodegas Schenk SA (a branch of a large Swiss company that makes, among other wines, Don Cortez)
Cooperativa Agrica de Villa
Cherubino Valsangiacomo SA
Exportadora Vinícola Valenciana SA (Vinival)
Vincente Gandía Plá SA
Cooperativa Agricola Santa Bárbara
Antonio Arraez SL
Cooperativa Vinícola La Viña
Bodega Cooperativa La Baronia
Bodegas Murviedro

VALDEVIMBRE DOS OTEROS
There are some good claretes from here, often made by adding whole bunches of grapes to the fermenting must, to give an attractive prickle to the wine.

Main producer
VILE (Planta de Elaboracion y Embotellado de Vinos SA)

YECLA *(Denominación de Origen)*
The highly alcoholic wines from here are very similar in style to those of Jumilla.

Main producers
Cooperativa de La Purísma
Enrique Ochoa Palao

RIOJA

1970 Excellent. Stocks are low, but get them if you can find them. But don't keep them.
1971 Poor, with a low yield.
1972 Even worse.
1973 A good vintage, with the wines now coming to their peak.
1974 Average: not a year to choose.
1975 Fair to good.
1976 Originally rated below 1975, but the wines of the two years can sometimes be hard to tell apart.
1977 A rainy autumn, low yields and very poor wines.
1978 Excellent, but low yields.
1979 So-so: go for the years on either side.
1980 Good.
1981 Very good, but choose wines from Rioja Alta rather than Rioja Baja, given the choice.
1982 Excellent. The crianza wines are on the market but reservas and gran reservas will not appear yet.
1983 Good.
1984 Average but rather patchy.

Spanish Shopping List

Alella
Marqués de Alella white, Alta Alella

Alicante
Fondillon generoso, Bodegas Salvador Poveda Luz
Fondillon Alicante, Primitivo Quiles, NCR

Almansa
Tinto Selecto, Bodegas Miguel Carrión
Castillo de Almansa, Bodegas Piqueras – Mario Bonete García

Ampurdan-Costa Brava
Reserva Don Miguel, Cavas del Ampurdan SA
Gran Recosina rosado and red, Cellers Santamaría

El Bierzo
Santo Rosado, Bodegas Los Arcos
Vega Burbia and Almena del Bierzo, Bodegas Palacio de Arganza

Binisalem
Red reservas, from Bodegas José L Ferrer

Cañamero
La Cepa de Cañamero, Felipe Ruiz Parralejo

Canaries
Malvasia Seco, Bodegas Mozaga
Rosado El Grifo, Bodegas El Grifo

Cariñena
Puente de Piedra red, cooperativa Vinícola San José de Aguaron
Espigal clarete, Bodegas Joaquin Soria
Don Mendo, Bodegas San Valero
Cueva de Algairén Gran Reserva, Bodegas Enrique Lopez Pelayo

Cebreros
El Galayo, Grupo Sindical de Colonización No 795

Cigales
Older wines from Pablo Barrigón Tovar

Coniusa
Raimat wines, especially Abadia red

Huelva
Whites from Bodegas Cooperativa Vinícola del Condado, and their solera wines
Sherry styles from Bodegas Miguel Sales Acosta
Sherry styles from Hijos de Francisco Vallejo

Jerez
Croft Jerez, Palo Cortado

Don Zoilo Fino and other Zoiol Ruiz Mateos styles
San Patricio Fino, Garvey
Tio Pepe, Gonzalez Byass
Apololoes Oloroso Muy Viejo, Gonzalez Byass
Almacenistas from Lustau
La Iña, Domecq
Elegante, Sandeman
La Guita Manzanilla, Hijos de Rainera Perez Marin
Tio Diego, Valdespino

Jumilla
Castillo de Jumilla, Oro de Ley, Antonio Bleda García
Bullanguero, Asensio Carcelén NCR

Málaga
Colmenares Moscatel, Larios
Lagrima Viejo, Pérez Texeira
Solera 1885, Scholtz Hermanos

La Mancha
Yuntero dry white, Cooperativa Nuestro Padre Jesús de Perdón
White from Bodegas San Roque
Cueva del Granero, Bodegas Cueva del Granero
Zagarrón, Cooperativa del Campo Nuestra Señora de Manjavacas

Méntrida
Casarrubios red, Bodegas La Cerca SA

Montánchez
Viña Valdemantilla red, Bodegas Galan

Monterrey
White from the Cooperativa de Monterrey

Montilla-Moriles
Fino Festival, Alvear
Kiki Pale Dry, Gracia Hermanos
Flor de Montilla, Carbonell y Cia

Navarra
Monte Cierzo, Vina Zarcillo, Bodegas Cajo Simon
Chivite white, Bodegas Julián Chivite
Gran Vino del Sênorio de Sarria red reservas, Señorio de Sarría
Castillo de Tiebas red, Vinícola Navarra

Penedès
Extrismo Bach dessert white, Masia Bach
Still wines from Bodegas Bosch-Guell
Sparkling wines and red reservas, from Conde de Caralt
Sparkling wines from Cavas Hill
Jean León Chardonnay
Jean León Cabernet Sauvignon
Red Vi Novello, Cooperativa de Mollet de Perelada

Vin Natur blanc de blancs sparkling wine, Marqués de Monistrol

Viñedos Torres, Gran Coronas Black Label

Gran Codorníu Brut and Non Plus Ultra, Codorníu, both sparkling

Freixenet vintage sparkling wines, or their Brut Natur sparkling wine

Reserva Heredad sparkling wine from Segura Viudas (in spite of the bottle)

Blanc Flor, Ermita d'Espiells, Juvé & Camps

Mont Marçal Blanco Añada, Bodegas Manuel Sancho

Mont Marçal Primer Vi Novell, Bodegas Manuel Sancho

Mont Marçal Tinto Reserva, Bodegas Manuel Sancho

Priorato

De Muller Priorato red

Ribeiro

Red Pazo, Bodegas Cooperativa de Ribeiro

Ribera del Duero

Peñafiel, Cooperativa de Ribera del Duero

Vega Sicilia and Valbuena, Bodegas Vega Sicilia

Tinto Pesquera Gran Reserva, Alejandro Fernandez

Rueda

Campo Grande Fino, Dorado 61, and Verdejo Palido, all from Agricola Castellana Sociedad Cooperativa

Almirante de Castilla, Bodegas de Crianza Castilla la Vieja

Tarragona

Viña Solimar, De Muller

Tierra de Barros

Viña Amelia red, Bodegas Coloma

Lar de Barros red and white, Industrias Vinícolas del Oeste (Inviosa)

Utiel-Requena

Generoso wines from Casa de Calderon

Valdeorras

Godello, Cooperativa de Barco de Valdeorras

Pingadelo red, Cooperativa de la Rúa

Valdepeñas

Clarete from Cooperativa La Invencible

Copa de Oro, Bodegas Morenito

Reds from Félix Solis

Val de Salnes *(Albariño)*

Albariño de Fefiñanes

Albariño del Palacio

Albariño pétillant, Bodegas Chaves

Valencia

Viña Murviedro Blanco and Los Monteros Tinto, Bodegas Murviedro Monteros, Bodegas Schenk

Alto Turia, Cooperativa Agricola Santa Bárbara

Yecla

Viña Montana, Cooperativa de La Purisma

Sparkling List

THERE ARE SEVERAL DIFFERENT WAYS to make sparkling wine. Depending on which is used, the grapes from which the wine is made, and the temperature in which they are grown, fizzy wine can be one of the world's greatest luxuries, or a less pleasant alternative to lemonade. All sparkling wine – apart from the very cheapest 'bicycle-pump' examples which are simply made by pumping carbon dioxide from a canister into a tankful of wine – requires wine to ferment in a closed environment, thus trapping the CO_2 created by the fermentation process to be trapped in the wine itself, in the form of bubbles. White sparkling wine can be made from black grapes.

THE WORDS

Blanc de Blancs

White fizz made from exclusively white grapes.

Blanc de Noirs

White fizz made from exclusively black grapes.

Carbonation

Fizz made in exactly the same way as lemonade – with its bubbles pumped into it from a CO_2 cylinder.

Cava

The name adopted by the Spanish sparkling wine makers many of whom once called their wine Champagne. Cava is always made by the same method as Champagne.

Champagne

In Europe, and other countries sensitive to the feelings of the winemakers of the small region of Champagne in North-East France, this word exclusively describes wine made in that region, from strictly defined grapes and by the Méthode Champenoise. In the USA, the USSR and Austrlaia however, anything made of grapes and with bubbles in it can use the name; and nobody can see any reason why it shouldn't. What a pity the Champenois can't register Champagne as a trademark: those American 'Champagne' makers would become quite indignant at a French pop manufacturer usurping the name 'Coke' . . .

Champenoise

Describes wine made by the Méthode Champenoise. *qv.*

Charmat

The third best way to make sparkling wine – also known as 'Cuve Close', and 'Tank Method'. Wine undergoes its secondary fermentation in tanks rather than bottles.

Crémant

Less fizzy Champagne, and increasingly used as a name for fizzy wine produced elsewhere in France – e.g. Crémant de Bourgogne.

Cuve Close *(see Charmat)*

Dégorgement

The removal of the yeasty solids which accumulate in a bottle of Méthode Champenoise wine as it ferments.

Fermentazione Naturale

On Italian labels, this can mean Charmat or Méthode Champenoise.

Frizzante

Italian word for semi-sparkling wine.

Méthode Champenoise *(or 'Champagne Method)*

Any wine made this way has to undergo its secondary fermentation in the same bottle in which it is finally sold. In the USA, such wines often bear labels stating 'fermented in this bottle', rather than 'fermented in the bottle' which will feature on labels of Transfer Method *(qv.)* wines. In Italy these wines can be called Metodo Champenois or Metodo Classico Champenois.

Mousse

French word for the bubbles in sparkling wine.

Mousseux

French word for sparkling wine of any kind.

Pétillant

French for semi-sparkling wine.

Russian Continuous

A curious mixture between Charmat and Transfer Method, whereby the new wine passes from tank to tank in a literally 'continuous' system. Its supporters claim that this system provides a yeastier, more Champagne-like flavour than the Charmat system; unfortunately, until now, the only examples have been made in

Eastern Europe and are neither readily available in the West, nor particularly attractive. In 1985, Lancers' the Portuguese rosé plant, installed the first Russian Continuous system outside the Eastern Block. The quality of its wines will be of interest.

Sekt
German name for sparkling wine – which does not, even in the case of the apparently Germanic 'Deutsche Sekt' have to be exclusively made from grapes grown in Germany.

Spritzig
German word for semi-sparkling wine.

Spumante
Italian word for sparkling wine – usually for sweet Muscaty stuff made in the North-West, but increasingly for drier wines from other parts of the country.

Transfer Method
Very popular in the USA, this is a compromise between Charmat and Méthode Champenoise. The wine is fermented in the bottle, but it goes into a tank for the degorgement *(qv.)* before rebottling in a fresh bottle. Labels bear the words 'Fermented In The Bottle'. Wine is usually better than Charmat fizz.

VSQPRD
The European standard for sparkling wine.

THE GRAPES

In Champagne:

Chardonnay	Blanquette de Limoux *France*
Pinot Meunier	Ca del Bosco *Italy*
Pinot Noir	Château Remy *Australia*
Elsewhere	Clairette de Die Tradition *France*
Cabernet Franc *France*	Cremant de Bourgogne –
Chardonnay *USA, France,*	Delorme *France*
Italy, Spain	Deinhard Leila *Germany*
Chenin Blanc *Loire, USA*	Domaine Chandon *California*
Clairette *France*	Dopff au Moulin Cremant
Colombard *USA*	d'Alsace *France*
Perellada *Spain*	Equipe 5 *Italy*
Pinot Blanc *Italy*	Ferrari Brut *Italy*
Pinot Grigio *Italy*	Pinot de Pinot *Italy*
Pinot Noir *France, Italy*	Piper Sonoma *California*
Muscat *Italy, France*	Poniatowski Clos Baudoin
Ugni Blanc *France*	Vouvray *France*
Good Sparkling Wine (apart from Champagne)	Raimat Cava *Spain*
	Saumur Mousseux – Bouvet-Ladubay *France*
Asti Spumante	Schramsberg *California*
Fontanafredda *Italy*	

SWITZERLAND

IMAGINE the unimaginable: a heavily devalued Swiss franc. It could just happen, allowing us all to indulge in an orgy of Suchard chocolate, Rolex watches and, yes, Swiss wine. All three are well made, and the latter two at least, call for a considerable amount of effort. Switzerland's 12,000 hectares of vines are often planted in areas and on steep slopes which prevent the use of mechanical aids; hail can be such a problem that the Swiss army can regularly be seen firing into the sky to break up the approaching menace before it reaches the vines.

Whilst growing a wide variety of grapes, some of which are both indigenous to Switzerland and unknown elsewhere, the Swiss specialize in making a reasonably good white from the Alsatian Chasselas (which they call the Fendant) and Dôle, a pleasant light

Passetoutgrains-type red from the Pinot Noir and the Gamay.

Prices are unfortunately far too high for any of these wines to be exported for anything more than their novelty value; their quality is not considered sufficiently outstanding for cost to be no object. Those of us with no skiing holidays planned will just have to go on imagining . . . Matters may change though. At the time of writing Switzerland has her very own wine lake.

The Grape List

White

Riesling Sylvaner Clone of Müller-Thurgau. Produces dry, light rather fragrant wines.

Raeuschling Related to Alsace Knipperle. Rare, grown near Zurich; produces a dry austere wine that ages well in good years.

Chasselas The most common white variety in Switzerland; found mostly in French speaking cantons; often vinified 'sur lie'.

Johannisberg Related to the Sylvaner; grown in the Valais; also called the Rhin or Gros Rhin. Produces soft full dry wines.

Tokayer/Malvoisie The German and French names respectively for the Pinot Gris; very occasionally affected by botrytis, producing a sweet dessert wine.

Ermitage Related to the Marsanne, it makes some of the best wines in the Valais, dry, powerful and with a hint of sweetness.

Gewürztraminer Planted in small quantities throughout Switzerland. Various special varieties are grown in the Valais in very small quantities, many of them being indigenous:
Arvine – dry, robust and full-bodied wines.
Amigne – similar though richer in style.
Humagne – light, acidic wine – very rare.
Muscat – dry style, similar to Alsace.
Rèze – used to make Gletscherwein- matured up near the glaciers.
Petit Rhin – Rhine Riesling.
Pinot Blanc.
Païen or Heida – related to the Traminer – Grown at around 1,300 m. above sea level near Visperterminen in the highest vineyards in Europe.

Red

Pinot Noir/Blauburgunder Grown in virtually every wine-growing canton in Switzerland; light, fruity wines, sometimes with considerable alcohol.

Merlot Found only in the Ticino.

Gamay Planted mainly in the cantons of Valais, Vaud and Geneva.

Rouge du Pays another rarity from the Valais.

Protected Appellation

Clevner Wines produced from the Pinot Noir in the canton of Zurich.

Dôle Name used in the Valais for a blend of the Pinot Noir and Gamay (and a small amount of Pinot Gris); made from grapes averaging at least 85 Oechsle.

Dorin Wine made from the Chasselas in the canton of Vaud.

Fendant Wine made from the Chasselas in the canton of the Valais.

Goron Similar to Dôle though of lesser quality and with a higher porportion of Gamay; also comes from the Valais.

Oeil de Perdrix Rosé made from the Pinot Noir in the canton of Neuchâtel.

Perlan Wine made from the Chasselas in the canton of Geneva.

Salvagnin Blend of Pinot Noir and Gamay from the Vaud.

Viti Controlled appellation for the Ticinese Merlot.

The Wine Regions

WEST SWITZERLAND
Valais
vineyard area:	5390 ha. Vitis Vinifera
planted:	36% red 64% white
main varieties grown:	Chasselas, Gros Rhin, Malvoisie, Ermitage Pinot Noir, Gamay.
major villages:	Monthey, Martigny, Fully, Saxon, Saillon, Leytron, Chamoson, Ardon, Vetroz, Conthey, Sion, St Léonard, Sierre, Salgesch, Varen, Leuk, Raron, Visp, Visperterminen, Bramois.
best areas – reds:	Sierre, Salgesch.
whites:	Fendant – Vetroz, Sion, St Léonard. Johannisberg – Leytron, Chamoson.

Vaud
vineyard area:	3547 ha.
planted	18% red 82% white
main varieties grown:	Chasselas, Pinot Noir, Gamay
major villages:	La Côte – Between Geneva and Lausanne Coppet, Nyon, Begnins, Luins, Vinzel, Tartegnin, Mont, Fechy, Rolle, Aubonne, Perroy, St. Prex, Morges. Lavaux – Between Lausanne and Montreux Pully, Lutry, Villette, Cully, Rivaz, St. Saphorir, Grandvaux, Riex, Epesses, Dezaley, Chardonne, Vevey, Montreux. Chablais – Between Montreux and the Valais Villeneuve, Yvorne, Aigle, Ollon, Bex. Jura – Arnex, Orbe, Grandson, Champagne, Bonvillars, Onnens/Concise. Vully – on border with Canton Fribourg Vallamand.
best areas – whites:	Dezaley, Yvorne, Aigle.

Geneva
vineyard area:	1279 ha.
planted:	38% red 62% white
main varieties grown:	Chasselas, Riesling Sylvaner, Gamay, Pinot Noir.
major villages:	Dardagny, Russin, Essertines, Peissy, Satigny, Lully, Bernex, Cologny, Jussy, Corsier.
best areas:	none.

Neuchâtel
vineyard area:	583 ha.
planted:	28% red 72% white
main varieties grown:	Chasselas, Pinot Noir.
major villages:	Vaumarcus, St. Aubin, Bevaix, Cortaillod, Boudry, Colombier, Auvernier, Cormondreche, Corcelles, Neuchâtel, La Coudre, St-Blaise, Cornaux, Cressier, Le Landeron.
best areas:	Cortaillod – Rosé known as Oeil de Perdrix. Auvernier, Neuchâtel.

Bern
vineyard area:	249 ha.
planted:	19% red 81% white
main varieties grown:	Chasselas, Riesling Sylvaner, Pinot Noir
major villages:	La Neuveville, Schafis, Ligerz, Twann, Tuscherz, Erlach, Gampelen, Ins, Spiez, Oberhofen.
best areas:	Schafis, Ligerz, Twann.

Fribourg
vineyard area:	102 ha.
planted:	12% red 88% white
main varieties grown:	Chasselas, Gewürztraminer, Pinot Noir
major villages:	Vallamand, Motier, Praz.
best areas:	Praz.

EAST SWITZERLAND
Canton Zürich
major villages:	Lake of Zürich – Feldbach, Staefa, Maennedorf/Uetikon, Meilen, Herrliberg/ Erlenbach, Kuesnacht, Waedenswil. Valleys of Limmat and Furt – Weiningen, Otelfingen, Boppelsen, Buchs. Valleys of Wehn and Glatt – Regensberg/ Dielsdorf, Oberweningen, Stadel, Bachen- buelach/Winkel, Buelach. Toess Valley – Winterthur – Tuefen, Freienstein, Neftenbach, Wuelflingen, Wiesendangen, Winterthur/Stadel, Rickenbach, Dinhard. Thur Valley – Andelfingen – Berg, Flaach/ Volken, Dorf/Humlikon, Henggart, Andelfingen, Schiterberg, Alten, Ossingen. Rhine area – Dachsen/Uhweisen, Benken, Rudolfingen/Trullikon, Truttikon, Unter & Oberstammheim, Huentwangen, Wasterkingen, Rafz/Wil, Eglisau, Rheinau, Flurlingen.
best areas:	Staefa, Maennedorf, Meilen, Herrliberg, Erlenbach, Kuesnacht, Schiterberg, Rudolfingen, Rafz, Eglisau.

Canton Schaffhausen
major villages	Trasadingen, Wichingen, Hallau, Oberhallau, Gaechlingen, Osterfingen, Schleitheim, Siblingen, Loehningen, Beringen, Buchberg, Ruedlingen, Schaffhausen, Doerflingen, Bibern, Thayngen, Stein a. Rhein, Hemishofen.
best areas:	Wilchingen, Hallou, Osterfingen, Schaffhauser, Stein a. Rhein.

Canton Thurgau
major villages:	Berlingen, Mannenbach, Arenberg, Ermatingen, Nieder & Oberneunforn, Iselisberg, Warth, Ottenberg, Weinfelden, Goettighofen, Nussbaumen, Huettwilen, Herdern, Kalchrain, Schlattingen, Amlikon, Sonnenberg – Stettfurt.
best areas:	Ermatingen, Weinfelden, Sonnenberg – Stettfurt.

Canton St. Gallen
major villages:	Rhine Valley – Buchberg, Au/Monstein, Berneck, Balgach, Rebstein/Marbach, Altstaetten, Montlingen, Werdenberg. South and West of Canton – Wartau, Sargans, Mels, Ragaz/Pfaefers, Walenstadt, Quinten, Wil, Rapperswil.
best areas:	Berneck, Balgach, Sargans.

Canton Graubuenden
major villages: 'Buendner Herrschaft' – producing the best red wines found in East Switzerland – Flaesch, Maienfeld, Jenins, Malans.
Others – Zizers, Trimmis, Chur-Masans, Ems.

Canton Aargau
major villages: Thalheim, Kasteln-Oberflachs, Schinznacher-Dorf, Boezen/Hornussen, Elfingen, Remigen, Ruefenach, Villigen, Mandach, Hottwil-Wil, Klingnau, Doettingen, Tegerfelden, Ennetbaden, Wettingen, Birmensdorf, Seengen.

best areas: Schinznach, Thalheim, Birmensdorf, Klingnau.

Canton Baselland
major villages   Biel-Benken, Aesch-Klus, Arlesheim, Muttenz, Pratteln, Liestal, Wintersingen, Buus, Maisprach.

best areas: Arlesheim, Muttenz.

SOUTH SWITZERLAND
Canton Ticino
vineyard area: 656 *ha.*
planted: 99% red 1% white
main varieties grown: Merlot.
major villages: Locarno area – Maggia, Tenero, Gordola, Cugnsco, Gudo, Vira, Sementina, Lumino, Giubiasco, Magadino.
Lugano area – Pregassona, Lugano/Castagnola, Breganzona, Bioggio, Biogno, Castelrotto, Morcote, Arogno.
Mendrisio area – Tremona; Arzo, Besazio, Ligornetto/Stabio, Mendrisio, Coldrerio, Balerna/Mezzana.
Bellinzona area – SanVittore, Roveredo, Grono, Lostallo.

Major distributors

Bonvin, Sion
Bujard, Lutry
Fonjallaz, Epesses
Hammel, Rolle
Howeg, Grenchen
Landolt, Zurich
Fritz Lanz, Dietikon
Moevenpick, Bursins
Emil Nussch, Balgach   Schenk, Rolle
Obi-Kriesi, Bischofszell   Schuler, Schwyz
OWG, Waedenswil   Tavelli, Sierre
Provins, Sion   Testuz, Cully
Rutishauser, Scherzingen   VOLG, Winterthur

Swiss Labelling

NORTH AND EAST SWITZERLAND
White wines are named after the grape variety and the region, village or vineyard, e.g:
Riesling Sylvaner vom Zurichsee Sonnenufer *region*
Meilener Raeuschling *village*

Red wines, exclusively Pinot Noir, are named after the region or village with occasionally the vineyard or method of production e.g.:
Maienfelder Beerliwein *village*
Clevner Sternenhalder Staefa *vineyard*

WEST SWITZERLAND
White wines made from the Chasselas are named after the region, village or vineyard except in the Valais where they are called Fendant, with or without a regional label, e.g:
Twanner *village*
Dezaley Clos des Abbayes *vineyard*
Fendant de Chamoson *village*

Other white wines have their varietal or a local name, with or without a region specified, e.g:
Johannisberg du Valais *local name*
Ermitage *variety*

Red wines are normally labelled with their varietal or controlled appellation name, e.g:
Pinot Noir de Sierre
Dôle du Valais
Merlot del Ticino

Beware: Many Swiss wines are given brand names with no geographical or quality connotation at all, e.g:
Johannisberg RHINEGOLD
Malanser WILLKOMMSTRUNK
Gamay STERNEWY

Great Swiss Estates

Graubünden
Schloss Salenegg

Neuchâtel
Goutte D'Or

Vaud
Aigle Les Murailles
Yvorne Les Combettes
Dézaley Clos des Abbayes
Dézaley Chemin de Fer
Château de Malessert

Valais
Château Lichten
Clos du Château
Mont d'Or

Zürich
Sternenhalder, Staefa
Mariahalden, Erlenbach

SYRIA

THOSE who know their bible will remember Damascus being described as producing and exporting huge quantities of wine. Nowadays, despite the wartime demands of French troops based in Syria, winemaking is an activity which occupies few Syrians. Aleppo, Damascus and Homs all produce tiny amounts of full-bodied wine which never rise above table-wine quality. Those who drink more than a glass or two seldom rise above the table.

TANZANIA

WE are indebted to Mr P.R. Matthews who, in answer to a facetious comment in *What Wine?* magazine provided the following description of Tanzanian wines: 'the red varies from OK to bloody awful . . . the rosé can be compared to diesel. It's very much the luck of the draw though, and some bottles can be good. The white is of quite good quality and much sought after. All cost around £8 per bottle.'

TUNISIA

AS a Muslim state, alcohol was strictly proscribed here. It was the arrival of the French colonialists which heralded a renaissance of Tunisian winemaking which had been in full swing around Carthage in Punic and Roman times.

French vines, notably the Cinsault, Carignan and the hybrid Alicante-Bouschet, tended to produce wine of light colour and a propensity for early maderization – unlike some of the sturdier wines produced in Algeria. It was only the late arrival of phylloxera, the departure of the French, and a single-minded effort by the government which really set winemaking on a path towards quality.

The area under vine has been reduced from 50,000 ha in the 1970s to 30,000 in the mid 1980s, production has dropped to 1,000,000 hl, and a number of new varieties of grape have been planted, including the Pinor Noir, Mourvedre, Cabernet Franc, Sémillon and Sauvignon. Nonetheless Tunisia's finest wine remains its Muscat.

State control over the 900 small concerns which sell their wine through 13 state-owned, 14 cooperative and 10 private wineries is very strong. Whilst there is no formal definition of geographical wine regions, under the Office du Vin, which was established in 1970, there are now three designated levels of quality.

The Wine Regions

Almost all of Tunisia's vineyards are situated in the region following the coast of the Gulf of Tunis, behind the city itself. Amongst the best thought-of names are:

Cap Bon
Carthage
Côteaux du Khanguet
Saint-Cyprien
Sidi-Tabet
Tebourba

The Grape List

Red
Alicante-Bouschet (a French hybrid more noted for quantity than quality)
Alicante-Grenache (used for rosé)
Cabernet Franc (recent)
Carignan
Cinsault (also used for rosé)
Morastel
Mourvèdre (recent)
Nocera (recent import from Sicily)
Pinot Noir

White
Beldi
Clairette (producing dull wine)
Merseguera
Muscat (d'Alexendrie, de Frontignan or de Terracina)
Pedro Ximénez
Reldei
Ugni Blanc

TURKEY

TURKEY'S wine industry peaked in the 1890s, when the vineyards of Europe were decimated by phylloxera. In one year 15 million gallons were exported. It then fell into a sharp decline until in 1925 Kemel Ataturk began the drive to revitalize the industry, with the

formation of Tekel, the state organization which now has 21 wineries and dominates export. In addition there are now 118 private wineries, with Aral being the biggest and Doluca, Kutman and Kavaklidere amongst the best.

Turkey is divided into nine administrative zones for viticultural purposes, the most important are:

Ankara
Aegean
Thrace/Marmara
South-East Anatolia
Central-East Anatolia
Central South Anatolia

The Grape List

Ankara
Hasandede (white)
Kalecik (red)
Cubuk (red)
Dimrit (red)
Carignan (red)
Gamay (red)
Aramon (red)

Aegean
Irikira (red)
Tokmak (red)
Muscat (white)
Thompson's Seedless (white)

Thrace/Marmara
Beylerce (white) (one of better natives)
Yapincak (white) (related to Sémillon)
Altintas

Papazkarasi (red)
Karalhana (red)
Kuntra (red)
Adakarasi (red)
Karasakiz (red)
Cinsault
Aramon
Gamay
Cabernet Sauvignon (recent)
Pinot Noir (recent)
Sémillon – used for Trakya white
Riesling (recent)
Chardonnay (recent)
Sylvaner (recent)

Anatolia
Carignan
Aramon
Gamay
Okuzguzo
Bogazkere
Narince
Emir
Kabarcik
Dobulgen
Sergikerasi
Horozkerasi

URUGUAY

JESUIT priests quickly established vineyards after Uruguay's 'discovery' in 1516. Mainly sacramental wines were produced until the late 19th century, when three pioneers from Spain, Francesco Vidiella, Luis de la Torres and Pascual Harriagues laid the foundations of a modern wine industry. Harriagues introduced the Torda grape from Concordia, now known as the Harriague; and Vidiella the Tannat grape (a relative of the Folle Noire) which now bears his name.

Vinifera strains now predominate over labrusca, producing

mainly dessert, fortified and sparkling white wines, some deep rosés rather like the Spanish 'clarete' wines, and a little passable Cabernet Sauvignon. There seems to be no formal classification, though 'Gran Reserva' wines may possibly be better than others.

The Grape List

Red
Cabernet Sauvignon
Cabernet Franc
Pinot Noir
Merlot
Nebbiolo
Harriague
Alicante
Grenache
Cinsault
Vidiella
Barbera
Grignolino
Lambrusco
Carignan
Isabella
US hybrids

White
Sémillon
Sauvignon Blanc
Malvasia
Pedro Ximenez
Riesling
Pinot Blanc

The Wine Regions

Montevideo
Canelones
San Jose
Maldonado
Soriano
Paysandu
Florida

UNUSUAL WINE TASTINGS

THE WINE TASTING WITH NO WINE

You may have heard the story of the pub with no beer, well . . . When, in May 1985, the prestigious Bordeaux firm of de Luze invited Britain's most prominent members of the wine trade to congregate in London for a tasting of the 1984 vintage clarets, they had everything arranged: glasses, spittoons, tasting sheets. Everything except the wine, which was held up on its way from France. The wine trade enjoyed a hearty lunch, drank a few glasses of Champagne and returned to their offices no wiser about the flavour of the claret.

THE NUDE TASTING

We are indebted to the American magazine, *Wines & Vines*, for their report of a wine tasting held on 11 November, 1984 in Los Gatos California, by the Lupin Naturist Club. Mr Glyn Stout, organiser of the event was reported as saying 'there's lots going on here in the cooler seasons'.

USA

GOOD AMERICAN WINE does not all come from California. It's a fact that non-Americans often forget, and Californians forget all the time. This fixation on the west coast is very unfortunate, since it distracts the attention from the fascinating developments which are taking place elsewhere. Where unpalatable indigenous Labrusca (table) grapes were grown, hybrids and Vinifera are now being planted with increasing success: nowhere in the world has vinegrowing and winemaking been developed into such an exact science. Every time you taste a well-made wine from Europe, the chances are that a little of the know-how which went into its production came from across the Atlantic.

The United States is now arguably the most varied winemaking nation on earth: from the coolest to the most sun-baked states, vines are being planted by a set of people every bit as pioneering as were the men and women who first headed westwards in search of gold. Often climatic conditions provide an almost insuperable challenge; equally often there is another factor which stands in their path. Apathy: America is not yet a wine drinking nation. Coca Cola, beer, milk – yes, but not wine. There's no tradition of cork-pulling in the average American household, and wine – even the home-grown kind – is still often thought of as dangerously 'foreign'.

And there are two powerful lobbies which are actively campaigning against wine. They make odd bedfellows, the anti-alcohol brigade and the distilling companies whose livelihood depends on harder forms of liquor, but between them they are pretty effective at deterring would-be winemakers throughout the nation.

Over the last few years there has been an easing of local laws and licencing requirements in a number of states and in a growing number, people are now – and this is revolutionary – actually permitted to buy wine at the same supermarket as their groceries. Even so, some states are still 'dry' and others still live under the bureaucratic control of a state monopoly which decides just what people can and cannot buy. Until this archaic system is finally swept away, America will never really join the community of winemaking and wine drinking countries.

THE WORDS

Boutique Winery the non-pejorative term used to describe small,

commercial wineries.

Brix the unit of measurement used to indicate the sugar quantity in grapes when they are picked, or in their juice when it is crushed. 1 degree brix corresponds to approximately 9.54 grammes of sugar in a litre of water. An average, dry, wine of around 13% alcohol will have been picked at approximately 22.5 brix.

Crackling semi-sparkling wines made either by the Champagne or Charmat method. In the latter case, the words 'bulk process' must also appear on the label.

Skin contact Wine left to macerate on its skins before fermentation has had (enjoyed?) skin contact.

Toasty the flavour of American new oak barrels, often found in white wines.

Vinted this means virtually nothing at all. The fact that a winery has 'vinted' a wine can simply indicate that it blended the contents of two vats of bought-in wine to produce a third.

Vintner-grown used by an estate which bottles its own wine to indicate that the vineyards in question may be outside the viticultural region in which the estate itself is situated. The term may also appear on wines whose grapes were grown by members of a cooperative.

US Grape Varieties

Abbreviations

A	Aurora	Grig	Grignolino
Al	Aligoté	Johan	Johannisberg Riesling
Ang	Angelica	Lab	Labrusca
Barb	Barbera	M	Muscadine
BN	Baco Noir	Mal	Malvasia
Cab Fr	Cabernet Franc	MC	Moscato Canelli
Carig	Carignan	Merl B	Merlot Blanc
Cas	Cascade	Miss	Mission
Cat	Catawba	M-T	Müller-Thurgau
Ch	Chardonnay	Mus	Muscat
Ch B	Chardonnay Blanc	Mus Ott	Muscat Ottonel
Chamb	Chambourcin	N	Niagara
Chan	Chancellor	PB	Pinot Blanc
Charb	Charbono	PG	Pinot Gris
Chel	Chelois	PM	Pinot Meunier
Chen B	Chenin Blanc	PN	Pinot Noir
Col	Colombard	PS	Petite Syrah
Con	Concord	PV	Petite Verdot
CS	Cabernet Sauvignon	Ries	Riesling
Cyn	Cynthiana	Rkat	Rkatsiteli
D	Diamond	SB	Sauvignon Blanc
Del	Delaware	Sch	Scheurebe
Dut	Dutchess	Scupp	Scuppernong
FB	Fumé Blanc	Sem	Semillon
Foch	Maréchal Foch	Sey B	Seyval Blanc
Gam	Gamay	Sey Vill	Seyval Villard
GB	Gamay Beaujolais	St	Steuben
Gewürz	Gewürztraminer	Sylv	Sylvaner
Gren	Grenache	Syr	Syrah
		Vig	Vignoles
		Vill B	Villard Blanc
		Vill N	Villard Noir
		Zin	Zinfandel

We are indebted to Wines & Vines Magazine for much of the information on grape varieties used.

ALABAMA

What might have been . . . The first vines for winemaking were planted in the early 1800s by Napoleonic soldiers redundant following their defeat by Wellington at the battle of Waterloo. Unfortunately these Cabernet vines fared badly in the climate of the southern states. Other subsequent attempts were more successful but were scuppered by Prohibition. It was only the pioneering efforts of Jim and Marianne Eddins at their Perdido Vineyard which persuaded the state to license wineries.

Perdido Winery (1979) *Mus*
All was almost lost when the owners launched this winery: Hurricane 'Frederick' ruined that year's harvest completely. Since then however Scuppernong (Muscadine) grapes are flourishing as are red, white and rosé wines from Perdido's and other Alabama vineyards. The Rosé Cou Rouge is named after the local 'Redneck Riviera'.

ARIZONA

The Rip Van Winkle factor applies to Arizona as it does to so many other states which, 100 years ago, were happily and harmlessly producing wine. If Rip had fallen asleep in 1915, the year when Arizona went 'dry', he would have had to slumber till 1980 if he was to celebrate his awakening with a locally made wine.

Recent farm winery laws have done much to arouse winemaking Van Winkles, and several wineries have opened, or are soon to do so. The major problem is to decide where and what to plant. Heat and drought are not welcomed by many grape varieties (though the Muscat can be pretty tolerant) but vines require less irrigation than cotton for example. Arizona is now America's eighth most prolific state for table grapes; it is up to the University of Arizona to direct the conversion from table to bottle . . .

Sonita Vineyard (1983) *SB*
40 *ha* of vines have been planted at this high-altitude (5000 ft) ranch.

R.W. Webb Winery (1980) *Ch/Col/Johan/CS/PS/Zin*
The first to be opened in the state since 1915.

San Dominique Winery (1981)
A small enterprise, owned by an insurance company executive.

Peter Beope Vineyard (1983)
Brand new, and still waiting for its 8 *ha* of vinifera to be ready for winemaking.

ARKANSAS

At the turn of the century, the Concord grape held sway over Arkansas, covering some 4,000 *ha*. After Prohibition, the state legislature had to cope with a surfeit of grapes and instituted a tax on wine imported from other states to encourage local winemaking. Anyone hoping for a sudden blossoming of Arkansas Mondavis must have been very disappointed: the inhabitants of the state, used to moonshine whiskey, wanted their liquor powerful. Within no time at all, everyone was tottering around on doses of 'Sneaky Pete' grape hooch, and a little later sections of the state declared themselves 'dry'. The situation is easing somewhat now, but only gradually. Recently restaurants were generously allowed to serve local wine to diners. Eleven wineries make around 40,000 *hl* of wine from 2,000 *ha* of vines.

Post Winery (1880) *Cat/Con/Del/D/M/N/St/A/Sey B/Cyn*
Matt and Betty Post have 12 children, which must help with the multiple tasks of running a half million gallon winery. Wines include 'burgundy', 'champagne', 'port' and 'sherry' of higher than usual quality.

Wiederkehr Wine Cellars (1881) *Ries/Ch/Cat/Con/Cyn/N/Vill B/Mus*
Alcuin Wiederkehr is, to Arkansas, what Konstantin Frank was to

New York. Trained at the University of California at Davis, and in Bordeaux, he and his brother have taken over the family winery and succeeded with Labrusca, vinifera and sparkling wines. Particularly good Riesling and Cynthiana.

Other wineries
Mount Bethel Winery
Mount Kessler Cellars
Ozark Mountain Smokehouse
Sax Winery

NORTH CAROLINA

If you have ever enjoyed a wine made from the Catawba grape, you owe at least a toast to North Carolina where this native grape was first discovered. Better known there now though is the Scuppernong Muscadine, a vine which bears no evident relationship to any other. Behaving more like a bush than a vine, one Scuppernong can extend its leaves and fruit across a whole vineyard, producing literally tons of fruit. The tradition of this vine here is proven by the writings of the 16th century Florentine, Giovanni da Verrazano, who found it 'growing naturally', and of Sir Walter Raleigh's men who declared 'In all the world the like abundance (of grapes) is not to be found'. Grapes grow separately rather than in closely packed bunches, and were once picked by men walking though the vineyards beating the vines with sticks. Nowadays, mechanical harvesters perform a similar task. The renaissance of North Carolina winemaking dates back to 1965 when local studies into vinegrowing began.

Château Biltmore Winery (1978)
Hybrids and vinifera, including Cabernet Sauvignon and Chardonnay are grown in the elegant surroundings of Biltmore House, one of America's most classic 'stately homes'. A Vanderbilt enterprise, this winery first used the label 'Biltmore Estate' until it was decided to adopt the name 'Château Biltmore'. The wines have a very good reputation, and a recently developed 'Champagne' has proven popular.

Deerfield Wine Cellars *Scupp*

John Dockery's Winery *Scupp*

Duplin Wine Cellars (1976) *M*
Supplied with Muscadine and hybrid grapes by a group of local farmers, Duplin makes a range of table wines and a bottle-fermented 'Champagne'.

Germanton Vineyards (1981) *M/Carlos/Noble/Foch/Chan/BN*
Five dedicated winemakers, working as a cooperative, make old-fashioned wines from hybrid and a few vinifera grapes.

SOUTH CAROLINA

Whilst other states declared themselves 'Dry' and drank themselves silly, South Carolina did the opposite. There has been little to deter the winemaker here apart from an immensely strong anti-alcohol lobby. But any state with a town called Bordeaux proudly sited on its land must have something going for it. The 1764 British government, more vinously enlightened than its 20th century counterparts, and the local state authorities, gave Huguenot immigrants 12,000 *ha* on which to plant grapes and make wine.

Foxwood Wine Cellars (1976) *M*
Previously called 'Oakview Plantations', this is a 140 *ha* vineyard and

winery, converted from grape juice making, which specializes in Labrusca and Muscadine.

Tenner Brothers Winery (1953)
The oldest winery in the state, now belonging to Canandaigua, a New York winemaking company. Wines include 'Hostess', 'Richard's Wild Rose' and 'Richard's Peach'.

Truluck Vineyards & Winery (1976) *Ch/CS*
The dentist owner and his sons have progressed from growing South Carolina's first French hybrids to making wine from recently planted vinifera.

CALIFORNIA

ALMOST A COUNTRY ALL OF ITS OWN, California boasts a number of sub-regions, each of which has its own individual climate and character. The only problem this causes is the parochialism which can afflict some of these west coasters who have so much fine wine being made in their own back yard that they seldom see the need to glance over their shoulders at what is going on elsewhere. The great Californian winemakers – Robert Mondavi has to be the finest example – have been careful not to fall into this trap; they are also making wine which justifies the high prices it commands.

CENTRAL VALLEY

Sacramento Valley
As yet, this is an area where the emphasis has been on good, simple table wine. The summer temperature is, for the most part, too high for really fine wine to be produced, and the winter frosts provide their own set of problems. Some milder microclimates are being investigated but these will prove to be exceptions to the rule.

San Joaquin
A good place to grow raisins . . . It's warm, dry and possibly better suited to the making of 'port' style wines than of stuff to drink with dinner. To produce anything fresh and fruity requires *very* skilful winemaking indeed.

R&J Cook *Ch B/SB/CS/PS/Merl B*
Produce Petite Syrah rosé.

Crystal Valley Cellars/Consentino Wine Co. *Ch/CS/FB* Sparkling wines

Delicato Vineyards

East-Side Winery
Producing various branded wines.

Ficklin Vineyard
Here the emphasis is on 'port' and Emerald Riesling.

Franzia *CS/Ch/Ch B*
The Cabernet Sauvignon has been described variously as 'delicious', 'silly' and a 'Mickey Mouse' wine. It's inexpensive, ripe-tasting and slightly sweet. Anyone who likes blackcurrant cordial should love it.

Frasinetti Winery

E & J Gallo
An enormous concern, making many generics including 'Chablis' and 'Burgundy', whose flavour would be unrecognizeable to Europeans used to the original French versions. But the Cabernet Sauvignon is of good quality, and reasonably priced.

Harbor Winery *Ch/CS/Zin*
Belonging to an English teacher, this company has no vineyards of its own, and buys in grapes from growers.

Quady Winery
Renowned for two very individual sweet wines: 'Essencia', made from California Orange Muscat, and 'Elysium' made from the Black Muscat.

Winters Winery *Zin/SB/PS/PN*
The winery here dates back to 1897 – almost prehistoric in Californian winemaking terms.

MENDOCINO & LAKE

Mendocino & Lake
Irrigation may be the answer here. Until recently the land was so dry in the hills, and the prospect of piping in water so remote, that until relatively recently almost no-one bothered to try to make fine wine. This situation has been altered completely by the use of farm ponds and the discovery of cool microclimates. Parducci is probably the best known winemaker here.

Château du Lac *Ch/Johan/CS/Zin*
White Gamay is also made.

Cresta Blanca Winery (1882) *PS/CS/Grig/Sylv/Ch/Zin* 10,000 cases
The oldest and first 'premium' winery in California, and one which won medals in Paris in 1893. It's run by a cooperative of growers, and produces varietals, dessert and sparkling wines.

Dolan Vineyard (1980) *Ch/CS* 800 cases

Edmeades Vineyard (1968) *Zin/CS/Ch/Gewürz/PN/PB/Col* 20,000 cases
California's first Eiswein was made here from Colombard; a generic white is called 'Rain Wine' because the winery is situated in the rainiest part of the state. Zinfandel is worth looking for.

Fetzer Vineyard (1968) *SB/Sém/Ries/Gewürz/GB/CS/PN/Zin/PS*
A family run winery with generally reliable wines, both under this and its Bel Arbres Label.

Frey Vineyard *Ch/Col/Gewürz/Grey Ries/SB/Johan/CS/PN/Zin*

Greenwood Ridge Vineyard (1972) *Johan/CS* 20,000 cases

Guenoc Winery *SB/CS/Ch*
Once owned by British actress, Lillie Langtry.

Handley Cellars *Ch*

Hidden Cellars Winery *SB/Johan/Gewürz/Zin/Ch*
Good late-harvest botrytized Riesling is made.

Husch Vineyard (1971) *SB/Ch/Gewürz/PN/CS* 6,500 cases
A self-taught winemaking couple, who also produce Pinot Noir rosé.

Konocti Winery (1974) *SB/Ch/Ries/CS/Zin/Gamay*
A cooperative of 30 growers, situated in 'frontier country' and
producing the above as well as white Cabernet and Pinot Noir. 60% of
the shares are owned by Parducci (qv).

Lazy Creek Vineyard *Ch/Gewürz/PN*
The husband-and-wife team declare that their objective is wines
which are 'pleasant in the mouth' rather than of a particular style.

Lower Lake Winery (1977) *FB/CS* 3,500 cases
The first post-prohibition winery in the district. White Cabernet is
made.

McDowell Valley Vineyards and Cellars (1978) *CS/Ch/SB/Col/
Gren/PS/Zin* 46,000 cases
The winery is solar powered, harvesting takes place at night . . . If
you'd like a glimpse of the future, this is where to come.

Milano Winery (1977) *CS/SB/Zin/Ch/Ries/Chen B/GB* 12,000 cases
The winery is a converted hop kiln. Chardonnay and late harvest
Riesling are particularly good.

Mountain House Winery (1980) *Ch/CS/Zin* 2,500 cases
A century ago, the present winery used to be an inn and stagecoach
stop. The Zinfandel is late harvested.

Navarro Vineyards (1975) *Gewürz/PN/Ch/Winery Ries/CS*
6,250 cases
The aim here is to make Alsace-style wines; Gewürztraminer is a
success.

Olson Vineyards *Ch/Col/SB/PS/Zin/white Gamay/white Zinfandel*

Parducci Wine Cellars (1933) *CS/Chen B/SB/Ch/PS/
Mendocino Ries/Carig/Merl/Col/Zin/PN* 250,000 cases
The first Mendocino winery, producing big reds and some sweet
whites. The Chenin is particularly good value.

Parson's Creek Winery (1979) *Ch/Gewürz/Johan* 10,000 cases

Pepperwood Springs Vineyards *PN/Ch*

Channing Rudd Cellars/Mont St Claire Vineyard (1976) 625 cases
A small but quite successful winery.

Scharffenberg Cellars (1981) *Ch/SB/PN* 4,000 cases
Brut sparkling wine is made.

**Tyland Vineyards Winery/Tijesseling Wine & Champagne
Cellars** (1979) *SB/Ch/CS/Chen B/Gewürz/GB/Zin* 6,000 cases

Whaler Wineyard *Zin*
White Zinfandel is also made.

NAPA VALLEY

Napa
Napa is Indian for 'plenty', and plenty is what there is here: plenty
good soil, plenty good weather and – in the past – plenty wealthy
investors eager for a prestigious slice of the vinous cake. The fact that
the hillsides which might make the best wine were left unplanted
whilst the flat land which, in the traditional vinegrowing regions of
Europe, would have been classified as second rate, is perhaps
unfortunate. As is the speed at which some of the first generation
wineries lost the humility which might have enabled them to learn by
foreign example. Million dollar wineries abound; wine is 'released' at
– in some cases – prices which would make the owner of a Bordeaux
classified growth blush (no easy task this) and at the time of writing,
'For Sale' boards punctuate the roadside with worrying regularity.

Apologists for the Napa and some of California's other excesses lay
the blame firmly at the door of foreign currencies which make
California's wines uncompetitive in both home and overseas markets.
What they often fail to consider is the 'Star System', based on how

well each winery has done with each of its wines in each of its
vintages, which shift producers in and out of the critical limelight like
Hollywood actors.

The hype which inevitably surrounds much of this stargazing leads
to extravagant prices being asked and paid for good, but not
superlative, wines. Opus One, the Mondavi/Rothschild co-production
is an example of a wine which, had it been launched under the name
of one of Philippe de Rothschild's several less well known châteaux,
would have commanded a fraction of its price.

Mondavi is still the man to watch though: at the head of the field at
every stage of the race, he is the man who is possibly doing most to
lead California as a whole back from its concentration on 'tasting'
wines which do well when sniffed and sipped against the European
competition – until the tasters want a glass of something to drink
with their lunch.

Acacia Winery (1979) *Ch/PN* 15,000 cases
Located in the cooler southern Carneros district, where conditions are
ideal for the Pinot Noir grape.

Alatera Vineyards *Ch/CS/Gewürz/Ries/PN*

Alta Vineyard Cellars (1878) *Ch* 2,500 cases
Refounded in 1979, the original winery was visited by Robert Louis
Stevenson on his honeymoon.

S.S. Anderson Vineyard (1971) *Ch* 2,000 cases
Still Chardonnay and sparkling wines (Cuvée de Noir and Cuvée de
Chardonney).

Artisan Wines Ltd *Ch/CS*

Beaulieu Vineyard (1900) *CS/PN/GB/Gren Rosé/Ch/SB/
Johan/Muscat de Frontignan* 250,000 cases
The famous Russian winemaker Andre Tchelistcheff, now retired,
gave this vineyard a lasting reputation for fine, classic wines,
particularly from the Cabernet Sauvignon grape.

John B. Beckett Cellars *CS/Johan*

Beringer/Los Hermanos Vineyards (1876) 150,000 cases
Over 20 different varieties. Owned by Nestlé. Table, dessert and
fortified styles are made.

Burgess Cellars (1972) *CS/Johan/PN/Ch/Zin/Ch Blanc* 30,000 cases
Owner Tom Burgess used to be a pilot.

Cakebread Cellars (1973) *Zin/SB/Ch/CS* 15,000 cases
Distinctive peppery BBQ Zinfandel is made by this family firm.

Carneros Creek Winery (1972) *Zin/CS/PN/PS/Ch/SB* 15,000 cases

Cassayre-Forni Cellars (1976) *Zin/CS/Ch Bl/CS* 6,500 cases
This winery, owned by two families, has no vineyards of its own.

Caymus Vineyards (1972) *CS/PN/Zin/LH Ries/FB/Ch* 20,000 cases
Has the same owner and winemaker as Wagner Vineyards, Charles
Wagner. Good Cabernet, and a 'partridge eye' blanc de noir from the
Pinot grape.

Chappelet Vineyard (1968 *CS/Ch/Johan/Chen B/Merl* 30,000 cases
Ultramodern winery built in a striking pryramid shape, sloping
upwards at 50°. In 1981 a jereboam of Chappelet Cabernet 1969
fetched a record price for a Californian wine – $6.000. Uses French
oak barrels to achieve a classic 'European' style.

Château Bouchaine *PN/Ch*
A new winery with an experienced winemaker, Jerry Luper, formerly
of Château Montelena.

Château Montelena (1881) *Ch/Zin/CS/Ries* 30,000 cases
The grounds of this estate, once owned by a wealthy Chinese
gentleman contain pagodas and an ornamental lake. The Château

Montelena Chardonnay beat all comers in a famous Paris tasting in 1976.

The Christian Brothers (1920s) *FB/Ch/CS/Gam/Chen B/Mus* 4m cases
Owned by a Catholic Order of Lay Brothers. When winemaker Brother Timothy is not occupied perfecting the consistent quality of the huge range of table, dessert and fortified wines, he spends time with his famous collection of corkscrews, reputedly the largest in the world.

Clos du Val Wine Co. (1973) *Zin/CS/Ch/Merl/Sem* 25,000 cases
Principal Bernard Portet, the son of the former manager of Château Lafite, is slowly placing more emphasis on his Bordeaux style Cabernets than on his heady, robust and famous Zinfandel. Portet's brother is having similar – some say greater – success at Taltarni in Australia. Both wines benefit from beautifully satirical posters by Ronald Searle.

Conn Creek Winery (1974) *CS/Ch/Zin/Ries* 20,000 cases
In partnership with Château La Mission Haut Brion, wine is made at Conn Creek by US and French 'technicians'.

Cuvaison Vineyard (1970) *CS/Ch/Zin/PS* 11,000 cases
Swiss owned, with a Swiss winemaker. 2nd label: Calistoga Vineyards.

Diamond Creek Vineyards (1972) *CS* 4,000 cases
Three different Cabernet wines from three vineyards, whose names reflect their different soils; Volcanic Hill, Gravelly Meadow, and Rock Terrace.

Domaine Chandon (1973) *PN/PB/Ch* 3,500 cases
Owned by Moët-Hennessy. Blanc de Noir and Napa Valley Brut méthode champenoise, still table wine and Panache, an aperitif. 2nd label: Fred's Friends.

Duckhorn Vineyards (1976) *Merl/CS/SB* 3,000 cases

Evenson Vineyard (1979) 800 cases
Specializes exclusively in Gewürztraminer.

Far Niente (1979) 30,000 cases
A revival of the famous pre-Prohibition name, meaning 'without a care', a sentiment manifested by its owner, whose other interest is racing Ferraris.

Forman Winery Newton Vineyards (1980) *CS/Merl/SB/Sém* 8,000 cases
Winemaker Ric Forman (formerly of Sterling Vineyards) left the winery with an already established reputation for its Sauvignon Blanc.

Franciscan Vineyards (1973) *CS/Ch/Merl/Ries/SB/Zin* 200,000 cases
German owned.

Freemark Abbey Winery (1875) *Ries/CS/PS/PN/Ch* 25,000 cases
The Chardonnay is noted, as is 'Edelwein', a botrytized riesling.

Frog's Leap Vineyards
A very new concern with a winemaker from Spring Mountain. Their Chardonnay is already attracting attention. The winery motto is 'time's fun when you're having flies' and a froggy museum is apparently planned to rival Philippe de Rothschild's in Pauillac.

Grgich Hills Cellars (1977) *Zin/Ch/Ries/Gewürz/CS/SB* 10,000 cases
The name refers to the two partners, Mike Grgich and Austin Hills, rather than to the vineyard's situation, which is actually on the valley floor. The wines have a fine reputation, particularly for Chardonnay and Gewürztraminer.

Inglenook Vineyards (1881) *CS/PN/Ch B/Ch/Gewürz/Col* 1,5m cases
One of the few vineyards that survived Prohibition intact. Has become very commercial since its takeover by Heublein.

The Jaeger Family Vineyard
Merlot only as yet.

Robert Keenan Winery (1977) *CS/Ch/PN* 7,500 cases
Now have their own vineyards, and ex-Chappelet winemaker Joe Cafaro.

Hans Kornell Cellars (1952) 100,000 cases
German owned, makes exclusively sparkling wines from Riesling, Muscat and red grapes. 7 types of méthode champenoise.

Charles Krug Winery (1861) *Ch B/Ries/P BL/Sylv/Ch/CS/Zin* 650,000 cases
The original Mondavi winery before Robert's departure to found his now-famous business. Excellent restrained whites and Cabernet.

Long Vineyards (1968) *CS/Ch/Ries/LH Ries* 1,400 cases
Zelma Long, the celebrated Simi Vineyards winemaker, owns this vineyard with her husband Robert, who makes the wine here with style.

Markham Winery (1972) *CS/Merl/Ch/Ch B/Jo Ries/GB/Mus* 20,000 cases
2nd label: Vin Mark.

Louis M. Martini Winery (1922) *CS/Ch/Gewürz/Merl/PN/FB/ Gamay Rosé/Zin/Barbera.* 350,000 cases
A wide range of table wines and sherries are made by the Martinis, who are amongst California's greatest winemakers.

Mayacamas Vineyards (1889) *Zin/Ch/LH SB/CS/PN* 5,000 cases
Refounded in 1941, makes a variety of extremely powerful wines from their mountain top vineyards. Pioneered the 'Late Harvest' style Zinfandel.

Robert Mondavi Winery (1966) *CS/SB/Sém/Ch B/Gamay/PN/PS/ LH Ries/Ch/Zin/Gamay Rosé* 500,000 cases
The single most important venture in California, and possibly the USA. The combined resources of the Mondavi family, and every new technological innovation known to man go together to produce their range of enormously successful, instantly recognizable wines. In 1979 Robert Mondavi and Baron Philippe de Rothschild joined forces, like two great nineteenth-century showmen, to bring the world their co-creation, Opus One – whose astonishingly successful launch has since been followed by diminishing box-office returns.

Monticello Vineyards *Ch/CS*

Mount Veeder Winery (1973) *CS/Ch B* 4,000 cases
Buys in Chard and Zin, wines from which are labelled MEV.

Napa Wine Cellars *CS/Ch/Zin/Gewürz*

Joseph Phelps Vineyards (1972) *LH Ries/Syrah/Ch/Gewürz/CS/ Zin/SB/PN* 50,000 cases
The owner, an ex-builder, built his own winery. His wines are amongst the finest in California, including Rieslings which have a clean, almost European quality, and first-class Chardonnay.

Pope Valley Winery (1972) *Chen B/Zin/CS/Johan/PS/SB* 12,000 cases
No vineyards. Make a Zinfandel rosé.

Quail Ridge Vineyards (1978) *Ch/CS/Col* 10,000 cases
Best known for their Chardonnay.

Raymond Vineyard and Cellars (1978) *LH Johan/Ch/CS/ Chen B/SB* 25,000 cases
A family concern. Oaky Chardonnay and Cabernet.

Round Hill Cellars (1978) *Ch/CS/Zin/Gewürz* 75,000 cases
Buy grapes from Napa, Sonoma and North Coast. Good value wines.

Rutherford Hill Winery (1972) *Johan/CS/Gewürz/PN* 100,000 cases
Not to be confused with Rutherford Ranch, Round Hill's second label.
Make a fruity Pinot Noir Nouveau. Partners also own Freemark
Abbey.

Rutherford Vintners (1976) *CS/Ch/PN/Johan/Mus* 15,000 cases
Ex-Louis M. Martini manager. Other names are Château Rutherford
and Rutherford Cellars.

St Clement Vineyards (1975) *CS/Ch/SB* 8,000 cases

Shafer Vineyards (1979) *CS/Zin/Ch/Merl/Cab Fr/PV* 9,000 cases
Owned by an ex-publishing executive from Chicago and his family.

Shown and Sons Vineyards (1971) *Ries/Ch/Chen B/CS*
Owned by Richard Shown, but no sons are visible.

Smith-Madrone Vineyard (1971) *Ries/Ch/CS/PN* 6,000 cases

Spring Mountain Vineyards (1976) *Ch/CS/SB/PN* 25,000 cases
Better known to TV viewers, and now virtually re-named, Falcon
Crest.

Stags Leap Wine Cellars (1972) *CS/Ch/Ries/PS/Merl/
GB* 20,000 cases
Owner Warren Winiarski is an ex-university lecturer in Greek. The
Carbernets are particularly good; the 1974 was a surprize winner in a
Paris tasting.

Sterling Vineyards (1964) *Ch/Chen B/Gewürz/SB/CS/Merl/Zin*
75,000 cases
The 'Disney World' winery built and formerly owned by a British
businessman, and now by the Coca Cola Company. Ric Forman built
up a certain reputation for the wines, which since his departure has
fallen off somewhat.

Stonegate Winery *Chen B/Zin/PS/CS/Ch*

Storybook Mountain Vineyards (1880s)
Planted by Adam and Jacob, the Brothers Grimm. Only Zinfandel,
notably the Estate Reserva.

Sutter Home Winery (1874) *Zin/Mus* 100,000 cases
Refounded in 1946. No vineyard. Grapes come from Amador County
and from abroad.

Trefethen Vineyards (1886) *Ch/CS/Ries/PN plus various for
blending.* 35,000 cases
Refounded in 1973 by the Trefethen Brothers, who kept the old name,
'Eshcol', for their blended wines.

Tulocay Winery (1975) *CS/PN/Zin/Ch* 2,000 cases
Specialized company making vintage wines of limited availability
from bought-in grapes.

Veedercrest Vineyard *Ch/LH Ries/Gewürz/Mus/CS/PS*
The grapes are grown at 2,000 ft in high mountain vineyards; the
wine maker is a former philosophy lecturer.

Vichon Winery (1980) *Ch/CS/Sém* 30,000 cases
A relatively new venture, possibly to be acquired by Mondavi.

Villa Mt. Eden Winery (1881) *CS/Ch/Chen B/Napa Gamay/
PN/Gewürz* 15,000 cases
Refounded in 1970. Good, dry white wines.

Vose Vineyards (1970) *CS/Ch/Zin/SB* 5,000 cases
The wine maker is the splendidly named Hamilton Vose.

Yverdan Vineyards *Ries/CS/Zin*
A small concern with only local distribution.

ZD Wines (1969) *Ch/Gewürz/PN/Zin/Merl* 10,000 cases
Has a tiny 4 acre vineyard, but buys in most of its grapes from all over
the place.

CALIFORNIA NORTH CENTRAL COAST

Monterey
Starting from right at the back of the field, Monterey is now far more
heavily planted in vines than the better known Napa. Whilst much of
the wine made here is still of jug rather than boutique quality, Paul
Masson with its Pinnacle Selection and Chalone with its Chardonnay
have proven than really first class varietal wines can be made here –
as the Gurus of the University of California at Davis predicted well
over 20 years ago.

Santa Clara/San Benito/Santa Barbara
Santa Clara county boasts the presdence of the huge wineries of Paul
Masson and Almaden, as well of that of Ridge, one of California's
Rolls Royce boutiques. The region was planted with grapes by the
Spaniards when they first settled here; its finest vineyards are those
sited at the highest altitudes.

Ahlgren Vineyard (1976) *Ch/CS/Sém/Zin*
Creditable Cabernet.

Almaden (1852) *CS/PN/Gewürz + 26 others varieties.*
It would be accurate to call Almaden 'big'. It would also be an
understatement: this is America's biggest quality-oriented winery,
producing literally dozens of generic and quite a few varietal wines.
None are superlative; none are less than adequate.

Bargetto Winery (1933) *Ch/Johan/CS*
A family-run winery, buying in grapes from other vineyards. The first
public tasting room and cellar tour in the region.

David Bruce Winery Inc (1964) *Ch/Johan/CS/PN/PS/Zin*
Blockbuster wines – the way California used to make them ...

Calera Wine Company (1975) *PN/Zin*
An ambitious winery aiming to make a variety of Burgundian-style
Pinot Noir and distinctive Zinfandels, but also producing an
extraordinary botrytized Zinfandel.

Chalone Vineyard (1969) *French Colombard/Ch/PN/CS/Chen B/PB*
Another pioneering winery ambitious to produce Burgundian-style
wines, and with a track record which now – at least to its fans –
warrants higher-than-Burgundy prices being paid for the wines. The
fact that many of the vines were planted just after World War I must
play a part in the wines' quality. A Californian superstar.

Château Julien (1983) *Ch*
The winery belongs to a New Jersey petroleum executive; its Private
Reserve Chardonnay is good, big wine.

Cloudstone Vineyards *Zin/CS/Ch*

Congress Springs Vineyards (1892) *Sém/SB/Zin/CS/Chen B/PB/PN*
Originally founded in 1892, this small winery belongs to two brothers
and a partner. Good Sauvignons.

Crescini Wines (1980)
A tiny winery making various varietals.

Cygnet Cellars (1977) *Zin*
No vineyards are owned, but an extraordinary late harvest Zinfandel.
If you like red wine as strong as sherry (17%), this is for you.

Devlin Wine Cellars (1978) *Ch/SB/CS/Zin*
No vineyards are owned here either, but there's some reasonable
Chardonnay.

Durney Vineyard (1968) *Johan/Chen B/CS/GB*
With 30 *ha* of steep vineyards in the Carmel Valley, the speciality
here is Cabernet Sauvignon.

Enz Vineyards (1973) *Zin/Pinot St George*
Although the winery's young, the 12 *ha* vineyard is 100 years old and

the Pinot St George planted in it is the oldest in California.

Felton-Empire Vineyards (1976) *Gewürz/Johan/Chen B/PN/CS/Zin*
With 18 *ha* of vines, this is one of California's best producers of late-harvest Riesling.

Fortino Winery (1970)
20 varietals are made here, but Zinfandel is the house speciality.

Frick Winery (1977) *Ch/PN/PS/Zin*
With what must be some of the silliest wording ever to appear on a bottle, blazened on its back label, this winery still produces some fine wine – particularly a truly first-class Chardonnay.

Gemello Winery (1934) *Ch/PN/Chen B/CS/GB/PS/Zin*
There are no vineyards, but some consistent white Pinot Noir and Zinfandel.

Grover Gulch Winery (1979) *CS/Carig/PS/Zin*
A very small winery, and one of the few to use the southern French Carignan.

Emilio Guglielmo Winery (1925)
Generics sell with 'Cavalcade' and 'Emile's' labels; varietals under the name of 'Mount Madonna'. This is a jug wine producer which is upgrading its quality.

Hecker Pass Winery (1972) *Carig/PS/CS/Gren/
French Colombard/Zin*
Apart from 'Chablis' and 'sherry', Frances Fortino the winemaker produces several varietals including Ruby Cabernet.

Jekel Vineyard (1978) *Ch/CS/Ries/PN*
With over 50 *ha* of vines, and excellent Cabernet, Riesling and Chardonnay, Jekel is one of the most reliable names in California. Is this the only winery in the world to be run by identical twins – Bill and Gus Jekel? Bill makes films when he is not making wine.

Kathryn Kennedy Winery *(1973)* *PN/CS*
Wines are sold under this, and the 'Saratoga Cellars' label. Try the pink Pinot Noir.

Kirigin Cellars (1976)
Nikola Kirigin Chargin came to California from Croatia, bringing his European origins to bear on a selection of varietal wines.

Thomas Kruse Winery (1971) *PN/Ch/CS/Grig/Zin/
French Colombard/SB*
Both Pinot Noir and Grignolino are used for rosé.

Live Oaks Winery (1912)
When everyone else is busy making Chardonnay and Cabernet, this will be the place to look for 'Burgundy' and 'Chablis'.

Llords and Elwood Winery (1955) *Ch/Johan/CS/PN*
The late-harvest Riesling is good – one of the first to be produced in California; the Cabernet is pink, and there is also 'port', 'sherry' (including 'Great Day Dry') and 'Champagne'.

Paul Masson Champagne and Wine Cellars (1852)
Sylv/Gewürz/Ch/Zin/Johan etc
Apart from the countless number of carafes, the contents of which must have been enjoyed throughout the world, Paul Masson also produces a number of excellent varietals under its 'Pinnacles Selection' label, 'port' and a great deal of 'Champagne'. Since 1942, the winery has belonged to Seagrams, and it is now the principal exporter of US premium wines.

McHenry Vineyards (1980) *PN/Ch*
A small winery, concentrating on Burgundy-style varietals.

Monterey Peninsula Winery (1974) *Zin/French
Colombard/CS/PN/PB/Barb/PS*
There are no vineyards but some pretty individual red wines, of which

the Zinfandels are probably the most interesting.

The Monterey Vineyard (1973) *Ries/SB/Gewürz/Sylv/PN/GB/Zin*
The winemakers here apparently indicate when you should drink various of their wines, calling them 'Thanksgiving Riesling' and 'December Zinfandel'. In fact, however, both names refer to the late harvesting which is a speciality. The whites are all worth trying, as is the Zinfandel. 'Taylor California Cellars' generic blends are also made here.

Mount Eden Vineyards (1975) *Zin/CS/PN/Ch*
Martin Ray, the previous owner of the land on which this winery is based, used to make what he reckoned to be the 'only fine wines in America'. The wine is now made by Richard Graff of Chalone who seems to be more successful with Chardonnay than with his other varietals.

The Mountain View Winery (1980) *Ch/Zin*
A small winery, concentrating on two varietals.

Nicasio Winery (1952)
Electronic engineer, Dan Wheeler has run his winery as a hobby, and for the delectation of his mail-order customers for over 30 years. Amongst the wines are generics and 'Champagne'.

Novitiate Wines (1888) *Ries/Mal/Chen B/PN/Black Mus*
Brother Lee Williams makes good dry 'sherry' and sweet muscat.

SAN FRANCISCO BAY AREA

Livermore Valley
Strong soil and a warm temperature have always made this a suitable region in which to make good, full-bodied wines rather than light, delicate ones. Skilful winemaking has enabled firms such as Wente to produce excellent Chardonnay however, and other firms are beginning to enjoy similar success.

Richard Carey Winery *Zin/FB/Gewürz*
Late-harvest Gewürztraminer is successful.

Concannon Vineyards (1883) *FB/White Ries/PS/Zin/Rkat*
Started by an Irishman, to make altar wine, this winery now belongs to a wealthy Chilean family. Here the international flavour is also evident in the first planting of Petite Syrah in California, a pink Zinfandel which is dubbed 'rosé', rather than 'white' as is more usual, and the Rkatsiteli, a characterful white import from Russia.

Cronin Vineyards (1980) *Ch/PN/Zin/CS*

Diablo Vista Winery (1977) *CS/Ch/Zin*
Collectors' item wines made by Leon Borowswki from bought-in grapes.

Fenestra Winery *CS/SB/Zin/PS/Ch*

Fretter Wine Cellars (1977) *PN/SB/Sem/Merl/Gam/Ch/CS*
Gamay Rosé is an unusual wine, made here with some success.

Grand Pacific Vineyard Co (1975) *Ch/Merl/CS*

Kalin Cellars (1977) *Merl/CS/PN/Ries/Sem/Ch*
A tiny winery, with no vineyards, but wonderful Chardonnay.

Livermore Valley Cellars (1978) *PB/Grey Ries/French Col/
Golden Chasselas*

Montclair Winery (1975) *CS/French Col/Zin/PS*

J.W. Morris (1977) *CS/Ang/SB/Ch/Zin/PN/PS*
The old name described this winery well: 'J.W. Morris Port Works'. Of course, it might have been a pretty effective advertising slogan too. Nowadays, port-style wines are still made, along with Amador Angelica for those who find ruby port a trifle dry.

Obester Winery (1977) *SB/CS/Johan*

Pacheco Ranch Winery (1979) *Zin/Chen B/Gewürz/Johan/Mus*
Also known – rather less romatically – as 'R.M.S. Cellars', this winery makes reasonable Cabernet rosé and some good dessert wines.

Rosenblum Cellars (1978) *Ch/CS/Gewürz/Zin/PS/Chen B/Johan*

Stony Ridge Winery (1887) *Ch/Sém/SB/Zin/Barb/PN/Cab*
This winery was refounded in 1975.

Villa Armando (1962)
If you like your red wines as sweet as some people like their whites – this is the place to find them.

Weibel Champagne Vineyards (1945) *Ch/Johan/PN/CS/Grey Ries/Chen B/Zin*
What's in a name? If the idea of 'Sparkling Green Hungarian', 'Crackling Rosé' and 'Crackling Duck' doesn't turn you on, remember that, in the 'good old days', wines like these were all the rage. Nowadays, the sparklers are more modestly titled, as are 'port', 'sherry' and several table wines.

Wente Bros (1883) *Ries/Ch/PB/SB/PN/Grey Ries/Sém*
A family dynasty has founded and run this winery for a century – the fourth generation is in charge now – and has built it up to around 350 *ha*, with a further 250 *ha* recently planted. Best wines are the Semillon, Chardonnay and late-harvest Riesling.

Woodbury Winery (1977) *PN/Cab/Zin/PS*
Russell Woodbury, who also acts as a 'négociant' concentrates on making a range of 'ports' of consistently high quality.

Woodside Vineyards (1960) *CS/Zin/PN/Ch*

SIERRA FOOTHILLS

Amador Foothill Winery (1980) *White Zin/Zin/Ch/Bl/CS/SB*
In the USA there is a well thought of regular publication called the 'Underground Newsletter'. This is the 'Underground Winery', dug into the earth to keep it cool.

Amador Winery
This is known for its blends: 'Sutters Gold' and 'Mountain Jubilee'.

Argonaut Winery (1976) *Zin/Barb*

Baldinelli (1972) *White Zin/Zin Rosé/Zin/CS*

Beau Val Wines (1979) *Zin/Barb/SB*
The speciality here is oak-aged Zinfandel which shows more class than is usually encountered with wines from this grape.

Boeger Winery (1973) *CS/Zin/Johan/Ch/SB/Chen B*
Sited in the heart of the Gold Rush country, the two well-known blends here are 'Sierra Blanc' and 'Hangtown Red'.

Montevina Wines (1970) *Zin/Barb/Ch/SB/Ruby Cab.*
The Alexander Valley's leading producer of Zinfandel (red and white) and well-regarded Sauvignon.

Nevada City Winery *PN/CS/Zin/Charb/Ries/Ch*

Santino Wines (1979) *Zin/CS/SB*
Up-and-coming winery, and one of the few to succeed with a 'white' Zinfandel.

Shenandoah Vineyards (1977) *Zin/CS/Chen B/Miss/Mus* 6,500 cases

Sierra Vista Winery (1977) *Zin/CS/Chen B/Chard/ SB/FB/PS* 2,000 cases

Stevenot Vineyards (1978) *Chen B/Zin B/PS/Ch/Ries* 11,000 cases

Wine made by Julia Iantasco.

Stoneridge (1975) *Zin/Zin B/Ruby Cab/CS* 1,000 cases.

Story Winery & Vineyards *Zin/CS*
Zinfandel is the principal grape.

SONOMA COUNTY

Sonoma County
Less well known outside California than the Napa Valley, this is nonetheless the region where you will find many of the state's very best wines. The county is subdivided between Sonoma Valley, Russian River Valley and Santa Rosa. Dry Creek and Alexander Valley are also generally reckoned to enjoy two of California's best microclimates. Sonoma Valley was dubbed 'Valley of the Moon' by Jack London when he lived here.

Alexander Valley Vineyards (1964) *Ch/Johan/Gewürz/Chen B/CS/PN/Zin*
One of the oldest wineries in the Alexander Valley, and certainly one of the best, with particularly fine Chardonnay.

Balyerne Winery & Vineyards (1980) *Gewürz/Ch/SB/Johan/Sch/CS/Zin*
Growing Scheurebe in California shows individuality.

Davis Bynum (1975) *FB/Gewürz/Ch/PN/Zin/PS*

The California Wine Company (1937) *Ch/CS/Johan/SB/French Col/Grey Ries/PN/Zin*
Using names such as Bandiera Wines, Potter Valley and Arroyo Sonoma, this firm was refounded in 1975 as Bandiera Winery.

Cambiaso Winery and Vineyards (1934)
Previously restricted to basic generics, Cambiaso is now owned by Thais.

Clos du Bois (1976) *CS/Ch/PN/Merl/Gewürz/Chen B/Ries*
The vineyard came first (the wine was made at Souverain) and the winery followed. Botrytized Gewürztraminer can be excellent, but the European-style Chardonnay and Cabernet Sauvignon are the real success stories.

Cordtz Brothers Cellars (1906) *Ch/SB/Gewürz/CS/Zin*
This winery was refounded in 1980.

Dehlinger Winery (1975) *CS/Ch/Zin/PN*
Small, but up-and-coming and situated at Sebastopol in the Russian River Valley.

Deloach Vineyards (1979) *FB/Ch/CS/Zin/Gewürz/PN*
Another young Russian River Valley winery with well-made wines. The Pinot Noir and 'white' Zinfandel are worth looking out for.

Diamond Oaks Vineyard *CS/FB/Ch*
Also several blends, red and white.

Domaine Laurier (1978) *Ch/Johan/SB/Zin/PN*
Good Burgundy-style Pinot Noir and Chardonnay.

Donna Maria Vineyards (1974) *Ch/CS/Gewürz/PN*
The Chardonnay is the wine to look for here.

Dry Creek Vineyard (1972) *Chen B/FB/Zin/Ch/GB/CS/Merl/S/Gewürz*
One of California's most quality-consistent 'boutiques' with a dazzling Fumé Blanc and an excellent pink Cabernet.

Georges Duboeuf & Son Ltd
The great Beaujolais négociant's toe-in-the-Californian-water.

Fenton Acres Winery (1979) *CS/Ch/PN*
A partnership of three winemakers.

Field Stone Winery (1976) *CS/Chen B/PS/Gewürz/Johan*

With its cellars dug into the ground like a French 'Chai', this winery makes a range of good wines, including pink Cabernet.

Fisher Vineyards (1974) *Ch/CS*

Foppiano Vineyards *CS/PS/FB/Zin*
Good quality 'White Burgundy' would sell well even without its appropriated name.

Chris A. Fredson Winery (1885) *Zin*

Geyser Peak Winery (1880) *CS/PN/Ch/Gewürz/FB*
One of California's oldest operating wineries, now belonging to Schlitz Brewery.

Hop Kiln Winery and Griffen Vineyard (1975) *Zin/French Col/White Ries/PS/Gewürz*
A Russian River Valley winery with some beefy, late-picked red wines – for those who like the style.

Horizon Winery (1977)
A tiny winery specializing in Zinfandel.

Hultgren & Samperton (1978) *Ch/CS/Gam/PS*

Iron Horse Vineyards (1979) *CS/PN/Ch/SB*
The effect of the Pacific Ocean fog on the grapes is thought to be responsible for first-class Cabernet and Pinot Noir. Pinot Noir Rosé and sparkling Blanc de Blancs Brut and Rosé are also produced. Latest arrival is 'Tin Pony', the winery's 'second wine'.

Italian Swiss Colony *CS*
Apart from the Cabernet, the concentration here is on jug wines and 'Chablis'.

Johnson's Alexander Valley Wines (1975)
PN/Ch/Gewürz/Zin/CS/Johan
Apart from the above listed, and a white Pinot Noir, this winery will be of interest to anyone who likes 1924 theatre pipe organ music (there are monthly concerts) and pear wine (of which a fair quantity is made).

Jordan Vineyard and Winery (1972) *Ch/CS/Merl*
The winery was built in 1976, a French-style château, in which ex-Château Lafite barrels are used to mature Bordeaux-style wine. The presence of Merlot in the blend seems to play an important part. When you're an oil millionaire/wine freak, like Tom Jordan, you can afford to aim for the very best.

F. Korbel & Bros Champagne Cellars (1882) *Ch/Johan/SB/Chen B/ Gewürz/Zin/PN/CS*
Don't confuse this century-old company with the far younger Kornell Champagne Cellars. This firm was founded by three brothers from Bohemia; here, the main effort goes into creditable fizz, but there are table wines and brandy too.

Lambert Bridge (1975) *CS/Ch*
Doubly named: after the family who own it, and the bridge of the same name next door, this is a source of first-class Chardonnay.

Landmark Vineyards (1974) *Ch/Johan/Gewürz/CS/PN/Zin*
William Mabry III having retired from the air force and architecture, took up winemaking.

Lytton Springs Winery (1977) *Zin*
If you like Zinfandel with all its animal, rubbery, steely character, you may be as impressed by this as the critics. Old vines – rare in California – play their part.

Marietta Cellars *CS/Zin*

Mark West Vineyards *Ch/PN/CS/Ries/Gewürz*
Burgundy is the goal which the Ellises who make the wine are aiming for. The Chardonnay used to be over-oaked, but is less so now; white Pinot Noir is another novelty.

Martini & Prati Wines Inc (1951) *CS and others*
Don't confuse with Louis Martini. This is predominantly a bulk, and generic wine producer.

Mill Creek Vineyards (1974) *Ch/CS/GB/Gewürz/Merl/PN*
Pink Cabernet is pleasant, and other wines reliable.

Pastori Winery *CS/Zin*

Pat Paulsen Vineyard (1980)
Ex-comedian Paulsen ran for President – as a joke – but takes his winery a touch more seriously, making good Cabernet and Sauvignon Blanc.

Pedroncelli Winery (1904) *CS/Ch/Zin/Ries/Gewürz/Gam*
A 'generic' producer which has turned varietal. Zinfandel rosé is successful.

Piper-Sonoma Cellars (1980)
With the impetus from Piper Heidsieck, and regular supervision from Champenois winemaker Michel Lacroix, this is arguably the source of some of California's finest fizz. Not surprisingly, the word 'Champagne' does not feature on labels.

Pommeraie Vineyards (1979) *CS/Ch*

Preston Vineyards (1975) *PN/Chen B/SB/Zin/Gam*
The Sauvignon is probably the wine to look for here.

A. Rafenelli Winery (1974) *Zin/Gam/CS*
Up-and-coming, but little-known.

River Oaks Vineyards
Generic and varietal wines, made at the Clos du Bois.

River Road Vineyards (1977) *Ch/FB/Johan/Zin*

Sausal Winery (1973) *Ch/CS/Gam/PN/Zin*
Good Zinfandel and interesting 'white' Cabernet.

Simi Winery (1876) *CS/PN/Zin/Gewürz/Ch/Ries/Chen Bl/GB/Merl*
Founded by two Italian brothers, and now the property of Moët-Hennessy, this is the source of good wines made of almost all the varieties used. The Alexander Valley vineyards may help to give the wines a 'European' style; winemaker Zelma Long has something to do with it too.

Soda Rock Winery (1980) *Chen B/Johan/CS/Zin*
Owned by a family of Hungarian immigrants named Tomka, this is the home of 'Charlie's Country Red', a label which does not refer to the politics of the Tomka's homeland.

Sonoma Vineyards/Windsor Winery (1959) *Ch/Johan/Zin/CS*
Rodney Strong, the owner, was once a ballet dancer; the company used to sell its wine exclusively by mail.

Sotoyome Winery *CS/PS/Zin/Ch*
The owner-winemaker is an ex-professor of history.

Souverain Cellars (1973) *Ries/Ch/Merl/CS/PN/GB/Col/MC*
Originally built by the Pillsbury flour-milling conglomerate, the winery now belongs to the North Coast Grape Growers Association, who also use the name 'North Coast'. Pink Pinot can be good, also the Moscato and Chardonnay.

Robert Stemmler Winery (1977) *Ch/SB/Ries/CS*
A tiny operation, making rather Germanic-tasting whites.

Joseph Swan Vineyards (1969) *Zin/Gam/PN/Ch*
A small, family-owned estate, where the speciality is Zinfandel.

Toyon Winery and Vineyards (1972) *Gewürz/Ch/CS/Zin*

Trentadue Winery and Vineyards (1969) *CS/Zin/GB*

Vina Vista Vineyards (1971) *CS/Johan/Ch/PS/Zin*

William Wheeler Winery CS/Ch
Recently established, and charging premium prices.

Willowside Vineyards (1970) Ch/Gewürz/Zin/PN

Stephen Zellerbach Vineyards CS/Ch

SONOMA VALLEY

Adler Fels (1980) Johan/Gewürz/CS/Ch
Small, recently established winery producing less than 5,000 cases.

Buena Vista Winery and Vineyards (1857)
CS/PN/Zin/Ch/Gewürz/FB
This claims to be the oldest 'premium' winery in California, and its
place in history is certainly ensured by the fact that it was built by
Agoston Haraszthy, without whom California might still be better
known for its oranges and avocados than for its wines. Today, Buena
Vista belongs to Racke, a German beverage company. Vineyards are
in the cool Carneros district. Good Zinfandel.

Château St Jean Inc (1974) Ch/SB/Johan/Gewürz/PB/Mus/PN/CS
If you really want to seem pretentious, refer to this in your best
French accent . . . The Jean here is not le Baptiste, but the wife of one
of the owning partners. Winemaker Richard Arrowood vinifies the
output of each vineyard separately, so sometimes produces as many as
seven different Chardonnays. Specializes in white wines (including
one from Pinot Noir, botrytized Riesling and Moscato Canelli) and has
now started to make méthode champenoise sparklers.

H. Coturri & Sons Ltd (1979) CS/Ch/Gewürz

Fisher Vineyards (1974) CS/Ch

Glen Ellen Winery & Vineyard (1982) CS/Merl/Zin
A very small winery with highly situated vineyards 1,500 ft up in the
Mayacamas mountains, named after the place rather than a person.

Grand Cru Vineyards (1886) Gewürz/Chen B/Ries/PN/Zin
Excellent late-picked Gewürztraminer is the speciality at this winery,
which was refounded in 1971.

Gundlach-Bundschu Winery (1856)
Ries/CS/PN/Johan/Ch/Merl/Zin
Possibly the oldest Californian winery to remain in the hands of one
family. The winery was refounded in 1973 and now belongs to the
great-great-grandson of the founder. Any resemblance to a dairy is
purely intentional: one of the partners used his experience in that
field when installing the stainless steel tanks. Zinfandel and late-
harvest Riesling are good.

Hacienda Wine Cellars (1973) Gewürz/Ch/Ries/CS/Zin/PN
Frank Bartholomew who owned Buena Vista, kept these 20 ha back
when he sold that winery. Winemaker Steve MacRostie is someone to
watch.

Hanzell Vineyards (1956) PN/Ch
Ex-ambassador James D. Zellerbach had the ambition to recreate a
slice of Burgundy, as well as its wines. The winery looks a little like a
scaled down Château du Clos de Vougeot and both wines are matured
in Burgundian oak barrels.

J.J. Haraszthy & Son (1978) Ch/Johan/Gewürz/Zin
Keeping the family name going, Val Haraszthy is making good-
quality wine.

Haywood Nursery (1980) Ch/CS/Zin/Johan

Kenwood Vineyards (1906 – as Pagani Bros) Ch/Chen B/Gewürz/
SB/CS/PN/PS/Zin
Renamed in 1970, specialities here include pink Cabernet and Pinot.

Kistler Vineyards (1978) Ch/CS/PN
A very young winemaker, producing very highly regarded wines.

La Crema Vinera (1979) Ch/PN
A small, up-and-coming winery aiming for Burgundy-style wines. The
single vineyard Pinot Noir is a success.

Laurel Glen Vineyard (1980) CS
Concentrating on good Cabernet.

Matanzas Creek Winery (1977) CS/Ch/Gewürz/PN/Merl/PB
Only a sexist would bother to mention that this winery is owned by a
woman, and boasts a woman winemaker. So we won't. We shall
however, mention really first-class Chardonnay and Pinot Blanc.

Ravenswood (1976) CS/Zin/Merl
No vineyards, but some good wines.

St Frances Winery (1979) Ch/Ries/PN/Merl/Gewürz
All the wine comes from own vineyards.

Sebastiani Vineyards (1825) CS/GB/White Ries/PN/Ch
Ever heard of 'Partridge Eye' rosé? Well here one can find an 'Eye of
the Swan' Pinot as well as a number of other generics and varietals.
Still family run.

Valley of the Moon Winery (1944) PN/Sém/French Col/Zin
Generic and varietal wines.

SOUTH-CENTRAL COAST

San Luis Obispo – Santa Barbara
Well established, but only now in the limelight, this is the area to
launch a winery if you want to be noticed – and to make good wine.
The sea breeze provides the cool air which grapes require if they are
not to produce big, blowsy wine. Proof of the potential of these two
counties lies in the success of a few of the Pinot Noir wines made here.

Ballard Canyon Winery (1978) CS/Johan/CS/Ch 6,000 cases
The winemaker's name is Robert Indelicato.

The Brander Vineyard (1979) Ch/SB 3,000 cases
The Sauvignon is particularly good.

Caparone Winery (1980) CS/Merl/Nebb/Zin 3,000 cases
One of the small number of wineries to use the Italian Nebbiolo grape.

J. Carey Cellars (1977) Ch/CS/Merl/SB 4,000 cases
The Cabernet shows promise.

Chamisal Vineyard (1980) CS/Ch 1,600 cases
Some sparkling wines are now being made.

Creston Manor Vineyards & Winery SB/Ch/CS

Edna Valley Vineyard (1979) Ch/PN 20,000 cases
There is no Edna, only the valley. Quality grapes are supplied to other
wineries.

Estrella River Winery (1977) Ch/SB/Chen B/Mus/Johan/CS/
Zin Barb/Syr 66,000 cases
One of California's most promising young wineries.

The Firestone Winery (1973) CS/PN/Merl/SB/Gewürz/Ch/Ries
73,000 cases
The first winery in the Santa Ynez area, it owes its foundation to the
tyre company fortune. More recently, there has been investment by
the Japanese Suntory company. Even if its wines weren't good –
which they are – the winery will always be regarded fondly by the
would-be wit: when guests query a vintage and ask if it's a good year,
the answer 'No, it's a Firestone' has been known to raise a smile. But
not many. The Pinot Noir is well regarded, but the Merlot (very good
value) Chardonnay and late-harvest Riesling are all notable. Rosé
Cabernet and Pinot Noir are made.

Hale Cellars (1972) 3,000 cases
Formerly the Los Alamos Winery, this is run by a lawyer and his wife.

HMR (Hoffman Mountain Ranch) *Zin/CS/Ch/PN*
Until recently this was owned by a Tchelistcheff-advised ex-heart specialist. Chardonnay and Pinot are 'powerful', Zinfandel good.

Lawrence Winery (1977) *Ch/Ries* 300,000 cases
16 different varieties of wine are sold, in large quantity. None is worth a large detour.

Los Vineros Winery *PB/Gewürz/SB/CS/PN*
White Cabernet is made here.

Martin Brothers Winery *Ch/Chen B/SB/Zin*

Mastantuono Winery (1980) *Zin/Gren/PN/Carig* 2,500 cases
Intense Zinfandel.

Pesenti Winery (1934) *Zin/CS* 33,000 cases
Variety is derived from making white and rosé versions of both grapes.

Ranchita Oaks Winery (1979) *CS/PS/Zin/Ch* 4,000 cases

Rancho Sisquoc Winery (1978) *CS/PS/Zin/Ch* 2,000 cases
Part of the massive (14,000 *ha*) James Flood Ranch.

Ross-Kellerei Winery (1980) *Ch/Chen B/SB/Johan/CS/PN* 3,500 cases
Grapes are bought in; wine is sold under brand names, such as Zaca Creek, San Carlos de Sonata. White Cabernet and Pinot Noir are made.

Sanford & Benedict Vineyards (1975) *PN/Ch/CS/Merl* 10,000 cases
A television executive and a biology professor are making very good Chardonnay and Pinot Noir.

Sanford Winery *Ch/PN/SB/PN*
Pinot is used to make Vin Gris.

Santa Barbara Winery (1962) (Chen B/Ries/Zin/CS 10,000 cases
Apart from the above varietals, 'sherry' is made.

Santa Ynez Valley Winery (1969) *SB/White Ries/Ch/Gewürz/ CS/Merl* 10,000 cases
A converted dairy barn – the winery belongs to three families; the winemaker trained at U.C. Davis. Whites, particularly Sauvignon, but also white Cabernet are particularly good.

Tobias Vineyards *PS/Zin*
White Zinfandel is made too.

Vega Vineyards Winery (1979) *White Ries/Gewürz/Ch/PN/CS/PS* 4,000 cases

Watson Vineyards *Ch/Johan/PN*

York Mountain Winery (1882) *Ch/PN/CS/Zin/Chen B/Ries* 3,500 cases
Owned by respected oenologist Max Goldman since early 1970's when it was bought from a New York family.

Zaca Mesa Winery (1978) *CS/Ch/PN/Ries/Zin/SB*
Pioneers in the Santa Ynez Valley, the makers here are using ungrafted vines. Results so far have been inconsistent but promising.

SOUTH COAST

This is basically desert land, ideally suited for growing Muscat grapes, less so for the varieties you need for good light drier wines. As elsewhere however, individual microclimates have been found which are already producing some happy surprises.

(Los Angeles, San Diego, San Bernardino, Riverside).

Ahern Winery (1978) *Zin/SB/Ch/PN* 3,500 cases

Bernardo Winery (1889) *Zin/Mus/Tokay/Carig/Miss/Rosa Peru* 4,000 cases
Ross Rizzo is the 5th generation of winemakers.

Brookside Vineyard Co. (1916) *Ch/Chen B/Col/Emerald Ries/ Mal Bianco/SB/Johan/CS/GB/Gren/PS/Zin* 835,000 cases
Formerly in Monterey, this is one of the oldest firms in California. Over 100 different varietals and blends are produced and sold to Japan, S. America and Canada. The Assumption Abbey label is also used.

Callaway Vineyard & Winery (1974) *Ch/Chen B/White Ries/SB/ Grey Ries/Col/PN/Zin* 75,000 cases
Situated in the desert, this is the most southerly 'serious' vineyard in California: it has been called 'the Miracle of Tennecula'. Possibly more money has been poured into this than any other winery in the history of US winemaking. With the assistance of Karl Werner of Schloss Vollrads in the Rheingau, Germanic whites are being made to balance the dark powerful southern-style reds. Late harvest, botrytized Chenin Blanc ('Sweet Nancy') is particularly notable.

Cilurzo & Piconi Vineyard & Winery (1978) *SB/Chen B/CS/PS/ PN/Ch/GB* 4,000 cases

Donatoni Winery *Ch/CS*

Ferrara Winery *SB/Johan/Zin*

J. Filippi Vintage Co. (1922) *Ch/Chen B/Col/Emerald Ries/Gewürz/ Green Hungarian/Johan/CS/GB/PS/Zin* 200,000 cases
Special 'natural' wines are made, as well as dessert and other table wines.

Filsinger Vineyards & Winery (1980) *Ch/FB/Emerald Ries/Zin/ PS/Gam* 8,000 cases

Galleano Winery (1927) *Miss/Zin* 84,000 cases
White Zinfandel is made. The emphasis here is on generic wines.

Glen Oak Hills Winery (1978) 650 cases
Wines are labelled 'Hugo's Cellar', after the winemaker.

Hart Winery (1980) *GB/CS/Merl/SB/PS* 1,700 cases

McLester (1979) *CS/Zin* 1,250 cases
Wines are from named vineyards.

Mount Palomar (1975) *SB/Chen B/Johan/PS/CS* 12,500 cases
Several branded wines are made. Also 'sherry'.

Rancho de Philo (1975)
A few hundred cases of 'cream sherry' are made at this 16-year-old hobby of the ex-president of the Brookside Winery.

San Pasqual Vineyards (1974) *PS/SB/Sém/Chen B/MC/Gam* 25,000 cases
The owners are a judge and a lawyer. Gamay is a speciality.

COLORADO

Winemaking is really in its infancy here, with a single winery which has been going for less than five years.

Colorado Mountain Vineyards & Winery (1978)
Ch/Chen B/Col/Sém/Johan/CS/GB/Zin
Wines are made from all of the above varieties as well as Pinot Noir 'white', Zinfandel 'white' and Cabernet Sauvignon Rosé. Most of the grapes are imported from California.

CONNECTICUT

The current social climate treats tobacco a little less kindly than it used to, and the tobacco fields of Connecticut are a less than exciting financial proposition. For this, and other, reasons, the 1978 farm winery law has done much to encourage the growing of grapes.

Clarke Vineyard (1983) *Ch/Johan/PN/Vidal/Foch/Sey B*

Haight Vineyard (1978) *Ch/Johan/Foch*
Wines have won awards at tastings. Sparkling wine is made too.

Hamlet Hill (1980) *Johan/Foch/Sey B*
Following training from New York winemaker Hermann Wiemer, Dr Howard Bursen is making several blends and now turning his hand to 'Champagne'.

Saint Hilary Vineyard
Peter Kerensky, an ex-chef, prefers to concentrate on making good Labrusca than on trying to produce vinifera like some of his neighbours.

Stonecrop Vineyards (1980) *Foch/Sey B/Vidal*
Award winning Foch.

DELAWARE

Despite having the same name as one of America's own, truly 'foxy' grapes, Delaware has only one winery.

Northminster Winery *Johan*
Richard Becker owns this, the only winery in the state.

FLORIDA

You cannot make wine from oranges. And there are those who say that you shouldn't make it from the Florida Scuppernong grape either. This indigenous variety, also known as the Muscadine, has been used to make wine since the 16th century, when the French Huguenots are reported as having been active vintners. More recently, other quaintly named varieties of grape have been planted, amongst them, the Florida H 18–37, the Stover and the Welder. These last two may do more to establish the acceptability of wine to rednecks than Madison Avenue ever could.

Alaqua Vineyard (1980) *M/Welder*
With 4 *ha* of vines this winery produces red and white wines. The owner's daughter trained in oenology at Lafayette.

Black Creek Farm Winery (1984)
A brand new commercial venture launched by two former home winemakers.

Chautauqua Indian Hill Vineyard (1980)
The newly-built winery (1985) belongs to an orthopaedic surgeon.

Florida Heritage Winery (1981)
Here the Welder is used to make dry and semi-dry red and white wines.

Grosz's Vineyard
Esmond and Malinda Grosz and meteorologist Dan Mills have achieved what many might consider the impossible: they have used the Stover to make sparkling wine not unlike the stuff they make in Europe.

Lafayette Vineyard and Winery *M/Stover/Florida H 18–37/ Vinifera and French hybrids.*
With nearly 30 *ha* this is one of Florida's largest estates.

Todhunter International (1972)
Formerly known as 'Fruit Wines of Florida' this winery, though still active in making non-grape-based wines, has some 25 *ha* of vines, mostly Stover. Winemaker Mary Studt has made some creditable table and dessert wines.

Wines of St Augustine (1983)
The man after whom this winery was named, said 'to many, total abstinence is easier than perfect moderation'. The non-abstainers may care to try Stover, Muscadine and 'Champagne' made from oranges – all of which are produced by Edward Gogel whose experience covers almost every major winemaking state in the USA.

GEORGIA

Georgia is Scuppernong country. There are now 400 *ha* of these Muscadine vines planted (including some close to Jimmy Carter's home in Plains), of which some produce table grapes, the rest rather poor wine for sale in other states. Amongst the more quality-conscious producers however, the concentration is on vinifera. It was the passing of the 1983 farm winery law which really sparked off a renewal of interest in wine production, exactly 150 years after the state's founder, General James E. Oglethorpe, obliged the settlers to plant grapes so that the English might drink wine . . .

Apalachee Vineyard (1983) *Johan/Carmine/Cab F*
The owner is an engineer; there are 5 *ha* of vines.

Château Elan (1983) *Johan*
Winemaker Edmund Friedrich was brought up in Germany and also trained in Arkansas and California.

Habersham Vineyards (1983)
12 *ha* of vinifera have been planted here.

Happy 'B' Farm Winery (1980) **Monarch Wine Co.** *M/Con etc.*
The main emphasis here is on peach wines and brandies. Amongst the grape wines produced, many are made from Californian grape concentrate.

HAWAII

Tedeschi Vineyard
Emil Tedeschi, who is presently making pineapple wine now plans to make wine from Carnelian grapes.

IDAHO

Very up and coming as winemaking states go, Idaho boasts several recently established wineries which have picked up major prizes in national tastings. Which ought to mean that you can find Idaho wines throughout the country. Just try . . .

Facelli (1982) *Ch/Johan* 1,000 cases
Lou Facelli used to be a musician and restaurateur, before turning his attention to making grape, fruit and berry wines in partnership with a local farmer whose 50 *ha* of land now has a wide selection of grapes, including a small amount of Chardonnay and Riesling.

Sainte Chapelle Vineyards (1976) *PN/Ries/Ch/Gewürz/Merl* 55.000 cases
Unquestionably Idaho's first and finest winery, making wines which are on sale in over 40 states. The Riesling and Gewürztraminer is a

particular success, the Merlot has won a gold medal and the Méthode Champenoise is good too.

Spokane River Winery (1982)
The tasting term 'solid structure' should mean something to the owner of this winery – he's a former building inspector. The grape varieties are chiefly Californian.

Weston (1982)
Film-maker Cheyne Weston has 6 *ha* of mainly Californian grape varieties.

ILLINOIS

The Prairie State used to make large quantities of wine, before Prohibition and subsequent restrictions did their utmost to kill off any attempts at vinous interest. The centre of production used to be Nauvoo, a town noted for its blue cheese, and the welcome it offered a succession of religious sects, all of whom fared better than the winemakers. One Nauvoo winery is now a museum. Recent law changes are, it is to be hoped, making it easier and more attractive for winemakers to plant their vines in Illinois.

Gem City Vineland (1887)
The owner is a descendent of a member of Etienne Cabet's Icarian sect who stayed in Nauvoo. Seven different wines are made including straight Concord and 'Sauternes'.

Lynfred Winery (1975)
Owned by former restaurateurs Fred and Lyn Koeler (hence the name of the winery) and making wine from Californian and Michigan grape varieties.

Mogen David Co.
One of America's biggest, producing around 75 million bottles of sweet sacramental wine, mostly made from Californian grape concentrate.

Thompson Vineyard and Winery (1965) *Del/Cat/hybrids*
Formerly known as Ramey & Allen, and famous for bottle-fermented 'champagne' which is still made by Dr John E. Thompson, a nutritionist and farmer who has, with some difficulty, persuaded the owners of neighbouring farms to stop using 2.4-D, a weedkiller which stunts vines.

INDIANA

With what may well be the most delightfully named winery in America – Possum Trot – Indiana is an absolute 'must' for the wine lover. Winemaking suffered its inevitable period of hibernation during Prohibition, but the renewed interest in grape fermentation in neighbouring Pennsylvania sparked off a similar trend here; indeed the 1971 farm winery law is based almost wholly on the one passed in that state three years earlier. There are now eight wineries in Indiana.

Banholzer Wine Cellar (1972) *Ch/CS*
Varietals are made from the above grapes, and a red Kaisertahl and white La Fleur hybrid blends.

Easley Enterprises (1970) *BN/De Chaunac*
Some vinifera is expected too.

Golden Raintree Winery (1975)
The words Indian and Indiana might appear to have been transposed when you see that the winemaker here is a Hindu called Murli Dharmadkari. But his experience was gained whilst obtaining a viticultural and oenological doctorate at the University of Ohio,

rather than on the banks of the Ganges. Labrusca and hybrids are used to make blends, including 'Chablis' and 'Director's Choice'. They win prizes.

Huber Orchard Winery (1978) *Cat/Chel*
The winery is a converted dairy.

Oliver Wine Company (1972)
Con/N/A/Cas/Chel/De Chaunac/Sey B/Vidal
Professor Oliver was responsible for getting the farm winery law passed. He also makes mead.

Possum Trot Vineyards (1978) *A/BN/Foch/Sey B/Vidal/Vig*
Ben Sparks is one of the state's most active campaigners and winemakers. His white is a blend, the red is mostly Foch.

Villa Milan Winery (1983)
Belongs to a former TV reporter. 4 *ha* of hybrids are grown.

IOWA

Here's yet another state which once had a flourishing wine industry but which has now had to abandon any thoughts of making this form of demon drink following the double blow of 'dry' laws and 2.4-D, an agricultural weedkiller which stunts vines. Do not despair however, there is some wine legally made in Iowa (by the Amana religious colony) from wild and bought-in grapes. Founded by a German sect, the Community of True Inspiration, Amana is one of the largest producers of fridge-freezers in the world. Their skill as vintners is less well chronicled.

KENTUCKY

The lunacy displayed by local bureaucrats knows few bounds. When F. Carlton Colcord believed winegrowing might help to bring money and employment to a particularly hard-done-by area of Kentucky he found an annual winery license fee of $1,500 a trifle excessive. However, he managed to have it reduced to $250, in return for which the state forbad him to sell his wine to shops or restaurants, and to supply any one client with more than one quart per wine per year. For some inexplicable reason, after a while, Colcord tired of this enterprise and sold up. In 1982, after great pressure – and having seen Mr Colcord leave and another winery close down – the authorities relented: you can now buy one case a year rather than a single quart, and wineries can now sell to retailers.

Colcord Winery (1977)
Question: name a winery in Paris.
Answer: there's the Colcord in Paris, Kentucky.
The first in the state; its owner originally sold his grapes to an Indiana winemaker, Bill Oliver, who became so impressed by the quality of his purchases that after studying at the University of Kentucky that he is now growing grapes here too.

Other wineries:

Kentucky River Products Winery

Laine Vineyards and Winery
Mostly grows hybrids. Winery closed at present.

LOUISIANA

There is no serious winegrowing here, though sacramental wines were produced in the 18th century. As in Florida, the trick in Louisiana is to ferment oranges and to call the result wine . . .

MARYLAND

Boordy *Sey B/Vidal*
Maryland's first winery. Until 1981 belonged to Philip Wagner.

Berrywine Plantations *A/Chan/Foch/Sey B/Vidal/Vill B*
Owned by a livestock farmer.

Byrd Vineyards (1977) *Ch/Gewürz/Col/Johan/CS/Sey B*
Concentrating on vinifera, there are still a few wines made from hybrids.

Montbray Wine Cellars (1966) *Ch/Johan/CS/Sey B*
In the competitive world of US winemaking, everyone wants a 'first'. Montbray has several: it beat the local competition with Cabernet, Riesling, Chardonnay and 'Eiswein'.

Provenza Vineyards (1974) *Cas/Chan/Sey B*
The owner here is an orthodontist with 6 *ha* of vines.

MASSACHUSETTS

There are many ways to dissuade the would-be winemaker from planting vines: charging an annual $4,500 for a license is pretty effective, and that's exactly what the state of Massachusetts used to do. That fee has now been reduced to $22, and future developments are eagerly awaited.

Chicama Vineyards (1971) *Ch/Ries/CS/PN/GB/PG/Merl/Gewürz*
Apart from the above varieties, Chicama also makes wine from two kinds of Russian vine and a couple of 'Chicama Champagnes'. The winery itself is situated on Martha's Vineyard, and its winemaker trained with Hans Kornell and at Domaine Chandon.

Commonwealth Winery (1978) *Ch/Gewürz/A/De Chaunac/Foch/Sey B/Vidal*
Grapes are also bought in; the owner and winemaker trained at Davis and in Germany.

MICHIGAN

Michigan plays an essential role in American wine history: it is the source of the first bottles of 'Cold Duck', the blend of New York 'Champagne' and California 'Burgundy' devised by a Detroit restaurant owner who had discovered a similar concoction in Germany. Slightly higher on the quality scale – but only slightly – Michigan also produces a great deal of Concorde table wine. Changes are, however, under way and the 15 wineries in the state are beginning to produce some creditable wine from a range of hybrids, particularly from recently planted vineyards close to Lake Erie.

Boskydel Vineyards *A/De Chaunac/Sey B*
Various wines are made from hybrids. Several blends.

Bronte Champagne & Wines (1933) *Cat/Del/A/BN/Foch/Vidal*
Over 8 million bottles are made from the above varieties.

Château Grand Travers (1974) *Ch/Ries*
Owned by a Canadian brewery millionaire, this is a deluxe winery with 18 *ha* of vinifera. The winemaker is a German, Karl Werner.

Fenn Valley Vineyards *Gewürz/Johan/BN/Chan/Foch/Sey B/Vidal*
You've heard of the Welschriesling of Eastern Europe? Well, here there's a real Riesling, made by Doug Welsch. And it's good.

Fink Winery *Con/Johan/CS/Zin*
Up-and-coming – despite a name which might deter some wine lovers.

Frontenac Vineyards *Con/N*
The claim here is for 40 varieties of 'fermented beverage'. Some are made of grapes.

Lakeside Winery *Con/Del/N/Foch/Sey B/Vidal*
Worth watching.

Milan Wines *Con/N*
Also of high potential.

Tabor Hill Vineyards *Ch/Gewürz/Johan/CS/PN/BN/Chel/Sey B/Vidal*
Chardonnay and Riesling were both served to Gerald Ford in the White House when he was President.

St Julian Wine Company *N/Chamb/Chan/Sey B/Vidal*
Michigan's oldest, making over 10 million bottles of blended wine.

MINNESOTA

The North Star State is as cold as its name implies. Thus far, vinifera have not proven successful, but hybrids are doing well and there are several successful experiments which attempt to cross French hybrids with the locally developed Swenson Red.

Alexis Bailly Vineyard (1977) *De Chaunac/Sey B/Foch/Leon Millot/Swenson Red*
David Bailly's early 19th century ancestor was a noted wine maker. Today, grapes are bought in from surrounding growers; Millot and nouveau-style Foch are the most successful.

Lake Sylvia Vineyard (1976)
Horticulturalist David Macgregor is working with Elmer Swenson to breed new varieties, and to find more effective ways to cultivate traditional ones. His Foch is quite successful.

MISSISSIPPI

Progress moves at different speeds in different states: in Mississippi, Prohibition was still in force until 1966. Until 1976, would-be winemakers had to pay a $1,800 winery license fee – which dissuaded many of those who felt otherwise tempted to satisfy the thirst of their neighbours, whose consumption was running at some 8 million bottles of wine every year. With the license fee reduced to a more sensible $10 and the local wine tax cut to a seventh of the 35 cents levied on wine brought in from elsewhere, there is every reason to hope for a continuing explosion of Mississippi wineries.

Almarla Vineyard Winery (1979) *M*
8 *ha* of vines are owned by the former director of scientific services for the Bureau of Alcohol, Tobacco and Firearms, the agency responsible for the regulation of the US wine industry. Red and white of various kinds are made from the Muscadine grape and French hybrids.

Old South Winery (1979) *M*
Owned by a veterinarian who uses Muscadine grapes grown on his own 5 *ha* of vines.

Thousand Oaks Vineyard & Winery (1978) *M/N/BN/Foch/Landot/Vill B*
Seven table wines are made, some from the 12 *ha* Muscadine vineyard The winery belongs to senator Robert Burgin; experiments are being carried out with vinifera.

The Winery Rushing (1977) *M* 15,000 cases
The first winery in the state, built when the new wine laws were introduced. There are 10 *ha* of Muscadine.

MISSOURI

Just imagine the Show Me State producing so much wine that it was second only to California. Nonsense? Well, back in the late 1800s Missouri was indeed Number Two winemaker, and one of its prominent sons, Professor George Husmann, penned *'The Native Grape and the Manufacture of American Wines'.* After Phylloxera hit Europe, Missouri rootstock was sent there to assist in replanting. Today, however, the picture has changed somewhat: a combination of over-production, disease and the vigour of local prohibitionists decimated the commercial wineries of the state (even Husmann himself moved to California) until 1978 when a Missouri Wine Advisory Board was formed to encourage a winemaking renaissance. Since then matters have progressed swiftly. In 1980, for instance, the Bureau of Alcohol Tobacco and Firearms allocated the first appellation in the USA to the community of Augusta, and tests by state oenologist Bruce Zoecklein and viticulturalist Larry Lockshin indicate that vinifera grapes will soon be joining the hybrids to produce truly first-class wine.

Bardenheiers (1873) *Cat/Con/N/Sey Vill/Foch/Chel/BN*
The biggest winery in Missouri, and the oldest in continuous operation. Until 1970 it was basically a blending and bottling plant for Californian wine, but more recently the 20 *ha* of vines which were planted then have begun to yield some worthwhile wine. Experiments with Riesling crosses should extend the range beyond its present exclusive concentration on red.

Bristle Ridge (1980) *Cat/Con/Diamond/Dut/BN/Chan/ De Chaunac/ Sey Vill/Vidal/Vill B*
Co-run by an engineer and a farmer, Bristle Ridge makes an impressively wide selection of different hybrids and Labrusca.

Bois d'Arc Vineyards (1982)
Seven separate vineyards have been planted, allowing this winery to expand radically.

Carvers (1979) *CS/BN/Chan/Vill N/Sey/Ries and Ch hybrids*
The research physicist owner is experimenting with cool-resistant hybrids which are as closely related to European vinifera as possible.

Edelweiss Vineyard (1982)
Rheinhessen-trained Gunther Heeb makes wines which display the Germanic influence so often encountered in the Missouri wine industry.

Ferrigno Vineyard & Winery (1982) *Cat/Con/Elvira/De Chaunac/ Sey B/Vidal/Chel*
The owner of Ferrigno is a part-time sociology lecturer.

Green Valley Vineyard *Cat/A/BN/Chamb/Chan/Chel/ Foch/Sey B/Sey Vill/Vill B*
Nicholas Lamb makes medal winning wines from the above wide variety of hybrids.

Heinrichshaus Vineyards and Winery (1979) De Chaunac/Cat/ Chan/Chel/Landot/Sey B/Vill B
The speciality here is French hybrids (despite the winery's Germanic origins) and a blended wine with the odd name of 'Prairie Blanc'.

Hermannhof (1979) *De Chaunac/Sey B*
With 25 *ha* of vines Jim Dierberg produces several blends as well as a 'Champagne' in a converted brewery.

Kruger Winery (1973)
Wines are made in a German tradition.

McCormick Distilling
This Kansas City distillery has been making wine since 1979.

Midi Vineyard & Winery *Cat/Con/Chan/Vill B*
Co-run by a structural engineer and a philosophy lecturer. Red wines are most worth seeking out.

Montelle (1969) *Cat/Con/Cyn/Del/A/Chel/De Chaunac/Sey B*
With Mount Pleasant, this is one of the first wineries to make

'Augusta Appellation' wine. Its first vintage was in 1973. There are now 40 different wines, of which the whites are certainly best. Once a family operation, now run in conjunction with the winery of the Little Hill (the former Kepprich Cellars).

Moore-Dupont Winery (1982) *Cat/Chamb/Chan/Chel/Foch/Sey B/ Vidal/Vill B*
Two vineyard owners have combined to experiment with a wide range of varieties, including vinifera.

Mount Pleasant (1881, refounded 1968) *Cyn/Del/St/Seibel/Sey B/ Vidal* 10,000 cases
Pioneer winemakers Lucian and Eva Dressel's wines have earned themselves a good reputation – particularly their botrytized Labrusca Missouri Riesling.

Osage Ridge Vineyard
The owner, a genetics professor, has plans to build an underground winery.

Ozark Mountain Cellars (1976)
A fast-expanding winery run by a group of farmer-growers.

Ozark Vineyards (1976) *Cat/Con/N/A*

Peaceful Bend Vineyards & Winery (1972)
Several French and US hybrids are grown by the owner (a gynaecology professor) to produce red, white and rosé blends. Planted in 1951, these are amongst the oldest vines in the state.

Rosati Winery *Cat/Con/Elvira/Chel/Foch*
A family-run business in a town settled by Italian immigrants. Eleven different (mostly Concord) wines are made by Ashby Vineyards, with whom Rosati is in partnership. Amongst the wines is a commendable dry 'Champagne'.

St James Winery 20,000 cases
Wines are made from native grapes, French hybrids and vinifera.

Stoltz Vineyards & Winery (1967)
Over 100 different wines are made from grapes picked from 50 *ha* of vines.

Stone Hill Winery (1847, refounded 1965) *Cat/Con/Sey B/ Missouri Ries/N/Chel* 9,000 cases
Sic transit . . . This was once the second largest winery in the USA, with wines which were frequent medal winners in the last part of the 19th century. A wine museum contains proof of these past successes; today there is a range of uninspiring fruit, still wines and 'champagne'.

Sunny Slope Vineyard (1984)
Too new to say much about.

Weston wineyards (1979)
With 5 *ha* of French hybrids and a winery housed in a former Evangelical Lutheran Church, Weston's Germanic traditions are so strong that a three-week Oktoberfest is held each year. It is less beery, and a little less licentious than the European original.

Winery of the Abbey (1979)
Co-owned by the Dressels of Mt Pleasant, this is a new venture to watch.

Ziegler Winery
Concord is used for a selection of wines.

MONTANA

It is a little like being present at a birth: Montana has just had its very first winery.

Mission Mountains Vineyard (1980) *Johan/Ch/PN*
Montana's first winery.

NEW HAMPSHIRE

There is still only one winery in New Hampshire (which is still one
more than many in other states might imagine). It is really very
strange though, when you consider that the one winery in operation is
so successful.

White Mountain Vineyards (1969) 25,000 cases
The foundation of this estate dates back to 1958 when pharmacist
John L. Canepa took a job at the clinic in Laconia, and began to
wander around the local woods with his wife, Lucille. The sight of wild
vines set their imaginations working and after testing American and
French hybrids they bought a farm and began producing 'New
Hampshire Burgundy', 'Lakes Region Dry White Dinner Wine', and
'Maréchal Foch'. In 1975 vinifera were planted, and grown with some
success. Although the winery was sold in 1982 to John and Florence
Vereen who had fled the warmth of Miami, Florida, both Canepas are
still involved with its progress. Blends are now known as 'Mont Blanc'
and 'Winnepesaukee'.

NEW JERSEY

New Jersey is not on anybody's list of top ten US wine-producing
states these days, so it is surprising to learn that in the 1960s it was
the ninth most productive in the country. As wine drinkers' tastes
became more sophisticated, the almost exclusively Labrusca-based
wines became less popular and two big wineries closed their doors. A
renaissance is now under way, with vigorous efforts to make good
vinifera and hybrid still wines and some fair quality sparklers.

Antuzzi's Winery
150,000 bottles of wine are made per year.

Bernard d'Arcy Cellars (1934)
Previously called Gross Highland, this winery used to make solely
Labrusca wines, but is now switching to vinifera and hybrids. Other
wines include Cuve Close sparklers, and a new project is to make a
Méthode Champenoise first produced in time to celebrate the winery's
half-century.

Gross Highland Winery (1934) 40,000 cases
This is a successful producer of Cuve Close sparkling wine.

Renault Winery (1864)
During Prohibition, Renault's 'Wine Tonic' was popular in every state
of the union (possibly because of its 22% alcohol content). The firm
was founded by Louis Nicholas Renault who arrived before the Civil
War as the agent for Montebello Champagne, and his successors
continued the tradition (almost) by making Cuve Close sparkling
wine from Californian and New Jersey Labrusca grapes. In 1972,
Renault launched a dryish 'New Jersey State Noah White Varietal
Dinner Wine', made from the Noah grape, one of the only varieties to
have been successfully planted in France. Johannisberg Riesling and
French hybrids are other recent developments, as is a collection of
European wineglasses on show to around 100,000 visitors every year.

Tewksbury Wine Cellars (1979) *Sey B/Cayuga White/Gewürz/Ch*
Apart from the above, veterinarian Dan Veron, his wife Lynn, and
computer expert Jack Schaller also produce a blend called Tewksbury
red. The winery is in a converted horse hospital, and can produce some
9,000 gallons.

Other producers:
Amwell Valley Vineyard
B&B Vineyards

Savo Balik
Del Vista Vineyard
Fennelly Farm Vineyards
Jacob Lee (1938)
Polito Vineyards (1978)
John Schuster & Son (1868)
Tomasello Winery (1933)

NEW MEXICO

Sometimes it takes outsiders to recognize potential which those closer
to hand cannot see. European investors think New Mexico an
attractive place to make wine, which must surprise the state's three
wineries which, until the end of the 1970s contented themselves with
making wine from Californian grapes.

Franciscan missionaries were making sacramental wines here in
the 17th century, and in 1880, New Mexico was the fifth most
important winemaking state in the Union. During Prohibition some
production was maintained, but after a peak of activity in 1945 there
was a steady decline. Lee Elman plans to build a winery in the town of
Truth or Consequences – is this an ideal name to print on a wine
label?

Binns Vineyard & Winery (1982) *Ch/Chen B/Col/Gewürz/*
Grey Ries/Johan/GB/Gren/Merl/PN/Ruby Cab/Zin/Zin 'white'/
Gam Rosé/Zin Rosé
You name it, this farming family (two brothers) have planted it. They
also make fruit wine.

Chiavario Vineyards Winery (1982) *BN/Chan/Sey B/Vill B*
The former air traffic controller owner makes blended red and white
wine under the 'Mi Amigo' and 'Paloma Blanca' labels.

La Chiripada (1982) *Hybrids*
Two brothers and their wives produce wines from several hybrids.

Joe P. Estrada Winery (1875)
The oldest winery in New Mexico, specializing in the pink 'Mission'
grape.

St Clair (1984)
The newest winery in New Mexico.

La Vina Winery *Col/Johan/Carig/Ruby Cab/Zin*
New Mexico's largest winery, this enterprise is nevertheless run
mainly as a hobby by its owner, a professor of physics. Zinfandel
'white' and rosé are made here.

Vina Madre Winery (1978) *CS/Napa Gamay/Zin/Barb/Ruby Cab*
The first of the 'New Wave' of wineries to open here, this now has a
well established estate of classic vinifera.

Westwind Winery *Col/Ruby Cab/Zin/Vidal*
Co-run by the former owner of Rico's Winery, and once famed for their
'Ojo de Perdrix' blanc de noir. Black vinifera are grown on
mountainside vineyards.

NEW YORK STATE

Until very recently, this was the place to look for some of North
America's very worst wines – and a fascinating selection of the
'foxiest' of 'foxy' Labruscas. To put it simply, nobody ever believed
that the climate of the land around the finger lakes in the northern
part of the state, where most of New York's vineyards are planted,
would support anything but these hardy but unpalatable indigenous
varieties.

Over three centuries ago, grapes were being grown on Manhattan itself, Peter Stuyvesant, the then governor, believing that wine was healthier than more alcoholic drinks and even prescribing it for drinking by seamen. A few decades later, the Lords of Trade in London were informed by their imperial representative that New York could supply all the drinking requirements of Britain and its dominions, and in 1846 a horticulturist named Spooner was making wine in Brooklyn. Unfortunately, none of these were what twentieth-century drinkers would call enjoyable wine.

Matters began to improve with the arrival of hybrid grapes from France and, for a short while, it appeared that the days of traditional table grapes like the Concord were numbered. Their rescue came in the unexpected form of the temperance movement which began in New York State. So strong was the zeal of the Hellfire and Damnation brigade that, in the 'Short Bible' published in 1924, every reference to wine was altered to 'cakes of grapes' – which made for occasionally amusing reading. Winegrowers became grape juice makers, and the Concord was the variety for the job. The fact that some of these bottles of juice came with labels saying helpfully 'Caution – do not add yeast or admit air, or the contents will ferment' helped to boost their sales – as did a sudden explosion in the number of believers in any religion which required wine for its ceremonies.

When Prohibition was repealed, it was replaced by a set of stringent local laws which did much to hamper would-be wine makers, and which were only eased in 1976. Since then progress has been both swift, varied and impressive. Under the influence of a Russian immigrant called Konstantin Frank, these new producers learned that western varieties could be grown successfully in New York, and bottles of delicious Riesling and even Chardonnay now stand shoulder to shoulder with increasingly good hybrids. As for the Labrusca, its future here seems to be in the production of juice, jams and jellies.

Hudson River Valley

Benmarl Wine Company (1971) *Ch/Sey/BN*
An old 19th century vineyard, run as a 'Société des Vignerons' cooperative for 400 member-enthusiasts who are variously involved in every aspect of the winery's day-to-day tasks. Each member has a 'Droit de Seigneur' over 12 bottles of wine, from his or her own two vines. Wines include Blanc Domaine, Rouge Domaine, Rosé Domaine, Cuvée du Vigneron.

Brotherhood Winery *Ch/Cat/Del/Dut*
Hybrids are now being used to make still table wine; altar and sparkling wines used to be the only ones made.

Cagnasso (1977)
Joseph Cagnasso has made wine in Italy, Mexico and at Gallo in California. Here he specializes in hybrids.

Cascade Mountain Vineyards *A/Chan/Sey B/Vidal*
Recently founded by writer William Wetmore. Light reds have a good reputation.

Clinton Vineyard (1977) *Sey B*
Ben Feder is a book designer. His success with 7 *ha* of Seyval Blanc now extends to a Méthode Champenoise sparkler.

Cottage Vineyards
Having tried to grow Riesling, owner Allan Mackinnon learned his lesson and planted hybrids.

Great River Winery/Marlboro Champagne Cellars/Windsor Vineyards
Vintage French hybrids and unexceptional fizz.

Green's Northeast Vineyard *Foch*
George Green is a heart surgeon, his winemaking operation one of the

smallest in the States. But small seems to be beautiful.

High Tor Vineyard
Once celebrated for its wines, by others as well as its sometime owner Everett Crosby, an author and playwright, this winery has lost its lustre. 'Rockland' is another label, used for Delaware whites and hybrid reds and rosés.

Hudson Valley Wine Company (1907)
Del/Con/Cat/Chel/Iowna/BN/Warden
Labrusca is used here mainly, to make wines unashamedly called 'Chablis', 'Burgundy' etc. Founded by the Bolognesi familly, this is now owned by Herbert Feinberg.

North Salem Vineyard (1979) *Sey/Foch*
Dr George Naumberg divides his life between winemaking and straightening out the problems of the inhabitants of Manhattan who stretch out on his psychiatrist's couch.

Walker Valley Vineyard (1978) *Ries/Sey*
Owner/winemaker, Gary Dross, is chairman of the physical education department at Orange Country Community College. The few bottles of wine he makes each year belie his name.

West Park Vineyards (1983) *Ries/SB/Ch*
If you can't find one of these wines in the Windows on the World restaurant, ask the cellarmaster why not. He (Kevin Zraly) is co-owner of the winery.

Chautauqua-Erie

This is another region to watch with interest. Until recently, this was the centre for the production of Kosher wine.

Chadwick Bay (1981) *Chamb*
Up-and-coming winery.

Frederick S. Johnson Vineyards (1962)
Sey/Del/Chan/A/Cas/Ives/Chel/Cat
Well-thought-of estate-bottled wines, including dry white and sweet late-picked Delaware, and various good hybrids.

Merritt Estate (1977) *Sey/A/N/Foch/Johan*
A well-made range of hybrids.

Schloss Doepken (1980) *Con/Ch/Gewürz/Ries*
Good varietal wines – some oak-aged – and the wonderfully named Chautauquabloomchen and Schloss Blanc.

Woodbury Vineyards (1979) *Ries/PG/PN/Gewürz/Ch/SB/CS/ hybrids/Lab*
One of New York's most promising wineries, with particularly successful Chardonnay. Also some fizz.

Niagara

Niagara Wine Cellars *Ries/Ch/Chan/Foch/Vidal/Siegfried Ries*
Paul Lops believes that the German Siegfried Riesling holds great promise for Niagara.

The Finger Lakes

Aggressively beautiful country in which the majority of New York's vines are grown. Until Konstantin Frank proved otherwise, Labrusca and hybrid-based 'champagne' was the principal product. Now, however, there are some excellent Rieslings, Chardonnays and even a Gewürztraminer and a Pinot Noir or two to be found, and the French hybrids are showing promise too. No one with a serious interest in American wine should miss the opportunity to head up here to see what is going on. But don't ask for directions in Manhattan – the chances are that no one will even have heard of the brave winemakers of the area.

Barry Wine Co
Originally a sacramental wine producer, now concentrating on developing hybrids and vinifera.

Bully Hill (1970) *Sey B/Ries/Ch/BN/Chel/Foch/A/D*
Walter Taylor, characterful owner and winemaker is one of the most staunch supporters of Labrusca and hybrid wines. He also enjoys expressing his views of the Taylor Wine Co which once belonged to his family.

Canandaigua *Various Lab*
A large (Finger Lakes' second biggest) winery specializing in quaintly named commercial, Labrusca-flavoured wines, including 'Richard's Wild Irish Rose', and 'Captain Paul Garrett's Virginia Dare'. Those with a taste for the unusual may like to try 'Almande', an almondy fizz.

Casa Larga (1978) *PN/Ch/CS/Ries/Gewürz/De Chaunac/A*
Andrew Colaruotolo grew up drinking Frascati in his native Italy – and helping his father make it. One of New York's most promising wineries.

Château Esperanza *D/A/BN/Sey B*

De May Wine Cellars *Con/Del/N/BN/De Chaunac/Landot*
Owned by a Frenchman, this small operation makes good wine from Labrusca and hybrids.

Frontenac Point Vineyard (1982) *Foch/Chel/Ries/Ch/PN*
James Doolittle is an agricultural marketing expert; his wife is editor of the journal of the American Wine Society. Try the late-harvested Chardonnay.

Glenora Wine Cellars (1977) *Ch/Ries/Cayuga/Foch* 10,000 cases
Good, and improving Riesling and Chardonnay by a winemaker trained at Spring Mountain in California. Foch Nouveau is another novelty, and 'Champagne' is a new development.

Hammondsport Wine Co (1870)
Owned by Canandaigua and making bottle-fermented fizz.

Heron Hill Vineyard (1977) *A/Sey B/Ravat/Ch/Ries* 5,000 cases
Good Riesling (particularly late picked) and Chardonnay and really foxy Aurora – for those who like that kind of thing.

Lakeshore (1982) *Ries/Ch/CS/Gewürz*
A small but ambitious family-run winery.

Lucas Family Vineyard (1974) *Cayuga/De Chaunac.*
Bill Lucas is still a tugboat captain (hence their 'Tugboat Red' and 'Tugboat White' wines). Some recent successes.

O-Neh-Da *Cayuga White/Chan/Ravat*
Also called Eagle Crest, this is the place to buy altar wine. Worryingly, O-Neh-Da means 'hemlock' in Seneca Indian, but this refers to the fact that the winery is on Lake Hemlock rather than any effect of its wines.

McGregor Vineyards *Ries/Gewürz*
Prize-winning late-harvested wines.

Plane's Cayuga Winery (1981) *Ries/Ch/Dut*
Persisting with Labrusca (Dutchess) Bob and Mary Plane are proving increasingly successful with vinifera and hybrids.

Poplar Ridge (1981) *Cayuga White*
Up-and-coming with some good vinifera.

Taylors, Great Western, Gold Seal, Pleasant Valley Wine Co
Ch/Johan/Gewürz/CS/Cat/BN etc. (all are separate labels, used for separately produced wines)
After a spell under the ownership of Coca Cola, these companies all belong to Seagrams who recently closed the Gold Seal winery, although planning to continue to use its name. Taylor specializes in hybrids and good quality 'sherry' and 'port' style wines. Great Western's Pleasant Valley winery is New York's oldest; here, apart from Labrusca and hybrid wines, the emphasis is on transfer method sparkling wine. Gold Seal's label used to denote good quality Chardonnay, Riesling and sparkling wine. Konstantin Frank was winemaker, then consultant, here.

Vinifera Wine Cellars (1962) *Ch/Johan/Gewürz/GB*
Konstantin Frank's own vineyard and winery owe their name to the pioneer's faith in European grape varieties. Frank's son has recently taken over; quality is expected to continue to improve.

Wagner Vineyards *De Chaunac/Ravat/Sey/A/Rougeon/Del/Ries/Ch*
Bill Wagner and his young team make half a million bottles of good-quality wine, and are progressing well with oak-aged hybrids. Worth a visit.

Wickham Vineyards (1981) *Cayuga*
A family-run winery, specializing in hybrids, and now turning its hand to sparkling wine.

Widmer's Wine Cellars Inc *Elvira/Del/N/Salem/Dut/Moore's Diamond/Vincent/Cat/de Chaunac/Ventura/Vidal/Rosette/A/Vergennes/Isabella/Con*
Situated in the oddly named Naples Valley, this is a large (3,000,000 gallon) winery, specializing in 'sherry', 'port', 'burgundy', 'sauternes' and 'champagne', but making surprisingly good wines from hybrid grapes. 'Sherry' is left to mature for a month in the open air on Widmer's 'cellar on the roof'. When he feels the cold of the New York winter, Widmer can always visit his new Sonoma winery in California.

Hermann J. Wiemer Vineyard *Ries/Ch/PN*
With his own roots in the Moselle, it is unsurprising that Wiemer is successful with Riesling. As a supplier of vines to other growers, however, he is taking every opportunity to try out other varieties of vinifera.

Long Island

Hargrave Vineyard (1979) *CS/Ch/SB/Merl* 5,000 cases
Alex Hargrave, a graduate of Chinese Literature, is making some of North America's most exciting wines on land previously used to grow potatoes. His Chardonnay is exceptional: deliciously clean, complex and 'European' tasting, his Cabernet and Merlot full-flavoured, complex and well-oaked. The Sauvignon is terrific too. One of the most exciting wineries in the USA.

OHIO

In the mid-19th century, this was America's principal wine-producing state. The climate is well-suited to vines, and the Catawba grape seemed to flourish here. Ohio was also the first state to produce 'Champagne'. In 1858, a reporter writing in the *Illustrated London News* dubbed the Ohio Catawba 'finer . . . than any hock that comes from the Rhine' and said that its sparkling version 'transcended the Champagne of France'. The tasting skills of the writer in question have never been established, but Nicholas Longworth, producer of both wines, accused New York hotels of swapping the French stuff for his more highly prized fizz. Longfellow helped to promote Ohio wines with an 11 verse poem, and the Ohio became became known as the 'Rhine of America'. Longworth single-handedly launched the Ohio wine Industry in Cincinnati, but a second area also developed further north, along the banks of Lake Erie, and on islands in the lake itself.

When mildew and black rot almost wiped out the Cincinatti vines in the 1860s, many growers moved north and continued to make wine, until their efforts were thwarted by Prohibition. Even so, all was not quite lost: policing the island wineries was far from easy, and winemaking never quite died during the 'dry' years. In the mid 1930s there was a brief renaissance of Ohio wines, but unfortunately the wines themselves (much of it Catawba fizz) and the prices asked, were no match for the vigorously commercial New Yorkers and Californians, and by the late 1960s there were only around a dozen firms making Ohio wine.

As elsewhere, it was in the 1970s that new attempts were made to recreate a wine industry, some concentrating on hybrids, others on European varietals including Chardonnay and Riesling. The Concord, once in almost total control, is losing its share of the state's vineyards with each year that passes. Since 1981, the state legislature has finally begun to encourage winemaking, by taxing local wines on a preferential basis.

Breitenbach Wine Cellars (1980) *Cat/Con/Del/N/BN/Chan/Sey B/Vidal*

Bretz Winery
A name to watch.

Brushcreek Vineyards (1975)
Labrusca and hybrids are made.

Buccia Vineyards (1981) *A/BN/Chel/Sey B*
The owner's name is Bucci. He is now planting vinifera.

Catawba Island Wine Company
Not surprisingly, Catawba is made here, but so is Chardonnay.

Cedar Hill Wine Co. (1971) *Ch/Johan/CS/Dut/S/Chamb/Chel/Foch/Sey B/Vidal* (Wines are sold under 'Château Lagniappe' label) 2,500 cases
Dr Thomas Wykoff is an Ear-Nose-and-Throat specialist, owner of a French restaurant, (which also houses the winery) and wine maker . . . Lagniappe is New Orleans patois for 'something extra'. 'Champagne' is made too.

Chalet Debonne Vineyards *Ch/Johan/CS/Cat/Con/Del/N/Sey B/Vidal/Vill B* 8,000 cases
The vineyard was planted with Concord before Prohibition.

Colonial Vineyards Winery (1977) *Ch/CS/Cat/N/A/BN/De Chaunac/Foch/Sey B/Vill B*
The owner is a computer analyst, so this is a computerized winery. His 'Chablis' is made from (and was previously labelled) Seyval Blanc.

Daughters Wine Cellar *Cat/Del/Dut/N/Chamb/Foch/Vidal*
No, this isn't named after the owner's nubile offspring, but after Mr Dana Daughters himself.

Dover Vineyards *Cat/Con/Foch/Sey B*

E & K Wine Co *Cat/N*
One of the biggest wineries in Ohio, once almost exclusively devoted to producing Labrusca wine.

Grand River Winery (1973) *Ch/Merl/Gewürz/SB/PN/GB/Vig*
Willett Worthy makes the above varietals, a few vinifera, and a white blend called Adrienne, after his daughter.

Hafle Vineyards *Con/N/A/BN/Chel/De Chaunac*

Heineman Cellar (1896) *Cat/Con/Sey B/Vidal*
The current owner's father was a German immigrant. Blends are made, including 'Sweet Belle', with Catawba and Concord.

Heritage Vineyards (1978) *Cat/Con/Del/N/A/BN/Chel/De Chaunac/Foch/Seibel/Sey B/Vidal/Vill B*
Belongs to an electronics consultant and a business consultant. 'Champagne' is a new project.

Hillcrest Vineyard *Ch/Gewürz/SB/Sém/Johan/CS/PN/Zin*

Louis Jindra Winery (1973) *Cat/Con/BN/Chel/Foch/Sey B/Vidal*
The owner is a physician.

Klingshirn Winery *Cat/Con/Del/N/Chan/Vidal*

Lonz Winery (1862)
A Gothic turretted folly, partly built by George Lonz, and partly destroyed by fire. 'Isle des Fleurs Champagne' is the tradition. High potential.

Mantey Vineyards Inc (1880) *BN/Sey B/Johan*
Produce a rosé from the Baco Noir. Also 'sherry', 'port' and 'sauternes' but a recent takeover (and merger with Meier's Wine Cellars) has led to an improvement in quality.

Markko Vineyard (1969) *Ch/Johan/CS* 1,000 cases
Named after the Finnish policeman who owned the land before it was bought by home-winemaker, Arnulf Esterer. Esterer had studied under Konstantin Frank in New York State. One of Ohio's best.

Meier's Wine Cellars *Ch/Gewürz/Johan/CS/PN/Cat/Con/Del/D/Dut/Elvira/N/St/A/BN/Chan/Chel/De Chaunac/Foch/Seibel/Sey B/Vidal*
The largest in the state, situated in the area which Nicholas Longworth considered America's Rhineland.

Mon Ami Wine Co. (1872) *Ch/Gewürz/Johan/Cat/Con/Del/Dut/N/St/BN/Chel/De Chaunac/Sey B*
The speciality here is 'Champagne'.

Moyer Vineyards (1973) *Chamb/Vidal*
The winery is in a converted dance hall, and the owner now has a winery in Texas. Bottle-fermented 'Champagne' is made.

The Pompeii Winery *Cat/Con/Del/N/BN/Foch/Seibal/Sey B*

The Steuk Wine Company (1855) *Cat/Con/Del/Elvira/N/Chan/De Chaunac/Foch/Sey B*
Claims to be the oldest winery in the USA still owned and operated by the founding family. 'Champagnes' and good Labrusca wines are produced.

Stillwater Winery (1981) *Cat/Con/Del/N/A/BN/Chel/De Chaunac/Foch/Vidal/Vill B*
'Champagne' is made here; the winery is built into the ground.

Tarula Winery (1965)
Hybrids are used to make wine by two high school teachers.

Valley Vineyards Farm (1969) *Cat/Con/N/A/BN/De Chaunac*
An expanding winery which runs annual festivals.

Vinterra Farm (1976) *A/BN/De Chaunac/Vidal/Vill B*
There are 6 *ha* of vines; the Baco Noir is particularly recommended.

Wyandotte Wine Cellars (1979) *Cat/Con/Del/N/A/BN/Foch/Sey B/Vidal*

OKLAHOMA

If only some wine loving fairy godmother would wave her wand over this state . . . there are vineyards and keen, would-be winemakers. The only problem is the authorities who have consistently done all in their power to hinder vinous progress. As Leon Adams describes in his

The Wines of America 'Professor Hermann Hinrichs of Oklahoma State University told me a decade ago that grapes are a dependable crop in the Sooner State. He believed there is a commercial future for Oklahoma wines. Apparently he had not studied the political climate of the state'. Perhaps the finest, and saddest, symbol of Oklahoma's vinous past is the 1889 Fairchild Winery in Oklahoma City which was rediscovered by former Mayor George Shirk – half buried in mud.

Arrowhead Vineyards Winery (1979)
Wayne and Susan Pool have a licence to grow grapes and run the above-named winery; the only thing state officials will not let them do is sell wine on the premises . . .

Caney
This is a 50 acre hybrid and vinifera vineyard, some of the fruit of which is sold to Texan wineries, some picked by home winemakers for their own use.

Okarche (1970)
Peter Schwarz imports Concord grapes from Arkansas and despite an unclear legal position, uses them to make wine he sells at the winery.

OREGON

If any winegrowing state can be said to have become 'fashionable' in recent years, it is Oregon. People who could once see no further than the Napa Valley, and who still refuse to believe in the existence of fine wine in the Finger Lakes of New York State, are beginning to talk of Oregon as 'The Future'. The regular success of Oregon wines at national tastings does much to support such attitudes. And yet, only a decade or so ago the owners of the traditional farm wineries would have shaken their heads in disbelief if you'd said that wine drinkers in countries as distant as Britain might want to taste their wine.

Unlike all those other states where the liberating effect of Repeal was watered down by the exaction of prohibitive license fees by state legislatures, Oregon only charges its would-be winemakers $25 a year. The coolish climate, the altitude of some of the vineyards, and the keen open-mindedness of Oregon's principal winemakers all conspire to make the European visitor more at home than he sometimes feels in even the most welcoming of Californian wineries. As one French visitor put it, the Oregon growers seem to have smaller heads than the Californians. (The Californian estimate of the French head-size were unrecorded).

Another factor which might inspire transatlantic kinship is the Oregon attitude towards appellation and labelling. Whereas elsewhere, many producers feel that their own names should be quite sufficient for the curious client – 'why shouldn't we call our white blend Chablis?' or 'I always put 25% Zinfandel into my Pinot Noir' – in Oregon, the rules are clear and strict. No vinifera wine can call itself 'Chablis', 'Claret', 'Sauternes' or any other European generic name; apart from Cabernet which is allowed a 25% admixture of Bordeaux grapes, varietals have to be made from 90% of the variety named; wines must be made exclusively from grapes grown in the appellation area which appears on the label; chaptalization is limited to 2°, as in Burgundy. Oregon wines are often recognizable from at least the more old-fashioned of Californians – by their leaner, less blowsy style.

Adelsheim Vineyards (1978)
Ch/SB/Sem/Johan/Gamay/Merl/PG/PN 5,000 cases
David Adelsheim was a sommelier.

Alpine Vineyards (1979) *Ch/Gewürz/Johan/CS/PN* 1,000 cases
Good varietal wines, made by a hospital doctor.

Amity Vineyards (1976) *Ch/Gewürz/Johan/CS/Merl/PN* 4,000 cases
The Pinot Noir is good (some of the grapes being brought in from Washington) and there is also a 'Pinot Nouveau'. The second label is Redford Cellars.

Arteberry Ltd *Ch/Gewürz/Sem/Johan*
Previously known as a cider producer, also makes sparkling Chardonnay.

Bjelland Vineyards (1969) *Ch/Gewürz/SB/Sem/Johan/CS/PN/Zin* 1,250 cases
Paul Bjelland was a teacher.

Century Home Wine
Ch/PN/Gren/Con/N
Owner David Mave also makes white Pinot Noir and Gamay Rosé.

Château Benoit (1980) *Ch/Gewürz/SB/Johan/Merl/PN/MT* 5,500 cases
Benoit is the owners' name; Pinot Noir white and rosé are made.

Chehalem Mountain Winery *Ch/Gewürz/Johan/PN/PN White* 2,500 cases

Côtes des Colombe Vineyards *Ch/Chen B/Gewürz/PB/Johan/CS/PN/PN White/CS Rosé*

Di Martini Wine *Gewürz/PB/SB/Johan/CS/PN/Zin/PN White*

Elk Cove Vineyards *Ch/Gewürz/Johan/CS/PN/PN White*

Ellendale Vineyards (1981) *Ch/Gewürz/Johan/Cab Fr/CS/Merl/PN/ PN White/PN Rosé/Con/N/A/BN/Foch* 1,000 cases

Henry Endres Winery *Con/N*

The Eyrie Vineyards (1966) *Ch/PG/PN/PM/Mus Ott/White Ries* 4,000 cases
Trained at U.C. Davis in California, David Lett has proven just how successful vinifera can be in Oregon. Pinot Noir is his great success story, and at a blind tasting, organized by Burgundian merchant Joseph Drouhin, in Beaune, his wine came within a whisker of beating a Chambolle Musigny. He is now turning his hand to Pinots Gris and Meunier.

Forgeron Vineyards Winery (1977) *Ch/Chen B/Johan/CS/PG/PN* 2,200 cases
Forgeron means 'smith' in French, so you do not need to guess the owner's name. Both Smiths have lived in France. White and rosé Pinot Noir are made.

Glen Creek Winery (1982) *Ch/SB*
The Dumms, who own this winery, used to run a wine shop.

Scott Henry Estate Winery (1977) *Ch/Gewürz/PN* 6,300 cases
An up-and-coming winery, now planning to make sparkling wine.

Hidden Springs Winery *Ch/Johan/CS/PN/PN White/White Zin* 2,500 cases

Hillcrest Vineyard (1965) *Ch/Gewürz/Johan/Sem/Zin/PN* 10,000 cases
Despite being told by local 'experts' that he should concentrate on Labrusca, Richard Sommer trusted his own instincts, and the lessons he had been taught at U.C. Davis in California, and planted vinifera galore at the state's first post-Prohibition vineyard. His success has proved him right and inspired dozens of others.

Hinman Vineyards (1979) *Ch/Gewürz/Johan/CS/PN/PN white* 3,000 cases
Ex-teacher Doyle Hinman learned his winemaking in Germany and at U.C. Davis in California. Some grapes are bought in from Washington.

Honeywood Winery (1934) *Con/N*
A large winery which also makes berry wine.

Hood River Vineyards (1981) *Gewürz/Sem/Johan/CS/PN/Zin/ N/A/Cas* 1,200 cases

Knusden-Erath Winery (1967) *Ch/Gewürz/SB/Johan/Merl/PN*
20,000 cases
Richard Erath, an electrical engineer, made his first wine with grapes
bought from Richard Sommer; Calvert Knusden, his partner, is an
executive with a lumber company. Each has his own vineyard, and
wines bear either one or both of the owners' names. There are now
around 40 *ha* of vines, which must help to keep prices low. Amongst
the wines are a white Pinot Noir and a 'Champagne'. This is Oregon's
biggest winemaking operation. Sparkling wine is now planned.

La Casa de Vin (1980) *Chen B/SB/Johan/CS/CS rosé*

Nehalem Bay Wine Co *Ch/Johan/CS/PN*

Oak Knoll Winery *Ch/Gewürz/Muscat of Alexandria/Johan/CS/PN/N*
5,000 cases
Grapes are bought in; the winery previously concentrated its
attention on fruit and berry wines. Pinot Noir white and rosé are
made.

Ponzi Vineyards *Ch/Johan/PG/PN/PN white 4,200 cases*
The blend here is called 'Oregon Harvest'. Chardonnay and Riesling
are good.

Reuters Hill Vineyards 12,000 cases
Merged with another winery in 1978. Quality of wines is variable.

Roseberg Winery (1976) 3,000 cases
Four wines are made, from grapes bought in from Jonicole Vineyards.

Serendipity Cellars Winery Ch/Chen B/CS/PN/PN white/Foch 420
cases
Delightfully named by its librarian owners, who found winemaking
an unexpected pleasure. Grapes are bought in.

Shafer Vineyards Cellars *Ch/Gewürz/SB/Johan/PN/PN white*

Shafer Vineyard Cellars *Ch/Gewürz/Johan/SB/PN*
Harvey Shafer's Chardonnay is particularly good.

Siskiyou Vineyards (1978) *Ch/Chen B/Gewürz/SB/Sem/Johan/CS/
PN/Zin/CS rosé* 6,000 cases
Founder Charles David died in 1982. His widow, Suzi, now runs the
winery.

Sokol Blosser Winery (1974) *Johan/Ch/PN/Merl/SB/M-T*
25,000 cases
William Blosser and his wife Susan (née Sokol) are helped by a
physiology professor who learned winemaking in the Napa Valley.
The wines have all been well received, particularly the Riesling.

Tualatin Vineyards *Ch/Flora/Gewürz/SB/Johan/PN*
Tualatin means 'flowing water' in the language of the Indians of the
region. Bill Fuller learned his winemaking at the Louis Martini
winery in the Napa Valley. Best wines are labelled 'Estate bottled',
e.g. Muscat, Pinot Noir, Riesling, Gewürztraminer; others are made
from Washington grapes. Pinot Noir, red and white, is good.

Valley View Vineyards (1977) *Ch/Gewürz/Muscat of
Alexandria/CS/Merl/PN* 6,300 cases
Frank Wisnovsky, founder of this winery, was killed in 1980; his
widow now runs the winery, producing the above-listed varietals and
white Pinot Noir and Cabernet Sauvignon Rosé.

Wasson Bros Winery *Ch/Gewürz/Johan/PN*

PENNSYLVANIA

This is another example of the way in which the founding fathers
were far more kindly disposed towards wine than the bureaucratic
sons of more recent times. William Penn would have liked to have
founded a vineyard in the 17th century. Unfortunately, he was no

more successful than Pierre Legaux, a Frenchman who tried to plant
vinifera at the end of the 18th century.

From both experiments, the only enduring result was the Alexander
grape, one of Legaux's vinifera which had originally come from the
Cape of Good Hope, and which was soon planted here and in neighbouring states. Other attempts (including one by a friend of Benjamin
Franklin) came to little, and by the early 20th century the principal
grape grown was the Concord.

Repeal might have brought with it a rekindling of interest in
winemaking. A prospect which evidently so filled the would-be
prohibitionists with dread that they gave themselves a monopoly over
liquor sales which persists to this day.

Lest anyone be in the slightest doubt about what the state monopoly
means to the would-be wine drinker, Leon Adams' tale of his visit to
winemaker Melvin Gordon describes the situation vividly: 'I tasted
his wines from the barrels, and they were good, but Gordon couldn't
serve me any at lunch. In order to drink his own wine, he would have
had to buy it at a state store'. In 1968, the manacles were (despite the
ardent opposition of the liquor board) loosened slightly when wineries
were finally allowed to sell to individual consumers and restaurants,
and in 1982, wineries were allowed to open up to three retail tasting
rooms in local cities. Nonetheless, the state maintains its monopoly
over all other retail sales.

The logic of this form of state control is very strong indeed; it is
applied in the USSR with some success, as well as in the socialist
countries of Scandinavia. Though whether the people who currently
run the system would like to be thought socialist is another matter . . .

Adams County Winery (1974) 3,000 cases
White hybrids and vinifera are made.

Allegro Vineyards (1978) *Ch/CS/Merl/Sey B/Vidal*
Tim and John Crouch were musicians. Their Cabernet/Merlot blend is
an award winner.

Stephen Bahn Winery *Ch/Gewürz/Johan/PN/N/De Chaunac/Sey B/
Vidal*

Brandywine *Cat/Con/N/A/Sey B/Vidal*

Buckingham Valley Vineyards (1966) *Con/N/BN/Chel/De Chaunac/
Sey B/Vidal*

Bucks Country Vineyards (also New Jersey) *Cat/Con/Dut/N/A/Chel/
De Chaunac/Sey B/Vidal*
Most grapes are bought in.

Buffalo Valley Vineyards *Cat/Con/N/Chamb/Chan/Sey B/Vidal*

Calvaresi Winery *Cat/Con/Del/Dut/N/St/A/BN/Cham/Chel/
De Chaunac/Landot/Sey B*

Conestoga Vineyards Inc (1963) *Cat/Con/Dut/N/Chamb/Foch/Sey B/Vidal*
Having founded the first Pennsylvania winery to be launched since 1900, owner Melvin Gordon finally tired of the struggle against officialdom and sold out.

Conneaut Cellars *Ch/Johan/CS/De Chaunac/Sey B/Vidal*

Country Creek Vineyards & Winery *Johan/Cat/Con/N/A/BN/Chan/De Chaunac/Foch/Sey B/Vidal/Vill B*

Franklin Hill Vineyards *Johan/De Chaunac/Foch/Sey B/Vidal*

Heritage Wine Cellars *Ch/SB/Johan/CS/PN/Cat/Con/Del/Dut/N/De Chaunac/Sey B/Vidal*

Kolln Vineyards *Sey B*

Lancaster County Winery (1972)
Suzanne Dickel's winery is in the midst of the Amish community.

Lapic Winery (1977) *Cat/Con/Del/BN/Chel/Foch/Sey B/Vidal*

Lembo Vineyards (1971) *Chel/De Chaunac/Sey B*
The owners are ex-restaurateurs.

Mazza Vineyards (1974) *Ch/Gewürz/Johan/CS/Cat/Con/Dut/N/Chel/Sey B/Vidal* 10,000 cases
Most grapes are bought.

Mount Hope Estate & Winery *Ch/Gewürz/Johan/CS/Foch/Sey B/Vidal*
Recently launched venture which is already proving successful.

Naylor Wine Cellars (1978) *Ch/Gewürz/Johan/Cab Fr/CS/Merl/Zin/Cat/N/St/A/BN/Chamb/Chan/Chel/De Chaunac/Foch/Sey B/Vidal*
The Naylors used to have to make their wine in a potato cellar; they have a modern winery now.

Neri Wine Cellars *Cat/Con/N/A/BN/Chel/De Chaunac/Foch/Sey B*

Nissley Vineyards (1978) *Ch/Gewürz/Johan/Cat/Con/N/A/BN/Chan/Chel/De Chaunac/Foch/Sey B* 8,000 cases
This family operation specializes in French hybrids.

Nittany Valley Vineyards *BN/Chan/De Chaunac/Sey B*

Pecqual Valley Vineyard & Winery
Recently established. Showing promise.

Penn Shore Vineyards (1969) *Cat/Con/Del/N/BN/Chan/Foch/Sey B/Vidal*
Owned by a group of growers, and producing 14 wines, including several sparklers.

Presque Isle Wine Cellars (1960) *Ch/Gewürz/Johan/Al/Barb/Cab Fr/CS/Gamay/PS/PN/Cat/Del/Dut/St/Chamb/Sey B/Vidal*
A cunning wheeze really: a group of would-be winemakers founded a company to supply home winemakers with grape juice etc . . . With the easing of the law in 1968, wine was then offered to the public. Good Cabernet.

Quarry Hill Winery *Del/D/Chel/Vidal*

Tucquan Vineyards (1974) *Cat/Con/N/St/Chan/Foch/Sey B*
With no pretentions to make vinifera, the Hamptons are very successful with their Labrusca and hybrids.

York Springs Winery *Ch/Johan/CS/PN/Foch/Sey B/Sey Vill*

RHODE ISLAND

Before Prohibition, this small state used to produce a reasonable amount of wine. There was then a dry period until the mid 1970s when new laws permitted winemakers to try again. They have every reason to be optimistic: the temperature is little different to that in Bordeaux.

Diamond Hill Vineyard Cellar (1979)
A smallish concern run by two brothers and their wives.

Prudence Island Vineyard (1973) *PN/CS/Merl/GB/Ch/Gewürz/Ries*
With 20 ha growing exclusively vinifera vines, Prudence Island has won several awards, particularly for Chardonnay.

Sakonnet Vineyards (1977) *Ch/Johan/PN/Sey/Chan/Foch/Vidal*
10,000 cases
Having expanded three-fold since it first opened, Sakonnet gives many of its wines names of a nautical bent, like 'America's Cup'. Some sparkling Vidal is made.

South Country Vineyards (1974)
Also known as 'Winery Number One' because it was the first on the island. It has a small plot of vinifera vines, but relies mainly on bought-in grapes from New York State. The first wine was made in the early 1980's.

TENNESSEE

In the latter part of the 19th century Tennessee produced a large number of prize-winning wines; Chatanooga was once a centre of vinous activity. As elsewhere, Prohibition slammed on the brakes, and, until 1977, there was little to encourage winemakers. When in that year the state legislature began to take steps to remedy the situation, changing laws and reducing the tax on wine from $1.18 a gallon to only 5 cents on locally produced wine, matters began to improve. The only hindrance to further progress was a number of restrictive clauses in the newly passed laws which prevented wineries from selling their wine to wholesale customers. These clauses were, it should be said, the responsibility not of the temperance brigade, but of the producers of hard liquor. Liberality and free enterprise are now beginning to correct the situation.

Highland Manor Winery (1980) *Ch/Johan/CS*
The owners, a retired Air Force sergeant major and his wife, originally made wine from Labrusca and French hybrids, but vinifera is now proving successful.

Laurel Hill Winery
A new winery producing wine from vinifera and hybrids.

Smoky Mountain Winery (1981)
The Smoky Mountain National Park attracts tourists, many of whom leave with happy memories of Tennessee wine. The winemaker here once owned a vineyard in Indiana.

Tiegs Vineyard (1980)
A young winery owned by a ceramic engineer who is making red and white blends from hybrids planted in his own small vineyard.

TEXAS

J.R. is never seen to pull the cork on a locally produced wine in 'Dallas', but he could . . . There are no less than 18 wineries in the Lone Star State and the figure is growing. Texans think big, and it only took an optimistic A&M University feasibility study in 1974 to set oil men and ranchers alike dreaming of the day when they could complete with California. Their dreams may be extravagant, but anyone who thinks of Texas as too hot for winemaking should visit the western mountains which are as cool as anywhere on the Californian coast. On the other hand, hail can be a major problem, with stones large enough to kill cattle. Winemaking isn't new to Texas either: the

Val Verde winery is over a century old, and several wineries were running quite successfully before the arrival of Prohibition. Whether the wines they were making then would find many fans today however is another question; thick, over-cooked tasting brews made from such mouth-watering grape varieties as the Lenoir, Herbemont and Black Spanish are not to every California Chardonnay drinker's taste. Now however, there are plantations of a wide range of different grapes, in various parts of the state, from the cool mountainsides of the far west, to the Turkish Bath humidity of the Rio Grande Valley. Some wineries are situated in 'dry' counties, and have to sell their wines in neighbouring 'wet' counties. The Texan winemakers are sufficiently determined not to worry about such inconveniences. Time will tell how their wines develop.

Buena Vida Vineyards (1978)
Owned by osteopath Bobby Smith (a useful skill in view of the effect on the backbone of bending to prune the vines) and with wine made by his son, Steven. Wines include 'Texas Gold Premium Red' Chambourcin and a recently launched sparkling wine. Hybrids are used mostly.

Château Montgolfier (1982)
Named after the French balloonist, and belonging to a keen modern counterpart who is also an orthopaedic surgeon.

Cyprus Valley Vineyard (1982)
A small concern (6,000 gallons) with wines and vines under the care of Penny Bettis, wife of owner Professor Dale Bettis, who studied horticulture at Texas A&M University and science at Fresno in California.

Fall Creek Vineyard (1979)
Producing Sauvignon Blanc and Villard Blanc.

Gretchen Glasscock Vineyard (1977)
Leon Adams describes the lady in question as 'onetime Texas "Oil Princess"'.

Gaudalupe Valley (1975)
Has no vineyards, but buys in Texan grapes as well as Californian wine. First reports are encouraging.

Llano Estacado (1976)
6 *ha* of vines planted by professors Clinton McPherson, Roy Mitchell and Robert Reed. Clinton's son, Kim, the winemaker, trained at the University of California Davis wine school. He plans to make sparkling wine. In 1980 there was a major setback when a hailstorm destroyed the entire crop.

Robert Oberhellman (1979)
A large 30,000 gallon winery founded by an ex-food broker, and making Chardonnay, Pinot Noir, and Cabernet Sauvignon.

Pheasant Ridge (1982)
Owned by Bobby Cox III, 27 acres, all planted in vinifera.

Sanchez Gill Richter Cordier (1983)
A co-production between the well-known Bordeaux merchants and château owners and Texans, with 1.5 million gallons of capacity, paying the University of Texas a percentage of its sales in return for the use of its experimental vineyards.

Sanchez Creek (1980)
Anthropology professor Ron Wetherington, his wife Judith and her father, Joseph Swift, make Cabernet Sauvignon from an eight-acre vineyard.

Val Verde (1883)
The Qualiu family have been running this winery for three generations. Traditional vines imported from South Carolina are being replaced by finer, more modern varieties, barrels with stainless steel tanks and screwtops with corks.

UTAH

Hungry wine-loving visitors to Salt Lake City are advised to drive the ten or so miles to Sandy where the La Caille restaurant is surrounded by vines. If you have the peculiar desire to drink a glass or two of wine with your meal however, you'll have to buy it from a state official at a booth in the restaurant: in Utah liquor can only be sold by the state monopoly.

The Mormon religion regards wine drinking in a different way to polygamy – though it used to permit wine to be made and sold to non-Mormons. Today, Utah has only one winery:

Summum (1981) *Col/Gren rosé/Zin rosé*
The winery is pyramidal – its owner believes in the supernatural powers of these structures and is the founder of the Summum church. The wine is made from Californian grapes and is not actually 'sold' – bottles are obtained in bookshops in return for 'donations' to the Summum church.

VIRGINIA

Virginia's history might lead the non-American visitor to expect to see a Californian expanse of vineyards stretching to the horizon. It was the first region of America to use grapes for wine – as early as the 17th century – and in 1773 Italian vines were planted in Thomas Jefferson's estate at Monticello. By the late 19th century Virginia had become one of the most important winegrowing states of the Union, famous for 'Norton Claret', made from an indigenous Labrusca vine, Catawba, 'sherry' and 'port'. Sadly though, the proponents of temperance gradually took hold of the state, and despite attempts by Captain Paul Garrett to persuade his countrymen to drink 'Virginia Dare' from the Scuppernong Muscadine grape in the 1930s, Virginia is only now beginning to rebuild its wine industry, and plantation of hybrids and vinifera is moving ahead very rapidly again. For the first time, since 1980, winemaking is actually encouraged. Jefferson loved wine and thought it a far more sensible tipple than harder liquor; he would be pleased to see its production encouraged.

La Arbra Farm & Winery (1976) *BN/Vill B*
Run by investment banker Albert Weed.

Barboursville Winery *Ch/Gewürz/Johan/CS/Merl*
Owned by Zonin, a huge Italian company, and the source of Virginia's first Cabernet Sauvignon.

Blenheim Vineyards *Ch/Johan/CS*

Château Naturel

Chermont Winery *Ch/Johan/CS*

Farfelu (1976) *Ch/Chan/Sey B*
The airline pilot owner named his winery 'farfelu', the French word for 'a little crazy'.

Ingleside Plantation Winery (1980) *Ch/Johan/CS/Chan/Sey B*

Laird & Co Wine Cellar (1780)
The oldest winery in the state, Laird frankly offers a 'Sly Fox' Labrusca.

Meredyth Vineyard (1976) *Del/A/De Chaunac/Foch/Sey B/Vill B/Ch/Johan/CS/Merl*
Dr Archie Smith III was a philosophy professor at Oxford; his winery is a converted stable.

MJC Vineyards *Ch/Johan/Del/Dut/Cham/Foch/Landot/Sey B/Vidal*

Montdomaine Cellars (1981) *Ch/CS/Merl*
The owners are a couple whose other occupation is as pilot and stewardess.

Monticello Cellars
Jefferson's old home, not to be confused with the California winery of the same name.

Naked Mountain Vineyard *Ch/SB/Johan*

Oasis Vineyard *Ch/Gewürz/SB/Sem/Johan/CS/Merl*
Dirgham Salahi was born in Jerusalem, hence the winery name. He has 12 *ha* of vines.

Piedmont Winery (1976) *Ch/Sem/Sey B*

Prince Michel (1984) *Ch/Gewürz/Johan/CS*

Rapidan Vineyards (1981) *Ch/Gewürz/Johan*
Owned by a German physician and founded with advice from a German, Geisenheim-trained wine planter, this is a converted dairy farm.

Rose Bower Vineyards & Winery (1980) *Ch/Johan/CS/Foch*
Owner, Poet Tom O'Grady, is proving successful with vinifera.

Shenandoah (1977) *Sey B/Chan/Chamb*

WEST VIRGINIA

Attempts to resurrect the century-old wine industry in West Virginia were hampered by Governor John 'Jay' Rockefeller IV who regularly vetoed a farm winery bill and the sale of wines in food stores. He was finally overruled in 1981, and West Virginian consumption (previously the lowest in the US) rose nearly fourfold in a year. Winemakers celebrated their victory for free enterprize by singing 'Bye Bye Jaybird'.

Fisher Ridge Cellar *Ch/Sey B/Vidal*
Hybrid, vinifera – Fisher Ridge White – first legally sold this century.

West-Whitehall Winery (1981) *Ch/A/Foch/Sey B*
Small.

WASHINGTON

Non-Americans find it difficult enough to understand that the Washington which serves as the nation's capital is on the opposite coast to the state of the same name. For them to have to learn that Washington is the third most prolific wine-producing state of the union must confuse matters even further. Winemaking has a shorter history here than in several other states (the first wine was made little over a century ago) but once started, the wine industry has enjoyed a steady expansion, despite the fact that, for many years, the state held a monopoly over wine sales.

If Washington wine has a 'founding father', it must be William B. Bridgman who was the first man to concentrate his attention on European vinifera, having established that the climate of his vineyard was even better suited for such wines than traditional areas of France and Germany. Sadly, this turned out to be something of a false start. Leon Adams reports that the wine made for Bridgman by a German he had imported for the purpose was of poor quality. Adams also recalls visiting the region in the mid-1960's and discovering that the winemakers, newly liberated by the removal of the monopoly, were still blending Concord grapes with fine vinifera. It was Adams who suggested importing a Californian expert, André Tchelistcheff, and commissioning him to tell the Washington wine producers what they should be doing. After initially dismissing all the wines he tasted, Tchelistcheff then tasted what he thought to be America's finest Gewürztraminer and immediately felt inspired to see how other grapes might fare.

Tchelistcheff sought out particular vines, directed their pruning and oversaw the way in which the grapes were picked, fermented and matured, doing for the Washington producers what Professor Emile Peynaud has so frequently done for individual Bordeaux châteaux. The results of this careful effort, labelled 'Ste Michelle' surprised all who sampled them; it was as if a member of the chorus line had suddenly moved into the spotlight – and proved how well she could perform. Since those first 1967 and 1969 wines appeared on the market, progress in Washington has been swift. The state is often lumped together with Oregon, and there is indeed a great deal of contact between the two, but they should not be confused. The point of contact between them is the climate which, with the exception of certain Californian micro-climates, is far cooler and more 'European' than that enjoyed further south. Both also share the advantage of inexpensive land, so are potentially able to produce some of America's most keenly priced high-quality wine.

Many believe that the Yakima and Columbia Valleys are the ideal places to make wine in Washington, but there is still much to be done: 80% of the state's vineyards are still planted in Concord. But just think of the potential . . .

Arbor Crest (1982) *Ch/MC/SB/Johan/CS/Merl*
A Cabernet Sauvignon rosé is made here.

Associated Vintners (Columbia Wines) (1962) *Ch/Gewürz/Sem/Johan/CS/Gren/Merl/PN*
Ten university professors, one of whom (Dr Lloyd Woodburne) had, as a home-winemaker, made the Gewürztraminer which had so impressed Tchelistcheff, formed a company to make wine. Since then, their wines have done well in several blind tastings and, with Canadian Master of Wine, David Lake, at the helm the company has become acknowledged as one of America's most exciting young wineries. Appropriately enough, Gewürztraminer is still a speciality. The name has now changed to Columbia Wines; grapes come from Yakima and Columbia Valleys.

Bainbridge Island Winery (1981) *Ch/Gewürz/Johan*

Champs de Brionne (1984) *Ch/Gewürz/Sem/Johan/CS/PN*
Literally 'Bryan's Fields' after Dr Vincent Bryan, its owner.

Château Ste Michelle (1967) *Ch/Chen B/Gewürz/MC/SB/Sem/Johan/CS/Merl/Gren*
The site of André Tchelistcheff's success is now marked by a touristic mock-château which belongs to the United States Tobacco Company of Connecticut. Tchelistcheff still visits four times a year and, under his guidance, considerable investment is still being made. This is Washington's biggest: its wines are generally worth seeking out. A rare Cabernet Sauvignon rosé is made, and there is also a good Grenache rosé.

Daquila Wines *Gewürz/SB/Sem*

E.B. Foote Winery (1978) *Ch/Chen B/Gewürz/Johan/CS/PN*
5,000 cases
Grapes are bought in; the wines win prizes.

Haviland Vintners *Ch/Gewürz/MC/SB/Sem/Johan/CS/Merl/PN/PN white*

Hinzerling Vineyards (1976) *Ch/Gewürz/Johan/CS/Merl* 8,000 cases
One of the wines is called 'Ashfall White' after the volcanic ash deposited on the vines in 1980 by Mount St Helens. Late harvest Gewürztraminer ('der Sonne') is worth seeking out.

The Hogue Cellars (1982) *Ch/Chen B/SB/Johan/CS/Merl*
The Hogue family are fruit and vegetable farmers with ambitious plans for their winery.

Kiona (1979) *Ch/Chen B/Sem/Johan/CS/Limberger*
The unique wine here is a red, made from the German Limberger grape.

Franz Wilhelm Langguth (1982) *Ch/Gewürz/Johan/CS*
This is a name familiar to buyers of German wine, as one of that country's biggest and best-known wine companies. The large winery has 200 *ha* and could produce around 3,000,000 bottles of wine per annum. It must be ironic for the German company to see Riesling grapes being planted, rather than uprooted as has been the case in the Rhine (where they are being replaced by 'easier-to-grow' varieties'). The winemaker is Swiss, and previously worked at Château Benoit in Oregon.

Latah Creek Wine Cellar *Ch/Chen B/MC/SB/Johan/Merl*

Leonetti Cellar (1977) *Johan/CS/Merl* 300 cases
What a California wine magazine called 'The nation's best Cabernet' was made here by machinist, Gary Figgins, in his spare time.

Lost Mountain Winery *Barb/CS/Merl/PS/PN/Zin*

Mont Elise Vineyards (1974) *Chen B/Gewürz/CS/GB/PN/PN rosé* 5,000 cases
Previously called 'Bingen Wine Cellars' but now renamed – officially after the owners' daughter, but also because of the way in which locals pronounced the previous name. The speciality is Gewürztraminer.

Mount Baker Vineyards (1982) *Ch/Gewürz/CS/PN/Foch/Sey Vill*

Neuharth Winery *Ch/Chen B/Johan/CS/Merl/Zin*

Preston Wine Cellars (1976) *Ch/Chen B/Gewürz/Muscat of Alexandria/SB/Johan/CS/Merl/PN/PN white/Gamay rosé* 60,000 cases
No less than 17 different wines are made: best of these are probably Chardonnay and Fumé Blanc.

Quail Run Vintners (1982) *Ch/Chen B/Gewürz/Johan*
With 40 *ha* of vinifera, planted by a group of Yakima Valley vineyard owners this is a winery to watch.

Salishan Vineyards (1976) *Ch/Chen B/Johan/CS/Merl/PN* 2,000 cases
The Salish Indians used to live here. The wine is made by former journalist, Joan Wolverton, with help from her husband Lincoln, an economist. The Pinot Noir is good.

Paul Thomas Wines *MC/SB/Johan*
This winery also makes fruit wine and a white Cabernet Sauvignon.

Tucker Cellars (1981) *Ch/Chen B/Gewürz/MC/Johan/CS*
Owned by fruit farmers.

Vernier Wines *Ch/SB/Sem/Johan/CS/Merl*

Manfred Vierthaler Winery (1976) *Ch/Chen B/Gewürz/Johan/CS/GB/PN/MT/Gren/PN white/PN rosé* 10,000 cases
The owner is a German restaurateur.

Woodward Canyon Winery *Ch/Chen B/Gewürz/SB/Johan/CS*
Situated in the attractively named Walla Walla Valley, this winery is noted for its Chardonnay. It also produces a Pinot Noir rosé.

Yakima River Winery (1979) *Ch/Chen B/Gewürz/MC/SB/Johan/CS/Merl/PN/Cat*
A small, medal-winning winery with a varied selection of wines.

AMERICA'S FINEST
A Shopping List

Any list of the finest wines and winemakers in the USA is bound to create differences of opinion. The availability of particular vintages is unpredictable, and the quality of future harvests unknown; even so, this list should prove invaluable to anyone buying American wine.

Acacia (Napa, California)
Pinot Noir, Chardonnay.

Adelsheim (Oregon)
Pinot Noir.

Almaden (San Benito California)
Pinot Noir.

Amity (Oregon)
Pinot Noir, Riesling.

Arbor Crest (Washington)
Riesling.

Beaulieu (Napa, California)
Chardonnay, Cabernet Sauvignon.

Beringer (Napa, California)
Chardonnay, Fumé Blanc, Cabernet.

David Bruce (Santa Clara, California)
Chardonnay.

Buena Vista (Sonoma, California)
Cabernet Sauvignon, Riesling, Pinot Noir.

Byrd (Maryland)
Cabernet Sauvignon, Chardonnay.

Calera (California)
Pinot Noir, Chardonnay, Zinfandel.

Callaway (Temecula, California)
Chardonnay.

Carneros Creek (Napa, California)
Pinot Noir, Chardonnay, Cabernet.

Casa Larga (Finger Lakes NY)
Riesling.

Cassayre-Forni Cellars (Napa, California)
Zinfandel.

Catoctin Vineyards (Maryland)
Chardonnay.

Caymus (Napa, California)
Cabernet.

Chalone (Monterey, California)
Chardonnay, Pinot Noir.

Chappellet (Napa, California)
Chenin Blanc, Cabernet Sauvignon, Chardonnay.

Château Benoit (Oregon)
Riesling.

Château Chevalier (Napa, California)
Cabernet.

Château Grand Traverse (Missouri)
Chardonnay.

Château Julien (Monterey California)
Chardonnay.

Château Lagniappe (Oregon)
Chardonnay.

Château Montelena (Napa, California)
Cabernet Sauvignon, Chardonnay.

Château St Jean (Sonoma, California)
Riesling, Chardonnay, Fumé Blanc.

Château Ste Michelle (Washington)
Chardonnay, Riesling.

Christian Brothers (Napa, California)
Fumé Blanc.

Clos du Bois (Sonoma, California)
Gewürztraminer, Cabernet Sauvignon, Riesling, Pinot Noir.

Clos du Val (Napa, California)
Cabernet Sauvignon, Zinfandel, Pinot Noir, Chardonnay.

Columbia (Washington)
Chardonnay, Cabernet Sauvignon, Gewürztraminer.

Commonwealth (Maryland)
Chardonnay, Riesling.

Concannon (Alameda, California)
Petite Syrah, Chardonnay.

Conn Creek (Napa, California)
Cabernet.

Cuvaison (Napa, California)
Zinfandel.

Domaine Laurier (Sonoma, California)
Chardonnay.

Dry Creek (Sonoma, California)
Fumé Blanc.

Durney (Monterey, California)
Cabernet.

Edmeades (Mendocino, California)
Pinot Noir.

Elk Cove (Oregon)
Chardonnay, Riesling.

Estrella (Pasa Robles, California)
Cabernet.

The Eyrie Vineyard (Oregon)
Pinot Noir.

Louis Facelli (Idaho)
Riesling.

Far Niente (Napa, California)
Chardonnay.

Felton-Empire (Santa Cruz, California)
Riesling.

Fetzer (Mendocino, California)
Carbernet Sauvignon, Petite Syrah.

Firestone (Santa Barbara, California)
Merlot, Riesling.

Flora Springs Wine Co (Napa, California)
Chardonnay, Cabernet.

E.B. Foote (Washington)
Gewürztraminer, Chardonnay.

Franciscan Vineyards (Napa, California)
Cabernet Sauvignon, Riesling, Chardonnay.

Freemark Abbey (Napa, California)
Riesling, Cabernet Sauvignon, Chardonnay.

Frick (Monterey, California)
Chardonnay, Pinot Noir.

Frontenac Point (Finger Lakes, NY)
Chardonnay.

E & J Gallo (Stanislaus, California)
Cabernet.

Glen Creek (Washington)
Chardonnay.

Glenora (Finger Lakes, NY)
Riesling.

Gold Seal (Finger Lakes, NY)
Riesling, Chardonnay.

Grand Cru Vineyards (Sonoma, California)
Gewürztraminer.

Grgich Hills Cellar (Napa, California)
Chardonnay, Riesling.

Emilio Guglielmo (Santa Barbara, California)
Riesling.

Hanzell (Sonoma, California)
Pinot Noir, Chardonnay.

Harbor Winery (Sacramento, California)
Chardonnay, Zinfandel.

Hargrave (Long Island, NY)
Chardonnay, Cabernet Sauvignon, Sauvignon Blanc Pinot Noir.

Haviland (Washington)
Pinot Noir, Chardonnay.

Haywood (Sonoma, California)
Cabernet Sauvignon, Riesling.

Heitz (Napa, California)
Caberent Sauvignon, Chardonnay.

Heron Hill (Finger Lakes, NY)
Riesling.

Hidden Springs (Oregon)
Pinot Noir.

Hillcrest (Oregon)
Pinot Noir.

Hinzerling Vineyards (Washington)
Gewürztraminer.

Hogue (Washington)
Riesling.

Hood River Vineyard (Oregon)
Riesling.

Inglenook (Napa, California)
Cabernet.

Ingleside Plantation (Virginia)
Chardonnay.

Iron Horse (Sonoma, California)
Cabernet.

Jekel (Monterey, California)
Riesling, Cabernet.

Jordan (Sonoma, California)
Cabernet, Chardonnay.

Kendall-Jackson (California)
Chardonnay, Riesling.

Kenwood (Sonoma, California)
Cabernet Sauvignon, Chardonnay.

Knusden-Erath (Oregon)
Pinot Noir, Chardonnay, Riesling.

Charles Krug (Napa, California)
Cabernet Sauvignon, Chenin Blanc.

La Crema (Napa, California)
Pinot Noir.

Latah Creek (Washington)
Riesling.

Leonetti Cellar (Washington)
Cabernet Sauvignon.

J. Lohr (San José, California)
Cabernet Sauvignon, Chardonnay.

Lower Lake (Lake Country California)
Cabernet Sauvignon.

Macgregor (New York)
Gewürztraminer, Riesling.

Marietta (Sonoma California)
Cabernet.

Mark West (Russian River, California)
Chardonnay.

Louis Martini (Napa, California)
Cabernet Sauvignon, Gewürztraminer, Moscato Amabile.

Paul Masson Pinnacles Selection (Santa Clara, California)
Chardonnay.

Matanzas Creek (Sonoma California)
Chardonnay.

Mayacamas (Napa, California)
Zinfandel, Cabernet.

Meredyth (Virginia)
Cabernet Sauvignon, Chardonnay.

Louis K. Mihaly (Napa, California)
Chardonnay.

Milano (Anderson Valley, California)
Riesling.

Mirassou (Monterey, California)
Chardonnay.

MJC (Virginia)
Chardonnay.

Robert Mondavi (Napa, California)
Cabernet Sauvignon, Chardonnay, Pinot Noir, Fumé Blanc, Riesling.

The Monterey Vineyard (Monterey, California)
Riesling, Zinfandel.

Montevina (Amador, California)
Zinfandel.

Mount Eden (Santa Clara, California)
Chardonnay.

Naked Mountain (Virginia)
Chardonnay.

Navaro Vineyards (Mendocino, California)
Gewürztraminer.

Newton (Napa, California)
Cabernet.

Opus One (Napa, California)
Cabernet.

Oak Knoll (Oregon)
Pinot Noir.

Pacheco Ranch (Marin California)
Cabernet Sauvignon.

Papagni (Madèra, California)
Chardonnay, Moscato d'Angelo, Zinfandel.

Parducci (Mendocino, California)
Zinfandel.

Pedroncelli Winery (Sonoma, California)
Gewürztraminer.

Joseph Phelps (Napa,
California)
*Chardonnay, Cabernet
Sauvignon, Riesling,
Gewürztraminer.*

Pine Ridge (Napa, California)
Cabernet.

Ponzi (Oregon)
Pinot Noir.

Preston (Washington)
*Cabernet Sauvignon,
Chardonnay.*

Preston (Sonoma, California)
Sauvignon.

Quail Run (Washington)
Riesling.

Raymond (Napa, California)
Chardonnay.

Ridge (Santa Clara, California)
Cabernet Sauvignon, Zinfandel.

Roudon-Smith (Santa-Cruz,
California)
Chardonnay.

Round Hill (Napa, California)
Cabernet.

Ste Chapelle (Washington)
*Cabernet Sauvignon,
Chardonnay, Riesling, Chenin
Blanc.*

Saintsbury (Napa California)
Pinot Noir.

Salishan (Washington)
Pinot Noir.

Sanford (Santa Maria Valley,
California)
Chardonnay, Pinot Noir.

**Santa Cruz Mountain
Vineyard** (Santa Cruz)
Pinot Noir.

Sarah's Vineyard (Santa Clara
California)
Chardonnay.

Sebastiani (Sonoma, California)
*Cabernet Sauvignon, Pinot Noir,
Zinfandel.*

Seghesio (Sonoma, California)
Cabernet Sauvignon, Zinfandel.

Sequoia Grove (Alexander
Valley, California)
Cabernet.

Shafer (Napa, California)
Chardonnay.

Shafer Vineyard Cellars
(Oregon)
Chardonnay, Riesling.

Charles F. Shaw (Napa,
California)
Chardonnay.

Shenandoah Vineyards
(Virginia)
Cabernet Sauvignon.

Simi (Sonoma California)
Zinfandel, Gewürztraminer.

Sokol Blosser (Oregon)
*Chardonnay, Riesling,
Sauvignon Blanc.*

Sonoma-Cutrer (Sonoma,
California)
Chardonnay.

Souverain Cellars (Sonoma,
California)
*Cabernet Sauvignon, Gamay
Bjls.*

Smith-Madrone (Napa,
California)
Riesling.

Spring Mountain (Napa,
California)
*Cabernet Sauvignon,
Chardonnay.*

Stag's Leap (Napa, California)
*Cabernet Sauvignon,
Chardonnay, Riesling, Merlot.*

David S. Stare (Dry Creek,
California)
Chardonnay.

Robert Stemmler (Sonoma,
California)
Cabernet Sauvignon, Pinot Noir,

Sterling (Napa, California)
Cabernet Sauvignon, Merlot.

Stony Hill Vineyard (Napa,
California)
Chardonnay.

Stony Ridge (Monterey,
California)
Cabernet.

Sutter Home Winery (Napa,
California)
Zinfandel.

Tewksbury (New Jersey)
Chardonnay.

Trefethen (Napa, California)
*Chardonnay, Pinot Noir,
Cabernet.*

Tualatin (Oregon)
Pinot Noir, Chardonnay.

Turner (San Joaquin,
California)
*Chardonnay, Cabernet
Sauvignon.*

Valley View (Oregon)
Pinot Noir.

Vichon (Napa, California)
Chardonnay.

Villa Mt Eden (Napa,
California)
*Gewürztraminer, Chardonnay,
Cabernet Sauvignon, Chenin
Blanc.*

Vinifera Cellars (Finger
Lakes, NY)
Gewürztraminer.

Wagner (Finger Lakes, NY)
Chardonnay, Riesling.

Wente Brothers (Alameda,
California)
Chardonnay, Semillon.

William Wheeler (Sonoma,
California)
Chardonnay.

Wheeler (Dry Creek, California)
Cabernet Sauvignon.

Whickham (Finger Lakes, NY)
Chardonnay

Whitehall Lane (Napa,
California)
Cabernet.

Hermann J. Wiemer (Finger
Lakes, NY)
Chardonnay, Riesling.

Woodbury Winery (Marin
County, California)
Zinfandel 'port'.

Zaca Mesa (Santa Barbara
California)
Chardonnay.

USSR

THE Russian taste in alcohol is for strong Vodka, strong sweet red wine and almost equally sweet red sparkling wine. (Over 75 per cent of all Russian wine is sweet). In order to wean the populace off the first, and most damaging of these beverages, the government instituted a plan between 1950–1972 which doubled the acreage of vines and gave the state a hand in wine production. The size of the nation, and its varied climate mean that, in some regions, irrigation is essential, and in others that only the hardiest of varieties can withstand the cold.

The USSR is now the world's number four wine producer, its 3,000,000 ha representing 10 per cent of winemaking vineyards planted worldwide. Even so, most of these wines are – to Western palates – as successful as the Concorski supersonic airplane.

Russia's sparkling wines are made by a process restricted (until its introduction in 1985 into Portugal) to eastern Europe, and known as the 'Russian Continuous' system. Explained simply, this process consists of a series of sealed tanks: fermented wine enters the first tank, has sugar and yeast added, before passing into the second which is packed full of oak chips. The yeast in the wine having caused the sugar to ferment (and thus creating CO_2 bubbles), the yeast autolyses on the oak, allowing clear wine to pass into the third tank where it is sweetened before bottling. This *should* make wine of a quality somewhere between that of the Cuve Close and Transfer Method used in the West. But, sadly . . .

The Grape List

White

Akastafa (like white port)
Aligoté (as grown in Burgundy)
Alupka
Chardonnay (dry white)
Feteasca (red, white and rosé)
Grifesti
Gurdzhaani
Italian Riesling
Kara-Tachanakh (red dessert
wine)
Manadis
Mukhuzani
Muscat
Muscatel
Mzvane
Napureouli
Pinot Gris
Rcatsiteli
Rhine Riesling
Sauvignon Blanc
Sercial
Sémillon
Sou-Dag (similar to white port)
Sylvaner
Traminer
Tsinandali

Verdelho
Voskheat (used to make 'sherry')

Red
Aiou-Dag (red Muscat type)
Alouchta (like port)
Bordo
Cabernet Sauvignon
Chemakha (sweet red wine)
Feteasca
Kuchuk-Lambat (like port)
Kuchuk-Uzen (like Madeira)
Kurdamir (sweet red wine)
Livadia (like port)
Malbec
Massandra (like port and
  Madeira)
Merlot
Pinot Noir
Rara Neagra
Saperavi

The Wine Regions

UKRAINE AND CRIMEA
The Ukraine is divided into two
main zones: the Dnieper, and the
region around the Eastern foothills of the Carpathians. The
Crimean regions are around
Simferopol and the coastal zone
from Sevastopol to Feodosiya.
  Massandra and Ay-Danil,
were once the names of the
estates of Prince Vorontsov.
They are now applied to white
and dessert wines from a
number of state cooperatives.
Sevastopol and Balaclava are
centres of sparkling wine
production.

Red wines
Chernyi (Chorny) Doktor (sweet,
  from Solnechnaya Dolina, the
  'Valley of the Sun')
Cabernert Livadia
Saperavi Massandra
Bordo Ay-Danil

White wines
Sémillon Oreand
Riesling Massandra
Aligoté Ay-Danil
Muscat Oreand
Muscat Livadia
Muscat Kuchuk-Lambat

Sparkling
Kaffia

GEORGIA

Tiflis
Pinot Noir and Chardonnay
grown.
Red wines from Saperavi and

Mukhuzaani grapes
White wines: Napareouli,
Tsinandali.
Sparkling 'Champanski'

Kakhtiya
Some Cabernet Sauvignon

E. Georgia
White wines from Rcatsiteli,
Gurdzhaani and Mtsvani grapes

OLD RUSSIA

Rostov
Reds, whites, sparkling wines

Black Sea Coast
Sparkling and dry table whites
Anapa Riesling
Also Cabernet from Anapa

Makhachkala/Derbent
Dessert whites.

Other grape varieties: Aligoté,
Sauvignon, Sémillon, Pinot
Noir, Pinot Gris.

ARMENIA
Borders on Turkey and Iran.
Ancient evidence of
wine-making.

Grape varieties:
Verdelho
Sercial
Aligoté
Muscat
Voskheat

Wines
Various dubious euphemisms –
'Port', 'Madeira', 'Brandy'
Ashtarak – a sherry-type wine
made from the Voskheat grape

AZERBAIJAN
Rcatsiteli and indigenous
varieties.
Mainly dessert wines – Matras
and Shemalch popular locally

MOLDAVIA
Mostly sweet whites (15–20%
residual sugar), and some reds

Grape varieties
Red: Cabernet Sauvignon,
Merlot, Malbec, Saperavi, Rara
Neagra
White: Feteasca, Aligoté,
Traminer, Rhine and Italian
Riesling, Muscat, Rcatsiteli,
Pinot Gris, Grifesti

Red Wines
Negri de Purkar (C.S., Merlot,
Malbec, Saperavi, Rara Neagra)
Cabernet Sauvignon
Bordo
Chumay (Ciumaj) – sweet red,
Cabernet and Grifesti

Romanovka – Cabernet, Malbec,
Merlot

White wines
Pinot
Aligoté

Sparkling
Fetysk

Turkmenistan, Kazakhstan,
Uzbekistan and Kirgistan grow
only table grapes.

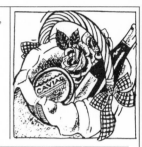

The Regions

Hectolitres p.a.

Moldavia	4.7m	Georgia	1.7m
Ukraine	1.7m	Azerbaijan	1.6m
Russia	10.7m	Armenia	0.9m

WINE TERMS

THERE are useful wine terms and useless ones. We have listed a
selection of both kinds, but would still suggest you stick to using
whichever words spring to your own mind when you smell or taste a
wine. After all, when you want to describe a film or a fine meal, you
don't generally seek recourse to a list of terms . . .

Fifty useful descriptive terms

Acidity The necessary component which keeps wine fresh.

Artificial Some wines taste as if the flavour chemists have visited the
winery . . . Also 'Confected' and 'Contrived'.

Astringent Tannic (q.v.) is characteristic of young red wine.

Attack A wine with good acidity and something to say.

Austere Some wines, although potentially excellent in the long term,
seem difficult to approach, making their fruit difficult to detect. An
over-used expression.

Balance A balanced wine has its fruitiness, acidity, alcohol and
tannin (for reds) in pleasant harmony. Balance can develop with age.

Body A full-bodied wine fills the mouth with flavour. Can also be
described as being 'Full' or having 'Weight'.

Bouquet The overall smell of a wine, often made up of several
separate 'aromas'. Like a bunch of different flowers.

Buttery The rich, fat smell, often found in good Chardonnay wines,
and sometimes associated with wine which has been left on its lees.

Classy Self explanatory, and often used, along with 'Fine',
'Breeding', 'Pedigree', 'Finesse' and 'Elegant' when the taster simply
wants to say that a wine tastes extremely good.

Clean Means what it says. Some wines can, and do, smell and taste,
'Dirty'.

Cloying The characteristic of cheap perfume and some sweets. A
sickly flavour or smell that hangs around.

Coarse Probably badly made, rough-tasting wine.

Complex Some wines have interesting and complex mixtures of
smells and flavours. Like a dish cooked with several different herbs.

Corked If a cork has, for whatever reason, allowed air to come into
contact with the contents of its bottle, the wine may be described as
corked, meaning 'Oxidized' (q.v.). Usually though, it will also have a
'Corky' (q.v.) character.

Corky The unpleasant musty cork smell and flavour caused by a faulty cork, or by one which has been 'got at' by a weevil.

Crisp Fresh wine with good 'Acidity' (q.v.).

Dumb As in 'Dumb Nose', meaning no apparent smell.

Dusty The tannic smell often found in young claret.

Farmyardy Not necessarily unpleasant, this smell is common in genuine mature Burgundy. There has to be some fruit there too though . . .

Finish Wine can taste very different when you first put it into your mouth from the way it does just before you swallow it. The 'Aftertaste' comes later.

Fresh What all young wines should be.

Flabby Lacking balancing acidity.

Fruity Self explanatory, but the one word which appears on tasters' notes less often than they would usually like.

Gamey A meaty smell, reminiscent of hung game, and often associated with wines made of the Syrah/Shiraz grape.

Hard Tannic, acidic wine.

Hot Over-alcoholic wine is described as 'hot' because of the burning sensation it has in the mouth. The strength may come from over-ripe grapes, or added sugar.

Length The flavour of some wines disappears very quickly whilst that of others lingers in the mouth. Also 'Short' and 'Long'.

Maderized An oxidized white wine is sometimes termed 'maderized' after the Madeira whose character is caused by the wine being intentionally exposed to heat and oxygen.

Mercaptan A rotten eggy, sulphurous smell resulting from sulphur dioxide having either been badly applied, or through a breakdown of the chemical with age.

Mousse The sparkle in fizzy wine.

Nose Polite word for smell.

Oaky The sometimes vanilla-like, sometimes savoury smell and flavour imparted by oak casks.

Oxidized Wine The air has 'got at' and destroyed the wine, turning it yellow (in the case of whites) or brown (for reds) and giving it a stale nutty aroma.

Palate The taste – and what you taste it with.

Petrolly a not unpleasant overtone often found in mature Riesling.

Powdery Slightly sweet, talcum-powdery smell.

Racy Crisp, lively wine.

Ripe Full-flavoured wine, evidently made from very ripe grapes.

Southern Fuller, sometimes more alcoholic wine, from hotter regions.

Sulphur The throat-tickling, sneeze-inducing evidence that the winemaker has been heavy handed with his sulphur dioxide.

Steely Also 'Firm'. Characterful wine with good acidity.

Stemmy or 'Stalky'. The flavour of the stalk rather than the juice.

Structure Wine with good structure is like a well-designed building all the parts fit together harmoniously. Wine with poor structure is probably falling apart.

Sweaty Saddle The Australian expression used to describe the character of the Shiraz grape. See 'Gamey'.

Tannic The mouth-puckering effect of tannin, the component which will enable a red wine to age.

Tart Generally over-acid.

Thin Self-explanatory.

Tired or 'Tiring'. Wine which has seen better days.

Unknit Wine whose flavours have yet to combine harmoniously. In some wines, the 'knitting together' never takes place at all.

Two silly tasting terms

Lacy 'Intricate, full of subtle, harmonious smells and flavours, delicately bound together.'

Loyal 'Term that is applied to a simple and honest wine.'

WORDS

Acidity
The essential natural component which gives wine its freshness and zing, and which prevents it from being cloying.

Appellation
The legal system operated in France and elsewhere which legislates where the grapes for particular wines should be grown, their yield per acre and, possibly, the way in which the wine must be made and matured.

Botrytis
The 'Noble Rot' of great sweet white wines. A welcome furry grey mould which can creep over ripe grapes at the end of summer, enabling winemakers to produce the finest sweet white wines, notably Sauternes and Trockenbeerenauslese.

Chaptalisation
Named after its official originator, the process of adding sugar to fermenting must to increase the alcoholic degree of the finished wine.

Cuve Close
(also Tank Method, or Charmat)
Sparkling wine of lesser quality than MÉTHODE CHAMPENOISE, whose bubbles are created by re-fermenting the wine in tanks rather than in bottles.

Fermentation
The process whereby yeast converts sugar into alcohol.

Fining
The process of removing solid matter from recently made wine by allowing an inert substance – e.g. egg white – to sink from top to bottom of the cask or tank.

Fortify
The process of adding alcohol – usually brandy – to wine.

Hectare *(ha)*
2.47 acres

Hectolitre *(hl)*
100 litres – or 133 75 cl bottles.

Hybrid
A cross between a LABRUSCA and a VINIFERA vine.

Labrusca
Table grape varieties – used for wine in some countries, but never making anything of fine quality. The flavour of such wines has been called 'foxy'.

Lie *(or Lees)*
The solid matter – yeast etc – most of which naturally drops to the bottom of casks or vats of newly made wines, and the rest of which is removed by FINING.

Maderized
A wine (generally white) which has been got at by air and heat.

Malolactic Fermentation
The process whereby the, appley, Malic acid found in newly made wine naturally transforms itself into the creamier Lactic acid. Unless prevented, this process will almost always occur.

Méthode Champenoise
The method of making fine sparkling wine by causing wine to referment in its bottle.

Microclimate
A small region enjoying a climate different to that of the surrounding area.

Must
Grape juice before it is changed by FERMENTATION into wine.

Negociant
A merchant – generally one who buys, blends and matures wine.

Oxidised
A wine which has been 'got at' by air.

Phylloxera
The vine-destroying beetle which devoured the vineyards of Europe in the late 19th and early 20th centuries.

Racking
The process of passing wine from one barrel or tank to another to 'refresh' it.

Sulphur
Bacteria-killing chemical. Sometimes overused

Vigneron
Winegrower.

Varietal
Used to describe wines made from specific grape varieties and sold under the name of those grapes, e.g. 'Californian Chardonnay'.

Vinifera
Wine-making grapes. All of the great varieties of Europe (Cabernet, Pinot, Riesling etc) are Vinifera.

YUGOSLAVIA

FOR many wine drinkers, Laski Riesling *is* Yugoslavian Wine (for example, according to 1983 figures, it accounts for one in every 20 glasses of wine drunk in Britain). This varietal, which is only slightly more closely related to the great Riesling of the Rhine than it is to the turnip, produces cheap, sweet and, at best, fairly innocuous white wine to be most sensibly enjoyed when standing at parties and eating very savoury food indeed. There is, however, a wide number of other grapes grown in Yugoslavia, many of which produce wine which is at the very least, far more *interesting* than Laski Riesling. Yugoslavia is the world's 10th biggest producer and exporter, making some 15 million gallons every year.

Fifty per cent of the wine is from the grapes grown by stated-owned farms; 50 per cent by small independent growers who give their crop to one of 12 cooperative groupings which vinify them and give the wine to a large regional centre which acts as blender, négociant and distributor.

The Words

Bijelo – White wine.
Crno – Red wine (actually means 'black').

Cuveno vino – Selected.
Stolno vino – Table wine.
Visokokvalitetno – High quality.

The Grape List

Red
Barbera
Blatina (grown in Mostar)
Bogonja (Gamay)
Cabernet Franc
Cabernet Sauvignon (the new success story)
Kadarka (most widely grown variety – particularly in Serbia)
Pamid
Pinot Noir (usually made sweet)
Plavac Mali (grown in Dalmatia and Slovenia to make Plavac and Dingac, Postup and Opul)
Plemenka
Plovdina (grown in Macedonia. Usually used with Prokupac)
Portugizac (Blau Portugieser)
Prokupec (grown in Macedonia and Serbia, and often used with Plovdina, and to make Ruzica rosé)
St Laurent
Teran (the Italian Refosco grape, grown in Istria and Slovenia)
Vranac
Zemelovka

White
Beli Pinot (Pinot Blanc – grown in Slovenia)
Bogdanusa (grown on the Dalmatian islands)
Burgundac Bijeli (Chardonnay)
Gravesina (Italian Riesling – also Laski, and Riesling)
Grk (used to make strong white, particularly on Korcula)
Kevedinka
Malvasia (particularly grown in Slovenia)
Mostarska
Muscat (Ottonel)
Neoplanta (Smederevka x Traminer)
Riesling Rhenen (Genuine Riesling)
Sauvignon Blanc
Sémillon
Sipon (Furmint)
Smederevka

Tokaj (Pinot Gris)
Traminac (Traminer)
Zilavka (grown in Mostar)

The Wine Regions

Bosnia-Herzegovina (less than 5% of total wine production)
Croatia (less than 30%)
Serbia (less than 40%)
Macedonia and Slovenia (less than 20%)
Montenegro (less than 5%)

SLOVENIA
Formerly an Austrian province, it produces quality white wines, particularly from the Slovenija Vino and Vinag Cooperative.

The main producer is the Slovin combine which has several model wineries.

Grape varieties
Merlot
Cabernet
Tokaj
Muscat
Malvasia
Pinot Blanc
Portugizac
Traminac
Sauvignon
Gewürztraminer
Sylvaner
Pinot Gris
Rhine Riesling
Italian Riesling

Drava
Contains Lutomer and Ormoz districts, known for Laski Riesling.

Vineyards
Jeruzalem (noted for late picked Riesling)
Svetinje (Beli Burgundec Spätlese)
Pohorje
Halozo
Ranina Radgona (Tiger's Milk)

Sava
Shows Austrian influence and produces mostly white wines from Italian Riesling, Sylvaner and Plavac. Some reds from St Laurent, Gamay, Portugizac, Cvicek rosé.

Coastal Region
Reds: Cabernet, Merlot, Teran
Whites: Rebula of Brda, Vipiva, Tokaj, Italian Riesling, Pinela and Zelen.

MACEDONIA

Two big cooperatives: Macedonija Vino (seven wineries) and Tikves. Quality red wines and dark reds mostly for blending.

Grape varieties
Prokupac
Smederevka
Zilavka
Cabernet
Merlot
Pinot Noir
Gamay
Vranac-Kratosija

BOSNIA HERZEGOVINA

Little domestic consumption. The chief producer is Kombinat Hepok in Mostar
Mostar produces what some consider to be Yugoslavia's finest wine: Mostarska Zilavka. A less distinguished red wine is made from the Blatina Grape.

MONTENEGRO

Chief producer: Agrokombinat 13 Jul (Titograd). Red Vranac has export potential.

SERBIA

Bordering on Hungary and Bulgaria, Serbia contains two autonomous provinces, both of which produce quality white wines.

VOJVODINA

Fruska Gora

Grape varieties
Italian Riesling
Traminer
Sauvignon
Sylvaner
Pinot Blanc
Sémillon
Plemenka
Smederevka
Neoplanta

The Navip cooperative has a huge central winery in Zemun where wine is prepared for export.
Fruskogorski Biser is a sparkling wine.

Banat
Similar to above

Subotica

Grape varieties
Italian Riesling
Ezerjo
Kadarka
Muscat Ottonel
Kevedinka
Prokupac
Gamay
Pinot Noir
Ruzica (rosés)

KOSMET

Borders on Albania and Macedonia and was hit by phylloxera in the early 20th century. Classic French varieties (Cabernet Franc, Gamay, Merlot, Pinot Noir) have been planted since 1960s. Cabernet wine exported to UK. Amselfelder brand exported principally to Germany but also to the UK.

Zupa
Zupsko Crno (red wine from Prokupac and Plovdina grapes) also Cabernets and rosés)

Vencac-Oplenac
Cabernet Sauvignon, Cabernet Franc, Merlot, Gamay, Pinot Noir, Prokupac, Plovdina

Krajdina
Dark heavy reds, Gamay.

Zilavka
The only noted white wine from this region is said to be slightly reminiscent of apricots.

CROATIA

Inland Croatia
Grape varieties

Italian Riesling
Sauvignon
Traminer
Sémillon
Pinot Blanc
Pinot Gris

Coastal Region
High alcohol red and white wines, mainly from diverse and eccentric grape varieties.

Istrian Peninsula
Formerly an Italian province. Its vines are still trained on pergolas. Wines are mainly produced by the Istravino Cooperative. Some sweet white wines from the Muscat and Malvasia grapes. Some sparkling wines.

Mainly reds

Teran
Cabernet
Merlot
Pinot Noir
Gamay

Dalmatia
Dalmacijavino coop in Split.

North
Reds from Plavina, Babie, Vranac. Marastina white has its own appellation at Cara Smokvica
Opol rosés

South
Red Plavac, e.g. Mali Plavac, also from Cabernet, Merlot. Dingac, made from part-dried grapes in delimited area; Postup; White Prosek (dessert wine).

Island wines
Faros (Hvar), Posip (varietal) Korcula; Grk; Bogdanusa; Vngara.

ZIMBABWE

BRITISH Prime Minister Harold Wilson's contribution to world winemaking has gone sadly unrecorded elsewhere. Had it not been for his decision to apply sanctions against Ian Smith's government of what was then Rhodesia, wines from that country might never have earned bronze and silver medals at the prestigious International Wine & Spirit Competition in 1983 and 1982.

Wines had been made in Zimbabwe since the 1950s with relatively little success. 'St Christopher', a wine produced by Rene Paynter, in those early days was pronounced a particular failure – perhaps it didn't travel well.

The Wine Regions

Matabeleland
Marondera

Major Producers

African Distilleries (Afdis)

Afdis' wines are generally bland and unimpressive, but Monis, whose winery is situated at Mukuyu, is proving increasingly successful. Under the supervision of David Simleit of Philips Central Cellars, (the principal wine and spirit wholesaler in Harare) research is being carried out on early-ripening varieties which will enable the growers to harvest before the rains which form their greatest hazard.

Monis
A Monis Mukuyu Cabernet 1982 won a silver medal at the 1983 International Wine & Spirit Competition, whilst the VAT 10 Colombard won a bronze medal and did creditably at the 1984 International Wine Challenge organised by What Wine? magazine in London. If exports to Europe are planned, Monis' 'Moselblumchen' will have to change its label. Is this the chance for the world's first African wine name?